Beginning
Visual Basic 6
Objects

Peter Wright

Wrox Press Ltd.

Beginning Visual Basic 6 Objects

© 1998 Wrox Press

First Published   October 1998

Published by Wrox Press Ltd, 30 Lincoln Road, Olton, Birmingham B27 6PA , UK.
Printed in Canada
1 2 3 4 5 TRI 99 98

ISBN 1-861001-72-X

Trademark Acknowledgements

Wrox has endeavoured to provide trademark information about all the companies and products mentioned in this book by the appropriate use of capitals. However, Wrox cannot guarantee the accuracy of this information.

Credits

Author
Peter Wright

Additional Material
Richard Bonneau
Mike Erickson
Jacob Sturm

Exercises
John Smiley
Barry Sturm

Managing Editor
Dominic Shakeshaft

Editors
Kate Hall
Dominic Lowe

Technical Reviewers
Darren Gill
Antoine Giusti
John Harris
Brian Henry
Dave Jewell
Rocky Lhotka
David Liske
David Rowlands
John Smiley
Mike Sussman

Cover/Design/Layout
Andrew Guillaume

Index
Diane Brenner
Andrew Criddle
Simon Gilks

Acknowledgements

Thanks to my friends and family. Thanks also to everyone at Wrox, I couldn't have done it without you.

Finally, above and beyond all the rest, this book is dedicated to my beautiful wife, Heather.

6

Beginning

VB6 Objects

Table Of Contents

6

Beginning
VB6 Objects

Introduction

Welcome to *Beginning Visual Basic 6 Objects*. This easy-to-use tutorial guide will give you a full introduction to object-oriented programming with Visual Basic 6.

In this book I will show you how the use of objects enables a programmer to produce robust, maintainable and re-useable applications. I'll show you everything you need to know to develop an object-oriented application, including the design process and how to go about implementing that design in code.

Who this Book is for

This book was written for programmers who want to learn object-oriented programming using Visual Basic. You don't need to be an expert programmer to follow this book, but you will need a grasp of Visual Basic's core.

Those of you who read my previous book, *Beginning Visual Basic 6*, will find that this book is the ideal next step. If you didn't read *Beginning Visual Basic 6*, but can find your way around Visual Basic's Toolbox and know what properties, methods and events are, then this book is ideal for you too. Just in case you're a little rusty though, I'll explain these briefly as we come across them.

More advanced topics such as classes, ActiveX components and ActiveX controls are discussed in sufficient detail to put any newcomer to them at ease. Don't despair if you've been using these for years though, you're in for a real treat as I show you to use them to create object-oriented applications.

What's Covered in this Book

Beginning Visual Basic 6 Objects is a great first step into object-oriented programming. The aim of this book is to introduce you to all the key techniques and ideas behind object-oriented programming, so that you can go away and use them in your future projects. This book is your launch pad into this world.

In the first chapter, I'll introduce you to objects. We'll take a good look at what they are, and how we can actually begin to implement them in Visual Basic. In preparation for what's to come, I'll give you an overview of design techniques that are used to support object-oriented programming.

In Chapter 2, I'll explain to you why programming with objects is so important. I'll show you a program built for a company called Northwind Traders. Northwind decides not to use object-oriented techniques, with disastrous results. Having seen the code nightmare produced, we'll be able to see just why object-oriented programming is so great in Chapter 3 when we visit the DataDamage Inc and its object-oriented gurus.

Chapter 4 follows with coverage of Object Hierarchies and we see more ways of designing our applications so that they are easier to follow, implement and manage.

In chapters 5 to 7, I'll lead you into the realm of ActiveX. We'll look at something called COM (Component Object Model) which underpins the ActiveX technologies we will discuss in depth over these three chapters. We'll explore ActiveX components and controls, I'll show you how to create them and we'll discuss the importance of these technologies in the world of object-oriented programming.

Then, in Chapter 8, we'll be taking a look at the topic of Object Persistence. This is a very useful programming technique that increases the power and flexibility of our objects. You'll find out how to implement Object Persistence, and why it's so useful in Visual Basic.

The final few chapters of the book are devoted to designing and running realistic applications. In Chapter 9, I'll show you how to design an application in preparation for the object-oriented application we will start to build in Chapter 10. I'll introduce you to design methodologies, which reduce the time, effort and pain needed to design an application, to a minimum. Using our design, we'll work through a tutorial to help create part of this application, enabling you to put into practice what you've been learning about object-oriented programming in this book.

Then, for those of you who really want to get stuck into object oriented programming, the final chapter contains an introduction to the **Business Objects** and **Utility Objects**. This is then followed up with a real life project for you to play with. We shall be visiting XYZ Financial Planners and creating a suite of applications to help them with their finances. We shall take this project from the design stage, implement it, and then test our results. You should leave this chapter with a great understanding of how OOP works in the real world.

What You Need to Use this Book

You need an enthusiastic commitment to learning the subject matter and a fair amount of time. To complete all the examples you'll need a PC running the Professional Edition of Visual Basic 6.0 and Microsoft Access. If you have the Learning Edition then you should still be able to do some of the exercises. And of course, you won't need a computer at all for the theoretical bits.

All the source code for the examples in this book is shown in the chapters. Other than the Nwind.mdb which comes with Microsoft Access, you do not need any extra files to create the programs we discuss. However, if you do want to avoid the finger ache that comes with a lot of typing, you can download the examples from the Wrox web site.

```
http://www.wrox.com
```

In this book, we'll take a brief look at Visual Modeler (available with the Enterprise Edition) which is an application designed to assist with object-oriented design. However, there isn't anything taught in this book that you can't do on pencil and paper. When you are ready to build a ten thousand page set of documentation, you may need a few tools to make your life easier, but for now a stiff piece of papyrus, a sharp stick and a pool of ink will do.

Conventions

I use a number of different styles of text and layout in the book to help differentiate between the various types of information. Here are examples of the styles I use along with explanations of what they mean:

Try It Outs - How Do They Work?

1 Each step has a number.

2 Follow the steps through

3 Then read *How It Works* to find out what's going on.

- Bulleted information is shown like this:
- **Important Words** are in a bold font.
- Words that appear on the screen, such as menu options, are in a similar font to the one used on screen, e.g. the File menu.
- Keys that you press on the keyboard, like *Ctrl* and *Enter*, are in italics.
- All file, function names and other code snippets are in this style: Nwind.mdb.

FYI **Extra details, for your information, come in boxes like this.**

- When discussing code, we have two conventions:

> *These boxes hold important, not-to-be forgotten, mission critical details which are directly relevant to the surrounding text.*

while,

Background information is shown like this.

When documenting use cases,

I've used this style.

Visual Basic code has two fonts. If it's a word that we're talking about in the text, for example, when discussing the `For...Next` loop, it's in a bold font. If it's a block of code that you can type in as a program and run, then it's also in a gray box:

```
Private Sub cmdQuit_Click()
    End
End Sub
```

Sometimes you'll see code in a mixture of styles, like this:

```
Private Sub cmdQuit_Click()
    End
End Sub
```

There are two reasons why this might be so. In both cases I want you to consider the code with the gray background. The code with the white background is either code we've already looked at and that we don't wish to examine further, or when you're typing code in, this is code that Visual Basic generates and doesn't need typing in.

These formats are designed to make sure that you know what it is you're looking at. I hope they make life easier.

How to Get the Most Out of this book

Beginning Visual Basic 6 Objects is written as a hands-on tutorial. That means you have to get your hands on the keyboard as often as possible. Throughout the book I use Try It Outs to teach you step-by-step, all the new concepts that we'll come across. There are also some end of chapter questions. However, in the final chapter we will develop a large sample project. This will give you a much better understanding of how you can apply the techniques and ideas learnt earlier in the book to your own object-oriented application. This is something that's hard to appreciate from any number of more trivial examples.

To help you get the most from the chapters, I would really like you to try out the examples as you read. It really does make a difference. The examples also provide a good base for experimentation and will hopefully inspire you to create programs of your own. It's important to try things out - you will learn as much (if not more) from your mistakes as you will from the things that work first time. It's a cliché but it's true!

I recommend reading through *Beginning Visual Basic 6 Objects* in sequence. As Humpty Dumpty said, "Begin at the beginning, proceed to the end, and then stop." On the other hand, it is your money and more important, your time. Feel free to skip over sections that you see as either a review or as superfluous. I won't be insulted...

Feedback

I've tried to make this book as accurate and enjoyable for you as possible, but what really matters is whether or not *you* find it useful. I would really appreciate your views and comments. You can return the reply card in the back of the book, or contact Wrox at:

feedback@wrox.com
http://www.wrox.com
or
http://www.wrox.co.uk

6

Introducing Objects

Overview

In this first chapter, we'll take a good look at what objects are, and how we can actually begin to implement objects in Visual Basic. We'll also see how objects have effected the language of Visual Basic itself. After that, we'll take a brief look at some of the design techniques that support object-oriented programming, and begin to consider the new ActiveX technologies that we'll be exploring in the rest of the book. Specifically, we'll review:

- What are objects?
- What is object-oriented programming?
- Why objects are good news for Visual Basic
- The relationship between classes and objects
- Implementing objects in Visual Basic 6.0
- An outline of object-oriented program design
- An outline of ActiveX technologies

What are Objects?

Objects, in computing, are abstractions of the real-world entities that are all around us in our day-to-day life: our houses, our cars, our desks, and the pieces of paper we may shuffle around at work.

In programming terms, objects are self-contained units that have their own **data** and a related set of **behaviors** that will effect that data:

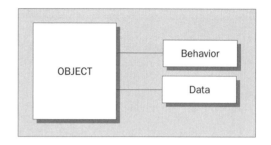

An abstract representation of a real-world object that we can all recognize, in today's age, is the wordprocessing document. Wordprocessor documents have size and content, like their real-world counterparts. We can also perform actions on these abstractions of documents - which parallel those that we might perform on real-world documents. For instance, we can add words to them, and we can throw them away. Word processor documents therefore have their own data (such as the words they contain), and a related set of behaviors (such as deleting words from a document).

Let's consider object data and object behavior in turn now.

Objects Contain Data

The data about an object is all the information we know about that particular object. If the object we were representing was a car, for instance, then we might have some data about its color, its make, how many doors it had, etc. We might also know whether it was locked or not, and how much petrol it had in it.

Following this car example through, we might actually have several cars we wished to represent, each with their own color, make, number of doors, etc. Each particular car would be an instance of a *Car* object.

*In programming terms, data is stored in **variables**. Each instance of an object (each car, in our example) has its own set of variables, quite distinct from the variables of any other objects - be they* Car *objects,* Desk *objects, etc.*

Objects Have Behaviors

The whole idea of representing objects is so that our programs can interact with them. We therefore need some way to allow programs to access the data that our objects hold. We do this by providing a set of behaviors that will allow the rest of the world to interact with our objects.

The behaviors of an object effectively form the **interface** that an object presents to the world.

An object can also have more than one interface, allowing it to interact more appropriately to various different objects.

In Visual Basic, the behaviors that create the interface of an object are the **methods**, **properties**, and **events** of that object.

Methods

Objects need to provide services for when they interact with other objects. Using their own data, or data from other objects, they manipulate information and yield a result.

> *When I drive my car, for instance, I interact with it in a particular fashion. To allow me to control my car and direct where I travel, it has a number of services that I can use: a steering wheel allows me to control my direction, for instance. Furthermore, there are certain driving procedures that I can implement (such as changing gear), and there are certain mechanical systems built into the design of the car (such as a gearbox) to help me determine the behavior of my car and where I travel.*

This type of behavior is implemented by the methods and functions that we create within our programs. Methods are simply routines that we write within our programs to implement the services or procedures that we want to provide.

In Visual Basic, methods are implemented using `Sub` or `Function` routines, and we'll be seeing a lot more of them throughout this book.

Properties

Object properties are attributes that describe an object. Critically, properties allow us to select what information we want to make available about our object. We can also choose which property values can be changed by our object's users.

For instance, a *Car* object may have a *Speed* property.

> *It's important to see that an object's properties are not the same as its data. While our **Car** object may indeed have a **Speed** property, the underlying data used to derive that property could be, say, the number of axle rotations per second. The number of axle rotations per second may or may not be available as a property of our **Car** object. The point is that we have arranged, in this case, for the **Speed** property to be made available from a complex set of underlying data.*
>
> *Since properties can just as easily be the product of complex processing as they can be single elements of raw data, it's useful to consider properties as object behavior - effecting object data to yield specific information about that object.*

Visual Basic supplies us with several types of `Property` routines to support object properties: `Property Get`, `Property Let`, and `Property Set`.

> *It's understandable that some of you may feel a little doubtful about whether properties are really a form of behavior. But just consider the similarity, in Visual Basic, between `Property Get` routines and normal `Functions` - the latter of which are clearly related to methods and behaviors.*

Events

Every Visual Basic programmer is familiar with writing routines that respond to events: the controls on our forms generate events, and we write code to take appropriate action when those events occur. The `Click` event is probably the most widely used event in Visual Basic forms. Nothing particularly new here.

However, an object can also raise **events**, just like the controls on a form in Visual Basic. These raised events provide us, the developers, with feedback on what's happening to our objects when our program is running. A user, for instance, may be providing a value for one of our objects, or another object may be calling one of our object's methods.

In Visual Basic 6.0 we are able to define and raise our own events, using the `Event` *statement to declare an event and the* `RaiseEvent` *command to raise that event.*

It's as important to be able to monitor when something happens to one of our objects as it is to know when something happens to our of our controls on a form.

As an example of how important events are to our cause, consider an Invoice object that accessed a property, Tax, which belonged to another object. Now if that other object was altered such that its Tax property changed, then unless we were alerted to the changing Tax rate by an event signalling that change, our Invoice object would deliver the wrong calculations until the new Tax rate was read.

Later in this chapter, we'll take a step-by-step look at setting up an object with its own related events.

Objects and Classes

All objects are defined by a **class**. A class is essentially a template from which an object is created. This means, as we saw with our *Car* object earlier, that we can create many objects based on a single class.

Classes allow us to classify objects. For instance, if we have a couple of objects, *Jeep* and *Van*, they could both be instances of our *Car* class. In Visual Basic, we can define classes using **class modules**. We can then create objects based on a particular class module, with each object being an instance of the class:

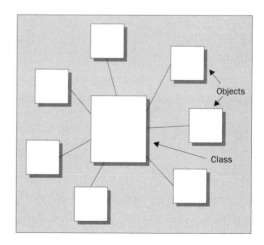

A little later in this chapter, we'll be stepping through the process of creating our own classes in Visual Basic. For now, however, I'd just like you to hang on to the idea that classes are templates for our objects.

What is Object-Oriented Programming?

Object-Oriented Programming (OOP) is a new way of thinking about, and tackling, programming problems - using objects. Actually, it's really been around for quite a while now, but it's only in the last 10 years or so that it has really started to gain ground with the programming community. Like anything new, there was a fair amount of resistance to it at first, and some people claimed it was obscure and difficult to use.

The basic idea behind OOP is very simple: abstract representations of real-world objects are used within our programs. It's worth appreciating, however, just how different OOP is from the more traditional, structured approach to program development.

> *With the traditional structured approach to development, a programmer looks at the data that the application needs to deal with, and then works out what needs to be done to that data.*

In Visual Basic, the structured approach to programming invariably results in a number of forms being produced for the user interface of the application. There will also be a set of routines that do the main work - either as events, or as subroutines that are called by events. The essential thing, here, is that the focus of this structured approach lies purely with the data - and providing the user with the appropriate tools and facilities to maintain that data.

This traditional approach has been orthodox for some time now. The data in an application will often relate directly to the forms and paperwork used in a business. This can create the illusion that an application developed with the structured approach is being tailored to the way the business works. Unfortunately, this is often just not the case.

> *We'll be taking a trip, in the next chapter, to Northwind: a company that still uses structured programming techniques. While we're there, we'll see how badly things can go wrong with the traditional structured approach, and how object-oriented programming can help make everyone's life happier.*

Object-oriented programming, on the other hand, approaches things from a totally different angle.

> *Instead of looking at the business data, and bolting an application on top of that data, OOP relies on identifying the objects around which everything in an application takes place.*

Object-oriented programming involves identifying the objects that we are going to need in our own applications. Then, as programmers, we attach properties and methods to those objects and make events available on them. The result is that we provide an interface so that the rest of the world can know what our objects are up to and what's happening to them.

The Black Box Idea

Think of a black box, something sinister like a military box of some kind. It has a rack of buttons on the top that represents the box's interface, and it has some kind of display system that displays information to the user. The box belongs to the military, so how it does what it does is secret. All a user is given when they get the box is a set of instructions. These basically do nothing more than describe what the box does, and how to use the black box's interface (that rack of buttons on top) to get it to do things. When the buttons are pressed, the results are displayed on the screen mounted on the box. The box should do everything that it was designed to do, no more and no less, and it should do it well. The user will never have to apply a crowbar to it to open it up and fiddle with its insides to get it to work the way they want. They shouldn't care. All they care about is that predefined interface and the results that the box kicks out.

> *The basic idea, in object-oriented programming, is that our objects should behave just like black boxes.*

As we've seen, the interface of a black box is the collection of properties, methods and events that we give to the object. Our users are other developers who will want to make use of our object in their own projects. The purpose of the object should be pretty clear to these people, and the interface should be as simple to use and effective as is humanly possible. In this way, they will never ever have to worry about how our object does its job at all. Our users can simply take for granted that our object does do what we say it does, and that they can kick it into life by playing with the interface.

In many ways, this is much like the controls that we use in Visual Basic to form the user interface of our applications. I don't suppose there are very many of us who have ever run the text box through a decompiler to look at the C code that makes it work! We know what the text box does, and we're happy with the properties, methods and events that it provides in order to fit it into our applications. So it is with object-oriented programming.

Why Objects are Good for Visual Basic

For a long time now, people have been saying that Visual Basic makes it difficult for programmers to program well. Visual Basic was the first of the new Windows Rapid Application Development (RAD) tools, and it just didn't fit nicely with established methods of writing software. It was a rebel among the ranks.

The event-driven model that Visual Basic uses, for example, led many people to believe that Visual Basic would result in the creation of unstructured code. They were probably right.

You see, the problem has not been that Visual Basic ever *forced* programmers to write bad code - that is simply not the case. The situation is simply this: early versions of Visual Basic failed to provide many of the constructs that programmers had come to expect and that would direct them to well-ordered code.

Why did this happen? Well, the emphasis within Visual Basic has always been to provide a powerful set of tools to get a user interface up and running as fast as possible. Other 'purer' languages, on the other hand, have been less concerned with this fast development theme, instead providing better facilities to encourage nicer code.

So consider some of the ways in which we can write code. In the old days, programmers would break a problem down into groups of smaller problems, and keep doing so until they were eventually happy that they could sit down and write code for these smaller problems. All that code would then be tied together with a single routine, which would feed the user deeper and deeper into those smaller routines, forcing the user down a known route in order to solve the larger problem in question. Visual Basic, on the other hand, has allowed us to focus on a user interface, with bits of code attached to the visual elements of that user interface. There is no predefined route through our code in Visual Basic - it's left to the user to determine which code will run and when, based on the controls the user interacts with on screen.

Now because it's quite easy to set up a user interface and implement some basic event-driven functionality behind that interface in Visual Basic, the language has been recognized as a neat tool for quickly creating **prototype** systems. We can quickly set up the user interface for the application and present it to our users - checking whether it's developing along the right track. Then, according to this prototyping strategy, the application could be re-written in a "real" development environment, such as C++.

> *I'm writing this book on the assumption that we all know there's a lot more scope to Visual Basic than prototyping. I'm talking to you now, as one programmer to another, to remind you that we have a powerful language to work with. My basic premise, in this book, is that you understand how great a tool Visual Basic is, and how far we're going to go with objects.*

Visual Basic 4 started down a path designed to change this perception of it being a prototyping language. It did this by providing developers with object-oriented development facilities.

> *Let me repeat that: object-oriented development facilities were responsible for finally changing the common perception that Visual Basic was merely a prototyping language.*

These OOP facilities gradually drew Visual Basic towards the current state of the art in terms of development techniques. In Visual Basic 4 there was a definite push in the right direction.

It wasn't plain sailing at first. Visual Basic 4 made an attempt, an unsuccessful attempt, to move the growing army of VB developers further into object-oriented development. It fell short on many fronts, however, and as such was not widely adopted by the Visual Basic community.

Visual Basic 5 came next and took much more confident strides into the world of objects. Now, the further support given by Visual Basic 6 for object-oriented programming is powerful and integrated enough to really encourage developers to make good use of it! We're on our way.

It is these advances which we shall cover in this book. And if you have never developed an object-oriented application in Visual Basic, then this is definitely a good place to start.

Implementing Objects in Visual Basic 6

So, just what does Visual Basic 6 bring to the object-oriented table that has so many people drooling on their keyboards? That's a good question, especially since object-oriented development tools were first introduced back in Visual Basic 4. The differences are subtle, but very powerful indeed.

Visual Basic itself is now totally object-oriented. The controls that we use to create our user interfaces are in fact a special type of object known as an **ActiveX Control** (more on these later).

The code editor that we work in now recognizes whether our code is dealing with an object or not. In response, the code editor will automatically show us a list of properties and methods relating to the object as we type.

The ability to create our own objects has also been improved. We can now create our own events, as well as force one object to implement the same interface (properties and methods) of another object. Why this particular feat is so important becomes clear much later - bear with me!

Visual Basic 6 also fits nicely into the new ActiveX-enabled world in which we now find ourselves. This means that our code can use objects from separate programs and DLLs, just as if they were within our own project. Creating these ActiveX servers is also simplicity itself with Visual Basic 6. But hey, I'm getting ahead of myself. All these things, and more, are covered in much more detail throughout the rest of this book. For now, let's just get back to basics with a quick refresher on what all these things are and mean, and how we can get at them. We'll cement it all together with plenty of working code and background information throughout the book.

Creating a Class

The root of this object-oriented fountain, from a VB standpoint at least, is the **class module**. To all intents and purposes a class module looks very much the same as any other code module in Visual Basic. Let's go ahead and drop one into an application now.

Try It Out - Adding a Class Module

1 If you don't already have Visual Basic running, then now would be a good time to start it. Make sure that you have a new Standard Exe project created before you do anything else.

2 To add a class module to your project, simply select Add Class Module from the Project menu within Visual Basic. After a short pause, a dialog will appear looking much like the one in the screenshot:

3 Select Class Module and then click on the Open button and voila - your new class module appears:

So, what's so special about it? Well, a class is nothing more than an uncreated object. That sounds horrible. Let me try again. A class is where our objects come from. Nope - still not there. Hmmm...try this.

If you have a pile of dough, and a cookie cutter, then the cookie cutter is a class. The cookie cutter defines the shape and appearance of something very specialized - a cookie. However, until you actually apply the cookie cutter to the dough then you don't have a cookie. Class modules are basically the same. We write the code that defines the methods, properties and events of an object in our class modules. However, this code itself will never run until we actually create an object based on the class.

For example, we might have a class in our project called Class1 (in fact, if you've been following along so far, you really do have a class in your project called Class1). If we wanted to actually use any code inside that class module at runtime, then somewhere in our code we would need to **instantiate** (long word - means create) an object from that class. It works like this (but don't type anything in just yet):

```
Dim MyFirstObject As New Class1
```

This code would go ahead and create an object, called `MyFirstObject`, that we could then interact with in our code. Using this object, we could access the code that's contained within the `Class1` Module. You'll get plenty of opportunity to see this all working a little later.

We can change the name of a class by simply editing the name property in the property window, just as if we were dealing with a form, a control, or even a standard code module.

Try It Out - Renaming A Class

1 Go ahead now and change the name of the class in your project to clsVehicle. We'll use this class to get a simple *Vehicle* object working, which we'll be able to use in a real application:

The cls in the name clsVehicle is quite common - most people like to prefix their class names with cls so that when they come to write lots of code it's easy to see when a class is being used.

Adding Properties to Classes

Properties represent the data of an object. However, as we know from the properties that we deal with on controls, they are far more than just variables.

With properties, we can write code to deal with storing data into, and retrieving data from the class. Now this may sound like a lot of hassle (and there is a way around it) but believe me the benefits far outweigh the pain. Since we need to write code to do the retrieving and storing of data, we're effectively creating variables with a custom 'front end'. The code we write can check attempts to store data to make sure that the data to be stored is valid, and raise an error if it is not – now that's not something a simple variable can do!

Producing the properties is actually very simple. Let's add a *Wheels* property to our `clsVehicle` class to show how many wheels our *Vehicle* has.

Try It Out - Adding a Property to a Class

1 Type this line into your `clsVehicle` class module:

```
Private m_intWheels As Integer
```

The first thing we do here is set up somewhere to hold the actual data about a vehicle's *Wheels* property. In this case, we declare a private variable at the top of the class, called m_intWheels:

```
Private m_intWheels As Integer
```

It's a weird name, and quite possibly not a naming style you're familiar with using. The m_ bit means that this is what is often referred to as a **member variable**.

> *Any variable that we declare to be* Private *within a particular class is called a member variable. Member variables cannot be accessed by anyone using our class: it exists purely for the sake of the code within the class, as an internal reference.*

And just in case you were wondering, the **int** prefix in m_intWheels is quite typical: it just tells anyone reading the code that this variable is set up to hold an integer value.

2 Now that we have somewhere safe to store the *Wheels* property value, it's time to write the *Wheels* property routines themselves. So enter this Property Get Wheels routine:

```
Public Property Get Wheels() As Integer
    Wheels = m_intWheels
End Property
```

Property Get routines are very much like functions. They have a name (which always needs to be the name of the property itself) and they return a value. Property Get routines can also have parameters, just like Visual Basic functions - but we'll leave that topic for later in the book!

Our code just needs to access, or calculate, the value to return. It then goes ahead and returns that value in the same way that a standard function would. In this case, all we need to do is set the Property name to be the value of the m_intWheels member variable that we declared a little while ago.

If someone were using an instance of our clsVehicle class (something that we will do ourselves later), then they could now access the value of the *Wheels* property with something as simple as this:

```
NumberOfWheels = MyVehicleObject.Wheels
```

where MyVehicleObject is the particular instance of our clsVehicle class, of course. This code would, in turn, cause the Property Get Wheels routine we just wrote to be executed.

3   Okay, so much for getting data out; but what about putting it in there in the first place? That's where a `Property Let` routine comes into play, so now add the following code to your project:

```
Public Property Let Wheels(ByVal intWheels As Integer)

    ' First check that the wheel count is valid
    If intWheels < 2 Then
        Err.Raise vbObjectError + 1, , "Number of wheels invalid"
        Exit Property
    End If

    ' If we reach this point then the number of wheels is valid
    m_intWheels = intWheels

End Property
```

As this code exemplifies, all `Property Let` routines need a name, and that name is the name of the property itself. `Property Let` routines must also take one or more parameters: the first parameter being the value that the user is trying to set into the property. Therefore, if we had a line of code like this:

```
MyVehicleObject.Wheels = 1
```

then the `Property Let` routine would roar into life, with the value `1` being the value of the parameter that's passed into it.

The ultimate aim of any `Property Let` routine is, of course, to store the data that is passed to it somewhere. In the code above, we store this data in our member variable `m_intWheels`.

Notice, however, the validation code around `intWheels` we apply before going ahead and storing this data in `m_intWheels`. We check to see if the value of the parameter passed in through `intWheels` is less than `2`. If it is, then we raise a normal Visual Basic error:

```
If intWheels < 2 Then
        Err.Raise vbObjectError + 1, , "Number of wheels invalid"
        Exit Property
End If
```

Notice the bit that says `VBObjectError+1`. When we raise an error of our own, Visual Basic expects us to give it a number, and provides the `VbObjectError` constant as a good starting value. We can add anything to this number without resulting in an error number that conflicts with any of Visual Basic's default error numbers.

We'll look at error handling in more detail through the book. If you have a craving for knowledge then you could do worse than look at the Err object and its Raise method in Visual Basic's online help.

If the `intWheels` value was valid, the remaining lines of code simply copy the value passed in through `intWheels` to our member variable `m_intWheels`, ready for later retrieval.

Adding Methods to Classes

A method is simply a public function or subroutine within a class. Let's create a method in our `clsVehicle` class module.

Try It Out - Adding a Method to a Class

1 Go ahead and type this into your `clsVehicle` class module:

```
Public Sub ShowInfo()

    MsgBox "This vehicle has " & m_intWheels & " wheels"

End Sub
```

As you can see, it's really nothing more than a `Public` subroutine that displays a Message box. However, the very fact that it's `Public` makes this subroutine exist as a method of the class. So there you have it, we've added a method to our `clsVehicle` class.

2 If we want to be able to call our method from within our code, however, we still have some work to do.

Since we've added our `ShowInfo` method to a class module, it can't be called until the class module to which it belongs has been instantiated as an object. We still need to breathe life into our `clsVehicle` class module by instantiating it - and only then can our `ShowInfo` method be called.

> *Let me repeat: if we want to call methods from within a class module, we must first instantiate an object variable of that class.*

Let's take an example. You needn't type this in, but consider the following code very carefully:

```
Dim MyVehicleObject As New clsVehicle
MyVehicleObject.Wheels = 4
MyVehicleObject.ShowInfo
```

In the first line, here, we create a new variable, `MyVehicleObject`, to be of type `clsVehicle`. This effectively creates a new object, `MyVehicleObject`, based on our code template `clsVehicle`. (That's our first glimpse at creating objects! Don't worry, there's much more to come.)

The second line of this code assigns the value 4 to the `Wheels` property of our new `MyVehicleObject` object. The thing to notice here is the prefix before the `Wheels` property that we must explicitly define: we need to tell Visual Basic which object the `Wheels` property belongs to (`MyVehicleObject` in this case). Notice also how we use the dot (`.`) to separate the object name from the property name in this notation.

> *Although this line assigns the value **4** to the `Wheels` property, it does so through the `Property Let` routine for `Wheels` that we wrote in the `clsVehicle` class.*

Finally, we call the `ShowInfo` method from our class in the third line of our code. Once again, notice that we must prefix the method's name with the name of the object; in this case, `MyVehicleObject`. This line would result in our Message box popping up on screen to tell us how many wheels we've assigned to our vehicle.

Implementing Events in Classes

The last thing we'll take a quick look at, before we actually put the class to use, is implementing events in classes.

Visual Basic 6 actually allows us to create our own events, instead of forcing us to respond to a set of existing events.

Creating events in classes is really a very simple process. All we need to do is to tell Visual Basic which events can occur, and then just raise them at the appropriate points within our code for that class. It's then up to the user of the class to deal with those events in whatever manner they see fit.

That said, events can be a tricky area to get one's head around when there are objects around. Prior to working with objects in Visual Basic 6, most people's experience of events comes from the user-side of things: writing code to respond to objects, instead of actually raising them.

> *Think of an event, in your object, as a flag on a motor racing track. Whenever something nasty happens, a marshal starts waving the flag frantically until somebody does something to respond to the situation (alert the press, **then** call the ambulance usually). Your code is the track marshal. When something happens, you raise an event, which is the code equivalent of waving the flag. It's up to the user of your object (the other chunks of code in the application, which actually create the object) to respond to your code's frantic flag waving in the way they see fit.*

So, how is it all done then? Well, let's go ahead and drop an event into our `clsVehicle` class - an event that gets raised whenever the number of wheels is set.

Try It Out - Adding an Event to the Module

1 The first thing that we need to do is to actually tell Visual Basic that a new event is likely to occur.

Bring up the code window for our `clsVehicle` class and, at the very top in the `Declarations` section, type in these two lines:

```
Option Explicit
Public Event WheelChanged(ByVal intWheels As Integer)
```

The top of your code window should now look something like mine:

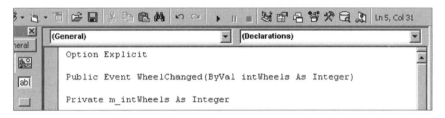

As you can see, it's really not that difficult to declare a new event. We simply type `Public Event`, followed by the name of the event (in this case `WheelChanged`), and then list any parameters that the event might pass to a user of the object.

2 Once we've declared an event, like this, the next thing we need to do is put some code into the class to actually raise that event when the appropriate conditions arise. In this case, it makes sense that the `WheelChanged` event could appropriately be raised immediately after someone has successfully set the `Wheels` property. So let's go ahead and add a line to the bottom of our `Property Let Wheels` property routine to do just this:

```
Public Property Let Wheels(ByVal intWheels As Integer)

    ' First check that the wheel count is valid
    If intWheels < 2 Then
        Err.Raise vbObjectError + 1, , "Number of wheels invalid"
        Exit Property
    End If

        ' If we reach this point then the number of wheels is valid
        m_intWheels = intWheels
        RaiseEvent WheelChanged(m_intWheels)

End Property
```

As you can see from this new line, when we need to raise an event we simply use the `RaiseEvent` keyword. After the keyword, we simply specify the name of the event to raise, followed by any parameter values that the event might expect. Since we declared the `WheelChanged` event to expect a parameter describing the new value of the `Wheels` property, we go right ahead here and pass the event the `m_intWheels` variable, which holds the new `Wheels` value.

21

From Classes to Objects in Visual Basic

So far, we've created a class module with a lot of code in it; but if we were to go ahead and run the application right now, nothing would happen. Remember the cookie cutter example earlier? We have our cookie cutter nicely created, but we need to apply it to some dough before anything even remotely cookie shaped will appear. So let's write a working program that uses our class module to create our first object. Since we're back in the land of working programs and user interfaces, we'll need to develop a form to work with, but our real interest lies with the objects that these forms will be interacting with.

Try It Out - Turning Classes into Objects

1 The project in which we created our `clsVehicle` class module should have a blank form supplied with it. You should be able to see it from the Project explorer window:

Double click on **Form1** in the explorer window to bring it into view, and drop a couple of buttons onto it, and a text box, so it looks like this:

2 Don't bother renaming the controls: we're only really interested, at this point, in seeing how we can actually turn a class into an object and then use that object.

What we're going to do is create `MyVehicleObject` from the `clsVehicle` class, and use the Text box in `Form1` to obtain a value for the `Wheels` property. Then we'll get the `MyVehicleObject` to put up its message box using the `ShowInfo` method that we added to the `clsVehicle` class earlier. First, let's create the object.

3 Here's the plan: we'll create our `MyVehicleObject` when the user clicks the `Command1` button.

So, click on the `Command1` button on your form. The code window should swing into view (well, it pops actually, but you know what I mean) with the `Click` event sitting in it - patiently waiting for some code.

Now add a line to the `Command1` button's `Click` event so that it reads like this:

```
Private Sub Command1_Click()
    Dim MyVehicleObject As New clsVehicle
End Sub
```

We glimpsed at this technique for creating objects from classes a little while back. It's just like declaring a variable. We use the `Dim` keyword to start the declaration, then give the object a name, in this case `MyVehicleObject`. Next, we tell VB that the variable is to be declared as a `New clsVehicle` type object. This lets VB go away, create a brand new object from the `clsVehicle` class, and assign it to our `MyVehicleObject` variable.

4 With that done, we can actually use the methods and properties that belong to the `MyVehicleObject` - that is, the methods and properties we defined in our `clsVehicle` class. We can use these methods and properties just as if `MyVehicleObject` was a control - or any other kind of object that we might come across in Visual Basic.

So let's finish off the `Click` event so that it looks like this:

```
Private Sub Command1_Click()

    Dim MyVehicleObject As New CVehicle

    MyVehicleObject.Wheels = Val(Text1.Text)
    MyVehicleObject.ShowInfo

End Sub
```

In the first new line, we assign the `Wheels` property of `MyVehicleObject` to be the text value of the `Text1` Text box. We then call the method `ShowInfo` that now belongs to `MyVehicleObject`.

5 At this point, we can actually run the program. Type a number into the Text box and then hit the `Command1` button. The code behind our button will now call the code that we wrote into our `clsVehicle` class:

23

6 Run the program again, however, and enter a number into the Text1 Text box which is less than 2. Notice that we get an error, just as we coded it:

7 Polite error handling is as important in object-oriented programming as it is anywhere else. So let's put an error handler in our code to catch this kind of mistake properly:

```
Private Sub Command1_Click()

    Dim MyVehicleObject As New CVehicle

    On Error GoTo Command1_Error

    MyVehicleObject.Wheels = Val(Text1.Text)
    MyVehicleObject.ShowInfo

    Exit Sub

Command1_Error:
    MsgBox "Try a realistic number of wheels!", _
    vbExclamation, "Ridiculous user error"
    Exit Sub

End Sub
```

This code shows a standard approach to handling errors in Visual Basic. First, we tell Visual Basic what we want to happen, within this Click routine, if an error occurs. We do this using the On Error Goto statement, which specifies the line label where our error handling routine will start - in the case, we've called that line label Command1_Error:

```
On Error GoTo Command1_Error
```

Two things can now happen. As the routine moves on to the next line and attempts to read a value from Text1.Text, this in turn invokes the Property Let Wheels routine. If our error is not raised within this Property Let Wheels routine, then the Click routine here will run through to call the ShowInfo method and then exit with the first Exit Sub statement:

```
MyVehicleObject.ShowInfo

Exit Sub
```

However, if our `Property Let Wheels` routine does raise that error, control will automatically be transferred to the `Command1_Error` line label, where a polite Message box will report the error:

```
Command1_Error:
MsgBox "Try a realistic number of wheels!", _
   vbExclamation, "Ridiculous user error"
```

8 For our error handler to actually kick in, we also need to change the way that Visual Basic deals with errors. By default, if there is an error in a class module, then VB will stop, no matter what error handlers we have in place, to show us the offending line of code. It's easily changed though.

Go to the <u>T</u>ools menu in Visual Basic and select **Options**. When the **Options** dialog appears, click on the **General** tab at the top of the dialog and then set the **Error Trapping** box to **Break on Unhandled <u>E</u>rrors**.

9 Now try running our program again, and enter some invalid number into the `Text1` Text box. You'll see our object in action, with error handling now in place:

So far, we've seen a simple way to create an object and do things with it. What about those events though - how do we write code to respond to events on an object? Well, that's actually a lot simpler than you might think. Time to code the second button.

Try It Out - Programming Objects with Events

1 To get an object working with events, there is a catch in Visual Basic: we need to declare the object in the **Declarations** section, not within a subroutine.

Let's work with a second object, now, that will deal with events. Right at the top of the code window for `Form1` (which is the **Declarations** section), type this in:

```
Private WithEvents AnotherVehicleObject As clsVehicle
```

This declaration of `AnotherVehicleObject` has three very important differences from the other object declarations we've seen. Let's consider these now.

First, we've declared this object in the **Declarations** section of our code, whereas earlier object declarations have taken place within the actual method where they were being used. Second, there is a `WithEvents` keyword here. This just tells Visual Basic that we are willing to deal with events on the object - hence the name. The third difference, here, is the lack of the `New` keyword. If we declare an object using the `WithEvents` keyword then we can't use `New`.

> *So if we're going to use an object `WithEvents`, we need to create that object for ourselves, by hand. We cannot rely on Visual Basic to do this automatically for us.*

To recap: thus far, we've declared our new object in the **Declarations** section; we've indicated to Visual Basic that there will be events related to this object; but, without the `New` keyword available to us, we have not actually created new instance of `AnotherVehicleObject`.

2 So how do we create an actual instance of our new object? Bring up the form's `Load` event and add the following code:

```
Private Sub Form_Load()

    Set AnotherVehicleObject = New clsVehicle

End Sub
```

Even if you've never seen this technique before, the code should be fairly obvious. We're just setting `AnotherVehicleObject` to be a `New` instance of the `clsVehicle` class.

3 Now something cool has happened. If you drop down the object Combo box at the top left of the code window you will see that AnotherVehicleObject is listed in there, just as if it were a control on a form:

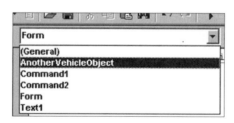

4   Select AnotherVehicleObject from this Combo box list, and the window will change to show you the `WheelChanged` event, ready to code:

5   Code up the event so that it looks like this, much as before really:

```
Private Sub AnotherVehicleObject_WheelChanged(ByVal intWheels As Integer)

    MsgBox "HEY! The number of wheels changed to " & intWheels

End Sub
```

6   Finally, code up the Command2 button's `Click` event so that it looks like this (if you want to go ahead and add your own error handler, like before, then please feel free to do so):

```
Private Sub Command2_Click()

    AnotherVehicleObject.Wheels = Val(Text1.Text)

End Sub
```

7   Now run the program once again, feed a number into the Text box, and hit the Command2 button. A Message box will appear courtesy of the event handler we just coded:

You might like to adapt this demonstration so that if we entered the same number of wheels twice in a row, the Message box wouldn't still tell us that we had changed the number of wheels.

That's really all there is to it! Okay, yes, there's a lot more stuff hidden away behind the scenes, and there are some really neat tricks we can do with the whole thing - that's where the rest of the book comes in!

By now, though, you should be fully refreshed with the wonders of classes in Visual Basic 6. We'll be seeing a lot more of them, and performing some very interesting object-oriented programming with them.

Object-Oriented Program Design

As any good developer will tell us, our programs will only ever be as good as the effort we put into our **program design**. It doesn't matter what method we use to get that code written (structured development, object-oriented development, or "Hey - let's see if this works" development), design work is the foundation of programming success.

When I first started out, one of the things that I found myself mumbling over and over was "There must be an easier way of doing this". Despite the fact that talking to oneself is the first sign of madness, I happened to be right. Enter stage left, the **design method**.

It seems that all over the world, brighter sparks than I were thinking, mumbling and screaming the same thing. A few of them sat down in their respective code-caves and came up with design methods: preset rules and techniques for working out the design of an application on paper, before the programmer sits down and starts to program.

Now, to many programmers, this sounds like a right royal pain in the backside. After all, we are programmers, not artists: why should we even bother with all this design nonsense? Think about this. Let's say you earn 20 bucks an hour and, after shipping the application, someone finds a tiny bug in your program. No problem - load up VB and fix it, change some code here, add a new variable there, 1 hour and 20 bucks later you have a happy user. The next day you get a call from a different user, but this time the problem lies with your understanding of the program, the design that's nestling in your head. It seems you didn't quite have the right grasp on the situation, and a huge lump of the application is now totally wrong and needs changing. That's going to cost your employer a few bucks more than the $20 it took to fix the simple bug isn't it?

Now, if you had done a design on paper before you started coding, and shown the users the design at that point in time, they would have spotted the problem and you could have changed it in an hour, instead of a month. Less heartache for you, less bother for the users, and less reason for your employer to start calling round recruitment agencies for your replacement.

Although there are quite a few techniques out there to assist in the design of object-oriented applications, I'm just going to whiz over a couple right now. Later in the book, in Chapter 9, we'll look at them in much more detail. For now, I just want you to know that these issues are out there waiting for us. All the great and powerful things that we're going to cover about object-oriented programming, between now and Chapter 9, are all dependent upon a good program design to help them work logically and successfully.

Okay, now you know how important program design is, let's take a quick look at a couple of the most popular design methods in use today.

> *Don't forget, if you want to know more about these techniques, we discuss them more thoroughly in Chapter 9.*

Use Case Techniques

The first technique worthy of mention is the **Use Case** technique. Despite the rather ominous sounding name, it really isn't all that difficult to get to grips with.

Rather than being a technique aimed at designing a final application, use case modeling is a **requirements gathering technique**. The use case technique provides a neat and effective way of obtaining a list of requirements for any new system, based on the way the current one works.

The use case technique is particularly useful in the world of object-oriented development, which is a very good reason for us to talk about it. Use case analysis provides a very easy way of identifying which objects will be required in a system and, therefore, which methods and properties those objects are going to need to support.

Take a look at this, a use case statement from a system we'll be developing towards the end of this book:

1 ORDERING A PRODUCT

Northwind maintains a catalogue of products, which is distributed to existing customers. Those customers may then call sales representatives to place an order, using the product IDs in the catalogue.

The customer calls a sales representative and asks to place an order. The rep starts a new order form and enters his or her employee ID at the top, along with the customer's ID and the date.

The customer then lists the product IDs required, and the quantity of each. For each ID, the employee checks the stock sheet to determine if the product is in stock and advises the customer if it is or is not, allowing the customer to change his or her mind. The customer is also told if any items are now discontinued, although Northwind may still have them in stock. If a product requested is discontinued, then the rep has to check other outstanding orders to ensure that it is not already due to be dispatched - and let the customer know.

When all the product IDs are entered, the customer chooses a preferred shipping company from a list that the representative gives. The rep enters the shipping company's ID onto the order sheet, and informs the customer of the total cost and shipping cost. The employee also enters the "required by" date onto the order and hangs up the phone.

The order form is then sent to the warehouse for dispatch. An order acknowledgement sheet is produced and dispatched to the customer.

As you can see, the format of the use case statement is quite simple. The first paragraph outlines the general problem area that the statement covers, while the rest of the statement explains in very clear terms what goes on in the real world for that problem area.

This particular statement is a very high-level one. It is a **requirements use case**. Typically, this would be used when you're talking to users, to get a grip on what they do in the real world. The requirements statement provides us with a starting point to begin drawing up a list of objects and their functionality in the final system.

Once the user is happy that the requirements use cases are correct, and that they reflect all the operations of the real world that are to be mirrored by the application, the statements can be broken down into more and more detailed ones, known as **functional use case statements**. We call these functional use case statements because they're sufficiently detailed to be able to outline specific functions the system may require.

> *I mentioned earlier that these things make it easy to spot the objects that will eventually appear in the system. Simply go through the statement looking for obvious nouns.*

So, from this use case statement, it's easy to see that some of the objects required will be *Customer*, *Order*, *Product*, *Supplier*, *Shipping-Company* and *Sales-Rep*. In Chapter 9, where we'll look at this technique in a lot more detail, we'll see how the use case statements can be transferred into a working design, and finally into code. It's not that tough, but it really is an essential part of object-oriented software development.

UML (Unified Modeling Language)

UML (**Unified Modeling Language**) is a true object-oriented design technique.

> *UML provides us with a way to draw diagrams that explain the relationships between our objects, as well as how these objects fit into the application as a whole.*

Take a look at this:

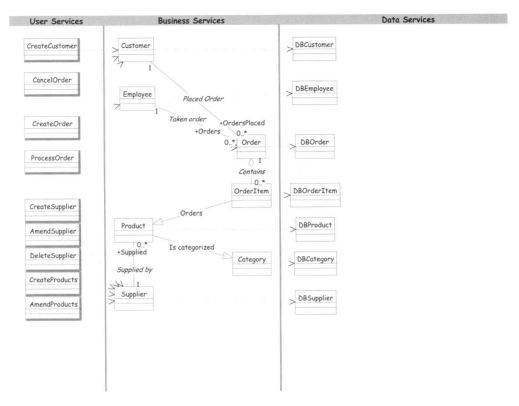

All the classes are listed in the diagram above. Where there is a relationship between one class and another, the name of the new property or member of the class that needs to be coded to represent that relationship is shown as well.

UML is more than just a way to produce a set of pretty pictures to go with a design though. Seeing the design on paper, and the relationships between all the objects in the system, provides vital information to developers on where their part of the development effort rests within the application. The graphic design provides a direct link between the final code and the somewhat ethereal design.

Furthermore, there are increasing number of design tools out there that let us produce UML designs for applications on our computer. These tools will then quite happily take the design that we've produced and turn it into a framework for an application in Visual Basic. In fact, we can get started with these tools almost for free.

> *If you have the Enterprise Edition of Visual Basic or Visual Studio then you should have access to Microsoft's own UML design tool, **Visual Modeler** (see Appendix A for more details). Visual Modeler is actually a cut down version of a bigger commercial product known as **Rational Rose**, and Rational provide a free downloadable trial version of this from their web site.*

As with use case modeling, however, UML is not something that we can do full justice to right now. For the moment, just keep these techniques ticking away in the back of your mind - they will come to affect everything else you learn about object-oriented programming. As I mentioned earlier, we'll be coming back to these techniques in Chapter 9 - but for now, I want you to become acquainted with another key area of object-oriented programming in Visual Basic - ActiveX.

ActiveX and Object-Oriented Programming

Ah, the 'A' word. You may be a little surprised to see **ActiveX** mentioned here in the opening chapter of a book about object-oriented programming. After all, ActiveX has been hyped beyond belief in the press as one of the next big things for the Internet. Nothing could be further from the truth.

> *ActiveX is the general name given to a set of technologies, within Windows, that allow applications to share data and functionality. ActiveX is, in effect, a way for one application to share its objects with another application.*

The reason ActiveX is here in this book is simple: Visual Basic 6 is fully ActiveX-enabled, and a great deal of our programming will make use of objects "served" from ActiveX server applications.

The Data Access Objects (DAO), for example (which we need to use if we want to get at Access databases from within Visual Basic), are not actually part of Visual Basic. They are objects contained in a separate application, an ActiveX component server. Likewise, most of the controls that we use to develop the user interface of our applications are not actually native parts of Visual Basic either. They are ActiveX controls: controls that live within separate OCX files on our computer.

Visual Basic 6 is more than just a user of other people's ActiveX efforts, however. Visual Basic 6 actually lets us go and create our own ActiveX servers (executable programs, or DLL files, which expose objects they contain to other applications). Using Visual Basic 6, we can go ahead and create any type of ActiveX object - from an ActiveX control, then ActiveX components, and right up to ActiveX documents. Let's take a quick tour to see what all these ActiveX elements are and how they affect the world of object-oriented programming.

> *We'll be learning a lot more about ActiveX and how its elements take us further into the world of object-oriented programming throughout the book.*

ActiveX Controls

ActiveX controls are what we use within Visual Basic to build our user interfaces; they are, in effect, the objects that we manipulate to build those user interfaces. We can therefore see ActiveX controls within Visual Basic's toolbar, like any other control that helps us to build new application interfaces:

When we create ActiveX controls with Visual Basic 6, they look very similar to normal Visual Basic applications, but instead of forms, we work with UserControls which ultimately show up in the Visual Basic toolbar.

ActiveX Components

ActiveX components are applications that let other applications use the classes they contain. In the following diagram, we have some code using a class from within one Visual Basic project, passing its results to a class in a second project:

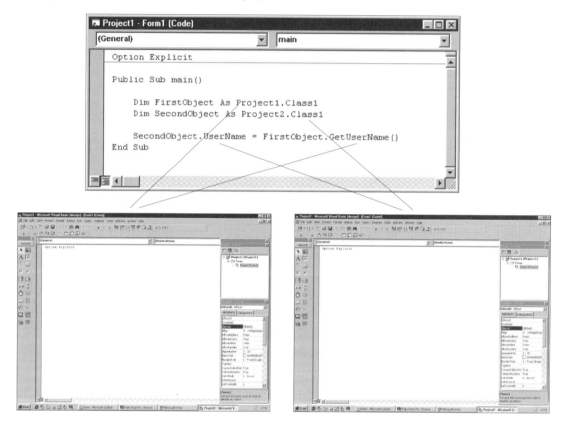

ActiveX components include the Data Access Objects (DAO) that we use to deal with databases within Visual Basic. As we noted earlier, the DAO is not actually part of Visual Basic - the DAO objects themselves are contained in a separate application, known as an ActiveX component server. Visual Basic is simply allowed to use the classes (and therefore the objects) contained within the DAO ActiveX component server application.

ActiveX Documents

ActiveX documents enable us turn a normal Visual Basic form into something that actually lives on the Internet and works within the confines of an ActiveX-enabled web browser, namely Microsoft Explorer. This is one way to bring objects to the Internet:

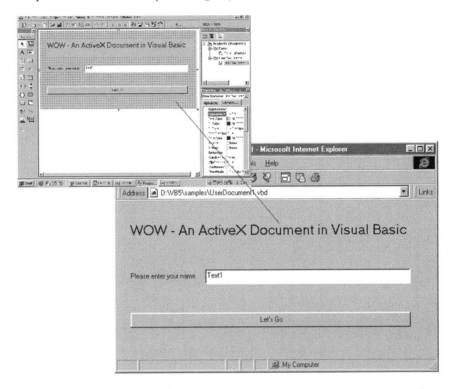

ActiveX truly opens up the world of object-oriented programming. It enables developers to ship applications that consist of more than one EXE or DLL file, where each file contains objects that are vital to the working of the application as a whole. This, in turn, means that other developers don't have to re-invent the wheel every time, since they can call upon the functionality contained within ActiveX servers residing on their own machines and the machines of their users.

From a maintenance point of view, things are also really cool. Changes to the functionality of the application no longer mean that the entire application needs to be reshipped and re-installed, since users need only update the servers themselves. A further benefit of this is that any other applications on a computer that make use of the same updated ActiveX objects will effectively be updated themselves.

ActiveX is a big area to truly get to grips with - so we'll be covering a lot of ground in more detail throughout the book.

Summary

In this first chapter, we've explored what objects are, and we've seen some techniques that will allow us to implement simple objects in Visual Basic 6. We learned about the relationship between objects and classes in Visual Basic, and we looked at object methods, object properties and object events.

We then explored object-oriented programming as a concept, considering its impact on Visual Basic as a language. We also acknowledged the importance of program design, which is fundamental to successful object-oriented programming. More of that in Chapter 9, when we come to consider object-oriented design in its full glory.

Finally, in this chapter, we overviewed the ActiveX technologies that Visual Basic makes available to us, and considered how those ActiveX technologies effected object-oriented programming in Visual Basic. A whole host of object-related programming activities open up with ActiveX technologies in Visual Basic.

Hopefully, then, I've whetted your appetite to learn more about object-oriented programming and the ActiveX technologies that we will return to again and again through the book.

Now that we've familiarized ourselves with the fundamentals of object-oriented programming in Visual Basic, in the next chapter we're going to take a ride to a company called Northwind. We'll learn a lot of valuable information about object-oriented programming while we're at Northwind - and what can happen without it! See you there.

Why Not Try....

1 What's the difference between an object and a class?

2 What's the difference between an object's methods and its properties?

3 What's the difference between an object's methods and its events?

4 What is the difference between object-oriented programming and the more traditional, structured approach to program development?

5 When a programmer develops an object through a Visual Basic class, who are the users of the object?

6

Why Program With Objects?

In this chapter, we'll look at why it's such a good idea to program with objects. We'll do this by paying a flying visit to Northwind Traders, a small company who embark on a programming project without recourse to any object-oriented programming techniques. By taking a look at what goes wrong for Northwind, we'll be able to see why programming with objects is such a great idea.

In this chapter, you will learn:

▶ Some of the history behind object-oriented programming

▶ How bad things can get when people program without an object-oriented philosophy

▶ The weaknesses of traditional structured programming methods

▶ How programming with objects can make life better

▶ Some of the key benefits of object-oriented programming

The Bad Old Days

Have you ever come across the concept of a chain letter? Yes, I know it's a strange way to start talking about object-oriented programming, but bear with me for a second.

The idea behind a chain letter is simple. There are some names on a list at the bottom of the letter, and it's your job to send them a buck or two, put your name on the list and then forward the list on to 6 or 7 people you know with the same instructions.

The theory is sound. Providing everyone you send the list out to follows the instructions precisely, sending you a buck and then sending the letter out to 6 or 7 of their friends, you should make quite a bit of cash. The first time you send the letter on you get 6 bucks. When it gets sent on again you end up getting another 36 dollars. When it goes again you get 216 dollars, and the next time 1296 and so on until pretty soon you are really quite well off.

As you can see, after only a short bout of letter forwarding there are suddenly a lot of letters out there, and a lot of people with your address. The amount of people that have the letter, and respond to it, grows exponentially until you quite quickly find that you can no longer calculate easily in your head the next amount of money to arrive.

This is very much how a piece of software works. We have a program with a few forms in it. Each form has a number of subroutines in it. Each subroutine has a number of possible routes through the code inside, and out to yet more subroutines. It doesn't take a genius to realize that the complexity of the permutations inside that code grows exponentially, just like the chain letter. Another similarity is that even the brightest human mind out there can soon lose track of what's going on, what should be where, and when. How on earth, then, can anyone ever deliver a bug-free system, on time and to specification?

The simple answer is that they can't - and that includes me. There's simply too much going on in your average business solution for you to realistically expect to hold every detail in your head.

I've never ever met a programmer who's been able to deliver on time, produce quality systems, remove all the bugs in an application, and still retain a very clear idea of what's going on inside every nook and cranny of the application.

The very best that any of us can probably hope for is some compromise, where we do well on most of the programming aspects that I just mentioned, but very rarely excel at all of them. The various programming techniques that have evolved through the history of programming have all been tools that have attempted to help us defy that compromise. Object-oriented programming is now the latest tool in that noble lineage.

When Wilbur Wright pulled back the yoke on his plane on that first flight at Kittyhawk, the world saw the state of the art in travel: a historical breakthrough in avionics. In the here and now, we know that there were a lot of things wrong with that first flight, the least of these not being that the plane only stayed airborne for a few seconds. Sure - things evolve: it's the nature of the world around us; and, as programmers, the nature of the industry we live and work in.

This book, and indeed object-oriented programming itself, is not going to solve every programming problem that you're going to encounter. What this book will do is show you where the current state of the art is: how object-oriented techniques can make everything run more smoothly in your programming career.

And more than that, this book is going to take all the boring dry theory and put it into something real, showing you how to turn that theory into a reality with the tools that Visual Basic 6 makes available.

Before we go any further, here's something else to ponder. Your average child today grows up, sees airplanes, jumps on one when they get a little older, and thinks those planes a pretty neat way to get around. But if we could send a time machine back a few years and drag Wilbur Wright into the present, he'd probably faint a few times and make some very strange noises when faced with a Boeing 747 or a Concord. Having experienced the previous state of the art, Wilbur would be totally awestruck by the fantastic standards of today: the shape of the wings, the cockpit layout, and the hydraulics underneath the plane. To Wilbur, these would probably all seem so brilliant, so right, so much more than simply a neat way of doing things.

With Wilbur Wright in mind (and he's no ancestor of mine), the rest of this book is going to take you on a journey around everything that's cool about VB6 in the new world of objects and deliverable applications. The state of the art moves on - no matter how comfortable we are with the old ways. Those older methodologies, such as structured programming, may well be cool tools - just like Wilbur's plane was pretty neat in its day. But the simple truth is this: Objects are to programming as the Boeing 747 was to the world of commercial flight. We're in a new paradigm now.

To answer the question 'Why Program with Objects?' in this chapter, we're going to be adventurous and take a flight in one of those old airplanes! We're going to study a business scenario where traditional programming techniques still prevail - and believe me; it's going to be a rough ride. Then we'll take a look at what made the flight so difficult, and we'll see how object-oriented programming techniques could have made the programming journey a whole lot smoother.

If you're an old hack then this flight will probably be all too familiar to you. You know how bad it can be. If you're a newcomer though, this rocky old flight will help you truly appreciate the modern tools you have before you.

Welcome to Northwind

We're about to find out how bad it can get when we don't program with objects. Our business scenario centers on a small company known as Northwind Traders, a specialist importer and re-seller of exotic foods and other goodies. In case you're wondering, these are the same guys whose database, `Nwind.mdb`, is supplied with Access and Visual Basic - which is kind of useful for us.

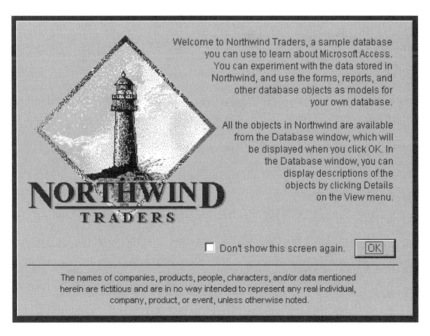

You can find the Nwind.mdb database file in the directory where you installed Visual Basic on your computer.

The Northwind database is a collection of eight interrelated tables of information that Northwind Traders keep about their business activities. As you can see from the screenshot below (taken within Access), Northwind keep database tables detailing such things as their customers, their employees, products, orders, and other related information:

Almost every one of these tables became very large over time. Here's a quick glimpse at a section of the Orders table, just so we get an idea of what Northwind were up to:

Order ID	Customer	Employee	Order Date	Required Date	Shipped D
10248	Vins et alcools Chevalier	Buchanan, Steven	04-Aug-94	01-Sep-94	16-Au
10249	Toms Spezialitäten	Suyama, Michael	05-Aug-94	16-Sep-94	10-Au
10250	Hanari Carnes	Peacock, Margaret	08-Aug-94	05-Sep-94	12-Au
10251	Victuailles en stock	Leverling, Janet	08-Aug-94	05-Sep-94	15-Au
10252	Suprêmes délices	Peacock, Margaret	09-Aug-94	06-Sep-94	11-Au
10253	Hanari Carnes	Leverling, Janet	10-Aug-94	24-Aug-94	16-Au
10254	Chop-suey Chinese	Buchanan, Steven	11-Aug-94	08-Sep-94	23-Au
10255	Richter Supermarkt	Dodsworth, Anne	12-Aug-94	09-Sep-94	15-Au
10256	Wellington Importadora	Leverling, Janet	15-Aug-94	12-Sep-94	17-Au
10257	HILARIÓN Abastos	Peacock, Margaret	16-Aug-94	13-Sep-94	22-Au

In fact these tables got so huge, that after years of development, re-development, fixing and amending, their invoicing and order entry system (written entirely in Access Basic) was beginning to creak and groan. The massive collection of Access forms, Access reports, custom queries and the odd code module could simply no longer cut it. What they needed was a Visual Basic system.

Although they had Visual Basic 6, the guys and girls at Northwind were better versed in traditional **structured development** techniques than they were in the newfangled object way of doing things.

Structured and Object-Oriented Programming

With a traditional structured approach to development, we tend to focus on the data that is managed by the application. We then start work on the code that maintains that data, breaking it down into smaller and smaller chunks until we finally reach a point where we're confident enough to start coding.

The object-oriented approach, on the other hand, has us focus on the real-world objects that the application is replacing or emulating - an invoice, for example; or perhaps a supplier, a customer, or a product. All these are objects with their own data and with their own code to work on that data. We'll be following object-oriented programming techniques throughout this book. As you'll see, it's a much nicer way of working.

In addition, the crew at Northwind were up against a fairly tight deadline, so the powers that be had decided "Better the devil you know" - and they went down the structured development route.

The first stop along their voyage of discovery was the GUI (Graphical User Interface). "Microsoft seems to know what they're doing with user interface design," the team had said one day, and proceeded to set about producing a Microsoft standard user interface, complete with menus, toolbars, buttons, status bars and much more besides. In fact, I have an early development shot of the product right here:

At this early stage, they hadn't managed to get any buttons on the toolbar; but you can see quite clearly that it's a pretty harmless user interface. A menu at the top of the form provided the users with a text based way to start up functionality in the program, while the toolbar underneath would ultimately provide a fast entry point for expert users. In addition, a cool status bar at the bottom of the form would be used to provide all users, no matter what their level of expertise, with advice and non-critical system messages.

> *The Northwind project quickly grew very big indeed, so we're just going to concentrate on the invoicing side of things, to keep it simple.*

The team decided that, initially, all they needed were two functions to deal with invoices:

- A function to create new invoices
- A function to review cashflow - based on invoices between a certain period.

The Northwind employees were very fortunate in that they never had a customer pay them late or fail to pay them at all, so they didn't need any functionality to deal with tracking invoices. Some companies have all the luck!

Creating the System

Two people were assigned to the invoicing side of things: one for each form. With some pretty rigid standards dealing with form design and layout of code, nobody could foresee any problems - all the code would look pretty similar and would be easily supported by anyone else on the team.

> *If you think everything worked out as easily as that for the Northwind employees, then stay tuned. Don't forget - we're paying a flying visiting to Northwind so we can find out how bad things can go wrong when you program without using objects!*

To keep things simple, we're just going to briefly overview the programming tasks performed by each Northwind employee. Believe me, Northwind ends up in a huge mess, so we'll just look at the details that will help us understand where things went wrong.

Creating Invoices

The invoice creation process at Northwind was real simple:

1 Take an order that's already been processed

2 Work out the value of everything in the order

3 Print it out on a sheet of paper labeled invoice

The form to do this was also pretty simple. The only thing the Northwind programmers needed to do, at first, was take an order number from the user. Once the user was done, the program then needed to go out to the database, grab the order information, and work out the financial details. The following screenshot shows you some of the solution they came up with.

> *Don't worry about creating any part of this Northwind program yourself - we're just here to take a theoretical look at a bad old-fashioned way of doing things!*

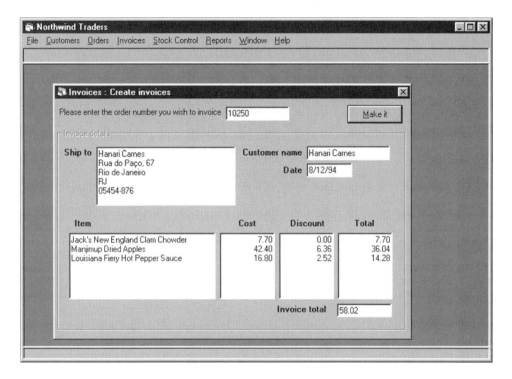

Once the details had been pulled from the database, the user could review the information on the form. If everything was OK, they would then select a menu item to print the invoice out on to the invoice printer.

The Northwind programmer decided to have a disabled frame in this form, with all the information inside it. This way, the user wouldn't be able to edit it, and potentially knock thousands of dollars off the company's bottom line in the process.

There were really two technical aspects to the form:

1 The user interface itself plus the code to deal with it

2 The functionality that dealt with the database and the order stuff

For the user interface, eight text boxes were used to display the actual information from the database. This decision was made because textboxes could be set up to align data to the left or right (which wouldn't be possible with list boxes, by the way).

In terms of finding out which order the user wanted to deal with, a text box was provided for the user to enter the order number, with some code behind it to make sure that the user only entered something numeric. When they were done, the user would click on a button at the top of the form, which contained the code to go out to the database and do the processing.

Our Northwind programmer wrote some code to ensure that the user entered only numeric information, and that code looked very much like this:

```
Private Sub txtOrderNo_KeyPress(KeyAscii As Integer)

' Need to filter out all keypresses with the exception of
' numbers.

    ' Allow control keys, such as tab, delete, return
    If KeyAscii < 32 Then Exit Sub

    ' If key pressed is not numeric, cancel it
    If KeyAscii < Asc("0") Or KeyAscii > Asc("9") _
Then KeyAscii = 0

End Sub
```

Pretty standard stuff: this code just looked at the key that was pressed, and only let through control keys (such as the cursor keys, backspace and delete) along with the number keys 0 to 9.

The nasty stuff lived in the Make It button's click event - a huge mass of code that accessed a database, built a recordset, copied field values to the controls on the form, and did a whole heap of other stuff. I wouldn't dream of exposing you to the whole thing in one go - it was so messy:

This code broke some very important rules that we'll be covering in the rest of the book:

➤ Keep your code cohesive - one routine for one job, not one routine that does 8 or 9 different things. The Make It button code, above, tried to do a lot of things in one routine: hit a database, load data, perform a search, fill text boxes... I'm sure you get the idea.

➤ Keep your code loosely coupled - you should be able to easily move code from one application to another, and not have any code that's explicitly linked to user interface controls and so on. When Northwind programmed this code, they wrote database code that was explicitly linked to the actual user interface button to make the invoice.

➤ Keep your code simple - big routines, and believe me the code in the Make It button was huge, are big problems from a maintenance and debugging point of view. Keep it small and keep it simple, always.

We'll be looking at these rules in more depth a little later - but let's admit something straight up. Let's go ahead and admit that when our back is against the wall and deadlines are looming, or when we get assigned a piece of work that we really aren't that keen on, things just don't run like this. We just try to get the application finished - at any cost.

Is that the way our programming has to be? No - in fact, object-oriented programming methodologies actually force us to do things in a nicer way, no matter what's happening around us. We have no choice but to do things properly! Trust me, our lives will be happier for it, and by the end of the book, you won't want to look back.

So let's now take a deep breath and see how this Make It button code works. We're going to get our hands dirty here - this is old technology.

Some Turbulent Invoice Code

The first chunk of code should be pretty clear if you've done any database work with Visual Basic. If you need a quick refresher though, take a peek at *Appendix B*

To begin with, our friendly Northwind programmer set up a slew of variables that they thought would be useful later on - for when they'd be performing the invoice calculations:

```
Private Sub cmdMake_Click()

' When this button is clicked, recordsets are opened in the
' database and the necessary values are calculated

    ' Declare the 4 recordset objects that we will need to
    ' work out the invoice details.

    Dim recCustomers As Recordset
    Dim recOrders As Recordset
    Dim recOrderItems As Recordset
    Dim recProducts As Recordset

    Dim curRunningTotal As Currency
    Dim curLineTotal As Currency
```

Next came some code that cleared out the text boxes on the form, ready for them to get some new data:

```
' Clear out all the text boxes - this way, if the
' user has entered an invalid order number then all
' they will see is a blank form

txtItems.Text = ""
txtCosts.Text = ""
txtDiscounts.Text = ""
txtTotals.Text = ""
txtShipping = ""
txtDate = ""
txtCustomer = ""
txtGrandTotal = ""
```

The following bit of the routine validated the order number that the user entered, making sure that they had entered something that actually existed in the database:

```
' First, open the orders recordset, so that we
' can check the order number entered by the user

Set recOrders = gDB.OpenRecordset("Orders", dbOpenTable)
recOrders.Index = "PrimaryKey"
recOrders.Seek "=", txtOrderNo

If recOrders.NoMatch Then
    MsgBox "You entered an invalid order number. Please " & _
    "try again", vbExclamation, "Error"
    recOrders.Close
    Exit Sub
End If
```

All that this section of code really did was open up the Orders table in the database and use the PrimaryKey index to find an order that matched the one that the user had entered on the form.

Now if that's not something crying out to be put into a reusable routine then I don't know what is! But, like I said before, our friends at Northwind were under pressure, keen to get the work done, and definitely not talking to each other about what the other had done, was planning to do, or needed.

It's just too easy, with structured programming, to forget that communication and teamwork are as important to getting a project out the door as is good solid code.

If there was no match between the order number the user entered in the form and any records in the database, then an error message was displayed and the routine exited. What happened to the user interface if the routine exited like this? Well, as we've already seen, there was code in place which cleared out the textboxes on the form, so an invalid order number resulted in the error message being displayed and the form being cleared of data.

Let's assume that the user did enter a valid order number. In this case, the next section of code shown below was run. This section pulled up the customer record that went with the valid order number. If it couldn't find a customer to match the order (something that should *never* have occurred) then the user would have been told that something really nasty had happened - the advice would be go get some painkillers and someone with a bit of technical knowledge:

```
    ' This point in the code will only be reached if we
    ' have a valid order number entered

    ' Now find the matching customer,
    ' or throw a serious headache if there's no match!

    Set recCustomers = gDB.OpenRecordset("Customers", dbOpenTable)
    recCustomers.Index = "PrimaryKey"
    recCustomers.Seek "=", recOrders!CustomerID
    If recCustomers.NoMatch Then
        MsgBox "There was a serious error - the customer and " & _
          "orders tables are out of sync", vbExclamation, "Error"
        recOrders.Close
        recCustomers.Close
        Exit Sub
    End If
```

At last, now, we get to see some code that actually meant something to someone dealing with invoices. First up, our Northwind programmers grabbed the items that corresponded to the valid order number the user had entered.

The Northwind database used quite a common arrangement, where the actual items that someone ordered were stored in a separate file from the order header information (customer number, shipping address, and so forth). This arrangement meant that Northwind needed to open yet another table to work out how much an order was really worth:

```
    ' Now we can open a snapshot with all the order
    ' detail records in

    Set recOrderItems = gDB.OpenRecordset _
  ("SELECT * FROM [Order Details] WHERE OrderID = " & _
  rsOrders!Orderid, dbOpenSnapshot)
```

For those not too familiar with SQL, what we have here is an `OpenRecordset` command that was issuing a SQL statement to `"SELECT"` a group of records from the `Order Details`. In this case, the `SELECT` statement was retrieving all records (*) from `Order Details` where the `OrderID` was a match against the order id (`Orderid`) of the current order:

Order ID	Product	Unit Price	Quantity	Discount
10248	Queso Cabrales	$14.00	12	0%
10248	Singaporean Hokkien Fried Mee	$9.80	10	0%
10248	Mozzarella di Giovanni	$34.80	5	0%
10249	Tofu	$18.60	9	0%
10249	Manjimup Dried Apples	$42.40	40	0%
10250	Jack's New England Clam Chowder	$7.70	10	0%
10250	Manjimup Dried Apples	$42.40	35	15%
10250	Louisiana Fiery Hot Pepper Sauce	$16.80	15	15%
10251	Gustaf's Knäckebröd	$16.80	6	5%
10251	Ravioli Angelo	$15.60	15	5%
10251	Louisiana Fiery Hot Pepper Sauce	$16.80	20	0%
10252	Sir Rodney's Marmalade	$64.80	40	5%

Orderid 10250

So in the example here, if the Orderid number was 10250, then all three records with the OrderID field of 10250 would have been selected. That's sounds like a fine meal.

By this stage, our Northwind programmers had collected several pieces of information together: the order selected by the user, the customer record that related to that order, and the set of items on that order. Now Northwind was at last ready to go ahead and start printing these details out on the form:

```
' Now at last we're ready to start putting
' information on the form

txtCustomer = recCustomers!CompanyName
txtDate = recOrders!ShippedDate

txtShipping = "" & recOrders!ShipName & vbCrLf
txtShipping = txtShipping & recOrders!ShipAddress & vbCrLf
txtShipping = txtShipping & recOrders!ShipCity & vbCrLf
txtShipping = txtShipping & recOrders!ShipRegion & vbCrLf
txtShipping = txtShipping & recOrders!Shippostalcode & vbCrLf
txtShipping = txtShipping & recOrders!ShipCountry
```

All that remained then was to work out the actual name of each product that the order item lines applied to, and to calculate those item prices ready to add into the grand total:

```
' Now we can loop through the items and put them on
' the invoice form

curRunningTotal = 0
Set recProducts = gDB.OpenRecordset("products", dbOpenTable)
recProducts.Index = "Primarykey"

Do While Not recOrderItems.EOF

    ' First find a product matching this item
    recProducts.Seek "=", recOrderItems!ProductID
    txtItems = txtItems & recProducts!ProductName & vbCrLf
    txtCosts = txtCosts & Format$(recOrderItems!UnitPrice, _
"#,##0.00") & vbCrLf
    txtDiscounts = txtDiscounts & Format$ _
    (recOrderItems!UnitPrice * recOrderItems!Discount, _
"#,##0.00") & vbCrLf

    curLineTotal = recOrderItems!UnitPrice * _
    (1 - recOrderItems!Discount)
    txtTotals = txtTotals & Format$(curLineTotal, _
"#,##0.00") & vbCrLf
    curRunningTotal = curRunningTotal + curLineTotal

    recOrderItems.MoveNext

Loop
```

It's worth noting, here, that the Northwind developer used what was quite a common trick from the traditional days of structured programming (before objects hit the scene). Notice that line near the top that reads:

```
Set recProducts = gDB.OpenRecordset("products", dbOpenTable)
```

The programmer has actually already declared a global variable gDB (somewhere else in the code) to hold a global database connection. You can tell it's a global from its g prefix, and you can tell it's a database connection from the DB bit. OK, so the programmer had to define this global variable him or herself, but in doing so they made sure that the currently connected database was available to any and all of the code in that application. Very handy I suppose - but I really don't recommend it at all.

> *In the world of object-oriented programming, each object would handle its own unique connection to whatever database it needed to use. You'll see this later in the book.*

Finally, the Northwind code printed out the running total and let the user continue with another order ID if they so desired:

```
txtGrandTotal = Format$(curRunningTotal, "#,##0.00")

recOrders.Close
recCustomers.Close
recProducts.Close
recOrderItems.Close

End Sub
```

Looking over this whole routine, it doesn't take a genius to realize that it's a huge amount of code for something so simple. OK, the Northwind team could argue that every line was required, but there really are quite a lot of problems with this code. Critically, it breaks those three very basic rules about code that we glimpsed at earlier - cohesion, loose coupling, and simplicity.

We'll discover ways to avoid breaking these rules as we venture deeper into the world of object-oriented programming through the rest of the book. For now, though, let's review these important issues as they occur within the Make It routine we've just seen.

Cohesion

First, there's the issue of **cohesion**. This is an incredibly simple principle that can add a great deal of value to our code, but one which many experienced programmers know little about.

Basically, we're aiming to write code that is strongly cohesive, which means that each routine, function, property, form or whatever else we may have in our project, should focus on one thing and one thing only.

> *It wouldn't surprise me if you were to go away and look at some of the things you've written to find that they were pretty light on cohesion. That's not a bad thing in itself, but to continue doing something, once you know that it's wrong, is definitely a bad thing in my books.*

In the above code, the Northwind programmers just went ahead and added code straight on to the Make It button - code that was doing a whole load of stuff that it shouldn't have been doing. The code behind that button was creating recordsets from the database, performing calculations, updating fields on the form, and whole host of other things on top of that! Each of these separate tasks should have been put in its own routine, with the Make It button's own code having nothing more than 4 or 5 lines to call those other routines.

Why? Well imagine what would have happened if an item name in the Northwind database had changed. Some poor lowly programmer would have had to go through *every single* routine in the code, checking that every reference to the database was still compatible with the new changes. Now if the programmer had written modules that contained a set of tightly cohesive routines, then it would have been a whole lot easier to keep track of the necessary code changes. Each routine would only have been performing one focus action, so the programmer would more easily have been able to select just those routines that were relevant to any database access.

Loose Coupling

The next problem lies with **coupling**. As well as tightly cohesive routines, we should also be aiming at loosely coupled ones. Again, this rule is nothing too complex: any routine we develop should be as loosely tied to the application as is practically possible - so we should be able to move our routines from one application to another without too much trouble.

Let's go back to that Make It button again. You'll recall that the code for this button goes to the database to retrieve information on a single order. And I just happen to know that, elsewhere in the Northwind application, this same task is done over and over again in other sections of code. Now if Northwind subsequently decided to move the Make It button's invoice-generating code to another invoice-based application (maybe to save time and money by reusing the same code), things would definitely not go well. The problem would be that the explicit references to the database would bind the Make It button to a particular set of assumptions about the database it was accessing. If the database in the new application had a different configuration, the Make It button's code would need to be extensively rewritten.

It would have been so much easier if our Northwind programmer had written just a single (highly cohesive) routine to retrieve information on an order. The Make It button could then have called this code rather than perform the actual database access itself. Two great advantages would have arisen from this:

▶ The Make It button would have been loosely coupled to the first project, so it's code could have easily been used within a second project. The second project would simply have needed to supply a separate routine to perform its own database access if the configuration was incompatible with the first project. The ability to reuse the Make It button code with relative ease like this would have saved much coding effort.

▶ By writing a highly cohesive database access routine to retrieve information on an order, whenever it became necessary to perform that task the new routine could simply have been called - instead of having to repeat the same sort of code over and over again.

It's worth noticing that the concepts of 'tightly cohesive code' and 'loosely coupled code' can dovetail with each other very well. For instance, we've talked about separating the database access code within the Make It button twice now. This same change first of all achieved a tighter cohesion within the Make It button code; and then it also happened to achieve a looser coupling of the Make It button code. This is no accident, but it does make life a lot easier.

Complexity

Another problem with the <u>Make</u> It button's code, as it stands, is its sheer complexity. It's huge! It's longer than anything you'd want to read through in one block.

There's a general rule of thumb here - if your code goes over 15-20 lines, then there's a strong chance that it could be broken down into smaller routines. This may seem like a rule designed just to give you more work, but trust me: shorter routines add a lot to the readability and therefore the maintainability of your code. If somebody needs to alter your code, life's going to be a lot easier for them if your routines are clear and well organized.

It's surprising how easy it is loose track of our own code (remember what I was saying about chain letters?) and an incredible amount of wasted time and effort is spent trying to fix code that's been put together in an unnecessarily complex fashion.

> *I'll leave you to ponder the full set of relationships between uncomplicated code, tightly cohesive code, and loosely coupled code. The only thing I will say is that all three lead to a happier life for us programmers.*

The rest of the problems with the <u>Make</u> It button are all fairly minor, but annoying nonetheless. That global database variable, gDB, for instance: I told you it would create some turbulence. With VB6, database access is so quick that we really can have our application open and close the database on the fly, whenever we need. The permanent open database connection, gDB, is just an additional memory overhead. If that wasn't bad enough, Access is not renowned for its stability when an application crashes with an open connection to one of its databases.

As you can see, our friends at Northwind were heading for some bad code and some bad headaches. Let's see how the other half of the programming team progressed.

Reviewing Invoice Cashflow

As you'll recall, the second form that the Northwind programmers decided they would need to write was a cashflow review form. The user would be able to enter a couple of dates and then get a complete list of all the invoices/orders between those two dates. This would allow the user to see at least one side of their business's cashflow situation.

The form that the Northwind designers came up with looked something like this.

> *Once again, you don't have to worry about coding this thing up - we're taking a hand-held tour of coding hell so that you can truly appreciate how heavenly object-orientation is in the rest of the book.*

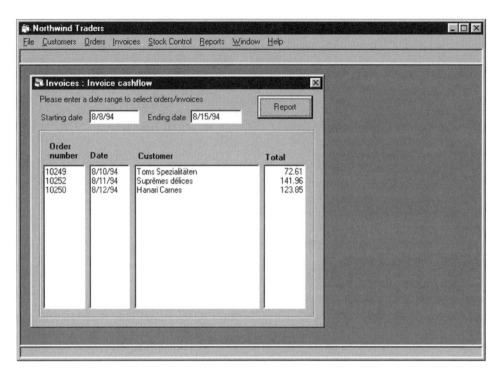

Pretty simple stuff - and if the user wanted to see some more detailed information, they could run up the other form and enter the order number shown in the list.

We're not going to go over the code behind this form line by line - I think you already have a pretty good idea of the kind of thought processes that were going on over there at Northwind. Take a look at the code for yourself though, and I'll see you afterwards - where we examine just what's been going wrong with this whole thing.

> *I wanted you to see this code in its raw state. To make it a bit more palatable, I've made sure there are plenty of comments in there to help you get an idea of what's going on.*

```
Private Sub cmdReport_Click()

' Get orders from the database between the two entered dates

    ' Declare some recordsets to access the database
    Dim recOrders As Recordset
    Dim recOrderItems As Recordset
    Dim recCustomers As Recordset
    Dim curSubTotal As Currency
    Dim curItemTotal As Currency

    Set recOrders = gDB.OpenRecordset _
("SELECT * FROM orders WHERE shippeddate >= #" & _
txtStartDate & "# and shippeddate <= #" & txtEndDate & _
"# ORDER BY shippeddate", dbOpenSnapshot)
```

```
        ' Clear out the boxes on the form
        txtOrders = ""
        txtDates = ""
        txtCustomers = ""
        txtTotals = ""

        ' Now we can loop through the orders and work everything
        ' out. First, open up the customer table in order that we can
        ' match the customers against the orders as we work through
        ' the loop

        Set recCustomers = gDB.OpenRecordset("Customers", dbOpenTable)
        recCustomers.Index = "PrimaryKey"

        ' Now start the loop
        Do While Not recOrders.EOF

            ' Grab the order items that match this particular order
            Set recOrderItems = gDB.OpenRecordset _
            ("SELECT * FROM [Order Details] WHERE orderid = " & _
            recOrders!OrderID, dbOpenSnapshot)
            curSubTotal = 0
            Do While Not recOrderItems.EOF

                ' Calculate the item total, taking the discount into
                ' effect, and add it to the total
                curItemTotal = recOrderItems!UnitPrice * _
                    (1 - recOrderItems!Discount)
                curSubTotal = curSubTotal + curItemTotal

                recOrderItems.MoveNext
            Loop
            recOrderItems.Close

            ' Add in the freight
            curSubTotal = curSubTotal + recOrders!Freight

            ' Finally, find a match with the order to the customer
            recCustomers.Seek "=", recOrders!CustomerId

            ' At this point we can add the invoice information into
            ' the text boxes on the form.
            txtOrders = txtOrders & recOrders!OrderID & vbCrLf
            txtDates = txtDates & recOrders!shippeddate & vbCrLf
            txtCustomers = txtCustomers & recCustomers!CompanyName _
            & vbCrLf
            txtTotals = txtTotals & curSubTotal & vbCrLf

            recOrders.MoveNext

        Loop

        recCustomers.Close
        recOrders.Close

End Sub
```

Same old problems as before - those guys were really on a roll weren't they? This time it was even worse though, since this one piece of code actually dealt with processing on **three** tables within the database!

Right at the start of the routine, the code opened a recordset requesting all orders placed between the two dates entered on the form:

```
Set recOrders = gDB.OpenRecordset _
 ("SELECT * FROM orders WHERE shippeddate >= #" & _
 txtStartDate & "# and shippeddate <= #" & txtEndDate & _
 "# ORDER BY shippeddate", dbOpenSnapshot)
```

This, in itself, could have been be a routine all on its own; if you're in any doubt, please review our earlier discussion on the topic of cohesion.

Half way through the code, we can see a loop finally kicked off, which was designed to go through each order held in the `recOrders` recordset:

```
' Now start the loop
Do While Not recOrders.EOF
```

For each order in the `recOrders` recordset, yet another recordset was built, which consisted of all the items that went to make up the order itself:

```
' Grab the order items that match this particular order
    Set recOrderItems = gDB.OpenRecordset _
 ("SELECT * FROM [Order Details] WHERE orderid = " & _
 recOrders!OrderID, dbOpenSnapshot)
```

The whole looping procedure to build up these recordsets is another terrible example of cohesion - the code to select those items relating to a particular order really should have gone in a separate routine entirely. As it stands, the loop is overburdened with disparate tasks.

The rest of the code is one horrendous mess of simple math to work out how much in total the order is worth, what the value of the discount is, and so on. For such simple math, it's an absolute travesty that Northwind wound up with this terrible code.

At the very least, the whole of this routine should have been broken down into a number of smaller routines. In an ideal world, the programmer would have called on someone with more database experience to produce the relevant database access code (such as a single SQL query, which could have been stored in the Access database itself). This neater approach would have created simpler, more cohesive code, since the code for the Make It button would be distinct from the database code. The project code would also have been more loosely coupled, since the Make It button's code could be transported more easily to another project.

> With object-oriented technology, the Make It button's code wouldn't care at all what code actually supported its database access. Instead, it would just call methods and properties on the relevant objects to get at the database information it needed, without a care in the world as to what went on in the database 'black boxes'. Much nicer!

Problems, Problems, Everywhere!

OK, so the ride with Northwind has been a bit bumpy so far. Actually, we haven't seen anything yet - but the real problems are, I'm afraid, just about to start. Please fasten your seatbelts.

For anybody who's ever done any development work, it should already be quite clear that there are a number of ways to improve the structure of the code in these two forms - even without having to turn to objects. As I mentioned earlier, however, this really isn't a thought that most programmers entertain when their deadline approaches and their boss starts getting tense. That's a shame.

So yes - the code could have been written better, even within a structured programming methodology. But my point, here, is that Northwind did write bad code - and they wrote bad code for some very regular reasons:

▶ They didn't use object-oriented programming techniques

▶ They had deadlines and pressures from their bosses

The whole of this book is about using object-oriented techniques. The Northwind programmers should have read this book (never mind the temporal problems). And Northwind had deadlines; but then who doesn't? So regardless of how nice or nasty the code has been so far, the fundamental programming methodology at Northwind let them down. Under pressure, they produced bad code - and we're about to see the unfortunate consequences.

We're going to consider two key phases where object-oriented programming would have produced significantly better results. The first of these is within the original development phase, while the second is within the subsequent maintenance and fixing issues that followed… read on.

Issue 1 - The Totaling Bug

It wasn't long after the Northwind application was deployed that a chilling bug was spotted - something that the testers had not come across (shame on them).

On the surface it was quite simple: pull up an invoice in the Create invoices form, and the total would be different from the one that you saw in the Invoice cashflow form.

 Bugs are bugs are bugs are a pain in the butt, and whichever methodology you decide to use (object-oriented programming or structured programming) you're still going to get them. Resolving them and fixing them is easier with the object-oriented approach.

You see, on the surface, this bug would appear to be nothing more than a simple calculation error, a spelling mistake or an omission of some kind. However, there were problems resolving it. With two distinctly separate pieces of code responsible for calculating the totals of the invoices, which one was wrong? In addition, the two programmers were now hard at work on something else, but the quickest way to resolve the problems would surely be to get them each to go over their own code.

Eventually, after many forays into Access to print out data, and trying to work out the figures by hand, the problem was traced to an error in the cmdMake_Click routine. It wasn't including the necessary code to add in the cost of shipping to the invoice total, something resolved with just a few lines of code a little later on.

The Object View

This was a fairly simple bug, so how on earth could an object-oriented approach have prevented it? Well, the truth is that it could not have been prevented at all - if a programmer is going to make a mistake like this, then they will do so whatever development methodology they follow. However, an OOP approach would have made fixing it a whole lot easier.

Because there were two programmers responsible for the two distinct forms in the application, it was impossible to pinpoint exactly where the error lay. What if there had been ten forms dealing with invoicing, or fifty? Then the problem would have been proportionately worse, with nobody having a clue where exactly the faulty code might be.

With an object approach to development, however, the code to calculate the invoice total would live in just one place - in an InvoiceTotal property or method. If the invoices were kicking out silly figures, then just one programmer would be needed to look over just this one routine.

Furthermore, since objects in an application are designed to model the real-life objects involved, it would be very easy to pinpoint exactly where a bug might be in an object application - without even having to look into the code. This makes it much easier to debug programs written with OOP techniques.

Issue 2 – The Extension Issue

After the application had been in the field for a while, it became apparent that some method of logging what each user was doing, particularly with regard to invoicing, was necessary. Specifically, a competitor seemed to be aware of just how much money Northwind was making with certain customers and at certain periods of the year - information that they were not so sure that they wanted to share with the world!

After much pondering, Northwind decided that the easiest thing to do would be to log every time a user ran up an invoicing form, or feature, out to a log file (just something as simple as a text file listing any and all important operations that a user kicked off). In addition, management wanted to be able to log which invoices were examined - and by whom. In time, hopefully, this would deter users from casually browsing through the financial records of the company, and would thus stop the leak of information. This meant that, one day, there would also need to be some way to turn the logging on and off.

Once again, the result was that a programmer was pulled back into the invoicing code. She spent weeks on the new feature. She added it to each and every form, and made sure she was totally happy with how all the forms worked with the new code. Eventually, she was happy that the new code did not introduce any new bugs into any of the forms.

And yet, despite all her diligence (even to the point of putting the new code in modules and calling single routines from the modules), she had to change the code in the invoicing forms. That, in turn, meant that everything to do with invoicing had to be tested and checked once again. This involved not only checking that her new code was working, but also checking that she hadn't screwed up anything that was previously working... it took ages.

The Object View

As I mentioned before, with object-oriented programming the code to do something with an object lives entirely in one place (which leads to highly cohesive code).

The result is significant. Take that Northwind extension to develop an audit-logging feature and add it to every form that deals with invoices. With object-oriented programming, this requires little more than loading up the code for the Invoice object and changing just that one piece of code. All the other forms dealing with invoices would, after all, simply be accessing methods and properties on that Invoice object.

What about Northwind's plan to turn logging on and off? With object-oriented programming, this could be achieved with a simple Boolean property on the Invoice object. Interfacing that Boolean property to the main application would require a simple line of code like this:

```
MyInvoice.Logging = False
```

Testing would also be reduced, and more focussed. Tests could be run prior to the change, perhaps even with an automated test program written in VB, which would pass values into the properties and methods of the object - and then log the results. Provided the results from the object's interface were the same after the logging code was added, there would be no real need to test the various forms and modules which made use of the object.

This would mean less time spent plowing through code to ensure that nothing was missed. It would mean less time spent learning the format of other programmers' work - which can be quite indecipherable. And it would mean less chance of introducing errors into the application.

Issue 3 - The Code Sharing Issue

Northwind began to grow, and pretty quickly appointed a full-time financial department to handle much of the day-to-day financial work. As they became more and more adept at using the technology around them, they took to using Excel to produce forecasts, charts, and more detailed interim reports. In fact, Northwind became so hungry for data that its needs could only be satisfied by a whole party of programmers.

One programmer was assigned to produce a routine that would export data to a file that could later be read into Excel. This took quite a while, and of course it resulted in the inevitable testing/bug fixing cycle. When complete, the rollout disrupted all the users - who had to stop work while someone installed the new software on their machines.

The Object View

If the development team had taken a more object-oriented approach from the start, then they could have realized the benefits of ActiveX deployment in VB6.

VB6 allows you to take a class, or a group of classes, and wrap them inside an ActiveX DLL or EXE. The additional complexity to the code is marginal, changing lines that look like this:

Dim MyObject As New clsInvoice

...to lines that look like this:

Dim MyObject As New BusinessServer.clsInvoice

As we'll see later, if our servers are named so that they are unique on our system (BusinessServer may well be a unique application name on many systems) then we wouldn't even need to change the code in the application - we could just add a reference to the server.

There are a number of benefits to this approach. If the Northwind programmers had taken all their business-based code (like Invoice objects, Order objects, and so on) and put them into an ActiveX DLL, then the code inside that DLL could have been used by any ActiveX enabled system, such as Excel.

The application itself would not need to have been changed. Instead, the financial Excel users could have had some training in how to get at the code within the DLL from within Excel using Visual Basic for Applications (VBA), which is embedded within Excel.

Issue 4 - The Database Issue

Years later, Northwind had grown again, and this was something that was causing some serious problems for the existing VB application. Instead of the one or two people that used to be logged on to the application, at the time when it was written, there was now a need to have 50 people online together. Limitations with the Access Jet engine simply didn't make this feasible.

After a big sales pitch from Microsoft, it was decided that Northwind should upgrade their database from an Access database to a SQL Server database. The application, as it stood, was fine - and most of the users were really quite happy about it. All that had to change was the database access code; something that the advertisements for Visual Basic had claimed was an easy task.

An easy task it was not. Every reference to a recordset had to be changed to deal with an RDO resultset. In addition, code that was previously just grabbing a record and setting field values on it now had to be changed so that it would call a SQL Server stored procedure to do the dirty work.

For those of you who haven't a clue what I'm talking about here, let me explain. Many Visual Basic programmers are quite happy to limit all their database work to the wonderful world of Access databases. With Access databases, as you know, we have tables, and queries to those tables, all within a single file. VB allows us to get at table data by creating recordsets.

*Unfortunately, Access has its limitations. It just can't handle very large amounts of information very well. For larger projects, like the one at Northwind, it eventually becomes necessary to upgrade from Access to something known as **SQL Server**.*

*SQL Server and its VB sidekick **RDO (Remote Data Objects)** are a very different setup from Access. SQL Server is a full-blown database server system, designed to reside on a powerful networked machine. Users access SQL Server across a network from their own machines. While we can use the same code in our applications to get at a SQL Server database as we would an Access database (the format of the open command is slightly different) there are some serious benefits to getting hold of Visual Basic Enterprise edition and using RDO.*

*With RDO (which is several evolutionary steps ahead of DAO), we use resultsets instead of recordsets. Resultsets are basically the same as recordsets, but resultsets are normally not updateable. To update the database, we would call a **stored procedure**, which is a block of code stored inside the SQL Server database. We would also very often create our resultsets by using stored procedures. This means, rather happily, that there's no more need to mess around with SQL code at the programmer's end of the knife. Database programming therefore becomes distinct from user-interface programming, for instance, which leads to more cohesive programs and a happier life for us all. I'm sure you get the general idea now, but the whole thing is a little out of the scope of our work here, so let's move on.*

Rather than enjoying the benefits that SQL Server should have brought to their project, the result was a complete nightmare for Northwind. What was initially going to be a simple task ended up taking six months, with every single form in the application having to be substantially changed; and then, of course, each form had to be tested before the application was finally shipped.

The Northwind team at that point vowed never to use Visual Basic again.

The Object View

In this case, the team was severely hit by their lack of object-oriented experience and development, and made the decision to ditch Visual Basic through a lack of knowledge. It's an interesting aside that the same cycle of trauma and pain was experienced when they made the switch to a new development tool, a tool in which they had even less experience.

> *The beauty of object-oriented development is that it allows programmers to take a black box approach to software development. The core of the application is coded into classes, which at runtime become objects. These are the black boxes, each with their own clearly defined interface of properties and methods. Just like any other black box that you may come across in your life, such as your TV set, the only thing that users of the classes/objects are really concerned with is the interface to the object, not how it works inside.*
>
> *For Northwind's project, had the bulk of the code resided in objects distinctly separate from the user interface, the team could have limited their work to changing the database access code in those objects. The user interface appearance, and the code behind the user interface, could have remained intact and would not have needed to be re-tested. Our friends from Northwind would then only have needed to test the interfaces to the objects, to check that the inputs were causing the right outputs.*
>
> *It gets better though. If Northwind had deployed these objects as ActiveX DLLs, then the upgrade process for the users would have been as simple as copying a new DLL onto their system - something that could even be done automatically over the network when they next logged on. No pain, no fuss, no worry, and no stress.*

Summary

In this chapter, we've been on a flying visit to Northwind Traders, and we've seen how things can go very wrong for a programming project - as well as how object-oriented programming can move us towards an easier and happier programming life.

We've seen some of the weaknesses of traditional structured programming methods, and we've learned about the important issues of cohesion, loose coupling, and complexity of code. Hopefully, you'll now have a sense of how highly cohesive code and a clearer, object-oriented approach can really improve the way you code your applications. At the very least, you'll know what to avoid in the future.

While they don't do absolutely everything a programmer will ever need, they do move us closer to the goal of delivering bug free, painless systems quickly and easily.

Throughout the rest of this book, we'll be seeing exactly how we can implement object-oriented programs using Visual Basic. Our ride will be a smoother one than Northwind, so let's move on now to take a more detailed look at object-oriented development.

Why Not Try....

1 Which rules did the NorthWind programmers break when they coded their Invoice program?

2 Discuss this statement: Each procedure should be designed to complete a single task. Is there a problem with this statement?

3 Discuss coupling in the NorthWind database application.

4 Let's tackle the issue of complexity here. Can you think of any guidelines that can alert you to the fact that you are writing code that is a bit too complex?

6

OO Development

Overview

In this chapter, we're going to explore some of the key programming techniques that will take us to the heart of object-oriented development with Visual Basic.

We saw, in the last chapter, just how badly things can go wrong without the good principles of object-oriented programming behind us. And we're familiar, now, with some of the key benefits of working with objects - so the techniques we learn here will be prepare us well for our future programming careers.

We're actually going back to another company, but this time I think you'll find that DataDamage Inc. are a much more aware bunch of people, and that they appreciate the value of the object-oriented techniques available to today's Visual Basic programmers.

In particular, in this chapter we'll be looking at:

- Developing a real-world object-oriented application
- Object Interfaces
- Multiple interfaces
- The Implements keyword
- Inheritance
- Containment and Delegation

Real Object-Oriented Programming

With Visual Basic 6, objects are here to stay. Love them or hate them, we can't get away from them. Without exception, everything we deal with in Visual Basic is an object. The forms we draw our user interfaces on, the controls that we put on to the form, and even most of the system objects that we use, from time to time, to complete the shine on our applications - they are all objects.

Visual Basic's support for object-oriented development has come a long way since previous versions. We now have the ability to expose more than one interface from within an object, thanks to the `Implements` keyword (more on that later), and we can create our own custom events at runtime. Visual Basic has a lot to offer real-world programming situations.

> *The problem with the whole thing, though, is that the object-oriented programming world is still populated by PhD-toting gangsters. These guys would have you believe that objects represent a different world, as opposed to just a neat way to design and develop applications. We covered a lot of the theory in my previous book (Beginning Visual Basic 6, also published by Wrox Press), but this time around we're going to see it used in anger, see some real-world development done with object-oriented programming.*

Let me tell you: OOP isn't that hard. It doesn't need that much in the way of background training, or patterns of deep thought. It's all a matter of common sense. Let's take a look at a real problem.

Welcome to DataDamage Inc

Our client, DataDamage Inc, has decided that something needs to be done to keep abreast of their `Biblio` database, which is a database containing a vast array of information on programming books, authors and publishers. They've decided to break down the development of this project into phases, with Phase 1 covering nothing more than the maintenance of the Authors table in the database, as well as simple browsing of the `Titles` table.

Sounds simple enough - nothing a few well-placed Data controls and some bound Text boxes won't handle. But wait a minute. Although the database is currently in Access format, a quick peek at the long-term plans for the system reveals some worrying elements. Not only are DataDamage going to want to migrate this system from an Access database up to a SQL Server database at some point in time, but they're also going to be using the code we write as the foundation for other developers to get started on the system. Anything we do now must remain useful under the new architecture.

In addition, it's quite likely that they will want to split the application itself across multiple machines on the network to improve the performance of the system. A few data controls and a couple of bound Text boxes aren't going to be much help here.

From Design to Object Analysis

Normally, at this point, we'd hit the paper and produce a full design of the application. This design would be from the point of view of the way things are done now (user requirements), the way they should be done in the new system (system requirements), and the way that it's all going to actually work (functional requirements).

My goal within this chapter, however, is to concentrate first and foremost on getting us through the technical aspects of OO development with Visual Basic. As we saw in Chapter 1, program design is a crucial part of object-oriented development, which is why I've devoted the whole of Chapter 9 to design techniques.

In this chapter, I'm going to speed us through the design phase so we can focus on the practical aspects of object-oriented development. If you're madly keen to learn about object-oriented program design, then take a peek at Chapter 9.

So the simple design I've prepared for us in this chapter looks like this:

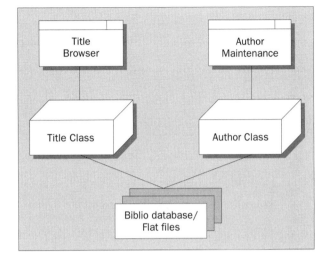

We have a data source (the `Biblio` database), which is going to be accessed by two classes. As we saw in the last chapter, the beauty of classes is that we can hide the data source in a neat black box with a simple interface.

Remember, an interface in object-oriented terms is the collection of methods, properties and events that go towards unleashing the power of our objects in a way which is easy to get to grips with.

These classes are then used in two forms to provide the `Title Browser` and `Author Maintenance` functions that we'll require.

Our next step (and this is really where we swing back into the design process), is to come up with the interface for these objects: the properties and methods that will be used to provide access to the underlying data. In the interest of keeping things real simple for the moment, let's just take a look at the `Titles` class:

Method	Description
MoveFirst	Moves to the first title in the data source
MoveNext	Moves to the next title in the data source
MovePrevious	Moves to the previous title in the data source
MoveLast	Moves to the last title in the data source

Pretty clear I think: we're going to provide some very similar functionality to something we might find in a recordset object itself, albeit without the ability to update the underlying data. Ah, the data... we're going to need some properties in there to get at that underlying data:

Properties	Description
BOF	Boolean to indicate if we're at the beginning of the `Titles` table
EOF	Boolean to indicate if we're the end of the `Titles` table.
Title	The Title field from the `Titles` table
Year_Published	The Year Published field from the `Titles` table
ISBN	The ISBN field - `Titles` table
PubID	The PubID field - `Titles` table
Description	The Description field - `Titles` table
Notes	The Notes field - `Titles` table
Subject	The Subject field - `Titles` table
Comments	The Comments field - `Titles` table

So there we have it. A simple interface that exposes the underlying data as well as the functionality to manipulate that data.

Creating a Class

Now we've designed our interface, let's go ahead and translate all of these ideas into some real code with some real functionality behind it. Once we've created our class, we'll build a test framework to see it in action.

Try It Out – Creating a Class for DataDamage Inc

1 Start up a new project and, when it appears, add a new class module in the usual way. If you can't remember how to do that, then now might be a good time to re-read Chapter 1, or consult my other book, *Beginning Visual Basic 6*.

2 The next step is to start adding code into our new class module to implement all the methods and properties that we've just discussed. For now, just key in the following code so that your class module looks like mine. By typing this lot in you're sure to come up with some questions of your own as to how things work, and I can go ahead and start answering them when the code is done.

> *There is a lot of code here, but the interface is real simple, and the bulk of it is quite repetitive and easy to follow. We'll take a closer look at how it works once you've typed it in.*

```
Option Explicit

' clsTitles - wraps up the Biblio Titles table. By keeping the
' interface consistent it should be possible to move the class
' to point at some other data source, such as an RDO Resultset,
' or flat file, without users of the class ever noticing.
```

```
Public Event DataChanged()

' Public members to implement properties
Public strTitle As String
Public intYear_Published As Integer
Public strISBN As String
Public lngPubID As Long
Public strDescription As String
Public strNotes As String
Public strSubject As String
Public strComments As String

' Private members to hold connection to database,
' and to the recordset itself

Private m_recTitles As Recordset
Private m_dbDatabase As Database

' Class event handlers

Private Sub Class_Initialize()
' When an instance of the class is created, we want to
' connect to the database and open up the Titles table.

    On Error GoTo Class_Initialize_Error

    Set m_dbDatabase = Workspaces(0).OpenDatabase _
(App.Path & "\Biblio.mdb")
    Set m_recTitles = m_dbDatabase.OpenRecordset("Titles", _
dbOpenTable)

    Exit Sub

Class_Initialize_Error:
    MsgBox "There was a problem opening either the Biblio " & _
"database, or the Titles table.", vbExclamation, "Problem"
    Exit Sub

End Sub

Private Sub Class_Terminate()
' When the instance of the class is destroyed, we need to
' close down the recordset, and also the connection to the
' database. Error handling is needed since there could have
' been a problem in the Initialize routine making these
' connections invalid

    On Error Resume Next

    m_recTitles.Close
    m_dbDatabase.Close

End Sub

' Generic Data management methods

Private Sub Reload_Members()
' Reloads the member variables (properties) with the field
```

```vb
' values of the current record

    On Error GoTo Reload_Members_Error

    With m_recTitles

        strTitle = "" & .Fields("title")
        intYear_Published = .Fields("Year Published")
        strISBN = "" & .Fields("ISBN")
        lngPubID = .Fields("PubID")
        strDescription = "" & .Fields("description")
        strNotes = "" & .Fields("Notes")
        strSubject = "" & .Fields("subject")
        strComments = "" & .Fields("Comments")

    End With

    RaiseEvent DataChanged

Reload_Members_Error:

    Exit Sub

End Sub

' Class methods

Public Sub MoveNext()
    If Not m_recTitles.EOF Then
        m_recTitles.MoveNext
        Reload_Members
    End If
End Sub

Public Sub MovePrevious()
    If Not m_recTitles.BOF Then
        m_recTitles.MovePrevious
        Reload_Members
    End If
End Sub

Public Sub MoveLast()
    m_recTitles.MoveLast
    Reload_Members
End Sub

Public Sub MoveFirst()
    m_recTitles.MoveFirst
    Reload_Members
End Sub
```

3 Don't forget to give the class a name when you are done typing. In order for your code to work the same as mine, it makes sense that you set the name property for your new class to `clsTitles` (reminding us that this is a class related to `Titles`).

4 You've probably noticed that there's quite a lot of database code in there. In order for this code to compile properly, we need to let Visual Basic know that we intend to use a database, and that it's going to involve setting a reference to VB6's Data Access Objects (DAO).

> *You may recall, from Chapter 1, that DAO in Visual Basic 6 is an ActiveX component. As such, the DAO doesn't reside within Visual Basic itself, which is why we have to build a reference to it now.*

From the <u>P</u>roject menu in Visual Basic, select Refere<u>n</u>ces, and the references dialog will appear. This provides us with a way to show Visual Basic which external objects (objects that live in DLLs or separate EXE files from your own app) that we intend to use. Scroll down the list of items until you see Microsoft DAO 3.51 Object Library and select it, just as in the screenshot below. Then close the dialog down by clicking the OK button:

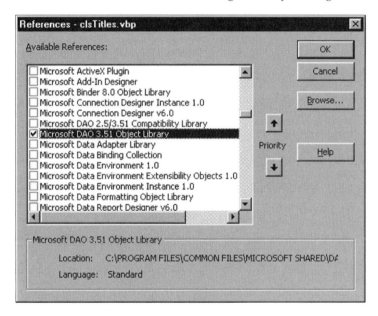

Now that everything is in place for our new `clsTitles` class to work, we'll take a look at the code and how it works.

How It Works

The first thing that any class needs is a way for its users to get at the important elements of the underlying data. We do this by declaring properties for the class.

Designing an interface for a class involves declaring a set of properties in very much the same way as how we interact with a set of properties when we design a user interface for our applications.

Since this class is supposed to wrap up a lot of functionality to deal with the `Titles` table in the `Biblio` database, it makes sense for us to have some properties in there to represent the fields in the underlying database. Then, no matter what format of database we use in the future, programmers using our `clsTitles` class will know that they can use these field properties to get at the underlying data.

Rather than spend ages typing in `Property Let` and `Property Get` routines, we've gone for a simpler approach this time:

```
' Public members to implement properties
Public strTitle As String
Public intYear_Published As Integer
Public strISBN As String
Public lngPubID As Long
Public strDescription As String
Public strNotes As String
Public strSubject As String
Public strComments As String
```

> *You don't need to key all this in again - we're reviewing the code we just entered for our* `clsTitles` *class.*

As you can see here, what we're doing here is declaring a set of `Public` variables within our `clsTitles` class. `Public` variables declared in a class in this way are, as far as Visual Basic is concerned, read and write properties. At runtime, a user of our `clsTitles` class can get directly at the `Title` property of the object, and at that point they will be reading from, or writing to, these `Public` variables.

FYI   **We still have scope though to expand and write full-blown property handlers later, should the need arise.**

Having variables acting as properties is great, but we still need code to get data from the database into those variables in the first place. That's where the `Reload_Members` routine comes in, reading data from the underlying recordset and storing it in our property variables:

```
Private Sub Reload_Members()
' Reloads the member variables (properties) with the field
' values of the current record

    On Error GoTo Reload_Members_Error

    With m_recTitles

        strTitle = "" & .Fields("title")
        intYear_Published = .Fields("Year Published")
        strISBN = "" & .Fields("ISBN")
        lngPubID = .Fields("PubID")
        strDescription = "" & .Fields("description")
        strNotes = "" & .Fields("Notes")
        strSubject = "" & .Fields("subject")
        strComments = "" & .Fields("Comments")

    End With
```

```
        RaiseEvent DataChanged

    Reload_Members_Error:

        Exit Sub

    End Sub
```

All we're doing here is pulling values from the fields in the `m_recTitles` recordset and putting them into our member variables. At the end of this, we raise a custom event, which we've called `DataChanged`, since the user interface needs some way of knowing when these member variables have changed and it needs to update itself.

The `m_recTitles` recordset itself is opened up when the class is first turned into an object. Take a look at the class initializer: first

```
    Private Sub Class_Initialize()
    ' When an instance of the class is created, we want to
    ' connect to the database and open up the Titles table.

        On Error GoTo Class_Initialize_Error

        Set m_dbDatabase = Workspaces(0).OpenDatabase _
    (App.Path & "\Biblio.mdb")
        Set m_recTitles = m_dbDatabase.OpenRecordset("Titles", _
    dbOpenTable)

        Exit Sub

    Class_Initialize_Error:
        MsgBox "There was a problem opening either the Biblio " & _
    "database, or the Titles table.", vbExclamation, "Problem"
        Exit Sub

    End Sub
```

This is pretty neat. Our `clsTitles` class is designed to deal with one specific table in a very specific database, `Biblio.mdb`. We therefore code the `Class_Initialize` event to make the class automatically connect to that database:

```
    Set m_dbDatabase = Workspaces(0).OpenDatabase _
    (App.Path & "\Biblio.mdb")
        Set m_recTitles = m_dbDatabase.OpenRecordset("Titles", _
    dbOpenTable)
```

This, in turn, reduces the workload for a user of the class: how many of us have written a class, for example, where we require a user of that class to pass in the pre-connected database object ready to use?

> *A point worth noting, though, is that the code prefixes the name of the database with*
> *App.Path. What this means, in English, is that the clsTitles class will expect to find*
> *a copy of the Biblio database in the directory the project lives in, or where the compiled*
> *program lives when we're finished.*

So now might be a good time to run up the Windows Explorer and make sure that there's a copy of the Biblio.mdb *database in the same directory that you intend to save this project.*

For any programs you write in the future that access databases, if you know the location of those databases then you can specify a particular path within your code, instead of using the App.Path *method. In some circumstances, it may even be appropriate to ask the user to enter a pathname for any databases they want your program to work with.*

The rest of our code for clsTitles provides an interface to support the common Move commands that we'd find on a recordset; in our case, this means just passing the call down to the recordset itself, before updating the member variables with the new information. Take a look at the MoveNext method, for example:

```
Public Sub MoveNext()
    If Not m_recTitles.EOF Then
        m_recTitles.MoveNext
        Reload_Members
    End If
End Sub
```

This code first makes a quick check to see if the end of the table has been reached. If we haven't reached the end of the table, we can move on to the next record - by calling the MoveNext method on the recordset itself. After that, our old friend the Reload_Members method is run, which will move the information from the underlying fields in the new recordset to our clsTitles member properties.

Using Our Class

Ok, let's get some forms up so we can actually use our clsTitles class.

Try It Out – Using Our clsTitles Class

1 Our application is going to be a traditional MDI (Multiple Document Interface) application.

Go ahead and add an MDI form to your project. Once again, if any of this form/module adding stuff seems a little strange then you'd do well to check out my last book, *Beginning Visual Basic 6.*

Since this is an MDI form, make it big enough to be able to hold the other windows that it's going to contain. If you make it too small, its child windows won't be completely visible within it - which isn't great for our users.

2 Set the name of this form to mdiMain. Then select **Properties** from the **Project** menu and use the **General** tab dialog to set the start-up form to be this MDI form, as in the screenshot here:

For the sake of completeness, you should also set up the project name to BiblioTech, just as I have done here.

3 Okay, so we have an MDI form in the application, and we have the `clsTitles` class that neatly wraps up the `Titles` table. We now need to add a menu to our MDI form that will allow us to access the other forms that we'll be adding to the application.

Add the following menu headings to the MDI form: File, Titles and Authors. Remember, you can do this in Visual Basic by selecting the MDI form in design mode, and then pressing *Ctrl* and *E* to bring up the menu editor. There's no need to worry about giving these things neat names since we aren't going to add any code to respond to events on them - it's the submenu items that we're more concerned with. I called mine `mnuFile`, `mnuTitles`, and `mnuAuthors`, respectively:

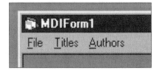

4 Use the menu editor again to add a menu item under the File menu. Set this new menu option caption to Exit and then name it `mnuFExit`. Underneath the Titles heading, put a Browse item in there and call it `mnuTBrowse`. Finally, underneath the Authors heading, put a Maintain item on there and call it `mnuAMaintain`:

5   The next step is to get the actual **Title Browsing** form up and ready, with code to start it up from the MDI.

As you've probably noticed, there's a lot here for us to do in this phase of our application development - such are the toils of creating a user interface. I'm not an unsympathetic guy! Take a break for this step, and just read what I have to say about user interfaces and object interfaces.

User Interfaces and Object Interfaces

While we're in the middle of building our user interface for DataDamage Inc, I'd like to point out to you how closely related user interfaces and object interfaces are to one another. This is really interesting.

Object-oriented programming does, in fact, fit in really well with the way Windows works. At the root of any programming problem there's a hideous mess of data and an equally unnerving set of code to manipulate that data. Dump that code in a class, though, and we can design a nice interface to that code and data - something more meaningful and more in tune with the real-world problem. Now in terms of the user interface of a Windows application, we usually provide graphical controls on a form that hook into some or all of the interfaces in our classes and objects. This is a case of a user interface marrying an object interface, if you like.

*Our **Title Browsing** form is going to provide users of the application with much the same interface as we can deal with in our objects. For **Title Browsing**, the interface will of course be in the form of buttons and text boxes, while our classes (such as* clsTitles*) and then our objects will interface through properties and methods.*

---

6 Let's get that **Title Browsing** form up and running. Add a standard form to the project, call it `frmTitle`, and set the `MDIChild` property on the form to `True`. By default, at runtime Windows will create this form in a default size, which can totally screw up our user interface.

Rather than write a lot of resize code to make the controls and the form appear as we intended at runtime, simply set the `Borderstyle` property to `Fixed Dialog`.

7 When you've done these things, go ahead and drop some controls on the form so that it looks like this:

Set the names of the text boxes to `txtTitle, txtYear_Published, txtISBN, txtPubID, txtDescription, txtNotes, txtSubject, txtComments` - names that fit quite nicely with the actual properties on the class. Likewise, set the names of the buttons to `cmdFirst, cmdPrevious, cmdNext` and `cmdLast`. Notice that I've also set the `Caption` property of the form to **Title Browser** - it would be rude not to, after all.

8 In order to get this working, we need to add a little code. Now the important thing to note here is that the hard work is done. We have a class with a very neat interface, and all we now need to do is to literally link the user interface elements to the class interface elements.

Click on the new form to select it, then hit *F7* on the keyboard to open up its code window. When it appears, key this code in:

```
Option Explicit

Private WithEvents Titles As clsTitles

Private Sub cmdFirst_Click()
    Titles.MoveFirst
End Sub
```

77

```vb
Private Sub cmdLast_Click()
    Titles.MoveLast
End Sub

Private Sub cmdNext_Click()
    Titles.MoveNext
End Sub

Private Sub cmdPrevious_Click()
    Titles.MovePrevious
End Sub

Private Sub Form_Load()
    Set Titles = New clsTitles
End Sub

Private Sub Titles_DataChanged()
' When the data changes, we need to load up the text
' boxes on the form

   With Titles
txtTitle = .strTitle
txtYear_Published = .intYear_Published
txtISBN = .strISBN
txtPubID = .lngPubID
txtDescription = .strDescription
txtNotes = .strNotes
txtSubject = .strSubject
txtComments = .strComments
   End With

End Sub
```

Incredibly simple huh? We just call single methods from the click events on those buttons. Take the First button, for example:

```vb
Private Sub cmdFirst_Click()
    Titles.MoveFirst
End Sub
```

The important part of this code, though, is the event handling.

FYI

It is most fortunate that Visual Basic 6 lets us create our own custom events. In the early days of VB, we could write an application that utilized classes, but we would still need to write nasty blocks of code to wait for conditions on our objects to occur. In Visual Basic 6 we can just raise a custom event.

We declared the `DataChanged` event, if you recall, right at the beginning of our `clsTitles` class like this:

```vb
Public Event DataChanged()
```

which is just a little note telling VB that there's a new event that can occur, and that it's called `DataChanged`. This event is triggered by the programmer with the `RaiseEvent` command; in our case, in the `Reload_Members` method within the `clsTitles` class:

```
RaiseEvent DataChanged
```

No great problems there I hope. However, dealing with the events in code elsewhere in the project does require a little thought. We need to declare the object WithEvents; this means that when we declare an instance of our Titles object, we just do the following (as you'll see right at the top of the code we just added to our Title Browsing form):

```
Private WithEvents Titles As clsTitles
```

At this point, the `Titles` object (which is derived from the `clsTitles` class) is available in the object drop down at the top of the code window, just as if it were a control on the form.

Using events like this greatly reduces the amount of code in the application. No more endless loops waiting for a specific condition to occur! There is a catch though, as we can see in the form's Form_Load event: when we declare an object WithEvents, we can't create the object at that point in time! So, where we would normally say:

```
Dim MyObject As New clsMyClass
```

we actually have to drop the New keyword when we use WithEvents. This isn't a big problem, but it can cause us problems if we forget to actually create the object! That's where the Form_Load event comes in:

```
Private Sub Form_Load()
    Set Titles = New clsTitles
End Sub
```

Here the object is actually created, and stored in our `Titles` object variable, which we declared earlier.

The beauty of objects and events is that they let us deal with the flow of our program in the same way that we might deal with the flow of events in everyday life. Very few people wait specifically for the phone to ring day in, day out: they prefer instead to respond to the phone's ring event.

9 Finally, we need to add some code to get the MDI form to load up the Titles browsing form. From the Project explorer window, double click on the MDI form, mdiMain, and select the Browse option from underneath the Titles menu. The code window will appear. Now code the event so that it looks like this:

```
Private Sub mnuTBrowse_Click()
    Load frmTitle
End Sub
```

10 At this stage, our program works just as we would expect it to. Run it up and have a play with the **Title Browsing** form to get a feel for what it's doing. There's a lot going on behind the scenes, however, that demonstrates some of the benefits of the object way of working. Just to recap:

▶ The application is now independent of its data

▶ Black-box development simplifies GUI code

▶ Custom events reduce code size at front end

But there's more good news: Visual Basic's support for object-orientation goes far beyond writing custom events, properties and methods. Let's take a look...

Interfaces

We've discussed interfaces a few times, now, when we've been talking about objects, classes, and black boxes; but what exactly is an interface, and why do we care?

Class Interfaces and Object Interfaces

Well, we already know that an interface is really nothing more than the name given to the collection of properties and methods within a class. That sounds simple enough, but it's worth looking at interfaces in some more detail now.

A **class interface** is the collection of properties and methods within a class: that's the public stuff, the public variables, property routines, subroutines and functions that we put into our classes.

The private variables and routines within our class, on the other hand, are typically called **Member routines**.

It's worth noting that since we create objects from classes in Visual Basic, there is a clear relationship between class interfaces and **object interfaces**. Once we've created an instance of a class, our object will have an object interface as defined by its underlying class interface.

The Implements Command

Visual Basic 6 comes with a special command that lets us do some neat things with class interfaces, and this is the `Implements` command.

Placed at the top of a class module, the `Implements` command forces us to write (or implement) the same methods and properties as those implemented in another class module.

In effect, this forces us to implement the same class interface for one class as that of another class. Consider this: if the class interface for `Class1` consists of three methods and four properties, and we use the following command at the top of a second class called `Class2`:

```
Implements Class1
```

then this forces us to implement the same three methods and four properties within `Class2` as those defined in `Class1`.

However, the methods, properties, etc. that make up a class interface do not have to be implemented using the precise same lines of code that were present in the original class interface.

The methods in the original class interface must all be defined within the implemented class interface, it's true, but the actual lines of code within those methods may be quite different from the original class interface that's being implemented. This takes us back to the theme of the black box: just as long as the buttons (or methods) on the outside of the black box work, we don't have to worry about what's going on behind the scenes.

Not every television, for instance, has the same internal workings inside it: all that matters is that the key functions we expect from a television are available to us. And so it is with our class interfaces: the lines of code behind each implementation of a class interface may be quite different.

If you are still a bit unsure about this idea of implementing, then you could take a quick peek at the section on **interface inheritance** that appears in a few pages time. It contains a good example of the use of the `Implements` command.

Right, I hope you've returned to this point, as we are about to consider the subject of multiple interfaces and see how handy the `Implements` command can be.

Multiple Interfaces

This concept is real simple: a class can support more than one interface.

Let's stay with our `Class1` and `Class2` example for a moment. Assuming we'd just implemented the interface for `Class1` within our code for `Class2`, we could then proceed to add a new set of methods and properties to `Class2` that were above and beyond the methods and properties implemented from `Class1`.

At which point, `Class2` happens to support more than one interface: first, the default class interface for `Class1`; and second, the class interface defined by the new methods and properties that belong to `Class2` itself:

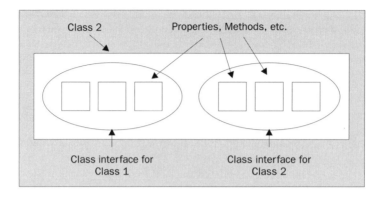

By arranging for a number of classes to implement the same interface, we're forcing the developers of those classes to conform to a particular set of standards. This makes life a lot easier for the people using those classes, since they can expect a certain interface to always be available.

Think about a car, a small van, and a large semi-truck. All have a common interface: press the gas pedal to go faster, press the brake to slow down, and turn the steering wheel to change direction. Each has at least one door, requires fuel, and contains a set of dials and gauges to show your current speed, fuel remaining, oil pressure and so on.

All of these classes implement a **common interface**: a Vehicle interface, if you like. Aside from implementing that Vehicle interface, however, each class has its own unique interface - which it bolts on to the base Vehicle interface. A car has rear seats, for example; a van has the ability to carry more goods than a car, but has less seats; and a semi has a detachable freight carrying device (its trailer), possibly a bed (if it's a long haul truck), and so on.

Let's carry this line of thought on for a little longer. A car and van could conceivably have the same chassis, the same engine, and to all intents and purposes they could be identical in every way if we ripped the bodywork off. A semi, on the other hand, is completely different underneath the surface. Now since all these cars implement the same interface as a basic Vehicle, we could take any qualified driver and tell them to *Drive* each of the vehicles from one point to another. *Drive* is a common method that most drivers know how to use, and the chances are that most drivers could get all three vehicles moving as requested. So despite the differences, and indeed the similarities, between these three vehicles, the *Drive* method will get us driving - whichever car we're in:

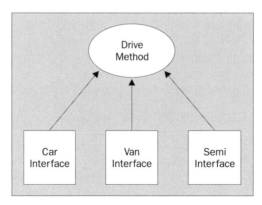

Visual Basic works the same way. If we have a `Vehicle` class defined with a `Drive` method (among others), we can implement the Vehicle interface within new `Car`, `Van` and `Semi` classes. Then, if we want to get our `Car`, `Van` and `Semi` objects moving, Visual Basic will allow us to pass each of these objects to a routine that simply expects a `Vehicle` type object and then calls its appropriate `Drive` method.

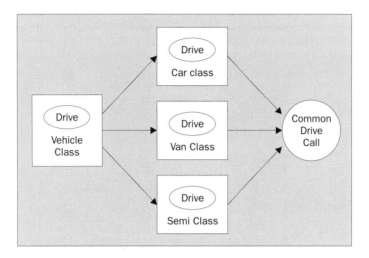

Implementing Interfaces in Visual Basic 6

In our example application for DataDamage Inc, multiple interfaces will be very useful. So far, we have a neat title browser. It works quite well, and this browser interface represents something that we would ideally like to see in the *Authors* class a little later.

So although we will ultimately need to produce both a `clsTitles` class (done that) and a distinct `clsAuthors` class, these classes will have some common methods. For instance, each class will allow the browsing of data. At the same time, however, each class will have its own unique properties, and the `clsAuthors` class will need to have its own unique methods of changing the underlying Author data (since Author data will be arranged differently in the database than the Title data).

So here's our plan: we'll define the common browsing interface between these two classes - that is, the interface that contains the `MoveFirst`, `Next`, `Previous` and `Last` methods. We'll then implement that common browsing interface in both the `clsTitles` class and the `clsAuthors` class.

Anyone who later modifies or deals with the code in our application will be grinning from ear to ear when they see that all data access objects in our application actually have a common object interface.

So how do we define a common interface between two classes? Well, the best way to do this is to start to think in terms of class **frameworks**.

The framework of a class is actually the bare bones of the interface for that class. A framework is therefore just a list of the public routines and properties that form the interface for a class or object, without any real code to actually implement that interface.

Frameworks are therefore the briefest possible description of a class interface or object interface, since they contain none of the actual code behind that interface - just empty routines and properties. Frameworks are useful things to know about, so let's get on with some code and see it all in action.

Try It Out – Using Implements

1 Since our `clsTitles` and `clsAuthors` classes are going to share a common interface, the first thing we must do is move the basic framework of the *Titles* interface out into another object.

Add a new class module to your project and call it `clsRecordset`. When that's done, add the following code.

```
Option Explicit

' clsRecordset object - a generic object designed to wrap
' up the functionality of a recordset in a generic re-useable
' object.


Private Sub Class_Initialize()
'
End Sub

Private Sub Class_Terminate()
'
End Sub

' Class methods
Public Sub MoveNext()
'
End Sub

Public Sub MovePrevious()
'
End Sub

Public Sub MoveLast()
'
End Sub

Public Sub MoveFirst()
'
End Sub

Public Sub AddAsNew()
'
End Sub

Public Sub SaveChanges()
'
End Sub
```

```
Public Sub DeleteCurrent()
'
End Sub
```

Be careful when you define your own interfaces like this though. The Visual Basic compiler has a real nasty habit of wiping out any empty routines that you might have in your project, hence the reasoning behind putting a single quote (comment) in each of the routines above.

Notice that all these routines are just bare definitions - with no real code in them. Also notice that we're adding three routines to this framework that weren't present within our original clsTitles class (AddAsNew, SaveChanges and DeleteCurrent) which are specifically concerned with adding, saving and deleting data. These are of little relevance for clsTitles, but will feature in our clsAuthors class.

2 With our clsRecordset framework interface defined, the next step is to actually let Visual Basic start enforcing it on our code - which is a perfect job for the Implements command.

Bring up the code for your clsTitles class and add a line just underneath the Option Explicit statement so that your code now reads like this:

```
Option Explicit

' clsTitles - wraps up the Biblio Titles table. By keeping the interface
' consistent it should be possible to move the class to point at some
' other data source, such as an Rdo Resultset, or flat file, without
' users of the class ever noticing.

Implements clsRecordset

Public Event DataChanged()
  :
  :
```

If we now try to compile this program and run it, we find that it no longer works: Visual Basic instead gives us a host of new error messages:

I wasn't kidding before, when I said that using `Implements` tells the compiler to force you to write certain routines! But this is just what we want, in our case, since we need to produce a consistent interface across the `clsTitles` class and the `clsAuthors` class that we're going to create shortly!

> *You may also notice how useful this could be in a team development environment where you would need to manage a group of developers and make sure that they were all developing to certain interface standards.*

3 The previous error message is telling us that, in order for the `clsTitles` class to implement the interface of the `clsRecordset` class, we need to write a method called `MoveNext`.

But hang on a second! We did write a `MoveNext` method; it does exist! If it didn't exist, then the application as it existed before we put that new `clsRecordset` class in would not have worked at all. The truth of the matter is that Visual Basic is just expecting a little more than we have already done. Time to find out just what.

Try going back to the code editor for the `clsTitles` source and drop down the **Objects** Combo box at the top of the editor:

Notice how the list now includes a `clsRecordset` object, just as if we had dropped a control on to a form and we were editing the form's code.

Select `clsRecordset` from this drop down list, just as I have done here.

4 Now drop down the **Events** list Combo box, which sits at the top right of the code window. You'll see a list of all the `clsRecordset` methods that we can implement in the `CTitles` class:

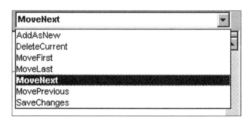

What does all this tell us? Something quite simple really: that our `clsTitles` class has two interfaces: the original `clsTitles` class interface, and now also the `clsRecordset` class interface that we added to `clsTitles` (we used `Implements` to do that).

The upshot is clear enough: all the routines in this drop down list for the `clsRecordset` interface will need to be defined within our `clsTitles` class.

> *As we noted before, it's perfectly true that there are routines by these names already present in our clsTitles class; but those routines are currently part of the default class interface for clsTitles. We now need to implement the clsRecordset class interface within clsTitles, which we committed ourselves to with the Implements clsRecordset command.*

Next question: how do we implement the clsRecordset class interface within the clsTitles class? Take a look at this routine (but don't type it in yet):

```
Public Sub clsRecordset_MoveNext()
If Not m_recTitles.EOF Then
    m_recTitles.MoveNext
    Reload_Members
End If
End Sub
```

This is our MoveNext routine all right, but notice that it's prefixed with clsRecordset_ which tells Visual Basic that this routine belongs to the clsRecordset interface. This prefix method is how we tell Visual Basic which routines and properties belong to which interface.

5 Okay, in order to get the clsTitles class working again, go through and change all the Public method names in clsTitles so that they're prefixed with clsRecordset.

Be careful though: you only need to do this for Public *methods that are also in the* clsRecordset *interface.*

You should end up with all your Public routines, which looked something like this:

```
Public Sub MoveFirst()
    m_recTitles.MoveFirst
    Reload_Members
End Sub
```

now looking more like this:

```
Public Sub clsRecordset_MoveFirst()
    m_recTitles.MoveFirst
    Reload_Members
End Sub
```

6 Since we added three new methods to the clsRecordset class, to create an interface for updating data (AddAsNew, SaveChanges and DeleteCurrent), we'll also need to code these routines into our clsTitles class.

Therefore add the following routines to clsTitles:

```
Public Sub clsRecordset_AddAsNew()
' Do nothing
End Sub

Public Sub clsRecordset_SaveChanges()
' Do nothing
End Sub
```

```
Public Sub clsRecordset_DeleteCurrent()
' Do nothing
End Sub
```

Notice that these routines are commented out again. We don't want them to actually do anything, at this stage, since our `clsTitles` class is just to allow browsing. We still need to implement them, however, since we've committed ourselves to implementing the entire `clsRecordset` interface within `clsTitles`.

7 When you're done, try running the application again, and you'll quickly find that it doesn't work. If you're in any doubt, try pressing the First button on our browsing form!

It's actually very interesting why things aren't working yet. Take a look at the code behind the First button on the browsing form:

```
Private Sub cmdFirst_Click()
    Titles.MoveFirst
End Sub
```

Visual Basic looks at this code and says "Ok, the programmer wants me to run the MoveFirst method on the Titles object". It then takes a peek at the default interface for the *Titles* object (which is the `clsTitles` interface) and sees that it doesn't actually have a `MoveFirst` method. There's one on the `clsRecordset` interface, which `clsTitles` implements, but not on the `clsTitles` interface itself anymore (we changed it, remember?). The net result: Visual Basic gives you an error.

As we've already seen, if we need to make calls to code that lives in an implemented interface, then we must prefix the method name with the name of the interface. Therefore, the code above should actually read:

```
Private Sub cmdFirst_Click()
Titles.clsRecordset_MoveFirst
End Sub
```

Also prefix the method name with `clsRecordset_` in the `cmdLast_Click`, `cmdNext_Click` and `cmdPrevious_Click` routines.

Okay, let's move on to the Author class of the DataDamage Inc application.

Try It Out - Adding the Author Class

1 On the whole, the `Author` class is very similar to the `Titles` class, with the simple addition that we'll allow the user to add, edit and delete records. Given the code that we have, this should be pretty easy to do.

Put a new class module into the application, and copy and paste the entire `clsTitles` class code into it. Change the name of this new class to `clsAuthors`.

Something called containment provides us with a workaround to save us doing this, but more on that later.

2 Once we have the `clsTitles` code pasted into our new class, there are a few routines that we obviously need to change: the Authors table in the `Biblio` database, for example, has a totally different set of fields. I've listed the entire class below, with the relevant changes highlighted:

```
Option Explicit

' clsAuthors - wraps up the functionality to browse and
' maintain the authors table in the Biblio database

Implements clsRecordset

Public Event DataChanged()

' Public members to implement properties
Public lngAu_ID As Long
Public strAuthor As String
Public intYear_Born As Integer

' Private members to hold connection to database,
' and to the recordset itself
Private m_recAuthors As Recordset
Private m_dbDatabase As Database

' Class event handlers

Private Sub Class_Initialize()
' When an instance of the class is created, we want to
' connect to the database and open up the Authors table.

    On Error GoTo Class_Initialize_Error

Set m_dbDatabase = Workspaces(0).OpenDatabase _
    (App.Path & "\Biblio.mdb")
Set m_recAuthors = m_dbDatabase.OpenRecordset("Authors", _
    dbOpenTable)

    Exit Sub

Class_Initialize_Error:
    MsgBox "There was a problem opening either the Biblio " & _
    "database, or the Authors table.", vbExclamation, "Problem"
Exit Sub

End Sub

Private Sub Class_Terminate()
' When the instance of the class is destroyed, we need to
' close down the recordset, and also the connection to the
' database. Error handling is needed since there could have
' been a problem in the Initialize routine making these
' connections invalid
```

```
        On Error Resume Next

        m_recAuthors.Close
        m_dbDatabase.Close

    End Sub

    ' Generic Data management methods
    Private Sub Reload_Members()
    ' Reloads the member variables (properties) with the field
    ' values of the current record

        On Error GoTo Reload_Members_Error

        With m_recAuthors

            lngAu_ID = .Fields("au_id")
            strAuthor = "" & .Fields("author")
            If Not IsNull(.Fields("Year Born")) Then
                intYear_Born = .Fields("Year Born")
            Else
                intYear_Born = 0
            End If

        End With

        RaiseEvent DataChanged

    Reload_Members_Error:

        Exit Sub

    End Sub

    Private Sub Save_Members()
    ' Assumes that the recordset is in either Edit or Addnew mode.

        On Error GoTo Save_Members_Error

        With m_recAuthors

            .Fields("Author") = "" & strAuthor
            .Fields("Year Born") = intYear_Born

        End With

    Save_Members_Error:

        Exit Sub

    End Sub

    ' Class methods

    Public Sub clsRecordset_MoveNext()
        If Not m_recAuthors.EOF Then
            m_recAuthors.MoveNext
            Reload_Members
```

```
         End If
End Sub

Public Sub clsRecordset_MovePrevious()
    If Not m_recAuthors.BOF Then
        m_recAuthors.MovePrevious
        Reload_Members
    End If
End Sub

Public Sub clsRecordset_MoveLast()
    m_recAuthors.MoveLast
    Reload_Members
End Sub

Public Sub clsRecordset_MoveFirst()
    m_recAuthors.MoveFirst
    Reload_Members
End Sub

Private Sub clsRecordset_SaveChanges()
'
    With m_recAuthors
        .Edit
        Save_Members
        .Update
    End With

End Sub

Private Sub clsRecordset_AddAsNew()
'
    With m_recAuthors
        .AddNew
        Save_Members
        .Update
    End With

End Sub

Private Sub clsRecordset_DeleteCurrent()
'
    m_recAuthors.Delete
    On Error Resume Next
    m_recAuthors.MoveFirst
    Reload_Members

End Sub
```

As you can see, it's really pretty similar to the Titles class. The obvious differences are the names of the member properties to get at the field values, as well as the name of the member recordset. Finally, we added some code this time around to handle the Add, Edit and Delete methods, as well as a new private routine, Save_Members, to copy the values of the member variables out to the corresponding fields.

3 Just as before, we now need to create a browsing and maintenance form. Add a new form to the project and place controls on the form so that it looks like this:

Once again, make the form an MDI child, and name it `frmAuthor`. Next up, name the two text boxes `txtAuthor` and `txtYearBorn` respectively, and the command buttons `cmdFirst`, `cmdPrevious`, `cmdNext`, `cmdLast`, `cmdAdd`, `cmdUpdate` and `cmdDelete`.

4 Now we're ready to add code. Because of the way we've designed the code so far, the code under this form should be quite familiar to you, and as brief as ever. Take a look at this and add it all to `frmAuthor`:

```
Option Explicit

Private WithEvents Authors As clsAuthors

Private Sub Authors_DataChanged()
' When the data in the Authors object changes (by moving to a new
' record, update the controls on the form with the revised data
    txtAuthor = Authors.strAuthor
    txtYearBorn = Authors.intYear_born
End Sub

Private Sub cmdAdd_Click()
    Update_Authors
    Authors.clsRecordset_AddAsNew
End Sub

Private Sub cmdDelete_Click()
    Authors.clsRecordset_DeleteCurrent
End Sub
```

```
Private Sub cmdFirst_Click()
    Authors.clsRecordset_MoveFirst
End Sub

Private Sub cmdLast_Click()
    Authors.clsRecordset_MoveLast
End Sub

Private Sub cmdNext_Click()
    Authors.clsRecordset_MoveNext
End Sub

Private Sub cmdPrevious_Click()
    Authors.clsRecordset_MovePrevious
End Sub

Private Sub cmdUpdate_Click()
    Update_Authors
    Authors.clsRecordset_SaveChanges
End Sub

Private Sub Form_Load()
    Set Authors = New clsAuthors
End Sub

Private Sub Update_Authors()
' Updates the members in the Authors object with the data currently
' on the form
    Authors.strAuthor = txtAuthor
    Authors.intYear_born = txtYearBorn

End Sub
```

The big difference between this and the code we have on the Titles form is that this has code to update the data in the class and ultimately the Authors database itself. When the application is running, we can enter data into the form and then click on the **Add** button, for example. This will trigger the Update_Authors routine to copy the fields out to the class members, and then run the AddAsNew method on the class to copy the information it holds out to a new record. The **Update** button works in exactly the same way, calling SaveChanges instead of AddAsNew.

> *Something for you to consider about this code: the DeleteCurrent routine that we've written will only be successful at deleting Authors that we've entered into the database ourselves. Other Authors in the database have further records in related databases, which prevents the simple deletion of an Author. A nice extension to this code would therefore be an error trapping routine so that our application doesn't crash out with an error message every time this occurs. We discuss error trapping at various points through this book.*

5 Toe To run this full application, you'll need to add some code to the MDI form to load the **Author Browser** form up.

Bring up the MDI form now, and click on the <u>M</u>aintain item under the <u>A</u>uthors menu heading. Just as before, the code window will come into view for the click event of that menu item. Just add a line of code so that it looks like this:

```
Private Sub mnuAMaintain_Click()
    Load frmAuthor
End Sub
```

Now run the program, and you'll be able to see both browser forms in action. DataDamage are clearly on their way to a great application.

The most important point to note, in all this, is that even though we have quite a lot of code in the form, it's all very simple stuff, really easy to understand and follow, and therefore really easy to maintain.

This is the benefit of the object-oriented design of the application. Although it took some effort at the start to get the code into the `clsTitles` and `clsRecordsets` class modules, and then to provide a neat interface to them from the code module, the result is that we have an application that is extremely easy to extend, should the need arise.

Inheritance and Containment

What is Inheritance?

With **inheritance**, a class gains all the properties and methods that make up the interface of the **base class**, and it can then extend the interface by adding properties and methods of its own. The new class can also extend or change the implementation of each of the properties and methods from the original base class.

Inheritance, in a nutshell, would mean that we could create an object and then use it (plus all its properties and functionality) as the basis for a new object.

For instance, if we had a *Vehicle* class that had all the properties and methods that apply to all types of vehicle, then inheritance would make it very easy to create classes for *Car*, *Van* and *Semi*. We wouldn't need to recreate all the code for a *Car* to be a *Vehicle*: it would inherit that automatically from the original *Vehicle* class. This technique could be very useful for comparing say, properties of *Cars* and *Vans* (such as color, number of wheels etc) – even though cars and vans are fundamentally different objects.

Inheritance at DataDamage Inc.

Consider our application for DataDamage Inc. If our application were a little bigger, then at some point we would reach a worrying situation. Given that the place where we stored the data would sooner or later change, we would eventually have to go through and change all our data access code to deal with that change. We would have work to do in both in the `clsAuthors` class and the `clsTitles` class - not to mention any other classes that may have been added over time which access the database directly. Not a pleasant situation, especially if you scale up the size of our application.

Inheritance would solve our dilemma here. We could simply put all the common functionality for accessing the database in one object, and then build on that object with new ones that inherited the old. This would be ideal in our case - we could have a `clsRecordset` object holding a lot of code to talk to the database, and then we could inherit that object into `clsAuthors` and `clsTitles`, just adding any appropriate code specific to those tables.

It seems we don't have that luxury yet, however. Maybe in a future version of Visual Basic we will find inheritance. For now, is all this just wishful thinking? Read on.

Interface Inheritance

As we've seen, VB6 comes complete with a fantastic command: `Implements`. When people first saw this command, the immediate reaction from a lot of them was to jump up and down proclaiming that Microsoft had at last brought inheritance to Visual Basic. This was not the case.

We can, however, gain **interface inheritance** by using the `Implements` keyword. The `Implements` keyword just tells Visual Basic that we would like to implement code for another object's interface - we don't inherit the original object's data or behavior. However, the big drawback is that we can't extend an interface that has been created with the `Implements` keyword, so with this method we don't gain one of the key benefits of inheritance.

So how do we use interface inheritance? Take a look at this example of a `Vehicle` class:

```
Option Explicit

Public Property Get Wheels() As Integer

End Property

Public Property Get NumberOfSeats() As Integer

End Property

Public Property Get Color() As String

End Property
```

Notice that there isn't any code in these routines. Remember that interface inheritance allows the inheritance of interfaces only. Any code in these routines would not be used anyway.

Now we can create classes based on the `Vehicle` class by using the `Implements` keyword to inherit the interface. Take a look at this `Van` class:

```
Option Explicit

Implements Vehicle

Private Property Get Vehicle_Wheels() As Integer
Vehicle_Wheels = 4
End Property

Private Property Get Vehicle_NumberOfSeats() As Integer
Vehicle_NumberOfSeats = 2
End Property
```

```
Private Property Get Vehicle_Color() As String
Vehicle_Color = "White"
End Property
```

We could do the same with a `Car` class:

```
Option Explicit

Implements Vehicle

Private Property Get Vehicle_Wheels() As Integer
Vehicle_Wheels = 4
End Property

Private Property Get Vehicle_NumberOfSeats() As Integer
Vehicle_NumberOfSeats = 5
End Property

Private Property Get Vehicle_Color() As String
Vehicle_Color = "Red"
End Property
```

Notice that we have to prefix the properties `Wheels`, `NumberOfSeats` and `Color` with `Vehicle_` so that Visual Basic knows that these routines belong to the Vehicle interface. Unfortunately we can't extend the interface, so if we want to add a property to the `Van` class for `StorageCapacity` we'll have to use a different technique.

Simulated Inheritance

It's possible to simulate inheritance by using a combination of two techniques, **containment** and **delegation**. So what do these terms mean?

The idea behind **containment** is that, in object-oriented analysis, an object can have a private instance of another object inside itself. For instance, a old *Television* object could contain a *Valve* object, but that *Valve* object would be private to the *Television* object, since no code outside of that *Television* object would be likely to interact with that *Valve*.

Delegation refers to the situation where one object delegates a task to another object rather than doing the work itself. Now when we elect not to call the methods in the base class, we are choosing not to delegate tasks down to the base class - and we write methods within the current class to perform the task instead.

Let's see how we can simulate inheritance with our `Vehicle` example:

```
Option Explicit

Public Property Get Wheels() As Integer
Wheels = 4
End Property

Public Property Get NumberOfSeats() As Integer
NumberOfSeats = 5
End Property
```

```
    Public Property Get Color() As String

    End Property
```

This time we've put some code into our `Wheels` and `NumberOfSeats` routines. With simulated inheritance these properties will be available in any new classes we create from `Vehicle`.

Now let's create a new `Car` class.

```
    Option Explicit

    Private objVehicle As Vehicle

    Public Property Get Wheels() As Integer
    Wheels = objVehicle.Wheels
    End Property

    Public Property Get NumberOfSeats() As Integer
    NumberOfSeats = objVehicle.NumberOfSeats
    End Property

    Public Property Get Color() As String
    Color = "Red"
    End Property
```

Notice that this time we don't use `Implements` and that we create a `Private Vehicle` object inside our new `Car` class. Our `Car` class contains an instance of the `Vehicle` class.

```
    Private objVehicle As Vehicle
```

In our `Wheels` and `NumberOfSeats` routines, the `Car` class is delegating the work down to the private `Vehicle` object.

```
    NumberOfSeats = objVehicle.NumberOfSeats
```

Now let's create a new `Van` class in the same way:

```
    Option Explicit

    Private objVehicle As Vehicle

    Public Property Get Wheels() As Integer
    Wheels = objVehicle.Wheels
    End Property

    Public Property Get NumberOfSeats() As Integer
    NumberOfSeats = 2
    End Property

    Public Property Get Color() As String
    Color = "White"
    End Property

    Public Property Get StorageCapacity() As String
    StorageCapacity = "A Lot"
    End Property
```

97

Now in this case the `NumberOfSeats` for a `Van` is different, so there is no delegation down to the `Vehicle` object. Instead, the `Van` overrides this functionality by implementing the routine itself.

```
NumberOfSeats = 2
```

We've also extended our interface for the `Van` object by adding a `StorageCapacity` property - something we were unable to do with interface inheritance.

```
Public Property Get StorageCapacity() As String
StorageCapacity = "A Lot"
End Property
```

Containment at DataDamage Inc.

In our application for DataDamage, the combination of containment and delegation allows us to move the basic functionality of the `clsTitles` and `clsAuthors` classes back into `clsRecordset`. We can then call that functionality from the methods in `clsTitles` and `clsAuthors`.

Try It Out - Using Containment in Our BiblioTech Project

1 Let's begin by moving the basic functionality that was in the `clsTitles` and `clsAuthors` into `clsRecordset`. Change the `clsRecordset` class so that it looks like this:

```
Option Explicit

' clsRecordset object - a generic object designed to wrap
' up the functionality of a recordset in a generic re-useable
' object.

' Class methods

Public Sub MoveNext(recRecords As Recordset)
  If Not recRecords.EOF Then
recRecords.MoveNext
  End If
End Sub

Public Sub MovePrevious(recRecords As Recordset)
  If Not recRecords.BOF Then
recRecords.MovePrevious
  End If
End Sub

Public Sub MoveLast(recRecords As Recordset)
  recRecords.MoveLast
End Sub

Public Sub MoveFirst(recRecords As Recordset)
  recRecords.MoveFirst
End Sub
```

2 Now we come to the interesting part! We're going to use containment in `clsTitles`, so that a private instance of `clsRecordset` is contained within our `clsTitles` object.

The top of our `clsTitles` class thus becomes:

```
Option Explicit

' clsTitles - wraps up the Biblio Titles table. By keeping the
' interface consistent it should be possible to move the class
' to point at some other data source, such as an RDO Resultset,
' or flat file, without users of the class ever noticing.

Public Event DataChanged()

' Public members to implement properties
Public strTitle As String
Public intYear_Published As Integer
Public strISBN As String
Public lngPubID As Long
Public strDescription As String
Public strNotes As String
Public strSubject As String
Public strComments As String

Private m_objRecordset As New clsRecordset

' Private members to hold connection to database,
' and to the recordset itself

Private m_recTitles As Recordset
Private m_dbDatabase As Database
```

Notice we've removed the `Implements` command from this code now: we no longer need to implement `clsRecordset` in `clsTitles`, since we can access the `clsRecordset` routines through our new `m_recRecordset` private member variable, which contains the private instance of the `clsRecordset` object.

3 Now we're able to remove the basic functionality from our `clsTitles` class - remember, we're delegating the recordset navigation tasks to our `clsRecordset` class. The end of your `clsTitles` class should look like this:

```
' Class methods

Public Sub MoveNext()
  m_objRecordset.MoveNext m_recTitles
  Reload_Members
End Sub

Public Sub MovePrevious()
  m_objRecordset.MovePrevious m_recTitles
  Reload_Members
End Sub
```

```
Public Sub MoveLast()
  m_objRecordset.MoveLast m_recTitles
  Reload_Members
End Sub

Public Sub MoveFirst()
  m_objRecordset.MoveFirst m_recTitles
  Reload_Members
End Sub
```

All we're doing here is delegating the navigation of the recordset held in the m_recTitles member variable, to our private instance of clsRecordset (i.e. m_objRecordset).

Notice also that we've deleted the following routines from our class. As we're using a combination of containment and delegation to simulate inheritance, instead of the Implements keyword, we're now able to extend the interface of our clsAuthors class. Therefore, these routines are no longer needed in our clsTitles class.

```
Public Sub clsRecordset_AddAsNew()
' Do nothing
End Sub

Public Sub clsRecordset_SaveChanges()
' Do nothing
End Sub

Public Sub clsRecordset_DeleteCurrent()
' Do nothing
End Sub
```

4 Now we must repeat the process with the clsAuthors class. Change the code at the beginning of clsAuthors so that it looks like this:

```
Option Explicit

' clsAuthors - wraps up the functionality to browse and
' maintain the authors table in the Biblio database

Public Event DataChanged()

' Public members to implement properties
Public lngAu_ID As Long
Public strAuthor As String
Public intYear_Born As Integer

Private m_objRecordset As New clsRecordset

' Private members to hold connection to database,
' and to the recordset itself
Private m_recAuthors As Recordset
Private m_dbDatabase As Database
```

Once again, the Implements command has been removed and we've declared a member variable `m_objRecordset` to hold our private instance of the `clsRecordset` object. No surprises here!

5 Now move to the bottom of the `clsAuthors` class and make the following changes:

```
' Class methods

Public Sub MoveNext()
  m_objRecordset.MoveNext m_recAuthors
  Reload_Members
End Sub

Public Sub MovePrevious()
  m_objRecordset.MovePrevious m_recAuthors
  Reload_Members
End Sub

Public Sub MoveLast()
  m_objRecordset.MoveLast m_recAuthors
  Reload_Members
End Sub

Public Sub MoveFirst()
  m_objRecordset.MoveFirst m_recAuthors
  Reload_Members
End Sub

Public Sub SaveChanges()

    With m_recAuthors
        .Edit
        Save_Members
        .Update
    End With

End Sub

Public Sub AddAsNew()

    With m_recAuthors
        .AddNew
        Save_Members
        .Update
    End With

End Sub

Public Sub DeleteCurrent()

    m_recAuthors.Delete
    On Error Resume Next
    m_recAuthors.MoveFirst
    Reload_Members

End Sub
```

Jus as with our `clsTitles` class, we can remove the `clsRecordset_` prefix from our method names. In addition, as the code for navigating the recordset is held within the `clsRecordset` class we just need to delegate these tasks to the base object, `m_objRecordset`.

Finally, we've extended the interface of our `clsAuthors` class with the `AddAsNew`, `SaveChanges` and `DeleteCurrent` routines. These routines need to be `Public` as they're being called from our `frmAuthor` form.

Now all that remains to be done is to make some minor alterations to our browsing forms.

6 Open the code window for `frmTitle` and change your code so that it looks like this:

```
Option Explicit

Private WithEvents Titles As clsTitles

Private Sub cmdFirst_Click()
    Titles.MoveFirst
End Sub

Private Sub cmdLast_Click()
    Titles.MoveLast
End Sub

Private Sub cmdNext_Click()
    Titles.MoveNext
End Sub

Private Sub cmdPrevious_Click()
    Titles.MovePrevious
End Sub
```

7 Now repeat the process with the `frmAuthor` form - it should look like this:

```
Option Explicit

Private WithEvents Authors As clsAuthors

Private Sub Authors_DataChanged()
' When the data in the Authors object changes (by moving to a new
' record, update the controls on the form with the revised data
    txtAuthor = Authors.strAuthor
    txtYearBorn = Authors.intYear_born
End Sub

Private Sub cmdAdd_Click()
    Update_Authors
    Authors.AddAsNew
End Sub
```

```
Private Sub cmdDelete_Click()
    Authors.DeleteCurrent
End Sub

Private Sub cmdFirst_Click()
    Authors.MoveFirst
End Sub

Private Sub cmdLast_Click()
    Authors.MoveLast
End Sub

Private Sub cmdNext_Click()
    Authors.MoveNext
End Sub

Private Sub cmdPrevious_Click()
    Authors.MovePrevious
End Sub

Private Sub cmdUpdate_Click()
    Update_Authors
    Authors.SaveChanges
End Sub
```

8 Now run the project! You shouldn't notice any difference as a user - but there's a whole world of difference in how the application is structured under the hood.

For the DataDamage application on its present scale, there wouldn't really be much code benefit to us at this stage in using these techniques. In the real world, though, should the database ever need to be moved to somewhere other than a nice simple Access database, these techniques would take on a new significance. Our trump card would be that we could easily redesign that base object in such a way that nothing else in the application would have to change.

Naturally, the code in the base class would have to change to reflect the change in database, but those changes would ripple up to any other classes which contained its functionality - and from there the changes would ripple up to the forms that used those classes. Now THAT is a maintainable system!

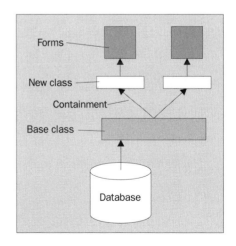

Here's a thought for you. Moving all that code out of the original class and into a new one might seem like a lot of work if the classes we were dealing with were a little larger and more complex. So what's the point? Well, the point does depend on your project and your needs. That's why we've looked at the different ways you can implement objects in Visual Basic. But I do have a real-life example that might help you make your mind up...

I did some consultancy for a large company that had a team of 10-20 inexperienced Visual Basic developers. In order to reduce the burden on them (they were all newbies after all) the Management decided that we would develop boilerplate code, which was pre-built blocks of code that the other developers would just fill in the blanks on. My suggestion was "Hey, why don't we do something with interface inheritance and containment of objects - that's going to save us a lot of time and effort, and the Visual Basic compiler can even help us enforce it all." The management answer was the age old "We don't have time to do that... it's too new."

The end result then was that we got on with the management's "quicker" solution. The rest of the team then took our boilerplate forms, added their minor changes, and then added them into the grand project. There were more than 90 forms in that project, all of which were based on the boilerplate code. Every time that boilerplate changed, the programmers had to stop and make the changes to their working forms by hand. Then they had to retest the forms for errors. This process took about an hour per form, each and every time the base code changed, which averaged out at once a month.

So, the management decision that we couldn't afford 2 days at the start to get it right resulted in them spending approximately 45 man days retro-fitting their code with boilerplate changes.

The moral of my story is this: containment may take some extra time in the short term, but in the long term it's usually worth every minute.

You have been warned.

Summary

Our time at DataDamage, in this chapter, has taken us over some of most essential object-oriented development issues within Visual Basic. We've been busy with plenty of program code, and we've taken a real-world programming scenario to explore the object-oriented issues.

Although there's a lot more to come in our journey through object-oriented programming in Visual Basic, we've covered some of the hardest areas already. In particular, we looked at:

- Class and Object Interfaces
- The Implements command
- Multiple interfaces
- Inheritance
- Containment and Delegation

In the next chapter, we'll have a look at a few more design aspects of object-oriented programming as we discuss object hierarchies.

Why Not Try...

1 In the exercise in this chapter where we created a class to browse the Titles table, what was the purpose of raising the event `DataChanged` in the `Reload_Members` procedure?

2 *When* does the procedure `Reload_Members` take place in the class?

3 In the exercise in the chapter where we created 'properties' for each field in the Titles table, did you find anything unusual about the way we created the properties?

4 In the exercise in this chapter where we designed a class to browse the Titles table, *when* is the recordset created?

5 In the second exercise in the chapter, where we 'instantiate' an object based on our class, *when* and *where* is the object instantiated?

6 In the second exercise in the chapter, where we 'instantiate' an object based on our class, how do we make use of the event `DataChanged` raised out of the class, and how is it used?

7 Prove to yourself that the code that was written in exercise 2 is really independent of the data source. Is there any way that you can tell whether the underlying data source for the form is an Access table, an Oracle table, a SQL table, or even a flat text file?

8 On a related note, if we were to change the location of the Titles data from a location on a Local Area Network to a remote Database Server, perhaps in the United Kingdom, what would we need to change in order to accomplish this feat?

9 I want to give you a chance to work with the `Implements` statement here, so that you can see how the Implements statement allows you to implement interface inheritance. In this exercise, you'll create a class, `clsPerson`, from which you will later, in our next exercise in fact, implement another class called `clsCustomer`. Create that new class called `clsPerson` now, with two properties called `Name` and `Address`. Then create a method called `ShowInfo` (sound familiar?).

10 Now create a new class, `clsCustomer`, that implements the properties and methods of `clsPerson`.

6

Object Hierarchies

Overview

Object-oriented applications are often built using several different objects that are all related to each other in some way. There are several types of relationships that can exist between these objects. The type of relationship we are going to look at is usually called a "has a" relationship. In a "has a" relationship, an object contains or is made of other objects. When an object is related to another object through the "has a" relationship this is the ideal situation to build a project with different levels, i.e. a project that has an object **hierarchy**.

The "Has A" Relationship

Just what is the "has a" relationship? If you look at a car you will see that it is composed of several objects such as an engine, a transmission, etc. The car has a transmission; the car has an engine. Thus, the "has a" relationship is simply when one object contains other objects.

Is an engine an object? Even though the engine is extremely complex you could still pull it out of the car, hook up a few necessary components (such as a fuel line and electric power) and the engine will work just fine outside of the car. Thus we can see that it is really a completely separate object that a car has. The car is not at all concerned with how the engine works internally, the car is only concerned with making the engine do a few things like starting, going faster or slower, or stopping. There are interfaces between the car engine and the car to do these things. For example, to start the engine your car has an ignition system, to make the engine run slower or faster the car has an accelerator pedal which is hooked into the engine through linkages. Just like in the real world, when creating applications where one object has a second object, the second object should be able to perform its functions simply by being told what needs to be done, not how to do it, through interfaces (methods in programming). In other words, the second object should be a true, real object.

Another more complex object in the car is the electrical system. The electrical system is actually composed of many electrical components that do very different things. For example, you have the ignition system, the electrical accessory system for radios, lighters, etc, and also a system to control all the lights including tail and head lights. All of these different electrical components could also be considered as objects. Thus we have an auto object that has an electrical object which has an ignition system object, an accessory object, and a lights object. This is how hierarchies are built.

You could build a car without a central electrical systems component, i.e. a car that has the car directly interfacing with the ignition system, accessory and lights objects. Would this make sense? No, because there has to be some central controlling object that will distribute the electricity evenly throughout all of the other objects. Some of these objects are dependent on each other (most modern cars will automatically shut of the lights if the car's ignition is shut off) and we therefore need an electrical object that manages all of the electrical components. The car itself will interact with the electrical system through the electrical object. We can see that a hierarchy of objects exists when one object contains another object, and this object contains yet another object. This is not the only reason we will build our objects within a hierarchy. Let us now turn our attention to hierarchies for a moment and see why they are so useful.

The Importance of Hierarchies

So, what is so great about hierarchies? Well, to begin with, hierarchies organize the information in your project in a way that is really easy for your user to understand. A hierarchy sets up a structured relationship between groups of objects. To get an idea of how grouping helps make things clearer imagine going into a food store where the food items are not grouped by different categories but simply placed randomly on the shelves. You could literally spend hours wandering aimlessly trying to find a few items. Even if the items were placed in alphabetical order shopping would still be a nightmare. Humans like to categorize things and group them together, it helps us visualize what they are and how they relate to each other.

When we want to find our favorite spaghetti sauce we know to go to the pasta aisle. The pasta aisle will have the pasta in one group, the tomato sauces in another section, and finally the spaghetti sauces in another group. The spaghetti sauces are then grouped by canned and jarred, and finally they may be grouped by brand. Once you understand how items are grouped in your local food store you can quickly find any item. The groups are placed in a logical order, a hierarchy, which makes it easy to find anything. The same will be true of applications built with hierarchies.

Anyway, enough of the theory, let's put some of this into practice. We're going to build the basics of a hierarchical application:

Building Hierarchies in a Company Database

Imagine that we are working for a company that is divided into different groups (database group, visual basic group, mainframe group...). Each group is working on one or more projects, each project has one manager and one or more workers. Each project is given a name, and a monthly and a yearly budget. Projects need the ability to add new workers and add a manager. Managers and workers are identified by their first and last name and have a salary. The information is stored in various databases. The company wants to build several applications that will access this information.

It sounds pretty hectic, doesn't it? Well, to make life easier for the application designers, and to speed up application design, we're going to make use of our new found friend – the hierarchy.

Well, where shall we start? Objects seem like a good place to me. We're going to need lots of them, so let's find them now.

Objects should be noun-like words. Looking at this we see that the noun words in this statement are groups, projects, workers and managers. Thus, we need group, project, manager, and worker objects. There is a "has a" relationship between group and a project. There is also a "has a" relationship between a project and the manager and the project and the workers. We can put these "has a" relationships together into a hierarchy where a group has a project, which has a manager and workers.

These are not the only objects we are going to need, though. There are many group objects, each group can be working on several projects, and each project can have several workers. Just like the car's electrical system, which contained a group of related objects that required an object to oversee all of the related objects, our groups of objects will also require an object to oversee them.

Thus we are also going to need a Groups object which will contain a collection of all of the groups and all of the required methods and properties to maintain the different groups. We will also need a Projects and Workers object that will hold collections of those objects and maintain them. Our Groups object will keep track of the total number of groups which is called group count. The Groups object will also allow you to retrieve a group. There will also be a projects count and a way of retrieving projects as well as a worker count and a way of retrieving a worker in the Projects and Workers objects. Thus we see that our hierarchy would be as follows:

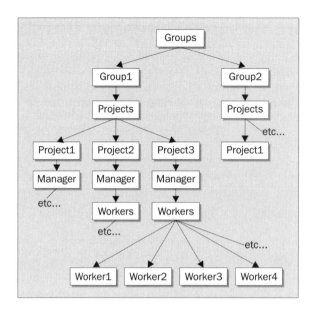

So, you can see that the Groups class is going to be right at the top of our hierarchy and the Worker class right at the bottom. You can also see why we need hierarchies to keep track of our objects – imagine what this tree would look like with twenty groups, or two hundred groups!

Next, we need to decide on properties for all our objects. Properties are adjective-type words that either describe or tell you something about the objects. We can see that the first and last names of the workers and managers are clearly properties. Their salaries should also be properties. The group count, project count, and worker count properties of the Groups, Projects and Workers objects also tells you something about these objects and should also be properties. The name of the project should also be a property.

When we've decided on properties, we need to look at the methods our objects will use. Methods should be verb-like words, such as "add" so actions such as adding a group, project or worker to our groups, projects or workers classes should all be methods. Retrieving is also a verb so we will need a method called Item that will retrieve a group, project or worker in our Groups, Projects, and Workers objects.

Now, we can think about coding our application. When writing the code it is easiest to start from the bottom of the hierarchy and work our way up. So let's fire up VB and get programming:

Try It Out – Defining Our Classes

1 First, create a **Standard.Exe** project in the usual way. Next, go to the **Project** menu and select **Add Class Module**.

Now, you should see the following screen:

2 Select **Class Module** and click **Open**. You now need to go to the **Properties** window for this class and rename it clsGroups.

3 Repeat the above process to create six more classes called clsGroup, clsProjects, clsProject, clsManager, clsWorkers, clsWorker.

4 Finally, rename the project ProjGroups and save it as prjGroups.vbp. Now take a look at the project explorer window. It should look like this:

Managing Information within the Classes

Now it's time to give our classes somewhere to store all their information. We will start with clsManager as it is the simplest class. As a manager has a first name, a salary, and a last name we will need private variables to store this information. Properties will be used to gain access to this information.

Try It Out – The clsManager Class

1 Bring up the code window for the clsManager class and enter the following lines of code in the General Declarations section for this class:

```
Option Explicit

Private m_strLastName As String
Private m_strFirstName As String
Private m_lngSalary As Long
```

All that we have done here is define a few private variables to store a Manager's First Name, Last Name, and Salary.

2 Now we need to create some properties – these will be used to gain access to the information stored in the above variables. Type this lot in:

```
Property Get LastName() As String

    LastName = m_strLastName

End Property
```

```
Property Let LastName(ByVal v_strLastName As String)

    m_strLastName = v_strLastName

End Property
```

```
Property Get FirstName() As String

    FirstName = m_strFirstName

End Property
```

```
Property Let FirstName(ByVal v_strFirstName As String)

    m_strFirstName = v_strFirstName

End Property
```

```
Property Get Salary() As Long

    Salary = m_lngSalary

End Property
```

```
Property Let Salary(ByVal v_lngSalary As Long)

    m_lngSalary = v_lngSalary

End Property
```

The first thing that is a bit odd about this class is that there are no methods. Technically speaking an object has properties and methods, so is this a legitimate object? Yes, it is. To begin with, this is a very simple example and it is likely that in a real application the manager object would have some methods. Imagine that there is going to be an application using this object that will calculate the total cost of a project by taking the number of weeks worked on the project and multiplying that by the weekly salaries of the manager and workers. The weekly salary may not be determined by the `Salary` property as some workers get paid on an hourly basis, sometimes in the middle of a week a worker gets a raise, etc. To handle this we could have a method that could go to the database and actually get the total amount of salary paid to the manager over this time period.

One other thing, the `Let` properties do not store the new information anywhere. To keep this example simple we won't include a real database to contain the information on managers, workers, projects and groups. We want to focus on objects and the relationship between them, not on building databases and doing database access and updating. In a real application, though, the new information being passed into the `Let` properties would have to be saved to the database. The `Let` properties should also limit who has this type of access; we do not want a worker to be able to change their manager's salary. It might also be a good idea to put security measures on the `Get` properties, as a worker should not know what their boss or fellow workers are earning.

> *Database programming is a large and diverse area, much too complex to deal with properly within this chapter. If you are interested in including database access into the example that follows, I recommend reading Beginning Visual Basic 6 Database Programming (ISBN: 1-861001-06-1), which is also published by Wrox Press.*

Try It Out – The clsWorker Class

1 The clsWorker class code is the same as that of the `clsManager` class. Of course, in the real world there would be additional properties and methods that would make them different, but we are trying to keep this simple. So again, we define some variables to store the information:

```
Option Explicit

Private m_strLastName As String
Private m_strFirstName As String
Private m_lngSalary As Long
```

2 Then we define some properties to gain access to this information:

```
Property Get LastName() As String

    LastName = m_strLastName

End Property

Property Let LastName(ByVal v_strLastName As String)

    m_strLastName = v_strLastName

End Property

Property Get FirstName() As String

    FirstName = m_strFirstName

End Property

Property Let FirstName(ByVal v_strFirstName As String)

    m_strFirstName = v_strFirstName

End Property
```

```
Property Get Salary() As Long

    Salary = m_lngSalary

End Property
```

```
Property Let Salary(ByVal v_lngSalary As Long)

    m_lngSalary = v_lngSalary

End Property
```

Collections of Objects

Collections were mentioned briefly in the main discussion about hierarchies at the start of this chapter. The idea is pretty simple, we all know what a collection is, and the idea of a Groups object managing a collection of individual groups is quite an easy one to imagine – but how do we go about using collections in Visual Basic?

Firstly, you need to create a variable, and define it as a collection. That's it, you've made a collection. However, as collections go, it's not particularly satisfactory – what if we want to add a new item to our collection or maybe even just look at objects already in our collection? It's become clear that as well as actually creating a collection we also need to create some methods to provide access to our collection.

So, what do we require from a collection? Most collections can be accessed satisfactorily with just four methods.

These are:

`Add` (Item):	Adds a new item to the collection.
`Remove` (Item):	Removes an existing item from the collection.
`Item` (Item):	Retrieves an item from the collection (for user inspection).
`Count` (Item):	Keeps a count of the number of items currently in the collection.

You should be aware that even if an object is part of a collection, it may still behave as a stand-alone object if required to do so.

Each individual item in a collection has it's own, unique, **key**. This key can be used to identify it to both the user, and the collection. A typical key could be, for example, a passport number.

All fairly straightforward, I'm sure you'll agree. Right, lets put some of this theory into practice and deal with some collections. We'll start with `clsWorkers`.

Try It out – The clsWorkers Class

1 The class `clsWorkers` is a going to be a bit more complicated then our two previous classes, as this class is going to have a collection of workers called `m_colWorker`. In the case of our workers we are using their last name as the key. Of course, this would not be a very good choice in the real world as many people share the same last name - the social security number or some other unique identifier should be used.

We need to code methods for adding new workers, retrieving workers from the collection and counting the number of workers in the collection. In this example we won't bother creating a method for removing workers as it is unnecessary at this stage. Right, let us see how these methods work. We'll start with declaring the collection object and creating a variable to store the worker count in the class' General Declarations section:

```
Option Explicit

Dim m_lngCount
Private m_colWorker As Collection
```

2 Next, we create a simple `Get` property to give the user access to the worker count. There will be no `Let` property as the class itself will be keeping track of what the count is. The user should not be able to change the value of the count.

```
Public Property Get Count() As Long

   Count = m_lngCount

End Property
```

3 Now we need to be able to add a worker to the collection. To do this we're going to create an `AddWorker` method. Type this section in, and then we'll see how it works.

```
Public Sub AddWorker(ByVal v_strWorkerLastName As String)

    Dim objWorker As New clsWorker

    If v_strWorkerLastName = "" Then
        Exit Sub
    End If

    objWorker.LastName = v_strWorkerLastName

    m_colWorker.Add objWorker, objWorker.LastName

    m_lngCount = m_lngCount + 1

    Set objWorker = Nothing

End Sub
```

What happens here is that the `AddWorker` method is passed the key for a worker, (the last name) along with the first name and salary. The `AddWorker` method builds a new `objWorker` object with these parameters and adds it to the collection. Once the `objWorker` object is created you can then get a reference to it using the `Item` method below and set the rest of the properties.

4 The `Item` method is one place where it is acceptable to use a variant. It is possible that a user of the application may want to retrieve a worker by the last name or they may want to retrieve a worker by using a numeric index. The numeric index would be used when they are simply looping through the entire collection. Therefore we use a variant, which can be either numeric or a string. If `v_vntIndex` is a number then `m_objWorker.Item(v_vntIndex)` will retrieve that number item from the collection. If `v_vntIndex` is a string it will retrieve the worker object with that key value.

```
Public Function Item(ByVal v_vntIndex As Variant) As clsWorker

    On Error Resume Next
    Set Item = m_colWorker.Item(v_vntIndex)
    If Err.Number <> 0 Then
        Set Item = Nothing
    End If

End Function
```

5 Perhaps one of the most important and most often forgotten parts of building a class like this is initializing all objects in the `Class_Initialize` section. We created our collection object without the `New` key word so we must now initialize the object. Bring up the initialize event in the code window:

Enter the following line of code into the sub-routine:

```
Private Sub Class_Initialize()

    Set m_colWorker = New Collection

End   Sub
```

Try It Out – The clsProject class

1 Just like like we built `clsWorkers` from the `clsWorker` class, we will build `clsProject` from objects that we already have, i.e. the manager object and the workers object. The `clsProject` class does not have to worry about keeping track of the workers; it simply creates a `m_objWorkers` object and uses the `clsWorkers` class' properties and methods to manage the workers. This is the advantage of programming in a hierarchy.

```
Option Explicit

Private m_objManager As clsManager
Private m_objWorkers As clsWorkers
Private m_lngMonthlyBudget As Long
Private m_lngYearToDateCosts As Long
Private m_strProjectName As String
```

2 We will also need an instance of the `clsManager` class and variables to store the `MonthlyBudget`, `YearToDate`, and `ProjectName` information. All of these variables will have properties that will give the user of the application access to these variables. We'll define the property get routine now.

```
Property Get Manager() As clsManager

    Set Manager = m_objManager

End Property
```

3 Since the `Manager` and `Workers` properties are objects, we do not use the `Let Property` but instead use the `Set`. We'll do this for all the properties:

```
Property Set Manager(ByVal v_objManager As clsManager)

    Set m_objManager = v_objManager

End Property

Property Get Workers() As clsWorkers

    Set Workers = m_objWorkers

End Property
```

118

```
    Property Set Workers(ByVal v_objWorkers As clsWorkers)

        Set m_objWorkers = v_objWorkers

End Property
```

```
    Property Get MonthlyBudget() As Long

        MonthlyBudget = m_lngMonthlyBudget

End Property
```

```
    Property Let MonthlyBudget(ByVal v_lngMonthlyBudget As Long)

        m_lngMonthlyBudget = v_lngMonthlyBudget

End Property
```

```
    Property Get YearToDateCosts() As Long

        YearToDateCosts = m_lngYearToDateCosts

End Property
```

```
    Property Let YearToDateCosts(ByVal v_lngYearToDateCosts As Long)

        m_lngYearToDateCosts = v_lngYearToDateCosts

End Property
```

```
    Property Get ProjectName() As String

        ProjectName = m_strProjectName

End Property
```

```
    Property Let ProjectName(ByVal v_strProjectName As String)

        m_strProjectName = v_strProjectName

End Property
```

4 Lastly, don't forget to initialize all of the objects in the Class_Initialize section.

```
    Private Sub Class_Initialize()

        Set m_objManager = New clsManager
        Set m_objWorkers = New ClsWorkers

    End Sub
```

Once again, we have a class with no methods, but as before this class could have some methods such as calculating out weekly or monthly costs, required budget, etc.

Try It Out - clsProjects Class

1 The class code for `clsProjects` is basically the same as that for `clsWorkers`.

```vb
Option Explicit

Private m_colProject As Collection
Private m_lngCount As Long

Public Property Get Count() As Long

    Count = m_lngCount

End Property

Public Sub AddProject(ByVal v_strProjectName As String)

    Dim objProject As New clsProject

    If v_strProjectName = "" Then
        Exit Sub
    End If

    objProject.ProjectName = v_strProjectName
    m_colProject.Add objProject, objProject.ProjectName
    m_lngCount = m_lngCount + 1

    Set objProject = Nothing

End Sub

Public Function Item(ByVal v_vntIndex As Variant) As clsProject

    On Error Resume Next
    Set Item = m_colProject.Item(v_vntIndex)
    If Err.Number <> 0 Then
        Set Item = Nothing
    End If

End Function

Private Sub Class_Initialize()

    Set m_colProject = New Collection

End Sub
```

Try It Out – The clsGroup Class

1 The class `clsGroup` is similar to our previous classes. This class will contain a `m_objProjects` object that will contain and manage all of the projects that the group is working on. It will also have a name for the group, which is held in `m_strGroupName`. Properties will give access to these variables. We'll start by defining these variables:

```
Option Explicit

Private m_objProjects As clsProjects
Private m_strGroupName As String
```

2 Now, we'll define the property `Let` and `Get` routines:

```
Public Property Let GroupName(ByVal v_strGroupName As String)

    m_strGroupName = v_strGroupName

End Property

Public Property Get GroupName() As String

    GroupName = m_strGroupName

End Property

Public Property Set Projects(ByVal v_objProject As clsProjects)

    Set m_objProjects = v_objProject

End Property

Public Property Get Projects() As clsProjects

    Set Projects = m_objProjects

End Property

Private Sub Class_Initialize()

    Set m_objProjects = New clsProjects

End Sub
```

This should all be quite familiar to you by now.

The Top of the Hierarchy

At last, it's time to code the big one – `clsGroups` is our main man as far as this project is concerned. This class will contain the code to access the information held by the group objects, which in turn, access the information held in the project objects, and so on (remember our hierarchy diagram near the start of this chapter).

Try It Out – The clsGroups Class

1 In order to manage all of the groups, our `clsGroups` class is going to need to store all of the groups in a collection. We will use the `Item` method to get a particular group from the collection. We will also want to know how many groups there are in this collection so we will also have a variable to keep track of the group count. Let's define a couple of variables.

```
Option Explicit

Private m_colGroups As Collection
Private m_lngCount As Long
```

This is pretty straightforward - `m_colGroups` stores all of the groups in a collection and `m_lngCount` simply keeps track of the number of groups.

2 Next, we need to define a property to access the information stored in the `m_lngCount` variable:

```
Public Property Get GroupCount() As Long

   GroupCount = m_lngCount

End Property
```

Nothing special here, this is a simple `Get` property that allows `clsGroups` to find out how many groups there are. Notice, though, there is no `Let` property. This is because the user should never be allowed to set the number of groups that are in the hierarchy. This number should be set internally every time a group is added to the collection.

3 Now it's time to set the code for the `Initialize` event. Bring up this event in the `clsGroups` code window and enter the following code.

```
Private Sub Class_Initialize()

    Set m_colGroups = New Collection
    GetGroups

End Sub
```

Again, in the declarations we did not use the New key word, therefore our object does not yet exist. Remember to use the Set_ObjectName = New in your Class_Initialize routine when you declare your internal objects without the New keyword in the declarations section.

We are also calling an internal method called GetGroups to retrieve all of the groups and place them into the collection. GetGroups will be discussed below, but first we must write the Item and AddGroup methods.

Try It Out - Adding Methods to the Class

1 We are going to start by adding the AddGroup method to clsGroups. This is similar to the AddProject and AddWorker routines that we created earlier. All we do is pass in the name of the group. The method creates the object and adds it to the collection using the name as the key. Type it in now.

```
Public Sub AddGroup(ByVal v_strGroupName As String)

    Dim objGroup As New clsGroup

    If v_strGroupName = "" Then
        Exit Sub
    End If

    objGroup.GroupName = v_strGroupName
    m_colGroups.Add objGroup, objGroup.GroupName

    m_lngCount = m_lngCount + 1
    Set objGroup = Nothing

End Sub
```

2 Next comes the Item method, when called, this method returns a clsGroup object. Using the Item method a user can get access to any group that is stored in the m_colGroups collection.

```
Public Function Item(ByVal v_vntIndex As Variant) As clsGroup

    On Error Resume Next
    Set Item = m_colGroups.Item(v_vntIndex)

    If Err.Number <> 0 Then
        Set Item = Nothing
    End If

End Function
```

3 The `GetGroups` method is actually one of the most important in the project. We will not actually be getting any information from a database in this example; our main interest here is to see how to develop a hierarchy. If we actually had a database with manager, group, project and worker information, we would create a class called `clsData`, which would have a `GetGroups` method to get all of the groups from the database, and `GetProjects`, `GetManager`, and `GetWorkers` methods to get the information on these objects.

As coding the `clsData` would require building a database, filling it with all of the required information, and then writing extensive database accessing code we will not make the `clsData` class (after all we're learning about objects here, not databases). Instead, I will show you below what the code would look like with the `clsData` class, and then we will rewrite the `GetGroups` method with some dummy code to fill our collections so we can test them and see how our project works. Don't type this lot in – just look at it for now.

```
Private Function GetGroups()

    Dim objData as New clsData
    Dim objGroup As New clsGroup
    Dim intGLoop as Integer, intPLoop as Integer, intWLoop as Integer
    Dim strWorkerName as string
    'Code using loop to get the groups from database.

For intGLoop=1 to objData.GroupCount
      strGroupName= objData.GroupData.Name(intGLoop)
     Me.AddGroup strGroupName
     'Code using loop to get the project information associated with
     'this group from the database

     For intPLoop=1 to objData.ProjectCount(strGroupName)
       strProjectName= _
       objData.ProjectData.Item(strGroupName,intPLoop).ProjectName
       Me.Item(strGroupName).Projects.AddProject strProjectName
       Me.Item(strGroupName).Projects.Item(strProjectName).MonthlyBudget _
       =objData.ProjectData.Item(strGroupName,intPLoop).MonthlyBudget
       Me.Item(strGroupName).Projects.Item(strProjectName). _
       YearToDateCosts = _
       objData.ProjectData.Item(strGroupName,intPLoop).YearToDateCosts
      'code to get manager for this project
       Me.Item(strGroupName).Projects.Item(strProjectName).Manager.Add _
       objData.ManagerData.Item(strProjectName).ManagerLName
       Me.Item(strGroupName).Projects.Item(strProjectName).Manager. _
       FirstName = _
       objData.ProjectData.Item(strGroupName,intPLoop).ManagerFName
      'get worker information for this project

        For intWLoop=1 to objData.WorkerCount(strProjectName)
          strWorkerName= _
          objData.ManagerData.Item(strProjectName, intWLoop).WorkerLName
          Me.Item(strGroupName).Projects.Item(strProjectName).Workers. _
          AddWorker strWorkerName

          Me.Item(strWorkerName).FirstName = _
          objData.ManagerData.Item(strProjectName, intWLoop).WorkerFName
        Next 'Worker
```

```
      Next 'project

      m_lngCount = m_lngCount + 1
      Set objGroup = Nothing

   Next 'Group

End Function
```

This function would retrieve information from the database. That information would be used to build the `objGroup` objects that will be stored in the `m_objGroups` collection. The result being that the users of our object hierarchy could have access to group information without having to access the databases directly. It works by building one `objGroup` object at a time with all of the information on the group in the properties, methods, and objects contained with the `objGroup` object. All of the objects we have made are accessible through the `objGroup` object. Can this be seen in this code?

Yes, but it is a bit hidden. `Me` refers to the `m_objGroups` object at the top of the hierarchy, so `Me.Item` refers to the `Item` method of this object. The `Item` method returns a group, so `Me.Item` is really an `objGroup` object. You can see that all of the properties, methods and objects start with `Me.Item`. You can think of the `objGroup` object as a doorway into all of the other objects. This doorway does not have to always swing open; you can place "gatekeepers" at the doorway. For example, the `objGroup` object can have code that will only allow pay information to be viewed if a person has a certain security level. A user gains access to all of your objects through the `m_objGroups` object and the `m_objGroups` object in turn can now control what manager, worker and project information is viewed, updated, added or deleted. A hierarchy allows you to protect and control your objects.

Okay, but what is this code actually doing? Well, it starts by using the `AddGroup` method to create an `objGroup` object. The `AddGroup` method sets the `GroupName` property of `objGroup`, and adds the group to the **m_objGroups** collection. We can reference this new group by using `Me.Item(strGroupName)`.

We now set all the properties of the objects within the group by retrieving their values from the database. First we use the `AddProject` method to add a project to our new group. The `AddProject` will also set the `ProjectName` property of the `objProject` object. Once we have done this, we use the `Add` methods of the `clsWorker` and `clsManager` classes to add the workers and manager to the project. Once this is done all the properties are set and we can create the next group and set its properties.

Now, the code looks a bit wordy but, as we will show shortly, using a `With` statement will make the code more compact and easy to read. Let's rewrite this code so that we don't have to do any data access by hardcoding some values into the code. Again, don't type this in – we'll tidy it up with that `With` statement in a minute.

```
   Private Function GetGroups()

'Code using loop to get the groups from database.
Me.Item(strGroupName).GroupName = "Visual Basic Group"
```

```
'Code using loop to get the project information associated with
'this group from the database
Me.Item(strGroupName).Projects.AddProject "Visual Basic Middleware"
Me.Item(strGroupName).Projects.Item("Visual Basic Middleware"). _
MonthlyBudget = 30000
Me.Item(strGroupName).Projects.Item("Visual Basic Middleware"). _
YearToDateCosts= 100000

'code to get manager for this project
Me.Item(strGroupName).Projects.Item("Visual Basic Middleware"). _
Manager.FirstName= "Santa"
Me.Item(strGroupName).Projects.Item("Visual Basic Middleware"). _
Manager.LastName= "Claus"

'This would be a loop to get all workers from data source
Me.Item(strGroupName).Projects.Item("Visual Basic Middleware"). _
Workers.AddWorker "Twist"

'Get next worker
Me.Item(strGroupName).Projects.Item("Visual Basic Middleware"). _
Workers.Item("Twist").FirstName = "Oliver"
Me.Item(strGroupName).Projects.Item("Visual Basic Middleware").
Workers.Item("Twist").Salary = 1

'Loop and get next worker
Me.Item(strGroupName).Projects.Item("Visual Basic Middleware"). _
Workers.AddWorker "Poppins"
Me.Item(strGroupName).Projects.Item("Visual Basic Middleware"). _
Workers.Item("Poppins").FirstName = "Mary"

'Loop and get another worker
'...Loop to get next project
'Loop and get information on next Group object

End Function
```

4   Okay, let's use that `With` statement and see what it looks like. Enter this lot into the `clsGroups` code window.

```
Private Function GetGroups()

  'Code using loop to get the groups from database.
  Me.AddGroup "Visual Basic Middleware"

  With Me.Item("Visual Basic Middleware")
    'Code using loop to get the project information associated with
    'this group from the database
    .Projects.AddProject "Visual Basic Middleware"

    With .Projects.Item("Visual Basic Middleware")
.MonthlyBudget = 30000
.YearToDateCosts = 100000
'code to get manager for this project
.Manager.FirstName = "Santa"
.Manager.LastName = "Claus"
```

```
'get worker information for this project
'This would be a loop to get all workers from data source

With .Workers
        .AddWorker "Twist"
        .Item("Twist").FirstName = "Oliver"
        'Get next worker
        .Item("Twist").Salary = 1
    'Loop and get next worker
    .AddWorker "Poppins"
    .Item("Poppins").FirstName = "Mary"
    'Loop and get another worker
    End With 'Worker

        End With 'Project

    End With 'Group

    m_lngCount = m_lngCount + 1
        'Loop to get next project
        'Loop and get information on next Group object

    End Function
```

Wow! Look how much neater and simpler the code becomes when we use the `With` statement. Not only is the code less wordy but everything is divided into neat, clean sections dealing with the different objects. The user will never have to worry about getting the information from the various databases, putting the information together, validating the information, etc. All of this can be done by our `clsGroups` class object.

If we add security to `clsGroups` to limit access to certain properties and objects, people can write code that accesses this information without worrying about the wrong people getting access to secure information. Most importantly, the user can focus on using the information without worrying about how to get it, how to maintain it, or even where it's coming from. That's the beauty of using hierarchies.

Try It Out - Testing the Project

1 Now the project is completed, let's actually give it a try and see if it works. Save all of your classes and save the project as `prjGroups`. If you have a form attached to your project, open its code window now. If you don't have a form, you can add one now by selecting **Add Form** from the **Project** menu.

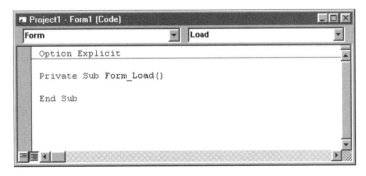

2 In the `General Declarations` section add this line:

```
Option Explicit

Dim CompanyGroups As clsGroups
```

3 In the form's `Load` event, type the following code:

```
Private Sub Form_Load()

    Set CompanyGroups = New clsGroups

    MsgBox "Group Count" & CompanyGroups.GroupCount & vbCrLf & _
    "Group Name:" & CompanyGroups.Item(1).GroupName & vbCrLf & _
    "Project Count:" & CompanyGroups.Item(1).Projects.Count & vbCrLf & _
    "Manager:" & CompanyGroups.Item(1).Projects.Item(1).Manager.LastName & _
    vbCrLf & _
    "WorkerCount:"&CompanyGroups.Item(1).Projects.Item(1).Workers.Count

End Sub
```

4 Run the application and you should see:

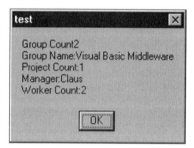

Congratulations! You have now built a set of objects all related by the hierarchical "has a" relationship.

As I said earlier, if you feel comfortable with doing database programming you could try building a database to hold the information. But the aim of this chapter was to build an object-hierarchy, not to develop our data access skills, so if you're not comfortable with database programming don't worry; all of the basic techniques of building hierarchies have been demonstrated and practiced at this point.

Summary

In this chapter, we've had a good look at object hierarchies, and how objects use collections to contain and access their dependent objects.

So, the obvious question is "What has been gained?" The answer to that question is that the user now has the ability to access information about the various groups without having to worry about where the information is coming from. In other words, the user can focus on the information itself, rather than the data access methods, which is how it should be.

You should now be familiar with the following:

- The "has a" relationship
- Designing a hierarchy
- Creating collections to manage information
- Creating methods to access collections

In the next chapter, we'll be exploring how ActiveX and COM technologies can be used to augment object-orientated programming.

Why Not Try....

1 Create an object hierarchy for a dog object. Consider the dog as the top of the hierarchy, which contains a body object, the body object contains leg objects, head object... First describe the dog object in words and then draw out the hierarchy. Make sure you include managing objects when there are multiple copies of objects (such as legs). Include in your description adjectives to describe your objects and verbs describing what your objects can do or what can be done to them. Using these verbs and adjectives list the properties and methods for of the objects.

6

Objects and ActiveX Components

Overview

In this chapter, we'll start to explore ActiveX components, and we'll see how ActiveX components extend the object-oriented programming techniques that we've already covered in this book.

So far, we've seen that objects are pretty neat: they allow us to produce representations of real-world objects as black box components. We've come to appreciate that these objects can have single or multiple interfaces, that they encourage highly cohesive code and loose coupling to any particular project, and that their self-containment supports the whole black box approach. Objects make our lives happier already.

Now the black box element to object-oriented programming means that some very complex technical solutions can be hidden behind an object interface. We can make our object-oriented solutions available to other programmers without them having to go through a very steep learning curve with our code. Furthermore, developers can effectively glue together our black box objects to create whole new applications. This is powerful stuff.

ActiveX components are the means by which we can take this whole black box idea further in Visual Basic. In this chapter, we'll explore what these ActiveX components are, their relation to object-oriented programming, and how we can implement them within our own Visual Basic code. This is going to take us right into the whole COM thing and the whole client-server way of programming - so get ready for the exciting world of components.

In this chapter, you'll learn about:

- Objects and ActiveX components
- Objects and COM
- COM behind the scenes
- Converting classes into components
- Creating components at runtime

> Clients and Servers in Visual Basic
> Threading Models and Load Balancing
> How to debug ActiveX components

What are ActiveX Components?

An **ActiveX component** is really nothing more than a standard class placed in its own application, totally separate from any other applications that make use of it. The situation is actually quite familiar to us now: it is the public objects within the ActiveX component that are available to other applications:

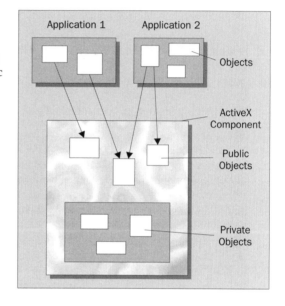

We call the ActiveX component application the **server** application, because it serves the other applications that call it. Meanwhile, those applications making the calls to the ActiveX server are known as **client** applications, since they are clients of our ActiveX component server.

This means that ActiveX components are our archetypal black box object: they are self-contained, discreet and separate from any other applications that may want to access their functions. We are in the heartland of object-oriented programming.

> *If you've done any work with OLE or ActiveX in the Microsoft Office suite, then you may have seen this at work already. Microsoft Excel, for example, exposes spreadsheets as Sheet components. This means that from within Visual Basic applications we can actually create instances of these Excel components, even though their code is contained in Excel. To do this, we rely on the public objects that Excel exposes for us to call.*

Using and creating ActiveX components is really quite an easy task with Visual Basic 6. We'll be working with ActiveX components in Visual Basic a great deal, later on. However, the more you read up on this topic, and the more time you spend dealing with ActiveX, the more you will come across a topic known as **COM**, the **Component Object Model**. You can get a lot more punch for your bytes if you understand exactly what is going on behind the scenes with this COM thing. So before we really get coding with ActiveX components, let's do things properly and take a good look at COM.

Exploring COM

COM is actually a set of DLLs, supported by a set of standards that allow developers to create objects that can work with each other, and which can expose their functionality in a uniform way to other application developers. This is black box nirvana.

> *If we can all work to a common set of standards within the Windows environment then, instead of writing applications from scratch each day, we can just produce components and tie them together to produce new applications.*
>
> *If a component already exists that does what we need to do, then we can use that component instead of re-writing our own.*

As time passes, we'll maybe one day find ourselves in possession of more and more components - until the time may come when there will be a component already written for whatever we need. At that point, programmers would be able to concentrate on getting the unique functionality of an application right, rather than getting bogged down in the heavy coding side of the application.

Now, essential as COM most certainly is, this stuff can get a little dry. COM is to computers what fanatical accountants are to life: somewhat dry but in many spheres vital. So don't be too surprised if you find yourself needing to read this stuff more than once, and remember, you'll be happier in the long run if you get to know this stuff. Luckily, you've got me to make this a sweeter ride for you, so let's go ahead and invite ourselves to the COM party.

COM and Interfaces

If we could get programmers to expose a common set of relations, or standards, between all their objects, then every developer out there would be able to create objects that could be used by everyone else. Reciprocally, those developers would themselves be able to make use of everyone else's objects - now what a great party that could be.

Hang on a second though. In order for this to work, we would need to get programmers to expose a common set of relations between all objects. But this just doesn't make sense. Surely we couldn't have the same relations available on every object, regardless of what that object did? Well, in fact we are able to do just that!

The way forward is to use **interfaces**. As we saw in earlier chapters, an interface is really nothing more than a name that refers to a group of methods and properties. In order for COM to work and party, every COM object must implement an interface called the IUnknown interface. This IUnknown interface consists of three methods, which every other programmer in the world can absolutely rely on to exist. It is these three methods of IUnknown that every COM programmer needs to be totally intimate with. It is these three methods of IUnknown, after all, that Windows and Visual Basic themselves use behind the scenes to get at the unique functionality of our classes. With these three magical methods, all other applications in the COM world are able to access the public properties and methods of our classes. That's quite something, don't you think?

Now it's a funny thing, but in real terms IUnknown is not actually anything that we need to worry about too much. When we create a class module in Visual Basic, and we tell Visual Basic that we're going to expose it as an ActiveX component, it puts the IUnknown interface in there for us: we never see it or have to deal with it.

> *However, knowing what the* IUnknown *interface does, and how it does it, is pretty useful when you come to talk to C++ developers, who will waffle on about* QueryInterface *all evening.*

Joking aside for one moment, knowing about the IUnknown interface also makes life a lot easier for us. If we actually know what's going on behind the scenes, we'll get a much deeper appreciation of how things tick, and our programming will be better informed. So let's clock this interface.

How the IUnknown Interface Works

Let's suppose that someone out there asks for an object known as Excel.Sheet. Here's a run through of what takes place:

1 Windows kicks in and looks up Excel in the registry to see where it lives, and then runs it. Excel is known as a component server in this instance, since it's an application that makes its objects and interfaces available to other applications. Maybe think of Excel as serving its classes and their public interfaces on a platter for us to pick through at our leisure.

2 Once Excel has been loaded as a server (the users don't see anything on the screen), the original program, now the client, is given access to Excel's IUnknown interface.

3 The client then asks the Excel server's IUnknown interface it if knows about an interface called Sheet. It does this by calling one of the three methods on IUnknown - in this case, a method called QueryInterface.

4 The result is that Excel does support an interface called Sheet, so the call to QueryInterface returns the Sheet interface to the client. In Visual Basic terms, we get something back that we can drop into a Visual Basic object variable, ready to use just as if it were an object native to our own project.

5 The client now has its Sheet interface, so it's ready to go on and call the methods and properties that make up that Sheet interface. Again, in terms of Visual Basic code, the object variable that holds Excel.Sheet is now ready for use.

6 Remember the Implements keyword from Chapter 3? It was there that we found we could declare more than one interface for an object. Now each and every interface implemented in an object also implements this IUnknown interface. This means that every single interface in our server also supports the three methods of IUnknown. The result is that we can find any other interfaces in a server from the one that we already have. So, again behind the scenes, if we have an interface called Excel.Sheet available to us in an object, then it's real easy to ask that interface at runtime what other interfaces the component server supports.

Without the IUnknown interface, and its three methods, a client application simply has no way of asking a server if it supports the interface that it needs to get its own work done. The corollary of this is clear enough: no IUnknown interface, no COM party!

So thanks to IUnknown, we have some relations established between client and server. The next question is - when do we tie the knot between them?

Component Binding

A glance at a few COM development magazines and newsgroups out there would soon suggest the topic of **component binding** for all but the most polite of conversational society. Contrary to popular belief, however, this is not a process whereby our code takes someone else's code and ties it to a bedpost.

Component binding is the process by which a client application loads up and uses a server's component. There are two types of component binding out there that we're interested in:

▶ Early binding

▶ Late binding

> *There are actually three types of binding, but only these two affect us as Visual Basic programmer types. For interested parties, the third type is very early binding.*

Which type of binding we use greatly affects the facilities that Visual Basic provides for us with during our development. Our choice of binding type also affects the speed of our final application.

To really understand what early binding and late binding are, and the differences between them, we need to take another look at how interfaces work behind the scenes. You see the first thing that needs to happen behind those scenes is that our client application needs to find the server itself. With late binding, this happens at runtime. With early binding, it happens in design time, but in a slightly different way. But I'm rushing ahead of myself - let's now take a closer look at these types of late and early binding.

Late Binding

Late binding between a client and server involves specifying the name of the server, and the name of the interface on that server that we wish to access, only once our program is actually running.

For late binding, Visual Basic talks to Windows and hunts through its registry for the server that we need. When it finds it, Visual Basic uses that hidden method on the server called QueryInterface to determine whether the server does indeed support the interface that we require.

> *With late binding, the Visual Basic compiler does not check whether our calls to objects on component servers are valid. All checking takes place when the program is running, as each call is made.*

Each time we call a method or property that is late-bound, there's a lot of work going on behind the scenes to find out exactly where the method or property we are after lives on the interface, just before it actually gets called. Now that's a big overhead. Every time we create the object, a lot of things need to go on to check that our code is correct in its assumptions. And every time we call a method or a property, there is yet more work going on behind the scenes to find the method we require and check its format. It's quite easy to see, then, that late-bound objects are relatively slow to work with - but the big plus is that they can be quite handy when we want to defer binding details until runtime.

In Visual Basic, we can bind late by using the generic `Object` type to define the interface we want to bind with, and this generic reference will remain unspecified until runtime. Here's an (admittedly rather contrived) example within some Visual Basic code. The following `ObjectPrint` method accepts a late-bound generic `Object` as a parameter, and contains a command to call the `Print` method of that `Object`:

```
Public Sub ObjectPrint(objPadObject As Object)
  objPadObject.Print "This is not a love song"
End Sub
```

Since the Visual Basic compiler cannot know what sort of `Object` will be passed to this method at runtime, no type checking or other validation procedures can take place. We might, for instance, have another method that feeds a `Form` object to this `DoObjectPrint` routine:

```
Public Sub DoObjectPrint()
 ObjectPrint Me
End Sub
```

This would work fine, simply printing some text on the `Me` object, our current form.

We'll be looking at some full-blown examples of implementing early and late binding in Visual Basic later in this chapter.

Early Binding

Early binding is very different. Early binding takes place as a program is being compiled, so type checking and object validation can take place before we run our program.

When we create a component server in Visual Basic it kicks out a file called a `TLB` file (**Type LiBrary**). This contains everything that we would ever need to find out about where a server lives, which interfaces it supports, and the methods and properties it contains - plus their syntax.

In Visual Basic terms, the difference between early and late binding rests with how we create the objects, as we'll see later. Suffice to say, because early binding is faster and slicker, and a more 'ActiveX' way of doing things, Visual Basic provides us with a great deal of help if we choose early binding for our components.

With early bound objects, Visual Basic pops up quick-fill help to guide us to the correct spelling of method and property names. Visual Basic will also show us the syntax of these elements - just as if they were built-in Visual Basic methods and properties.

Working with early-bound objects has the clear advantage of running faster applications and allowing Visual Basic to help us with quick-fill help. On the downside, since we must explicitly state the interface details we're binding to, early-binding is less flexible than late-binding.

In Visual Basic, we can bind early by specifying the object interface that we want to bind to explicitly within our code. Let's go back to that `ObjectPrint` example which we implemented with late binding just a few moments ago. To early bind `ObjectPrint`, we can specify a particular type of object within our code to indicate the binding. For instance, we might choose only to print `Form` objects:

```
Public Sub ObjectPrint(frmPadObject As Form)
    frmPadObject.Print "This is not a love song"
End Sub
```

> *We'll be looking at some full-blown examples of implementing early and late binding in Visual Basic later in this chapter.*

Early Binding ActiveX Servers

Let's consider how to bind ActiveX component servers. We'll first take a look at using the References dialog to achieve this, and then we'll consider the task from a code perspective.

Early Binding with the References Dialog

In order to early bind to ActiveX servers, which is something we'll be doing quite a bit later in the chapter, it's a good idea to get used to using the References dialog in Visual Basic. If you want to take a peek at it now, then by all means feel free. You can get at the dialog by choosing References from the Project menu within Visual Basic itself:

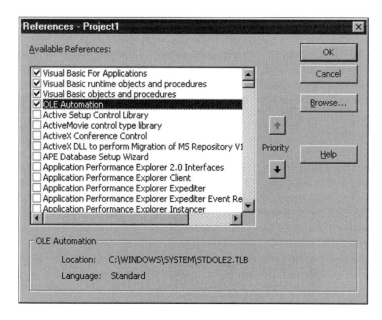

The References dialog shows us a complete list of all the ActiveX servers, be they component servers or ActiveX controls, that Windows knows about.

How are Windows and Visual Basic aware of these ActiveX servers? Simple - when we install an application that can provide others with access to its components, or when we compile an application ourselves that exposes classes to other applications as ActiveX components, the **Windows registry** gets updated.

> *The Windows registry is a mini database that holds references to all the servers on the system, the components within those servers, and the interfaces on those components. Think then of the References dialog as a market stall of ActiveX merchandise - just browse the available goods and pick and choose to your heart's content. If what you want isn't there, then you can even hit the Browse button to hunt down the actual server itself on your hard disk - hopefully, though, you'll never need to do this.*

To early bind an ActiveX server, simply select the ActiveX server you need from the References list, and close the dialog. You'll now be able to make use of the server's classes just as if they were native classes within your own application.

> *Don't worry if this all sounds a little too cloudy right now - we'll be using it a lot more, later in this chapter, and indeed throughout the rest of the book.*

Early Binding Through Code

If we're accessing a server, we will always need to set up a reference in the References dialog to that server. The basic code syntax for early binding to a server is then as follows:

```
Dim <objectname> As [New] <Servername>.<classname>
```

Wait a minute - what's this <Servername> thing? Well, if we have more than one server on our computer that has a class inside called <classname> then we need to prefix the name of that class with the name of the server that contains it.

It doesn't hurt to get into the habit of doing this anyway, as it happens, since it makes our code a lot more readable. I didn't bother earlier, just so you could get an idea of how easy it really is to deal with ActiveX component servers.

The New is optional (shown as square braces) because we can set up an object in our application to hold an ActiveX component - but choose not to create the component straight away. So while we would usually do this:

```
Dim MyObject As New MyServer.MyClassName
```

we could in fact use this technique:

```
Dim MyObject As MyServer.MyClassName

Set MyObject = New MyServer.MyClassName
```

Creating objects using `Set`, while heavier in terms of code and key tapping on our part, is actually faster at runtime. The technicalities of this are complex, so I'll try to be brief. If we `Dim` an object `As New` then Visual Basic will automatically add code to check to see if it has created the object already each time we call a method on it. We are, after all, telling Visual Basic, "I want you to go and create this object for me so I can use it later." Visual Basic won't actually bother creating this object until the first time we call a method or use a property on it.

By using `Set` to create the object manually in our own code, on the other hand, we're telling Visual Basic, "Hey, I have this object variable - I'll worry about creating it myself later." So Visual Basic doesn't have to worry about dumping code into our compiled project to check if the object has been created or not. If we haven't created that object by the time we need it, then Visual Basic will hit an error condition and tell us all about it - no niceties this way, but faster code.

In many applications, this isn't a huge thing to worry about. However, it's definitely worth bearing in mind for your own corporate developments, particularly if you find yourself working with projects that deal with a huge number of objects. In this case, the overhead can become quite significant, and you might choose to avoid the `New` keyword.

> *We'll be looking at some full-blown examples of implementing early and late binding in Visual Basic later in this chapter.*

A Short Story About ActiveX

Since we've covered quite a lot of COM ground, now, I thought you might appreciate a short break before we get back to it with a discussion about processes and addressing models in the next section. So here's a short story about how ActiveX makes everyone's life a whole lot easier.

Our story starts back in the days of Visual Basic 3. Things were tough then, but Visual Basic 3 had come out with the ability to talk to Access 1 databases; this was, at that time, a revolutionary step for a Windows development system. In fact it was a decision on Microsoft's part that would lead to the runaway success of Visual Basic.

There was a problem though. The problem was that soon after Visual Basic 3 was released, there came Access 2. Visual Basic 3 couldn't talk to this format of database, but there were a lot of benefits in Access 2 that the Visual Basic people really wanted to make use of (a dramatically faster database engine was one of them). Microsoft had to find a way to let Visual Basic 3 developers get at Access 2. Microsoft reacted, but what followed became a legendary mess.

You see, Microsoft decided to upgrade the set of the DLLs that originally shipped with Visual Basic so that Visual Basic code could deal with Access 1 and 2 databases. This update, which was known as the **Database Compatibility Layer**, had to be downloaded, it was absolutely huge, and it had something of a reputation for crashing the system. Developers had to recompile their applications to make use of the new DLLs, and if they didn't, there was a risk that older applications would not work on a system that had the new DLLs. In addition to that, people needed Access 2 on their machine in order to even install the compatibility layer, since it borrowed a couple of the DLL's that shipped with that application.

> *The Visual Basic programming world struggled forward, and thankfully made it to the next releases of Visual Basic - luckily for us.*

In the ActiveX world, today, things are a lot better. Take a good look at the References dialog, for example, and you'll see a reference to Microsoft's DAO 3.51 Object Library.

If Microsoft release a new version of Access today, and they want Visual Basic developers to be able to get at the databases it uses, all Microsoft needs to do is ship out a new ActiveX component server! The Visual Basic developers will then just need to pop open this dialog and reference the new server. Instantly, they will find the new functionality available to them. No more messing with different versions of DLLs. No more huge downloads. No more confusion and compatibility problems. That's a happy ending for us!

Compiling ActiveX Servers

As we've seen, when an ActiveX server is compiled, Visual Basic makes changes to the Windows registry so other applications on our system can create instances of our components.

Let's consider this neat trick with the Windows registry for a moment though. Isn't there a problem waiting for us here? Surely, every time we compile our ActiveX server, we will end up with a new, uniquely named entry in the Windows registry? Our registry will eventually get bulked up, our PC will come to a grinding halt, and the true definition of apocalypse will surely follow shortly thereafter.

It's precisely for this reason that there's a neat property for our ActiveX server projects that allows us to control how registry entries are made. This property is the **Version Compatibility** of our server.

Take a look at the Version Compatibility options - it's in the Project Properties dialog. You can navigate to this dialog, once you've started or loaded up any ActiveX server (EXE or DLL), by right-clicking on the project name within the Project explorer window and then choosing the Project Properties option. You'll now see the Project Properties dialog appear. Click the Component tab, and you'll see this dialog:

These three Version Compatibility options control what information gets stored in the registry every time we compile our ActiveX server:

▶ No Compatibility. With this option, we end up with a new, uniquely named entry in the Windows registry for every compilation. Clearly, we're back to our apocalyptic vision of a full registry, so don't select No Compatibility in this situation.

▶ Project Compatibility. This option should be selected while our servers are still in development, being debugged and so on. Then, each time we compile our server, Visual Basic will simply update that server's entries in the Windows registry. There's still one caveat, however: every time we compile, we do need to recompile any clients that talk to the server.

▶ Binary Compatibility. We use this option once we've compiled our server and we're happy that our server is complete, bug free and ready to roll. It's important that we set this option after we ship our working server. Any changes we make to the code, so long as they don't change method or property definitions, will not affect the registry in any way at all - so the clients that use our server will not need to be recompiled to take account of the changes we've made.

It's imperative, though, when we get to this shipping stage and we're using Binary Compatibility, that we **do not** change the definition of properties and methods in our class - if we do, then we absolutely must recompile the clients. If we don't recompile, then our clients will pop up a nasty ActiveX can't create component error message. Most users take this as a personal insult to their mother's background and jump on the phone to you immediately.

In-Process and Out-of-Process Servers

As well as there being two ways to bind to a server, there are actually two types of server that we can create: **in-process servers** and **out-of-process servers**.

This is an area where a lot of people get quite confused. It's a topic laced with terminology and overlapping definitions, but if you keep your wits about you, it's not that hard to grasp.

A **process** is basically an application. If we run up Excel and Word side by side on the same computer, each application is a unique process. It's like having two computers running different programs: each has its own data, its own screen display, its own user interface, and its own memory allocated to it.

In the Win32 world (Windows 95 and Windows NT), however, each process can actually consist of a number of **threads**.

> *A thread is like a mini process. Threads have their own data and code, their own memory, and so forth, but threads still always belong to a process.*

In Excel, for example, we can have a spreadsheet on display that contains a chart, as well as the numbers on the spreadsheet. The chart normally runs as a separate thread - it's responsible for maintaining its own display and doing its own calculations and such like; but it is still part of Excel. Close Excel down and any threads that it owns are closed down as well - including the chart.

So what are in-process and out-of -process servers?

> ▶ In-process servers run inside the client's process, and are actually a `DLL` (Dynamic Link Library). When we call a method on an in-process server's interface, our code loads up the `DLL` and transfers program control to the relevant part of that `DLL`. Our calling program, the client, sits and waits for the relevant code to finish running in the in-process server, and only then can this client continue running its own code.

> ▶ Out-of-process servers are effectively separate programs that contain objects, and they are `EXE` files. When we call a method on an out-of-process server, the `EXE` loads up in its own process space. A good example of this would be having our Visual Basic program make use of some of the ActiveX components that Excel provides. Obviously, our application and Excel are two completely different programs. If we need to run up Excel to use its `Sheet` object to do something, then we're effectively running a second program and asking it for help.

The downside to out-of-process servers is that they're usually somewhat slower than in-process servers. The advantage of out-of-process servers, on the other hand, is that they are independent from any client programs; they can be used to effectively create multitasking programs.

In Visual Basic terms, out-of-process servers also provide us with a lot more options about how our objects can be instantiated - a subject that we'll cover later on.

> *We'll be talking about in-process and out-of-process servers at various points through the rest of the book - we'll be putting all this good theory into practice soon enough!*

Processes and Global Variables

Because threads always belong to some process, there are some issues we need to think about concerning variable data types.

From your previous experience with Visual Basic, you'll almost certainly know that we can drop standard code modules into our projects, and that we can declare variables as `Public` within those projects.

> *In a normal application, a `Public` variable is one that can be accessed by absolutely any other code in our application. For example, we could have a `Public` variable called `g_intAge` to hold the user's age. We could set that from an **Age** dialog, and then get at it from any other form, class method, property, subroutine or function within our code.*

Traditional programming practice dictates that we really don't want to deal with `Public` variables too much: they add to something known as the **Global address space**, which, in real terms, means that they bulk out our application and its memory footprint. This leads to less efficient applications.

However, when we're dealing with ActiveX component servers, especially out-of-process servers (which run in their own process space), there are some neat tricks that we can perform if we do happen to use global variables.

In Win32 terms, global data is global to the process. Now, since all threads are owned by a process, it makes sense that all threads can access their parent process's global data. This means that if we were to declare a `Public` variable in a module that was inside an ActiveX component server, then we could conceivably access that data from any instance of a component provided by that server.

This opens up the possibility of something known as **load balancing**; a trick that they said couldn't be done in Visual Basic. It can!

> *You'll see some more of load balancing this later on in the chapter, when we look at some code that explores the domain of load balancing and load monitoring.*

For now, just be aware that unless we tell Visual Basic to run up a separate thread each time we create a component, the components we create from a single server will all share global data.

This is useful knowledge. Say, for instance, that we were dealing with a database application and we wanted the components in our server to instantly know what records in the database any brother and sister components were already dealing with. Given this technique, we can simply access the global data of our thread's parent process.

Creating Components in Visual Basic 6

Phew - theory out the way. What on earth does this all mean to Visual Basic programmers? Well, not a lot really. Visual Basic does a remarkable job of hiding all the tedious stuff behind a selection of mouse clicks, property windows and dialog boxes. But now that we know all that stuff, the material to come will be very easy indeed - and should ring a lot of familiar bells in your head.

Since an ActiveX component is nothing more than a public class contained within a server (`EXE` or `DLL`), making an ActiveX components is almost as simple as writing a class module in a standard Visual Basic application. Do you remember the `clsTitles` class that we worked on in Chapter 3? Let's turn it into an ActiveX component!

Converting Classes into Components

The first and foremost thing that we need to do if we want to convert a class into an ActiveX component is to store that class in some kind of server. In Visual Basic terms, this means that we need to create a new project - an ActiveX server project - and drop the class that we want to expose into that ActiveX server project. All that remains, then, is to set up something known as the `Instancing` property at runtime, and we're away!

Try It Out - Converting a Class into a Component

1 The first thing that we're going to need to do is create an ActiveX server project. There are two types of ActiveX server that we can deal with:

▶ ActiveX EXE servers

▶ ActiveX DLL servers

There's quite a difference between these two ActiveX server types in terms of the features that they provide us, and we'll be contrasting them in a little while.

For now, just start up a new project, by selecting File-New Project, and choose ActiveX DLL, as shown in the screenshot here:

After a short pause, you'll find your project created and ready to go.

A significant difference between a server and a normal application is that when a server is first created all it contains is a single class module. This makes sense when you consider that a server application does nothing more than expose public classes as ActiveX components, so our server is going to need at least one class:

2 Thinking back to Chapter 3, we already have some classes (`clsTitles` and `clsAuthors`) that we can use in this component server. So right-click on **Class1** in the Project explorer window and choose **Remove Class1** to get rid of the default class:

Say **No** to the question concerning saving changes to `Class1`.

3 Now we can go ahead and add in the `clsTitles` and `clsAuthors` classes that we wrote in Chapter 3. Click on the **Project** menu and choose **Add Class Module**. When the standard dialog appears, click on the **Existing** tab and find the `clsTitles` class that we worked on in the Chapter 3 and add it into the project. Repeat the process for the `clsAuthors` class and also the `clsRecordset` class that we worked on - don't forget, the `clsTitles` and `clsAuthors` classes relied on the `clsRecordset` class.

4 When you're done adding classes, the Project explorer window in Visual Basic will have changed to show you the new classes in your project. Click on the name of the `clsTitles` class in the Project explorer window and take a peek at the Properties window below. Notice anything strange?

When we're dealing with ActiveX component servers, we actually get an additional property available to us that we don't normally have: the **Instancing** property.

*We'll cover the **Instancing** property in a lot more detail later on in this chapter. For now, just take my word that this is a really important property and that it controls exactly how the server works in terms of its memory usage and other goodies at runtime.*

5 Click on the Instancing property and drop down the list of options. You should see a fairly large list of options, one of which is MultiUse - select it.

Be careful though - there's also an entry called GlobalMultiUse - we'll look at that one in a little more detail later in the chapter, but don't confuse it with the MultiUse entry.

When you've set the Instancing property of `clsTitles` to MultiUse, do the same for `clsAuthors` and then `clsRecordset`.

> *In an ActiveX component server such as the one we're producing right now, one class cannot implement another if the one being implemented is set as a **Private** class through the **Instancing** property.*

You may be surprised to learn that our server is now as good as complete. There are just a few project options that we need to take a peek at, and the job will be done.

6 Right-click on the name of the project in the Project explorer window, and select Project1 Properties to open the Project Properties dialog:

The first option that we absolutely must change here is the project name. As you can see from the screenshot, I changed my project name from Project1 to TitleServer. The project name is something we'll actually use in the client application later on to create an instance of our ActiveX component - so it's worthwhile spending some time thinking about a decent name.

You should also note that Visual Basic will get most upset if you try to name the project the same as any of the classes it contains. The name you use for the project must be unique in the project, just as it must be a unique filename when you save it (assuming you save the project in the same location on your hard disk as the classes, and so forth).

7 When you've done that, click on the Component tab of the Project Properties dialog to display the component server options for the project:

For now, all we need to do is follow this simple rule for ActiveX servers:

If you've shipped your server to end users already, make sure that the Binary Compatibility option is selected; otherwise, select Project Compatibility.

We'll look at the Binary Compatibility option later in the chapter, but it's worth knowing for now that in order to use Binary Compatibility we must have previously compiled the project. Visual Basic will then need us to specify the filename of the project when it was previously compiled - so that the Binary Compatibility option can ensure that the same IDs and references are used for the classes in our project. Again, don't worry about this too much for now - we'll go over it in a lot more detail later.

For now, just select Project Compatibility and click on the OK button to close down the dialog.

8 Our ActiveX component server is now ready to be compiled. Save our project as `TitleServer.vbp` using the File-Save Project As menu option. Then click on the File menu again and select Make TitleServer.dll. After a bit of disk whirring you should be presented with a nasty Visual Basic error, much like the one here:

```
Public intYea
Public strISB
Public lngPub
Public strDes
Public strNot
Public strSub
Public strCor
```

```
' Private members to hold connection to database,
' and to the recordset itself
```

```
Private m recTitles As Recordset
Private m dbDatabase As Database
```

Ah ha - one of your first exposures, albeit a nasty one, to the world of object references. Do you remember how I kept waffling on a while ago about how everything in Visual Basic is based around objects? Well, I wasn't kidding.

In this case, we have some code in the server that deals with databases, for the simple reason that we need to go to the database to build up the Invoice information. However, unless we **explicitly tell** Visual Basic exactly where to find the database objects, there's just no way we can do any database code.

The interesting thing about that the database objects is that they're all actually implemented as ActiveX components (it doesn't matter whether we use the more common Data Access Objects (DAO), or the Remote Data Objects (RDO)). So, what we need to do is tell Visual Basic exactly which database servers we're going to use. Or, in other words, we're going to **early bind** to those database servers.

Now while this may well sound like a pretty horrendous task, it's actually delightfully easy to do!

9 Click on the Project menu in Visual Basic and then select References from the list of items. This displays the References dialog. Now scroll down the list, and when you find the Microsoft DAO 3.51 Object Library reference, just click on the checkbox to its left to select it:

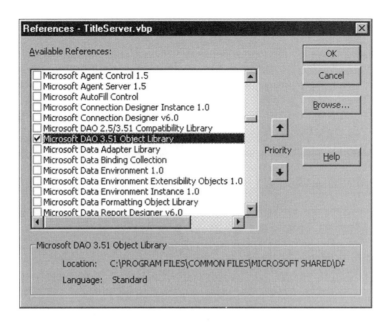

This is the server DLL on the system that contains the DAO database functionality in Visual Basic. Click the OK button to start using the new reference straight away.

We should now be able to create the server without any problems. Once again, go to the File menu and select Make TitleServer.dll. There should be a pause and, after a while, you'll find that you have a new DLL on your PC that happens to be our Invoice Server:

If you've come from a Windows 3 background, you may have been tempted to make sure that the DLL gets compiled into the Windows\System *directory. We don't need to do that with Windows 32 based systems like NT or Windows 95 though. When we compile the server, Visual Basic automatically puts entries in the Windows registry to indicate which facilities the server provides, and also to tell the system where on the machine the DLL lives.*

All that remains for us to do now is to write a client application, or at the very least a modification of our previous invoicing application, so that we can test out our new ActiveX DLL component server.

Creating Components at Runtime

Okay - now we have an ActiveX component server. It's no good, though, unless we know how to create objects from it within our own code at runtime. Thankfully, that too is a very easy task, and if we're converting classes out of an application and into a server, you'll be pleased to know that it requires us to change very little in our code.

Try It Out – Creating a Component at Runtime with Early Binding

1 Load up the BiblioTech application, the simple database application that we wrote in Chapter 3:

If you go to the Project explorer window, you'll see the familiar clsTitles, clsAuthors and clsRecordset classes in there. However, we don't need these any more, since we're going to use our new server. So right-click on the clsTitles class and select Remove to get rid of it. Then, do the same for the clsAuthors and clsRecordset classes - these also live on the server now.

2 If we now press *Ctrl* and *F5* to do a full compile of the application, you'll get one of several thousand inevitable errors. A typical and symptomatic one is shown here:

```
Option Explicit
Private WithEvents Titles As clsTitles

Private Sub cmdFirst_Click()
    MoveFirst Titles
End Sub

Private Sub cmdLast_C
    MoveLast Titles
End Sub

Private Sub cmdNext_C
    MoveNext Titles
End Sub

Private Sub cmdPrevious_Click()
```

Obviously what's gone wrong, here, is that we're trying to create objects from classes that no longer exist in the project, just the same as earlier when our server complained because it didn't know about the database classes.

Since we're using a server, now, we need to bring up the References dialog and reference our new server. So dismiss this error dialog, click on the Project menu and choose References to bring up the dialog that we saw earlier.

If you scroll down the list of servers you should find our TitleServer listed there. Now select it:

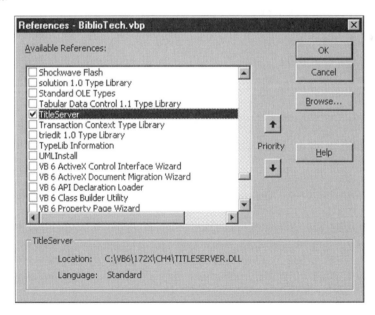

Now click on OK to close the dialog and establish the link to TitleServer.

151

3 Now that we have Visual Basic looking at the Title server, we can simply run the application, or Press *Ctrl* and *F5* again to do a full compile, and miraculously it works, just as it always did!

The obvious difference is that the `clsTitles`, `clsAuthors` and `clsRecordset` classes are no longer a part of this project - since they now live in our wonderful new ActiveX server.

Don't forget to save this `BiblioTech` *project - we'll be coming back to it later in this chapter when we look at debugging.*

Creating a Component at Runtime With Late Binding

So what about late binding? Well, let's look at our example application again. As we now know, declaring an object like this,

```
Dim objTitles As New clsTitles
```

is early binding, because we name the class (and optionally the server, although we must reference the server through the **References** dialog anyway) when we declare the object itself.

With late binding, Visual Basic has absolutely no idea of the type of component that we're dealing with, and so we must create our object variable as a generic object:

```
Dim objTitles As Object
```

All this does, though, is set up an object variable within Visual Basic that is capable of holding an object. It doesn't actually go ahead and create the object. To do that, we need to use the rather special `CreateObject` method, which those of you with some background in Visual Basic 4 might have come across when dealing with OLE. The `CreateObject` method works like this:

```
Dim objTitles As Object

Set objTitles = CreateObject("TitleServer.clsTitles")
```

It is by this method that we could, if we so wished, use late binding in our `BiblioTech` project. We won't step through to implement this, however - I'm sure you get the idea and, as we noted earlier, creating the object and calling its methods and properties is a lot slower with late binding.

Late binding does have its advantages, of course, in the right context. If we late bind then we don't need to set up references to servers within the Visual Basic development environment: the server name, the classes it supports, and the methods on them are resolved at runtime when we call the `CreateObject` method. In addition, with late binding we're free, at any point in code, to switch from one object server to another, just by making another call to `CreateObject`.

 FYI In applications where performance is the key, we really need to steer well clear of late-bound objects.

Exploring Components with the Object Browser

With Visual Basic relying so heavily on objects now, finding out which ones it knows about, and which ones it does not, can be rather useful. In fact, I often find myself scrambling for a document or help file that will show me a list of the methods and properties in the various objects that I'm using.

Visual Basic comes readymade with a utility to help: the **Object Browser**. If we are early binding to objects, and we have the references to their servers already set up in Visual Basic, then we can use the Object Browser to get a view of the classes (interfaces) in the server, and the methods and properties that they support.

This can be a great way to get 'help' on any object that we might want to use in Visual Basic, regardless of whether that object came in the Visual Basic box or if it was developed by ourselves or a colleague.

To bring up the object browser, just press *F2* within the design environment. If you don't still have our modified BiblioTech application loaded, then load it up now. When it's ready to go, hit that *F2* key. Here's what you'll see:

At the top left of the **Object Browser** is a combo box. This lists all the component and control servers that are currently referenced in your project. Drop it down and you should see the **TitleServer** component server there. Select **TitleServer** from this list and the **Object Browser** will show the classes, properties and methods that **TitleServer** contains:

Underneath the server Combo box at the top left, which we just used, there's a list of the interfaces that the server provides. In this case, we have the `clsTitles`, `clsAuthors` and `clsRecordset` objects listed. If we select either of these then the right-hand side changes to show the methods and properties that belong to the server.

Finally, selecting a method or property from the list on the right shows you the syntax of the method or property at the bottom of the browser.

This is where things can get interesting. If we're looking at a property of a built-in object in Visual Basic then the bottom of the screen will also show us a short note on what the method does - effectively providing us with some quick help on the method.

If we had created our objects using Visual Basic's class wizard utility then we'd also find that we could enter comments for any of the methods, properties, events and classes that we created. These comments would then be shown in the **Object Browser** underneath the format of the method - as the quick help message. You can even set these things up by hand, but I'll leave the explanation of that till a little later in the book (but for those who can't wait, you use the **Procedure Attributes** dialog).

Have a play with the **Object Browser** and find out what it can do. You'll find it very useful as you start to develop larger applications, especially in the object-oriented development arena.

More Advanced Components

So far, we've only touched on the surface of ActiveX components. We've seen how to make an ActiveX server, and we've seen how to create instances of objects in that server within our own code at runtime. You should be pretty comfortable with the whole process, so now it's time to take things a little further.

There's a lot more to learn about ActiveX components, and some of this stuff can radically change the way our servers and clients work. The main issues here can be summarized as follows:

- The speed of the servers
- The amount of system resources the servers consume
- How the servers are accessed by multiple clients

There's plenty of great code for us to explore as we begin to reach some of these more advanced ActiveX techniques, so let's get straight to it.

Component Instancing

The most important thing that can change the way our components work is the Instancing property. Recall how we changed the Instancing property on the classes that we put into that `TitleServer` DLL earlier:

These are only the options available to classes in DLL servers. EXE servers, on the other hand, provide a few more Instancing options:

So, what do all these Instancing options do? Well, they govern the functionality of classes on two levels:

▶ On the first level, the Instancing property controls the visibility of a class within a server. For example, setting the Instancing of a class to Private effectively hides the class within the server, preventing a client application from creating an object based on it.

▶ On the second level, the Instancing property controls the way in which memory is used by instances of that class within our PC, and the way in which multiple client applications interact with the instances of the class.

Keeping these two levels in mind, let's now take a look at each Instancing property in turn.

Private Classes

As we've already seen, the Private option effectively hides a class within a server, and this is ideal if we need to drop a class into a server application for the other classes to use, but which we do not want a client application to be able to create.

This is a very useful option, but surprisingly underused. Many people think that when they create a server application all they need to do is create classes in order to get their components exposed. Forget that! Object-oriented programming is about looking at an entire problem area and seeing how objects can be applied to it.

So don't look at servers and say that the only classes they should contain would be those that we expose. Private classes can be exceptionally useful in servers, in the same way that they are useful within normal applications: they provide a way for us to break down a large problem into concise, easy to maintain smaller objects.

PublicNotCreatable Classes

The next option, PublicNotCreatable, is an interesting one. Like a Private class, PublicNotCreateable classes cannot be created by a client application. However, PublicNotCreatable can be created by other classes within the server and then passed out to the client application.

This can be great in database applications. Look at our Invoice application for example. Using a PublicNotCreatable class we could easily get the Invoice object to create and pass out a Customer object containing all the information that we might ever want to get at to deal with a Customer. However, because the client could never explicitly create a Customer object on its own, we've ensured that the server makes the only Customer objects that are ever created. What the client application does with the object once it's got it is its own business, but only the server has the power to create objects of this type.

Global Classes

All the remaining Instancing options are public ones, resulting in components that can be created as objects by a client.

However, the two that are listed as Global (GlobalSingleUse and GlobalMultiUse) are pretty neat. With both of these options, we end up with methods and properties that can be accessed without having to specify the name of an object: the object gets created implicitly, without our help.

Let's say that our clsTitles class was set up as a GlobalMultiUse class. In our client application, all that we'd need to do to access the methods and properties of clsTitles would be to reference it, using the project References dialog. The methods and properties could then be used within that client application without having to specify the name of the server class. In many ways, the methods and properties appear to client applications just as if they were Public methods in a standard module in a normal application.

This seems nice and easy - but there's a caveat. We really shouldn't get into using Global components as a regular thing. There are some worrying issues surrounding Global modules that we should be aware of in our programming:

▶ The memory issue. Each class in a referenced server that is GlobalMultiUse or GlobalSingleUse is created quietly behind the scenes as soon as our application runs. Now in the object-oriented world, it isn't that uncommon to find applications with tens, if not hundreds of classes in them. If these are all set as living in a remote server and as Global then they will all get created the instant our application runs. This could create some serious memory problems.

▶ The performance issue. Each Global object is created without our help when the application runs, and that takes time. If we have a lot of objects like this then when our application runs, we might need to put a dialog on screen warning that the said application will take some time to get going.

The naming issue. We must ensure that the methods we create in Global classes do not have the same name as any other global methods within Visual Basic, or methods and properties of any other classes that we might want to use.

Global components are a neat thing to have, but we really do need to be careful how we use them. I can't think of a single time that I have ever absolutely desperately needed to use them, so unless you absolutely have to use them, steer clear of global components.

The other side of the Instancing property deals with how our objects are actually created, and how our object threads are created and managed.

SingleUse and MultiUse Classes

Many of the Instancing properties revolve around SingleUse and MultiUse. What do these property descriptions mean?

▶ With a SingleUse class, for each client that tries to talk to that class, a new instance of the server will be run in memory.

▶ For a MultiUse class, it doesn't matter how many clients access that class, it will always live in a single process space in memory.

So if we had 15 client applications running, all talking to a MultiUse class, only one instance of the server would ever be created.

> *For ActiveX EXE servers containing **MultiUse** classes, each instance of that **MultiUse** component will run in its own thread.*

MultiUse classes are more efficient than SingleUse classes: the fewer applications that we have running on a system at any one point in time, the faster that system will appear to run, and the less memory our client/server mix will use in the PC.

Okay, so now we can appreciate some of the distinctions between the different Instancing properties, let's write some code so that we can really observe these properties in action.

Client-Server Development

We're going to build both MultiUse and SingleUse client-server applications in this section, and we'll be able to see the how Instancing properties affect the behavior of these components.

We'll learn more about implementing ActiveX clients and servers, as well as gaining a lot more experience with the Instancing property. Enjoy the ride.

Try It Out - Creating a MultiUse Server

1 First we need to create a server. We're going to create an out-of-process server here, since these have that very special ability that in-process servers lack: we can run them just like any other application.

From the File menu choose New Project. When the new project dialog appears, select ActiveX EXE and click OK. You'll be faced with the now familiar sight of a project with a single empty class in it - all ready to go.

2 Before we start writing code, we need to change some options.

First, right click on the project name in the Project explorer window (it should currently say Project 1) and choose Properties from the pop-up menu that appears. After a short pause, the Project Properties dialog will appear:

Modify your dialog to look like the screenshot above: change the Project Name to ExeServerTest, and change the Startup Object box so that it shows Sub Main - this will enable us to run the server just as if it were any other application.

3 Now click on the Component tab to change to the Component server properties page:

The Start Mode box determines whether the application is a pure server application or whether it's a server that can actually be run as an application. In this case, we're going to need this server to run as an application that can serve, so click on the Standalone option, just as in the screenshot here.

Take a quick look at the Version Compatibility box at the bottom of the Component tab as well. This will probably be set to Project Compatibility, and that's where we're going to leave it for now.

As you'll recall from our earlier discussion about compiling ActiveX servers, Project Compatibility will update the server information in the registry for us each time we compile our server.

4 Once you've set up these Compatibility options, close down the dialog. Then click on the class (Class1) that comes with your new project, and use the Properties window to change its name to clsServerInfo. Set the Instancing property of this class to MultiUse.

5 When that's done, add a Form and a Standard Module to your project. Set their names to frmServerInfo and modGlobals respectively. Now the fun starts.

6 Bring up the code window for the **modGlobals** standard module, and type this in:

```
Option Explicit

Public g_strName As String        ' Variable to hold the server name
Public g_intClientCount As Integer ' Variable to count clients

Public Sub Main()
' Starts up the application
    Load frmServerInfo
    frmServerInfo.Show
End Sub
```

All that this is doing is declaring two `Public` (Global) variables called `g_strName` and `g_intClientCount`. We're going to use these to store a unique name for the server and to keep a track of the number of client applications that are currently talking to the server.

FYI

The `Main()` routine is where the code will start if we run this as a normal application, and it does little more than load up the form.

7 Bring up the code window for the class and type in this code:

```
Option Explicit

Private Sub Class_Initialize()
' Registers a client with the server
    g_intClientCount = g_intClientCount + 1
End Sub

Private Sub Class_Terminate()
' Unregisters a client with the server
    g_intClientCount = g_intClientCount - 1
End Sub

'//////// PROPERTIES TO GET TO GLOBAL SERVER DATA ////////
Public Property Get ServerName() As String
' Returns the name of the server, set by the user on the
' server's information form
    ServerName = g_strName
End Property

Public Property Get ClientCount() As Integer
' Returns the number of clients known to this server.
    ClientCount = g_intClientCount
End Property
```

The two event handlers at the top of the class just deal with increasing and decreasing that `g_intClientCount` variable in the global module. This count changes each time an instance of the class is created or destroyed. We then have two `Property Gets`: the first exposes the server's name, while the second exposes our client count (held in `g_intClientCount`). Nothing too complex there.

8 Finally, we need to sort out the form. Drop some controls on to it, and resize it so that it looks like this:

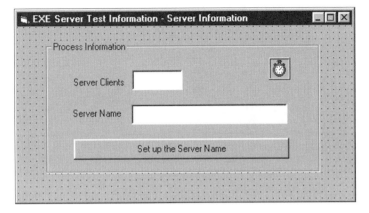

Set the **Locked** property of both text boxes to **True**, which will prevent the user from typing into them at runtime. Set up the rest of the properties this way:

Control	Property	Value
Server Clients Text box	Name	`txtClients`
	Text	<blank>
Server Name Text box	Name	`txtServerName`
	Text	<blank>
Timer control	Name	`tmrUpdate`
	Interval	1000
Command button	Name	`cmdSetName`
	Caption	Set up the Server Name

Don't forget to set that Interval property on the Timer control to 1000.

9 When you've done that, type this into the form's code window:

```
Option Explicit

Private Sub cmdSetName_Click()
' Displays an input box and gets the user to enter a name
' for the server.
    Dim strName As String

    strName = InputBox("Please enter a name for this server.")
    g_strName = strName
    Update_Information

End Sub
```

```
Private Sub Update_Information()
' Updates the information on display in the form
    txtClients = g_intClientCount
    txtServerName = g_strName
End Sub

Private Sub Form_Load()
    g_strName = "Unnamed"
    g_intClientCount = 0
    Update_Information
End Sub

Private Sub tmrUpdate_Timer()
' Automatically updates the form with client information
    Update_Information
End Sub
```

This code should be quite self-explanatory. When the user hits the Command button, we display an Input box and get the user to enter a name for the class. The Command button's Click event, the form's Load event, and the timer's Timer event all call a routine called Update_Information, which displays the client count and the server name in the controls on the form.

10 Save the project at this point - it's always a good idea to save before running a client-server situation.

11 Now run the application to get rid of any syntax errors that you might have introduced. Running the code like this is a useful way to verify that there are no typos or other mistakes in the code, which is quite useful.

Once you've verified that everything is OK, go ahead and compile the server. Do this by selecting File-Ma<u>k</u>e ExeServerTest.exe or File-Ma<u>k</u>e Project1.exe.

If you used the second of these menu options, Ma<u>k</u>e Project1.exe, then you still need to change the name of the ActiveX server to ExeServerTest.exe. You'll be able to do this in the Make Project window that comes up:

We now have a server that can count how many clients are using it, and display that information. Furthermore, this project could also be run as a standalone application, should we ever feel the need to!

Now that the application has been compiled, and effectively shipped off to a client, we should think about setting that <u>B</u>inary Compatibility option. This way, we're effectively locking the interfaces of the components - so any clients that use them will not have to be recompiled if we fix any bugs in our server (just so long as we don't change any interfaces on the server). It's time to go and write the client application.

Try It Out – Creating a Client for Our MultiUse Server

1 Start up a new Standard EXE project in the normal way. When the project is ready to go, right click on the name of the project in the Project explorer window and select the Properties option from the pop-up menu. Change the name of the project to ExeClientTest, then close the properties dialog down.

2 Change the name of the form to frmClientInformation, and drop some controls on to the form so that it looks like this:

Set the names of the two label controls to lblServerName and lblClientNo respectively. Then bring up the code window for the form and enter this code:

```
Option Explicit

Private m_objRemoteServer As ExeServerTest.clsServerInfo

Private Sub Form_Load()
' When the form loads up, we need to create our object, and display
' display global server data on the form
    Set m_objRemoteServer = New ExeServerTest.clsServerInfo

    lblClientNo = "Client Number : " & m_objRemoteServer.ClientCount
    lblServerName = "Server Name : " & m_objRemoteServer.ServerName

End Sub
```

The first thing we do here is declare a new object variable, `m_objRemoteServer`, to be of our server type. When the form loads up, our code creates this object, grabs the two property values from it, and displays them in that form.

3 Bring up the project **References** dialog and make sure that you've referenced the **ExeServerTest** project. Without this reference, we won't be able to call our server, and this code won't compile.

4 Save your code and run it to make sure that you have no errors. You should see the **EXE Client Test** form appear, and the server form should also appear at the same time!

How does this work? Well, when the client runs, it creates an instance of the server component. Since the server component requires that the server is running, and since we've set the server up to display its form no matter what happens, the server's form appears, displaying the same information as our client. It's good to see both client and server working, don't you think?

5 Close the client application down in the usual way. Notice how the server doesn't shut down - it stays running! Once you've enjoyed the show, go ahead and close the server down in the usual way - by closing its window.

6 Compile your client now, by selecting **Make ExeClientTest.exe** from the **File** menu. When that's done, minimize Visual Basic.

7 Now click on the Windows **Start** button and choose **Run**. Find your server on your hard disk, using the **Browse** button, and run the `ExeServerTest.EXE` server. Then do the same thing for the client application you just compiled. Then run the client again, and again, and again. You'll now see something like this:

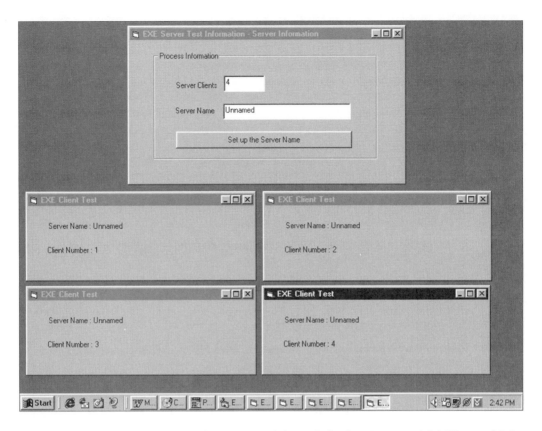

Since the Instancing property on the server's clsServerInfo class is set to MultiUse, multiple clients here can all talk to just our one server process. We have Global data in that one server process, which every client component can access. Therefore, the clients can find out how many other clients are using the server, and the server can also display how many clients it knows about.

> *Notice that the Server Name information on the existing clients is not updated if we*
> *changed the name of our server. Only new clients that call the server once we've renamed it*
> *pick up the new server name. I'll leave you to think about how you might adapt the client*
> *code to update itself when the server code changes.*

As you close these clients down, you should see the server update its display (remember there's a timer on there, which is constantly updating the display) to show that fewer and fewer clients are using it. Isn't it wonderful? Our objects communicating with each other!

165

Try It Out - Creating a SingleUse Server and Client

1 This has got to be the quickest piece of programming you've seen for some time! To convert our MultiUse client-server application to a SingleUse client-server application, load up the server in Visual Basic and change the Instancing property of the `clsServerInfo` class to SingleUse. Now recompile the server, using File-Make, keeping its original ExeServerTest name.

2 That's all we need to do, except recompile our client code as well - since we do not have Binary Compatibility set up yet, and we've just changed our server code. So load up the client code, and simply recompile using File-Make, keeping its original ExeClientTest name.

3 Everything else in our SingleUse client-server application is just the same as it was for the MultiUse version. So we're ready. Minimize Visual Basic and run the server, then several instances of the client application, and observe the differences in behavior.

In SingleUse mode, each client talks to its own server process, so each time we run up a new client we also run up a whole new server, each with its own global data and each totally unaware of any other servers and clients running:

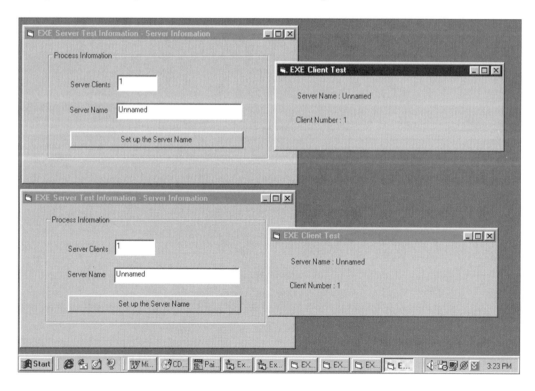

Now if you've heard about the Apartment Model threading (or you've noticed that it's one of the threading options within Visual Basic), and you want to find out more, it's time to think about reading Professional Business Objects with Visual Basic 6.0, *also by Wrox Press. This book is the best place to go when you've finished the one in your hand, and it covers advanced topics such as Apartment Model threading.*

For those of you who want to try and work out Apartment Model threading by yourselves for now, I'll give you a hint by telling you that each server thread has its own data in this threading model, rather like **SingleUse**.

Load Balancing

We're dealing with COM every time we create a component from a server, but in the real world of business many people prefer to use **DCOM (Distributed COM)**. DCOM is a little beyond the scope of this book, but what it allows us to do is register a server as living on a different machine.

The whole idea of putting servers on different machines is to spread the processing burden across a network and to make the application more resilient; maintenance and distribution burdens becomes easier, and superior performance is achieved. For very large systems, however, there's also a common requirement for something known as **load balancing**.

With load balancing, we monitor how many clients are talking to a specific machine - and when a certain limit is hit, we switch new clients to a different machine. This has traditionally been seen as something that's very hard to do.

Now before you start getting excited, DCOM provides no mechanism for switching the default location of servers on the fly - unless we want to go and mess with the registry of each local machine. In fact, Visual Basic doesn't really provide us with enough control over the registry to reasonably try that.

There is a solution, though, for those of you brave enough to take things a little further:

1 First off, we need to write our main server in the usual way.

2 If we want the processing burden to be borne by eight machines, we then compile our server with eight different names (Server1, Server2, Server3 etc.) and use the DCOM tools that are available to place each server on its own machine. (Alternatively, we could manually install each version of the server on the eight machines.)

3 We then write a control server (like the one in the last section) which counts how many connections there are to each server, and which handles requests for new components. Now if we were allowing just one client to connect to each machine, and a third client asked for a component, our control server could just use late binding to request the component from Server3 and then pass it back to requesting client. Naturally, we'd have to arrange for our client to be using late binding as well with this method.

This technique offers us a very rough but effective method of load balancing from within Visual Basic.

Debugging Components

Developing ActiveX components seems easy enough, but what about debugging? After all, what we're dealing with, here, is an application where the functionality is split across a client application and at least one remote EXE or DLL server. How do we follow the flow of a program that's split apart like this, and how do we work out what's going wrong when things do go wrong?

Thankfully, Visual Basic makes things very easy in this arena, and provides a way for us to continue using the built-in debugging facilities in Visual Basic. The way this works is that we can load up more than one project at a time - and step between them within the Visual Basic development environment. Want to know how it all works? Of course you do!

Debugging Client-Server Applications

The classic situation where many Visual Basic programmers start to feel they really don't want to do any debugging is within client-server applications. As we shall see, however, there's really nothing to worry about - it's as easy as debugging a normal application, once you've properly oriented yourself to having two projects alive at the same time.

Try It Out – Debugging a Client-Server Application

1 First, load up a client application: the revised `BiblioTech.VBP` project that we worked on earlier in this chapter. Visual Basic provides some wonderful little tools for debugging applications spread across more than one project, and that's what we're going to see here.

2 Now add the server to the project group. If you drop down the <u>F</u>ile menu, you'll notice that there is an A<u>d</u>d Project option on the list of menu items. Select it now:

The usual project dialog will appear, but with its caption showing that we're adding a new project, rather than opening or creating one.

3 Click on the Existing tab across the top of the dialog and find the TitleServer project we created earlier. When you've located it, select it and click on Open to load it up.

Take a look at the Project explorer window now:

Notice that there are now two projects loaded: the BiblioTech project and the TitleServer project.

The icons to the left of each project name show you what kind of projects they are. Looking at the screenshot, for example, you can see that **TitleServer** is an ActiveX component DLL, while **BiblioTech** is a standard EXE.

Notice also that BiblioTech is bold, even though it isn't selected. The reason for this is that when we have more than one project loaded, Visual Basic needs to know which one to run should the user hit *F5* or press the run button on the toolbar. The bold project in the Project explorer window is the default project. We can change this whenever we want (although I wouldn't, in this example) by right-clicking on the project that we want to make the default, and selecting Set as Start Up.

4 It's time to save the projects. Hit the save button on the Visual Basic toolbar, or select the Save Project option from the File menu:

A dialog appears for us to name a new file to save; in this case, a Project Group.

Basically, this saves the contents of the Project explorer window. Later on, you can load up the project group and Visual Basic will load up both of the projects that are currently visible in the Project explorer window. Whilst it's doing this, Visual Basic will also set the right startup project etc. This is a neat time saving feature.

That was a bit of a digression, but I wanted you know everything about how these project groups work in Visual Basic. Let's get on with the debugging stuff now.

5 Double click on the title form (frmTitle) in the BiblioTech project, and then press *F7* to bring up the code for the form:

Now find the line in the code that reads:

```
MoveNext Titles
```

This line is in the Next button's click event. It's calling a method in a module, which in turn calls a method in the clsTitles class, so this is an ideal place to start debugging the application. Click on the line and press *F9* to drop a breakpoint on it - you'll see the line highlight to indicate that the breakpoint is in place.

170

Now run the project, and when the MDI form appears, bring up the Title Browser form and click the Next button:

7 You'll quickly find yourself back in the code window, right where we placed the breakpoint. Press *F8* to single-step through the code and, as if by magic, after about three single-steps the code will jump from the client's source code into the server's source code at clsTitles. Is that useful, or what?

This, in a nutshell, is how we can use Visual Basic's debugging tools with ActiveX component servers. The only limit on the number of projects that we can have in a project group is the available memory!

> *You'll know when you're getting close to the limit since everything in Visual Basic will start to slow down a bit.*

Error Trapping

There is one other option that you need to be aware of in relation to debugging. Click on the Tools menu, and choose Options from the list of menu items. When the Options dialog appears, click on the General tab at the top:

Not surprisingly, the options that we're most interested in right now live in the Error Trapping group.

Normally, Visual Basic is set up to stop if it encounters an **unhandled error**. What this means is that if an error occurs and we don't have an `On Error Goto` active, the offending code will be displayed in the code window once we've acknowledged an error message on screen. We've all seen this before. It's a way of life with Visual Basic.

However, when we're dealing with ActiveX component servers this is a real pain. If an error occurs within the server, then the program will stop and show us the line in the client that called the faulty server method! That's not a lot of use to us, since we need to track down the error within the server.

Here's the good news. If we change the Error Trapping option to Break on All Errors, then the code will stop within the server's source code - provided, of course, that we have the server loaded in a project group. From there, we can start debugging.

ActiveX EXE Servers

There is a problem here though, and it's a little annoying but not insurmountable. This debugging technique will only work with in-process servers. So, we can't debug ActiveX EXE servers in this way, only ActiveX DLL servers.

For some of you, this might appear to be a real pain. It isn't! Just develop your servers as ActiveX DLLs for testing purposes, and when you're sure that you've got all the bugs out, compile an ActiveX EXE version. This DLL-EXE exchange over will not affect your server's code - it simply lives in a different project.

You can convert an ActiveX DLL to an ActiveX EXE within the **Project Properties** dialog. Simply use the pull down Comb box called **Project Type** to define the new type of project that you'd like your current project to be - for our purposes here, an ActiveX EXE:

There's also another option, although this one is slightly more complicated. We can have two copies of Visual Basic loaded, one with our server project in, the other with our client. We can set breakpoints in the server project and run it, just like a normal application. Then, when the client attempts to use the server, it will automatically see that there is already a copy of the server running in the other copy of Visual Basic, and it will use that.

I feel this second option is a convoluted approach in many ways though, and it is in fact a hang over from the old Visual Basic 4 way of working with OLE servers. Personally, I prefer to work with all the objects as early bound objects while I'm still debugging them and then, when I am sure they are happy, I can go over to the late bound way of working.

> *This also makes a lot of sense if you're working in a team environment, where the code that's actually going to use your server (which may be late bound) is being developed by someone else, and may thus not be available to you. In this case, all you need to do is write your own little test client that early binds to the server, and then you can make use of the debugging tools as Microsoft best intended them to be used.*

Summary

We've covered a lot of ground in this chapter. By now, however, one thing should be very clear indeed: ActiveX components are hot property for object-oriented programming in Visual Basic.

We've seen that ActiveX components take us to new and ambitious heights. We started to think about COM in this chapter, and how our own objects could interact with everyone else's objects - we considered what a great party that could be. We covered some dry COM stuff that I tried my best to make interesting for you, and I think that stuff will set you up well now for your time ahead with objects and components and clients and servers and all things interesting in object-oriented programming.

You should be feeling pretty comfortable with ActiveX components by now – they're really just another way to make classes available to applications, but of course with the great advantage that component classes and objects are not tied to any one project - but are available to anyone who can work with ActiveX. I think that's fairly exciting stuff, and it's all due to objects and changing the way we think about our programming.

In particular, you should now be quite happy with:

- ActiveX components
- What COM is and where it's taking us
- Client-server programming in Visual Basic
- Producing ActiveX DLL servers
- Writing your own ActiveX EXE servers
- Early binding to components
- Late binding to components
- Using the References dialog
- Debugging across multiple projects

All these tricks become more and more useful as we pan out from ActiveX components to deal with other aspects of ActiveX as well. We'll therefore continue our journey into objects, in the next chapter, by exploring ActiveX controls.

Why Not Try....

1 How is a Visual Basic class different from an ActiveX component?

2 How important is the `IUnknown` interface to a Visual Basic Programmer?

3 What is component binding, and how many types are there? How do they affect our Visual Basic application?

4 Take the class that you created at the end of Chapter 1, `clsEmployee`, convert it to an ActiveX DLL.

5 Create an instance of the Employee object using the `EmployeeServer` you just created.

6 You may be asking yourself, what about the event that the `clsEmployee` class triggers? Can we still get at that in an ActiveX DLL? The answer is yes! See if you can work out how to do this.

7 Use the Object Browser to explore the Properties, Methods and Events of the `EmployeeServer`.

6

Objects and ActiveX Controls

Overview

In the last chapter, we saw how ActiveX components can extend the way we think about objects when we program in Visual Basic. In this chapter, we'll take a look at ActiveX controls, which are another part of the exciting ActiveX genre guaranteed to take our object-oriented programming to new heights.

Visual Basic 6 actually lets us create ActiveX controls ourselves. No more C++ compilers, no more huge learning curves. Thankfully, like most other areas of Visual Basic, Microsoft has spent a great deal of time and research making it as easy as possible for us to develop ActiveX controls.

ActiveX controls are, of course, just another type of object - albeit a rather prolific type of object; what we're essentially doing then, in this chapter, is extending the inventory of objects that we know and understand - and can create for ourselves. ActiveX controls are fairly special objects: they very often have a visual element, they can encapsulate a great deal of functionality in a very neat and compact form, and they're wonderfully rewarding to create - as you'll find out in this chapter.

There are a few tricks and tips that we need to pick up if we're going to fully realize the potential of ActiveX controls, and gain access to every facet of them from within Visual Basic. So that's also what this chapter is about.

So in this chapter you will learn about:

- ▶ Objects and ActiveX controls
- ▶ Creating ActiveX controls
- ▶ Implementing ActiveX control events at design time
- ▶ Implementing ActiveX control properties at design time
- ▶ Establishing property persistence
- ▶ The PropertyBag object

In the early days of Visual Basic, if you wanted to actually write your own ActiveX controls, you needed to hit the books quite hard and learn everything there was to know about OLE and COM from a C++ programmer's perspective. You then had to spend a huge amount of time writing some very arcane code in C++ to get the control produced and ready to use.

VBXs, OCXs and ActiveX Controls

When Visual Basic was first released it caused real a stir in the development community, and not simply because it allowed developers to produce Windows applications in double quick time. The real stir was because Visual Basic provided a new way for programmers to extend the functionality that they already provided in their applications - using something known as **VBXs** (**Visual Basic Controls**).

VBXs were controls that we could copy on to our system and then add into Visual Basic to provide more user interface gizmos in our toolbox - thus providing more functionality to our users.

VBXs are quite a long way behind us now. They were a sixteen-bit invention and they were really little more than applications with some unique information built into them that allowed Visual Basic to use them as bolt-on controls.

We live in a 32-bit OLE/ActiveX world today, and we now have **OCX controls**, also known as **ActiveX controls**. The main difference between VBXs and ActiveX controls is actually just in the way they're implemented - something that we don't have to worry about too much within Visual Basic.

Since ActiveX controls are built around OLE (Object Linking and Embedding), the theory goes that a vast number of applications will be able to make use of them. And this is indeed an observable fact today: most of the applications in Microsoft's Office suite support ActiveX controls, as do almost all of Microsoft's Windows development tools. In addition, ActiveX controls are becoming a widely accepted way of adding extra functionality to web pages, with Internet Explorer 3 onwards and Netscape Communicator supporting them.

A whole industry is growing around ActiveX controls, as the world of computing gradually adjusts itself to an object-based way of thinking.

Introducing ActiveX Controls

Developing an ActiveX control isn't much harder than developing a normal application. The main difference is that we need to be aware that our control can actually run in two modes: **design mode** and **runtime mode**. In addition, the terms associated with controls can be a little confusing. But that's nothing to worry us - let's master the territory.

In this chapter, we are the **control developers** - the people writing the control in the first place. Everyone who uses our control in their own projects are the **users** - whether they're using our control to write an application, or they're using an application that makes use of our new baby.

> *Let's nail down two very critical terms: design mode and runtime mode. When we talk about design mode, we're referring to that phase of application development where we (or others) are working within the Visual Basic environment - adding forms, resizing elements, changing properties, etc. Runtime mode simply refers to the time when our application is being run.*

In design mode, when a user drags our control on to a form and resizes it, that's our resize code in the control running at that point. And when the user changes a property, once again it's our code that is running at that point.

You may also have seen controls with properties that will display entire forms for you to set and change property values. These are called **property pages**, and you need to design and write the code for these as well.

If you haven't seen property pages before, then here's an easy way to take a look. Make sure that the Microsoft Data Bound components are in your project - go to the Project menu, select Components, and from the dialog select Microsoft Data Bound List Controls:

Make sure the box is checked, as in the screenshot here, and then close the dialog by clicking OK. Now drop a DBCombo control onto a form in your project (a new icon for the DBCombo control will have appeared in your Toolbox). Right-click on the DBCombo control on your form, and select Properties. A set of property pages will now appear for the DBCombo control:

At runtime, our controls need to take all of these properties and use them to provide the application users with the functionality they're after. We also need to get the user interface of our control working, just as if it were a mini form: it needs to respond to user interface events intelligently, providing feedback to users when they do something right, and also when they do something wrong.

Furthermore, our controls need to be totally idiot-proof: development users and end users alike get mighty upset when an entire application is brought down by a faulty control. This does mean, of course, that we need to pay even more attention than usual to error handling.

It all sounds like an awful lot of work doesn't it? Don't worry, it's really not that hard to get to grips with, as we're about to find out.

Drawing ActiveX Controls

Let's do our old friends at Northwind, who we met in Chapter 2, a big favor. We'll create a Combo box control especially for Northwind, which automatically knows about the Nwind database supplied with Visual Basic. You'll immediately notice, here, that creating our own ActiveX controls is a great way to make new friends - and indeed a great way to keep old friends. I did tell you objects would make our lives happier, didn't I?

The first step in developing a control is usually to draw its user interface.

> *Later on in this chapter, we'll see that there's actually a valid use for controls that have no user interface; but at this stage, we'll keep things a bit more straightforward.*

So, what is our control supposed to look like? Our combo box will be able to provide, automatically, a dropdown list of customers to select from - displaying the customer name and the city that they're based in. In addition, we'll have to provide a way for the developer to control the number of customers on show. The developer will do this by electing to display either all of the customers, or just those that reside in a particular country. Other than that, no other setup should be required: developers should just be able to drop our control on to their form and instantly have customer selection capabilities added to their application. This sounds like interesting work - so let's follow through and draw our control.

Try It Out - Drawing An ActiveX Control

1 Firstly, create a new project in Visual Basic in the usual way. When Visual Basic asks you what kind of project you want to create, choose **ActiveX Control**. After the obligatory pause while VB internally stops playing Solitaire with itself, the project will be created and ready to go:

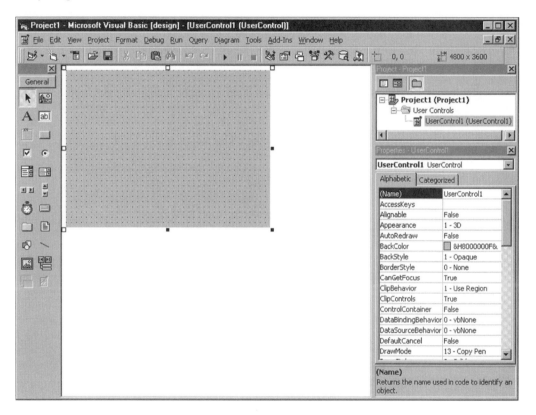

Looks pretty weird, doesn't it? ActiveX controls don't have forms, as such, but that gray area on display where the form should be. This gray area is actually something we can draw on. In fact, as far as Windows is concerned, it's a form with no border and no title bar.

This gray area is actually known as the **designer**, and it's where we draw the other controls that make up the user interface for our new control. It's also an area we can draw on and do things with from in our code, much like a painter splashing watercolors all over a rather nice piece of canvas.

2   For our Northwind Combo box control, we're going to need to put a Combo box on the control designer. So go ahead and place a standard Combo box right in the middle there:

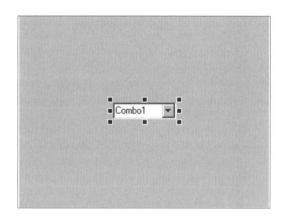

When a user comes along and adds our control to their application, the designer is the area of our control that they can resize and move around. So, for the moment, our Combo box is just sitting quietly in the middle of this area, which means that when a user draws our control on to a form, they're going to see a gray area with a Combo box in the middle of it.

> *Something worth nothing here is that the appearance of a control at design time is rarely the same as its appearance at runtime. In the case of our control so far, dropping this on to a form would result in a large blank area appearing, with a combo box in the middle.*
>
> *When people use our control in their own projects, they will almost certainly expect to be able to resize it to their heart's content, and expect it to still look pretty neat. So the control's final appearance is actually governed by code that we need to write to ensure that no matter what another programmer using our control does, it still looks wonderful.*

3   Just as if we were drawing controls onto a form in a normal project, the next step is to set the properties of the Combo box to control how it appears and functions to our end users.

For the Northwind Combo control, this engages us in nothing more than setting the name of the Combo box and its style. Set the Name property to cboCustomer and the Style property to 2 – Dropdown List. This means that, at runtime, all the user will be able to do is select from one of the items in the list. Critically, they will not be able to make up a customer of their own, which could potentially circumvent any data integrity features built into the database.

4   Now name the control designer itself, in the same way that we would name a form. In this case, we'll call it ctlCustCombo.

5   The final thing we need to do is give our control a name and save it. Naming the control is fairly easy: we just right click on the project name in the Project explorer window, and select Properties to display the Project Properties dialog:

Surprisingly, this still counts as part of drawing our control, a part of the definition of its user interface. This is because when a developer decides to use our control in their project, they'll need to go to their Project-Components dialog to select it, and the values we enter in the Project Properties dialog will have a dramatic effect on what the control user sees in their control palette.

The most important property is, of course, the Project Name property. This actually has two uses. On the one hand, setting this up to be MyControl would mean that when we compiled our control we'd produce entries in our Windows registry for a server called MyControl. If we left the Project Description box blank, this would also be the name that users would see when they went to their Components dialog to add our control to their project.

Normally, of course, we'd want to set up both properties. The Project Description text box allows us to enter some text that contains a more descriptive comment about our control, and this is what the users will usually see when they bring up their Components dialog.

For our Northwind Combo control, set the Project Name to CustCBO, and set the Project Description to be Beginning Objects Customer Combo.

6   When you're done, close the dialog down by hitting the OK button, and then save your project using File-Save Project. When Visual Basic prompts you, save your actual control as CustomerCombo.ctl. Then, for the project name, Visual Basic will automatically name it CustCBO.vbp, which is fine.

Our user interface is now complete, and we've finished drawing the ActiveX control. At this stage we could in fact use the control, although it would look rather awful and it would have no functionality. We'll wait until there's some more code in there, I think, and try it out in the next section.

ActiveX Controls at Design Time

Now we've sorted out the initial user interface of our Northwind Combo box control, the next thing we need to turn to is the design time support within the development environment.

How is our control going to respond when a development user resizes it? What properties are we going to expose for the user to play with? If we're going to expose any properties, should we develop property pages to make them easier to use? What about the design time events that occur, such as when the user runs the application and the current environment changes from design time to runtime? Let's extend our simple control to show how all these questions can be answered.

Design Time Properties for ActiveX Controls

Given the nature of our Northwind Combo box control, the properties that I suggest we expose are as follows:

New Property Name	Description
CustID	The ID of the customer selected
CustomerName	The name of the customer selected
LimitRegion	The region that is being used to limit the list of customers
LimitCountry	The country that is being used to limit the list of customers
CustomerCount	The number of customers currently held by the control

The idea is, of course, to apply the black box principle to our Northwind Combo object. We want to wrap up the bulk of any nasty code within the control itself - thus hiding as much of the complexity of the control as we can from the user. These five properties should be all that a developer will need to take control of the data presented to the end user, and to get an idea in their code of what the control is doing. These properties are the interface of our beautiful black box.

> *In addition, we really should make sure that the* CustID, CustomerName *and* CustomerCount *properties are all read only, while the two* Limit *properties are read/ write.*

Since all these properties deal with the actual data in the control, we need to establish some code that will load up this data in the first place. Let's get cracking.

Try It Out - Implementing Design Time Properties for ActiveX Controls

1 First, bring up our Northwind Combo control's References dialog and make sure that we have the **Microsoft DAO 3.51 Object Library** selected. We're going to need this because the control deals with a database.

> *If you can't remember how to do this, all you have to do is select* References *from the* Project *menu and use the* References *dialog that appears to select the appropriate* DAO *library. We covered this step by step in the last chapter, so if you're still having trouble then quickly run back there and take a look - we'll wait.*

2 Next up, we should code up the control's Initialize and Terminate events to load up the data it needs. Double click on the control's designer to bring up the code window and key this lot in:

```
Option Explicit

' Declare two variables to deal with the database and
' customer query results.
Private m_dbDatabase As Database
Private m_recCustomers As Recordset

Private Sub UserControl_Initialize()
' Connects to the database, and grabs the initial query.

    ' First, open the database itself.
    Set m_dbDatabase = Workspaces(0).OpenDatabase _
      (App.Path & "\Nwind.mdb")

    ' Next, select all the customers into a
    ' recordset ready for use
    Set m_recCustomers = m_dbDatabase.OpenRecordset _
      ("SELECT CustomerID, CompanyName, City FROM Customers", _
      dbOpenSnapshot)

End Sub

Private Sub UserControl_Terminate()
' Closes down the database and recordset connections

    ' Get rid of the customers query
    m_recCustomers.Close

    ' Then, lose the database connection
    m_dbDatabase.Close

End Sub
```

> *You may have noticed that, as with other examples in the book, the code in this control expects the* Nwind.mdb *database to reside in the same directory as the control. Before you go anywhere else, don't forget to run up Windows Explorer and copy the* Nwind.mdb *database from the directory where you installed Visual Basic into the directory where you're going to save our new control.*
>
> *As we progress through the development of this control, you might also like to consider adding some error trapping code to handle a situation where that* Nwind.mdb *database proved not to be available in the host directory.*

The Initialize and Terminate events work almost the same way in a control as they do in a class. Whenever a control gets created, the Initialize event is triggered; and whenever a control gets destroyed, the Terminate event is triggered.

There is a difference though. Within a class, the Initialize and Terminate events only ever get triggered when the project is run and an instance of the class is created or destroyed at runtime. Within a control, however, the Initialize and Terminate events get triggered whenever the project goes in and out of design mode. We'll see more of this later. We'll also find out how we can tell whether we're in design or runtime mode.

3 Now that we have these two events coded, and data loaded into our control (although not yet into the Combo box), we can begin to implement the control's properties. So bring up the control's code window once again.

We'll begin with the CustID property:

```
Public Property Get CustID() As String
' Returns the CustID field from the currently selected
' customer. If there is no customer selected, then "" is
' returned.

    ' Set up an error handler in case there is no current
    ' record to get    the ID from
    On Error GoTo Get_CustID_Error

    CustID = m_recCustomers!CustID
    Exit Property

Get_CustID_Error:      ' This error handler triggered when no
                       ' current record.
    CustID = ""
    Exit Property

End Property
```

All that's happening here is that the code is passing back the value of the CustID field from the current record. If there is no current record, a runtime error will occur and an empty string ("") will be returned.

4 The `CustomerName` property is almost identical, except that it deals with the `CompanyName` field in the database. Add the following code to our control:

```
Public Property Get CustomerName() As String
' Returns the CompanyName field from the currently selected
' customer. If there is no customer selected, then "" is
' returned.

    On Error GoTo Get_CustomerName_Error

    CustomerName = m_recCustomers!CompanyName
    Exit Property

Get_CustomerName_Error:

    CustomerName = ""
    Exit Property

End Property
```

5 The `CustomerCount` property needs to do a count of the number of records that we currently have. There are two ways we can do this: we can either use the `RecordCount` property of the recordset, or we can assume that the data is loaded into the Combo box and do a count of the number of items that the Combo box contains.

Let's choose the second option - it's not impossible that the control could be upgraded at some point in the future to support some kind of data container that might not have a count property attached to it. The second option would have less code to change, which is always a good thing.

So go ahead and add the following code to our control, which simply accesses the `ListCount` property to indicate a count of the number of items in the Combo box:

```
Public Property Get CustomerCount() As Integer
' Returns a count of the number of customers being
' managed by the combo box in the control.

    CustomerCount = cboCustomer.ListCount

End Property
```

6 All that remains now is to get those two `Limit` routines working (`LimitRegion` and `LimitCountry`). The `Limit` properties are really straightforward in principle. The control user will just enter a string into them, and our code will then rebuild the query to include only customers who are in the specified region or country.

Obviously, since the properties are read and write, we're going to need somewhere to store the strings that are being used. Our first port of call should therefore be back at the head of the control's code, to define two more member variables:

```
' Need two member variables to hold the limit strings
Private m_strRegion As String
Private m_strCountry As String
```

7 The `LimitRegion` and `LimitCountry` properties are then fairly easy to code up, especially if we delegate the responsibility for rebuilding the query to a separate subroutine. First, here are the two `Limit` properties coded:

```
Public Property Let LimitRegion(ByVal strRegion As String)
' Sets up the region to limit the customers to

    If strRegion <> m_strRegion Then 'If a new limit has been
                                     ' assigned then rebuild the query
        m_strRegion = strRegion
        Rebuild_Query
    End If

End Property

Public Property Get LimitRegion() As String
' Returns the current LimitRegion setting

    LimitRegion = m_strRegion

End Property

Public Property Let LimitCountry(ByVal strCountry As String)
' Sets up the country to limit the customers to

    If strCountry <> m_strCountry Then
        m_strCountry = strCountry
        Rebuild_Query
    End If

End Property

Public Property Get LimitCountry() As String
' Returns the current LimitCountry setting

    LimitCountry = m_strCountry

End Property
```

These `Property` routines should be straightforward enough. The responsibility for rebuilding the query is delegated out to a routine called `Rebuild_Query`, which is a pretty simple (but initially terrifying) routine that looks like this:

```
Private Sub Rebuild_Query()
' Routine to rebuild the query, taking into account the
' current applied limits

Dim strQuery As String
Dim strWhere As String
```

```
' First, set up the constant part of the query
strQuery = "SELECT CustomerID, CompanyName, City FROM Customers"

' Next, take a look to see if we need to add on anything
' to limit the regions
If m_strRegion <> "" Then strWhere = "Region = '" & m_strRegion & "'"

' ... then, take a look to see if we need to deal with
' a country
If m_strCountry <> "" Then

        ' If the WHERE clause already has something in it,
        ' we need to tack the word AND onto the end of it
        If strWhere <> "" Then strWhere = strWhere & " AND "

        strWhere = strWhere & "Country = '" & m_strCountry & "'"

End If

' Finally, if the WHERE clause has anything at all in it
' we need to tack it on to the end of our query
If strWhere <> "" Then strQuery = strQuery & " WHERE " & strWhere

    ' All that remains is to re-issue the query
    On Error Resume Next
    m_recCustomers.Close
    On Error GoTo 0

    Set m_recCustomers = m_dbDatabase.OpenRecordset _
(strQuery, dbOpenSnapshot)

End Sub
```

The comments should hopefully make this code fairly easy to understand. There is just a lot of string manipulation going on to build up a SQL query that takes into account the values of our LimitRegion and LimitCountry properties, putting them into a WHERE clause if they have been set.

I've left the data ordering in this code example at default, in order not to complicate the code further. Feel free to extend this code to handle data ordering if it appeals to you.

Design Time Events for ActiveX Controls

In addition to defining the user interface and setting up some properties for the control to expose, we also need to write a little code to respond to design time events on the control. The most common event that we'll use is the Resize event.

Remember that users can drag our control onto their forms, and at that point start to drag it around and generally mess with its size and shape. All the while this is going on, it's our responsibility to make sure there is some code sitting in the control that can see what's going on and make sure at all times that the control keeps its correct appearance.

189

When design time events take place like this, they happen on the `UserControl` object: the canvas we draw our new controls on. It's time to get our new control ready for these events.

Try It Out - Implementing Design Time Events for ActiveX Controls

1 Bring up the code window for our Northwind Combo control, select the `UserControl` object from the object dropdown at the top left of the code window, and drop the event combo at the top right down to see a list of the possible events:

As you can see, there are a lot of events here, many of which you should recognize from your time spent dealing with forms in normal projects.

However, ActiveX controls do bring with them a whole new set of events as well. These new events provide us, as control developers, with more information about what's going on with our control.

Here's a description of some of the most important of these new events:

Event Name	Description
AccessKeyPress	This is triggered when an **Access** key is pressed (which is a shortcut key, to you and me). For example, if our control had a Caption of <u>P</u>eter, and our user pressed *Alt* and *P* then this event would trigger. Likewise, if we had the Default property set to True and the user pressed the *Enter* key, this event would be triggered.
AmbientChanged	This event occurs when something in the environment of the host project changes that could affect the control. For example, when the control switches from design to runtime mode inside a client project, or when the user changes the ScaleMode, this event is triggered. More on this later.

Event Name	Description
ReadProperties	This event occurs when the control itself figures out that it needs to reload its properties. For example, when the container application goes from design time to runtime, the control itself gets destroyed and a new instance of it is created. The new instance will automatically fire a ReadProperties event so that we can write code to load up the property values that were set at design time. Visual Basic provides something known as a **Property Bag** for us to store our control's properties in when mode changes like this occur (more on property bags in the section headed *Property Persistence* later on).
WriteProperties	The reverse of ReadProperties above.
InitProperties	This event is fired whenever a new instance of a control is created, and it makes a great place for us to put some code to set up the default values of properties.

2 For now, all we're going to worry about is that Resize event. Find it in the drop down list Combo box at the top right of the code window, and code it like this:

```
Private Sub UserControl_Resize()
    cboCustomer.Move 0, 0, ScaleWidth
    Height = cboCustomer.Height
End Sub
```

That's it! When the user resizes our Northwind Combo box control, this code simply moves the Combo box to the top left corner of our control, and changes its width so that it matches the new width set by our user. Finally, we resist whatever the user does with the height of our custom control, since it isn't possible to resize the height of a combo box.

Hooking Up Data to ActiveX Controls

We now have the user interface for our Northwind Combo box control, we have its properties defined, and the code is in place to pull data from the database and into the control. All that remains is to get that data into the actual user interface elements. For our Northwind control, these user interface elements are simply our Combo box.

Try It Out - Getting Data into our ActiveX Control

1 We're going to need another small routine to load the data into the combo box, and a couple of extra lines of code to call that routine when the control gets initialized or the query is reproduced.

First, the Load routine. Bring up the code window for the control once again, and key this code in:

```
Private Sub Load_Data()
' Loads the data from the recordset into the combo box

' First, clear out any existing data in the combo.
cboCustomer.Clear
ReDim m_strCustID(0)

' Next, start a loop through the data and load it into
' the combo box  (remember, there could be no data to
' load, so an error handler should be used to catch that)
On Error GoTo Load_Data_Error
m_recCustomers.MoveFirst
On Error GoTo 0

Do While Not m_recCustomers.EOF

    cboCustomer.AddItem m_recCustomers!CompanyName & ", " & _
        m_recCustomers!City
    ReDim Preserve m_strCustID(cboCustomer.ListCount)
    m_strCustID(cboCustomer.ListCount - 1) = _
        m_recCustomers!CustomerID

    m_recCustomers.MoveNext

Loop

Load_Data_Error:
    Exit Sub

End Sub
```

This routine automatically maintains a list of CustomerIDs for each entry in the list, so that later we can find the customer record that matches the selected entry. It does this using a string array and a While Loop structure.

The keen-eyed among you may ask why I don't use the ItemData array that comes with the Combo box to maintain this list, instead of using the more longwinded While loop that's in place. The answer is simple: ItemData is great at maintaining a list of numbers to go with items in the Combo box, but the Nwind database stores CustomerID fields as strings rather than numbers, so we need to use our own array instead.

2 We're going to need to add another member variable to our code in order to support this maintenance of a CustomerID list within our control; so add these lines to the General Declarations section:

```
' Need an array to hold the customer ID's of the customers
' in the list
Private m_strCustID() As String
```

3 Now bring up the Rebuild_Query routine and add a line of code to the bottom of this routine which calls our Load_Data routine:

```
Set m_recCustomers = m_dbDatabase.OpenRecordset _
        (strQuery, dbOpenSnapshot)

Load_Data

End Sub
```

4 Now we can entirely rewrite the `Initialize` event handler so that instead of opening the recordset itself, it now just calls `Rebuild_Query`. So, alter the code for the `Initialize` event so it now looks like this:

```
Private Sub UserControl_Initialize()
' Connects to the database, and grabs the initial query.

    ' First, open the database itself.
    Set m_dbDatabase = Workspaces(0).OpenDatabase _
        (App.Path & "\Nwind.mdb")

    Rebuild_Query

End Sub
```

5 Finally, we can add a little more code to the control to automatically reposition the recordset when a new item gets selected in the Combo box that we just enabled. To achieve this, add the following routine:

```
Private Sub cboCustomer_Click()
' When an item in the combo box gets clicked we need to
' reposition the recordset at the selected record.
    If cboCustomer.ListIndex > -1 Then m_recCustomers.FindFirst _
    "CustomerID = '" & m_strCustID(cboCustomer.ListIndex) & "'"

End Sub
```

Now we're all ready to go. This means that it'll soon be time to look at how we can use and test our Northwind Combo box control. Personally, I'm looking forward to seeing our control up and running, but right now we need to take an important Time Out to think about the design time environment that we've been working within - and which our users will be working within.

The Design Time Environment

Take a look at your Toolbox at this point:

Notice that there are two grayed out controls at the bottom. The first one, the one on the left, is an OLE container control that's being used by our ActiveX control. (Remember that ActiveX controls are really OLE controls and, as such, make use of OLE services.) You can ignore this one for now. The grayed out control to the right is the important one. This is the Northwind Combo box control that we're currently developing. It's grayed out because we have it open in design mode, so Visual Basic is politely telling us that it isn't available for use.

Close down the code window, then close down the control's designer so that you have no windows open in the design environment other than the Project explorer and any of the usual explorers that you have hanging around. Now take a peek at the Toolbox:

Now that we've closed all the windows for the control down, you can see that the control has lit up on the Toolbox, meaning that it's available for use.

Running and Testing ActiveX Controls

Okay, so we understand our design time environment a little better now, and we've made our ActiveX control available from the Toolbar. But we still can't use it just yet, because we don't have a container project that could make use of it. So let's make one and finally get our Northwind Combo box control running and tested.

Try It Out - Running and Testing ActiveX Controls

1 Go to File menu and add a new project to the project group, just as we did in the last chapter. Make sure it's a **Standard EXE** project, or we're going to have a problem running it in a minute.

2 Before we can drop our new Northwind Combo box control on to the pristine new form, we need to change the way that Visual Basic deals with runtime errors. There is, after all, a strong likelihood that there will be errors from time to time - as the result of an empty recordset, for example. We therefore need to make sure that the error handlers in our code kick in, instead of Visual Basic stopping everything and bringing it all to a halt.

Click on the Tools menu in Visual Basic and select the Options item to bring up the Options dialog. Click on the General tab at the top of the dialog to show the error-handling options for Visual Basic:

Notice how I've selected the **Break in Class Module** option. This means that if there's a serious error which isn't handled by an error handler, Visual Basic will stop the code and show us the offending line, whether it's in the host project or in the attached ActiveX control code.

As long as all our errors are handled by error handlers, there shouldn't be a problem. So, select the B̲reak in Class Module option and then close the dialog by hitting the OK button.

3 Now go ahead and double click on the icon for our new custom control at the bottom of the Toolbar.

Because the control's project is already loaded, the icon automatically appears at the bottom of your toolbox without you having to go and play with the Components dialog in the usual way.

You should see the new control appear on your form, with our resize code kicking in instantly to make sure that the control is sized properly. You should also see that the Combo box that our control contains is set to the same width as the control on the form:

4 Try resizing the control on the form to see the code in action some more.

When you are done playing (it's incredibly good fun the first couple of times, but the novelty soon wears off), it's time to run the program. However, before you do this, there is one last thing to do. We need to set the form to be our startup window, otherwise the program will start running as a web document.

Right-hand mouse click on Project1 from the Properties window then select Set as Start Up from the menu. That's all there is to it. Now, we're ready to rock and roll. Run the program, and assuming you typed in all the code correctly, you should be able to see a list of customers and select from them:

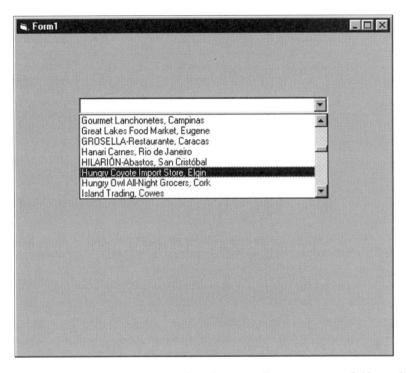

Congratulations! You just wrote your first (or second) custom control (depending on whether you read my first book or not).

6 There's yet more to this control though. Stop running the program and take a look at the Properties window for the `ctlCustCombo1` box:

Visual Basic automatically gives us a whole slew of properties that we would normally expect to find on a custom control, such as properties for the Index, TabIndex, Left, Top, Width, Height and all the other customary custom control delicacies. However, any read/write properties that we defined should also appear in the Properties window, such as LimitCountry and LimitRegion.

7 We can even set values into these properties if we like, although you're in for a little shock. For example, enter UK into the LimitCountry property. As soon as you hit *Enter* there will be a pause while the list is rebuilt. When it's done, run the application again and take a look at the list of the customers. Notice how nothing has changed???

> *The reason for this is something known as property persistence: as soon as we change from design time to runtime, the design time control is destroyed and a new, runtime control is created, with default property values. The control totally forgets about the values that we set into the properties at design time, unless we specifically write code to make the properties persist (stay alive). That little gem, along with a few other gotchas, is covered in the next section, ActiveX Controls At Runtime.*

8 Although a lack of object persistence has thwarted our plan to test the LimitCountry and LimitRegion properties, we can perform a quick test to see whether these properties really are working or not. With the application still running, put it in debug mode by clicking on the Break icon or by pressing *Ctrl* and *Break* on the keyboard. Now press *Ctrl* and *G* to bring up the Immediate window, and type this in:

```
ctlCustCombo1.LimitCountry = "UK"
```

Again, there will be a pause while the query is rebuilt. When it's done, hit *F5* to continue running the application and take a look at the list of customers again; this time, all you'll see are the customers that satisfy the query we just specified.

ActiveX Controls at Runtime

Design time operation of our ActiveX controls is only one side of the equation. We also need to think about how our controls will work at runtime. Rather strangely, there's a lot less work that needs to be done in runtime.

The properties that we set up at design time will often be used by developers at runtime to find out what the control is doing. These properties are also often used to manipulate the control.

It's quite likely, however, that sooner or later we'll want to expose one or two methods to the developer at runtime that do more complex things. We'll most likely also want to make events available, so that the developer can easily write code to respond to end-user interaction with our control. It looks like it's time to do some more coding.

Property Persistence

Properties have to be the single most important aspect of a control at design time. Visual Basic users expect to be able to pop open the **Properties** window and dynamically change the way the control looks (both at design time and runtime) and how it behaves (usually only at runtime). In fact, the more functionality we can wrap up in a control's design time properties, the less code the programmers will have to write - and the happier they will be again.

> *From the control developer's point of view, though, this means that we need to write a fair chunk of code. Thankfully, it's all rather similar stuff, so it's easy to get to grips with.*

Property persistence revolves around something known as a `PropertyBag` object. We don't actually ever get to create one of these, in fact we're given them by various events on the `UserControl` object that we saw earlier. These `UserControl` events provide:

 A convenient way to transport property values from design time to runtime

A way to save property values to disk when we're saving projects that make use of your custom control

There are two events that deal with property bags: the `ReadProperties` and `WriteProperties` events of our custom controls.

`WriteProperties` gets triggered whenever our control shuts down, or when the developer selects **Save** in their project within Visual Basic (or any other ActiveX-hosting development environment). Conversely, `ReadProperties` gets triggered when the developer loads up their project, and when an instance of a previously existing object is created.

This means that when our control goes from living in a design time project to living in a runtime project, we will first of all get a `WriteProperties` event, and then a `ReadProperties` event. So here's the trick: we can use these events to dump our property values into the `PropertyBag` object, and then grab them back out again 'on the other side' as it were. Voila - we've defied the change of state between design mode and runtime mode! We have property persistence. Let's take a look.

Try It Out - Property Persistence Using PropertyBag

1 Go back into our ActiveX control project, and bring up the code window. Find the **UserControl** object in the object dropdown at the top left of your code window, and the **WriteProperties** event in the event dropdown at the top right:

```
Private Sub UserControl_WriteProperties(PropBag As PropertyBag)

End Sub
```

As you can see, the `PropertyBag` is given to us in the event itself. It's therefore up to us, as control developers, to use the methods on `PropertyBag` to read and write our property values.

There are actually only two methods of the `PropertyBag`, and the one that we're most interested in, for this event, is the `WriteProperty` method.

`WriteProperty` takes just three parameters, one of which is optional:

▶ **Property name** - This first parameter is a name that we can assign to the property when it gets stored. It's actually very common for people to assign the same name to the value stored in the `PropertyBag` as the name of the property itself, but if we really wanted to be obscure and save our properties as A, B, C and so on, Visual Basic would let us.

▶ **Property value** - The second parameter is the actual value of the property that we wish to write into the bag. Naturally, it's a `Variant`, so we can store just about anything in it.

▶ **Default value** - The final parameter is the default value for the property that we're saving, and it's an optional parameter. It is, however, quite good practice to use it, if a little laborious at times. The reason for this is that the `WriteProperty` method checks to see if the value that we're writing is different from the default value for the property. It only gets written into the bag if it is different, thus saving time and disk space.

Microsoft actually recommends that we use default values all over the place. Personally, unless I'm dealing with a couple of hundred properties, there isn't that much benefit in terms of space saved or time spent executing in doing this. That's just my opinion, though, so probably not gospel.

2 Let's go ahead and code up that `WriteProperties` method:

```
Private Sub UserControl_WriteProperties(PropBag As PropertyBag)

    With PropBag

        .WriteProperty "LimitCountry", LimitCountry
        .WriteProperty "LimitRegion", LimitRegion

    End With

End Sub
```

Quite simple isn't it! Since there are only two properties in our Northwind Combo box control that we can deal with at design time, we only need to dump two values into the bag.

FYI The standard properties that Visual Basic automatically gives us with a control are saved and loaded automatically for us.

3 Now find the `ReadProperties` event and code that up so that it looks like this (you could just type this in without hunting for the event - do whichever is easiest for you):

```
Private Sub UserControl_ReadProperties(PropBag As PropertyBag)

    With PropBag
        m_strCountry = .ReadProperty("LimitCountry", "")
        m_strRegion = .ReadProperty("LimitRegion", "")
    End With

    Rebuild_Query

End Sub
```

The `ReadProperty` method takes just two parameters: the name of the property that we previously stored, and its default value. The default value again is optional, but in the case of the `ReadProperties` method, I really would advocate using it.

The reason for this is that the first time we draw our control on a form, the `ReadProperties` event gets fired. Since the control didn't exist, beforehand, to save itself into a property bag, all the results of all the reads will be the defaults that we specify.

> *`ReadProperties` is therefore a great way to set up our default property values, rather than dumping them into the `Initialize` event of every control we write.*

Notice, also, in that `ReadProperties` routine, how we read the properties directly into member variables rather than the `Property Let` routines that we wrote previously:

```
m_strCountry = .ReadProperty("LimitCountry", "")
    m_strRegion = .ReadProperty("LimitRegion", "")
```

Our reasoning is solid: we don't really want code to run in property handlers while we're reading values from property bags.

> *If we did read properties in through `Property Let` statements, we could end up in a real mess if one property relies on values in other properties that have not yet been read in.*

The last thing that we do in the `ReadProperties` routine, above, is set up the query again:

```
Rebuild_Query
```

We just loaded values into the properties that this routine uses, so it makes good sense to call it right there.

4 But hang on a second, the more astute among you cry: "If this event gets fired every time the control gets created, just like the `Initialize` event, why do we need to set up the query in the `Initialize` event?"

The simple answer is that we don't. We only did so previously because we hadn't come across property bags then. Find the `Initialize` event and get rid of the call to `Rebuild_Query` - no need to call it twice now.

5 When you're done, close down your code window, and any other code and form windows that you might have open. Then bring up our test project's form again (you remember, the one with the control on it!)

When it comes into view, go into the **Properties** window and set the **LimitCountry** to **UK**, then run the project. This time the list is limited to only UK customers, just as we had hoped. Our properties are now persisting, and they also get saved out when we save our source code within Visual Basic. We shall be finding out much more about persistance in Chapter 8.

Runtime Events

Visual Basic users expect the controls they use to provide their code with feedback as to what's happening at runtime. For example, where would the standard Command button be without its infamous `Click` event, or the Text box without its `KeyPress` and `Change` events?

However, it isn't good enough to provide just a flood of events and properties to the user that cover everything from mouse movement to what color shirt the end-user is wearing. The events that our controls raise at runtime really need to reflect the nature of the control.

 This is a fundamental concept of object-oriented programming, and we've already seen it expressed in many forms. Consider it carefully.

For example, Command buttons don't trigger `Scroll` events - why would they? Likewise, our Northwind Combo box control wouldn't really need to raise an `Unload` event, as a form would. However, an event like `CustomerSelected` could be quite useful in our Northwind control.

We saw events when we looked at classes and objects in general, earlier in the book. They work no differently here either. First, we declare our event; and then we `Raise` the event in our code wherever we see fit. Let's see this working.

Try It Out - Run Time Events in Action

1   If you have the project running at this point, stop it, and bring up the code for our Northwind Combo box control again. Scroll up to the top, to the Declarations section, and declare an event there like this:

```
Public Event CustomerSelected(ByVal strCustomerID As String, _
      ByVal strCustomerName As String)
```

2   Next, find the Combo box `Click` event that we coded up a while ago. Since this is where the customers get selected, it's an ideal place to raise the `CustomerSelected` event. Change the `cboCustomer_Click` event handler so that it looks like this:

```
Private Sub cboCustomer_Click()
' When an item in the combo box gets clicked we need to
' reposition the recordset at the selected record.
    If cboCustomer.ListIndex > -1 Then
        m_recCustomers.FindFirst "CustomerID = '" & _
            m_strCustID(cboCustomer.ListIndex) & "'"
        RaiseEvent CustomerSelected(m_recCustomers!CustomerID, _
            m_recCustomers!CompanyName)
    End If

End Sub
```

Now when an item in the Combo box gets selected, we automatically find the original record in the recordset and then raise a `CustomerSelected` event, passing to it the customer's ID and name.

3   We can try this new event out now. Close down the code window and the control window and bring up the code from our test project (that we developed earlier) for the Form where the control is located.

4   Select ctlCustCombo1 from the object dropdown at the top of the code window, and then take a look at the event dropdown. It should look like this:

Notice that, just as with the properties, Visual Basic automatically supplies a number of events for us. However, there at the top of our list (because it's an alphabetical list) is our `CustomerSelected` event that we've just created. Select that `CustomerSelected` event from the list.

5 Next, code up the `CustomerSelected` event handler so that it looks like this:

```
Private Sub ctlCustCombo1_CustomerSelected _
(ByVal strCustomerID As String, ByVal strCustomerName As String)
    MsgBox "Customer Selected : " & strCustomerID & ", " & _
    strCustomerName

End Sub
```

Now if you run the project, and select a customer, a message box will pop up and show you their name and ID!

Now none of that was very difficult, yet we've been accomplishing some very sophisticated maneuvers with a set of special objects that everyone's calling ActiveX controls. Visual Basic can be extremely groovy, don't you agree?

Summary

In this chapter, we've seen some of the great things we can do today with ActiveX controls, and you should now feel comfortable to start exploring more with your own ActiveX controls.

As a special favor, we developed a brand new ActiveX control for our old friends at Northwind, which combined the versatility of a Combo box with the convenience of having that Combo box hardwired in to the Northwind database.

Along the way, we learned about drawing ActiveX controls, working with design time properties and events, and then we moved on to some of the runtime issues of creating and shipping a new ActiveX control. We also took our first peek at the sometimes rather tricky topic of object persistence, but we came out in once piece, probably because Visual Basic is extremely cool when it comes to ActiveX. We shall be seeing more of object persistence in Chapter 8.

In particular, in this chapter we saw:

▶ How to create a custom ActiveX controls

▶ How to use those custom controls within a Visual Basic project

▶ How to make the properties persistent using the property bag

▶ How to write code to keep the appearance of our custom controls acceptable during design time and runtime

Custom controls are great things to develop, and are surely one of the most exciting features of Visual Basic 6. However, despite their ease, there's still a great deal more to learn about them if we want to really get the most out of them, and some neat tricks that you can pull too.

For example, there's a use for controls without a user interface. There's a whole set of events that we haven't covered yet. There's one event, for instance, which provides us with an object (Ambient) that lets us find out almost anything that we'd like to know about how our control is being used - and the environment that it's being hosted in. And what about those Property Pages? We never did get to the heart of those. Did you know that it's possible to create our own!

In addition, there are some things we need to know about how controls work with the registry - with regard to upgrades and things like that. Far too much to cover in one chapter, I think you'll agree, which is why we have two. Read on, and discover that you've only heard half the ActiveX story so far.

Why Not Try....

1 Explain what the author means when he says that when developing an ActiveX control, you need to be aware that the control can run in two modes - design mode and runtime mode.

2 Create an ActiveX control called ChangeColor that displays a Common Dialog control used to change the BackColor property of the form it is placed upon. For now, don't worry implementing any Design Time Properties for the control. Hint: You'll need to place both a Common Dialog Control and a Command Button on the designer.

3 Implement any design time properties for your new control that it may require. In this instance we need to create two properties for the control - Color and Caption. Color will provide a means for the control to communicate to the form it is placed upon the user's selection for a color. Caption will allow the programmer the ability to change the caption of the control. Hint: There's no need to provide a Property Let Procedure for the Color property, as we don't really need it to show up in the control's Properties Window. You should also declare a Click event procedure for the control so that the form can 'react' to the user's selection of a color.

4 Now it's time to tackle the Design Time events for our control---specifically, the Resize event that affects the way our control will look when the user places it on their form. By the way, the Initialize event procedure of the user control would be a great place to provide an initial value for the control's Caption.

5 Now, provide functionality to the control so that when it is clicked, the BackColor of the form is changed. Hint: Place code in the Click event procedure of the user control's command button. Don't forget to 'raise' the Click event of the user control!

6 Now it's time to test our control. Start a new project and drop the new control on it. Once the control is on the form, you can then place code in its click event procedure to change the BackColor of the form.

7 Our control is functional, but has some shortcomings. Specifically, changes we make to the control's properties (in our case, the Caption Property) are 'lost' when we run our project. Write code for the WriteProperties event procedure of the user control to 'save' the design time properties to the Property Bag, and for the ReadProperties event procedure of the user control to 'read' from the Property Bag.

6

Advanced ActiveX Controls

In the last chapter, we began to see just how powerful an expression of object-oriented programming ActiveX controls can be. Our controls are our objects, of course, and ActiveX gives us excellent control over how our objects interact with the rest of programming world.

There's a lot of great stuff about ActiveX controls that we haven't covered yet though. There are features that let us really take command of how our controls work - both in design mode and runtime mode - and these can allow our controls to become ever more sophisticated in their interaction with the developers who use them.

Of course, you can start producing professional working controls with the information that we covered in the last chapter. But if you want to produce really slick and intelligent controls then this is the chapter for you.

In this chapter you will learn about:

> ActiveX and Objects

> The AmbientProperties object

> How to create your own property pages

> How to perform error handling with ActiveX controls

> Interface-less ActiveX controls

It's worth remembering, when you read this chapter, that these ActiveX technologies are a highly developed expression of object-oriented analysis. The more you stop and think about ActiveX, the more I think you'll come to see it as an integral part of object-oriented programming in Visual Basic. We'll therefore start this chapter off with a little bit of object-related philosophizing. Now this may seem like a bit of a departure, but you'll see that because objects and ActiveX controls are really just the same approach, our thoughts will soon lead us into some of the most interesting areas of ActiveX control programming. We have a lot of ground to cover, so let's get started.

ActiveX and Objects

We're going to be doing some more of that philosophizing right now; I give you my word it will be worth every moment of extra brainpower. I'd like you to sit back for a moment and consider, with me, how an ActiveX control, which is a self-contained object, can ever find information about what's happening in its container object - that is, what's happening in the development environment where it's being used? Visual Basic does offer us an answer to this question, in the form of the `Ambient` object. But should there be an answer? Is Visual Basic telling us the truth? How do any of us really know what's going on in the environment we find ourselves in? We'll be considering the `Ambient` object in just a moment.

Now consider ActiveX error handling. There is a certain ponderous level at which error handling becomes most perplexing. It's just not enough for us to set up and send out some return values from one of our control methods to tell the outside world that errors are taking place within our objects. There's simply no guarantee that a developer will actually write any code to take notice of these values. It really is a question of "Is there anybody out there, and do you speak my language?" Like all good men and women, our controls must raise true error conditions when bad things happen, and they must be ready to express those conditions in whatever environment they may find themselves. But then how can we be sure that those error messages will appear meaningful in whatever development environment our users are working in? I'm sure you've all seen the Invalid property value dialog in Visual Basic. We need to present our errors in the format and style that ActiveX control users are familiar with - effectively adopting a common interface for our errors, as well as for the methods and properties in our controls.

ActiveX controls inhabit the strange world of objects that we all know, or at least think we know: clearly things can get a little less certain the more we think about them. So let's see how Visual Basic provides practical working solutions to these issues.

Ambient Properties

The `AmbientProperties` object, which all Visual Basic controls have access to, provides us with a huge amount of information about how our control is being used, and what the user is up to with it.

> *Remember, just because we're developing the control in Visual Basic that doesn't necessarily mean that our control users are going to be Visual Basic developers. There are a lot of other control containers out there, such as Visual C++, Access, Delphi, C++ Builder and many more. They don't all work the same way, and they don't all provide the same wealth of features to our controls that Visual Basic does.*

It's handy to be able to learn about the control container that our control is in, to know what it does and does not provide us with. It's also useful to know what the developer is up to - so we can make our control respond within the design time environment in just the way that the developer would expect.

There's nothing worse than setting a property and expecting it to do something to a control, and finding that the control just sits there. As control developers, our control may be totally aware of the change to its properties that were just made, but if the control doesn't provide any feedback to that effect, then the developer will probably reject our control as being buggy.

Want an example? In Visual Basic, when you drop a control on to a form and then click that control to select it, resize handles appear around the control for you to drag and resize that control. What if the development environment being used by some developers doesn't provide resize handles; that is, it expects your control to draw them instead? Nasty. Knowing things like this can really mean the difference between success and failure for our controls in the marketplace, and that's where the `AmbientProperties` object comes into play.

Responding to Changes in AmbientProperties

Let's make our Northwind Combo box control sensitive to changes within its immediate developer environment.

Try It Out - Responding to Changes in AmbientProperties

1 Let's go back to the Customer Selection Combo box in the Northwind Combo box control. Load up the Northwind control from the last chapter and go into the code window for the control itself. Select UserControl from the drop down Combo at the top left, and the AmbientChanged event from the top right, just as in the screenshot here:

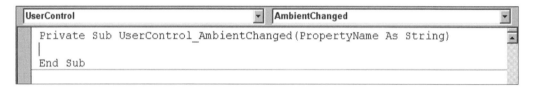

This is the event that gets fired whenever an ambient property, i.e. something in the development environment where the control is being used, gets changed.

2 Let's see what it does. Type in a `MsgBox` command so that our `AmbientChanged` event handler looks like this:

```
Private Sub UserControl_AmbientChanged(PropertyName As String)
    MsgBox "The " & PropertyName & " property", vbInformation, _
"AmbientChanged"
End Sub
```

3 When you've done that, save the control and close down its code window. If its form is open then close that too. Now bring up the form in our test project where the control is placed. Try changing the BackColor property of this form. This is what happens:

As soon as we change the **BackColor** property of the form, the `AmbientChanged` event gets fired on our control. Why? Why on earth would we want to know when the color of the form, upon which the control is located, changes? Well, in this particular control, we don't. However, if we had drawn our control so that there were areas where the user control's canvas was visible, then changing the color of the form would mean that our control would stick out like a sore thumb - its **BackColor** would be different from that of the form. By coding up the `AmbientChanged` event to recognize when the form color changes, we can make our control always blend seamlessly into the form on which it's placed.

If we wanted to be really flash, we could keep an eye out for colors that could conflict with the colors of text and stuff in the controls that we have inside our own control. We could make sure that there was never a nasty color clash - that's more one for the Gucci programmers out there though.

So, as you can see, the `AmbientChanged` event is really quite simple. It gets triggered when something changes which could potentially affect the appearance or operation of our control. `AmbientChanged` then passes a string to our control which is simply the name of the property that changed. Getting at this property value, however, does involve a little more code.

4   There is a property of our `UserControl`, called `Ambient`, which gives us the `AmbientProperties` object. We can use this `Ambient` object to get at the values of the property that has just changed and caused our `AmbientChanged` event to fire. So change the `AmbientChanged` event handler again once more:

```
Private Sub UserControl_AmbientChanged(PropertyName As String)

    If UCase$(PropertyName) = "BACKCOLOR" Then
        cboCustomer.BackColor = Ambient.BackColor
    End If

End Sub
```

All we're doing here is testing which property has just been changed within the developer environment. If it's the BackColor property that's changed, then we go right ahead and adjust the background color of the control to the new BackColor that's just been set. We access this new BackColor using Ambient.BackColor.

5 When you're done, don't forget to close down the code window and the control window. Then go to the form where the control is located and try changing the form's color. As you'll be able to see, our control can now automatically recognize when the container that it lives on changes in some way, and change itself to match!

Okay, that's no big deal right now. So let's take a look at all the properties of the AmbientProperties object to see if there's anything there that really does apply to our Northwind Combo box control.

Properties of the AmbientProperties Object

The AmbientProperties object provides a wealth of properties that we can use to find out what's going on in the development environment where our controls are being used.

Just in case you were wondering, we don't have to be within the AmbientChanged *event to use these properties.*

Property Name	Description
BackColor	This is the background color of the control container.
DisplayAsDefault	If the user makes our control the default control on a form, then this property indicates such. We'll need to change the appearance of our control to make it clear to the user that it's now the default control (normally, we would draw a different border around our control).
DisplayName	This is the name that the user has given to our control. Use this when raising errors (see later) to show the user which one of their controls has raised the error.
Font	This property contains the font of the container control where our user control lives. If we want our control to have the same font as the form it lives on, then we would look for a change to this property and respond to it accordingly.
ForeColor	Have a guess what this one does!
ScaleUnits	This contains the name of the co-ordinate system on the parent form (i.e. Pixels, Points, Twips, etc.).

Property Name	Description
ShowGrabHandles	If the container requires us to draw our own grab handles for resizing and selection, then this property will be set to True.
ShowHatching	When we load up our control's source code, or if the control breaks down, most containers expect hatching to be drawn across the control so that the user knows they can't use it. Visual Basic does this for us, but if the control is not being used in Visual Basic, then this property may be set to True to indicate that we need to provide some kind of visual representation to indicate that our control is no longer working.
TextAlign	This shows the default text alignment required of our control.
UserMode	If this is set to True, then the control is in a runtime environment. If it's set to False, then our control is in a design time environment.

This isn't the full list, by the way. There are more properties out there, but they mean little to us and are beyond our scope here - so I'm going to keep quiet about them.

Normally, we can watch the AmbientChanged event to pick up on when some or all of these elements change, and then we can do something in response. This works wonderfully well in Visual Basic's event-driven paradigm, of course. The only exception to the rule is the UserMode property.

UserMode is a Boolean property that gives us True if it's sitting on a form in a running application, and False if it's living on a form somewhere that's currently in design mode.

Now, as you may recall from the last chapter, when we switch from mode to mode the control is destroyed and then re-created. For that reason, we'll never see the UserMode value change in the AmbientChanged event; if it does change, then either the control doesn't exist yet (but it is about to), or the control is dying. For that reason, we need to check the UserMode property in the Initialize and Terminate events to see what mode we're running in, and then do something about it. Let's add some code to our Combo box control to see this in action.

Try It Out - Interrogating the UserMode Property

1 If you haven't already done so, load up the Combo control we were working on in the last chapter, and the test project that we also arranged for the control to be used in. Incidentally, when we created a project group in the last chapter, Visual Basic will have asked you at save time for a name to give to the group of projects. You can just load this group up to get your customer Combo control and the test project in which it's being used.

2 When the control is loaded, bring up the code for the control itself, and take a peek at the UserControl_Initialize event handler that we currently have in there, as well as the ReadProperties event handler:

```
Private Sub UserControl_Initialize()
' Connects to the database, and grabs the initial query.

    ' First, open the database itself.
    Set m_dbDatabase = Workspaces(0).OpenDatabase("nwind.mdb")

End Sub

Private Sub UserControl_ReadProperties(PropBag As PropertyBag)

    With PropBag
        m_strCountry = .ReadProperty("LimitCountry", "")
        m_strRegion = .ReadProperty("LimitRegion", "")
    End With

    Rebuild_Query

End Sub
```

Not very efficient if we think about it, are they? No matter whether the control is in the design time environment or if it's in a runtime environment, this code will always connect to the database and rebuild a recordset.

Always connecting to the database like this is fine for the moment - in fact when we get on to property pages we can even use that connection to our advantage by providing the development user with more information to set up their properties. However, rebuilding the query is totally unnecessary, since there's no way we can get at the data in the query until the application hosting the control is running.

3 We can make the control a lot more efficient with just a single line of code in the Rebuild_Query routine, which will check to see if the application hosting our control is in design mode or run mode. If it happens to be in design mode, we can forget about the query for now and just Exit. If the application does turn out to be in run mode, after all, then we can go ahead and perform the query just as the user would expect.

So add the line of code highlighted here to our Rebuild_Query routine:

```
Private Sub Rebuild_Query()
' Routine to rebuild the query, taking into account the
' current applied limits

    Dim strQuery As String
    Dim strWhere As String

    If Ambient.UserMode = False Then Exit Sub

    ' First, set up the constant part of the query
    strQuery = "Select CustomerID, CompanyName, City from Customers"
```

4 Great! Now all we need is an error handler in the Terminate event, and we'll be all ready to go. Add the highlighted line to your code:

```
Private Sub UserControl_Terminate()
' Closes down the database and recordset connections

    On Error Resume Next
    ' Get rid of the customers query
    m_recCustomers.Close

    ' Then, lose the database connection
    m_dbDatabase.Close

End Sub
```

This error handler is really nothing more than a catch-all line of code: if there was a problem opening up the Customers table at the start of the program, then trying to close it down here would cause a runtime error. This line of code basically tells Visual Basic to close the Customers table down and the database connection, and ignore any errors. The upshot is that we can be sure, by the time this routine finishes, that there will no longer be an open Customer table or an open connection to the database.

This `Terminate` event closes down the recordset and the database connection - but there will be times where there will be no recordset. Dropping a simple error handler in there like this will catch the inevitable error that occurs when we try to close an unopened recordset. The result is that our program will run just the way it should.

The result of these two changes is that, when the control is used in a design time environment now, it should appear on a form much faster than it did previously. This is because when our control is being created in design mode, now, we can skip building up the list of customers. We're talking objects for sale here.

Property Pages

There are times when we want to add our own personal touch to the design time interface of our controls. Perhaps the single line that the property window provides for each of our properties just isn't adequate for some of the properties in our control. Perhaps we just want to add a touch of flair to the whole deal.

This is where **property pages** come in. We took a quick look at property pages in the last chapter, and in a nutshell, a property page is a form that we can attach to a control and which will then be displayed when the user double clicks on a property in the property window.

The Font property of almost every control is a cool example of a built-in property page, and we can make those pages available for the font properties on our own controls. In fact, there are a great many built-in property pages ready for us to us in Visual Basic, as you're about to find out.

> *Despite their visual sophistication, if you know how to produce a form in Visual Basic then you know how to make a property page - they really are that easy.*

Using Built-in Property Pages

Visual Basic has a number of built in property pages which we can make use of in our own controls. In fact, if you've been using Visual Basic for any length of time, you've probably come across them already: the Font property page for selecting fonts, the Color page for colors, and so on.

Actually getting these things into our own controls is very easy indeed: Visual Basic automatically makes them available, based on the data type of the properties in our controls. Here's a complete list:

Data Type	Effect in the property window
StdFont	This makes the Font dialog available in the Properties window.
MousePointerConstants	This makes the mouse pointer list appear for the property in the property window.
OLE_COLOR	This is basically nothing more than a Long, but by declaring a property to be OLE_COLOR, Visual Basic automatically makes the Color dialog available from the property window, just as if the property were any other Visual Basic color property.
OLE_TRISTATE	Use this data type when you want a value property to be set to one of three values: 0 - Unchecked, 1 – Checked, and 2 - Gray.
OLE_OPTEXCLUSIVE	Properties of this type enable our controls to work the same way as the common Option button control. If we have a group of the same control on a form, with an OLE_OPTEXCLUSIVE property, then only one of the controls at any one point in time can have this property set to True; the rest are automatically set to False whenever anyone changes this property.
OLE_CANCELBOOL	This isn't actually a property type; we instead use it with events. Declaring an event parameter as OLE_CANCELBOOL means that developers using our controls can cancel an event by setting this property to True within their event handlers.

We can put a couple of these data types to good use in our Customer Selection Combo box control.

Try It Out - Using Built-In Property Pages

1 If it isn't already loaded, then load up the project group that has our Combo box and test application in it.

We're going to be adding properties to allow the user to change the font within the Combo box, and also to change the font color and background color. Thanks to the list of data types we've just seen, and the power that Visual Basic gives us, we're going to be able add a surprising amount of functionality to the Combo box - and with very little code.

2 Let's use the `TextFont` property first. Bring up the code for our `ctlCustCombo` control and add these `Property` statements:

```
Public Property Get TextFont() As StdFont
    Set TextFont = cboCustomer.Font
End Property

Public Property Set TextFont(ByVal TheFont As StdFont)
    Set cboCustomer.Font = TheFont
End Property
```

All we're doing, here, is using some pretty standard `Property` procedures, but with the added touch that we're specifying `StdFont` data types to invoke the property pages we're after.

3 Save your code now. Then close down the control's form and code window, and go to the form in the test project where the control is located. You should find something quite neat has happened in the **Properties** window!

There, under **T** in the alphabetical list, you'll find a new **TextFont** property, the one we just wrote in fact. If you click on this property, an ellipsis button (...) will appear, just as it does for a standard font on any control. Click on this ellipsis button and the familiar font dialog will come into view:

4 Some other properties, `ComboTextColor` and `ComboBackColor`, are just as easy to set up. Let's use them in our `ctlCustCombo` control, seeing as we have a Combo box control there just waiting to be jazzed up a bit. Bring up our `ctlCustCombo` control's code window once again and type this little lot in:

```
Public Property Get ComboTextColor() As OLE_COLOR
    ComboTextColor = cboCustomer.ForeColor
End Property
```

```
Public Property Let ComboTextColor(ByVal NewColor As OLE_COLOR)
    cboCustomer.ForeColor = NewColor
End Property

Public Property Get ComboBackColor() As OLE_COLOR
    ComboBackColor = cboCustomer.BackColor
End Property

Public Property Let ComboBackColor(ByVal NewColor As OLE_COLOR)
    cboCustomer.BackColor = NewColor
End Property
```

Once again, if you close down the code window and the control window, and return to your test project's form, you'll see new properties in the property window for our control. This time, though, we have color properties:

It's very easy to see how these data types can add a great deal of flair to our controls, and they really don't take any effort at all on our part to put them in.

> *Ignore property pages at your peril. Most developers would be unhappy to find a color property, for instance, which required them to type in the color value in Hexadecimal. On the other hand, they'll love you forever if you give them a nice neat color dialog as we've just done.*

Creating Property Pages

Of course, the built-in property pages are great for some things, but they can only take us so far. More often than not, we'll want to provide something more substantial in the form of a property page of our own. In the Customer Selection Combo box, for example, wouldn't it be neat if instead of having to type in the `LimitRegion` and `LimitCountry` values, the user could select them from a list of known values as well? This sort of thing is perfect for a property page, and it's well within our reach now as control developers.

Try It Out - Creating Our Own Property Pages

1 Property pages are really just like forms, and they need to be added into our projects before we can do anything with them. So select our `CustCBO` Customer Selection Combo box project for Northwind and then select the **Project-Add Property Page** menu option to add a property page to that control:

From this list, select **Add Property Page** and you should soon find yourself looking straight into the eyes of the new **Add PropertyPage** dialog:

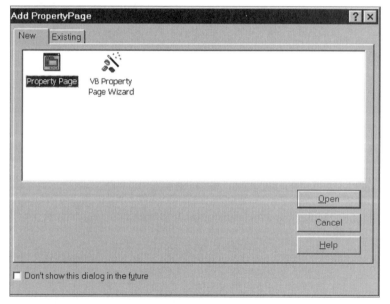

2 As you can see, there are two options: we can either create an empty property page, or we can use the **VB Property Page Wizard**. Since Wizards are for wimps (actually my only reservation is that they don't teach us anything useful about what's really going on behind the scenes), we'll just select the standard **Property Page** by double clicking on it:

Notice how it looks very much like an ActiveX control? The reason for this is that when the time comes to display the property page, Visual Basic will stick a frame around it for us and make it look nice. In addition, it needs to be done this way since the code we write forms a conversation with the innards of Visual Basic, so VB really wants to control every facet of our property page, including how and when it gets displayed.

3 Double click on the page to bring up the code window for it, and then drop down the list of events:

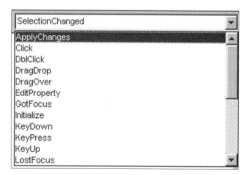

There are two very important events that we need to be aware of in this list: **ApplyChanges** and **SelectionChanged**. We'll look at them in a little more detail shortly. Right now, let's start drawing some controls on to the property page and get it working.

4   Drop some controls on to our property page so that it looks like the one in the screenshot below (the names of the two Combo boxes are shown in the screenshot, but you should set their style so that both are drop down lists):

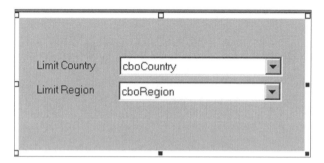

5   When you've done that, set the name of the property page to **propCustomer**, and set its caption property to **Data Limit Properties**. This caption will be displayed at the top of the property page when it finally appears.

Okay, now we have a property page, and it has some controls on it. The page's name has been set and it has a caption. Things are going well.

6   The next thing to do is attach the property page to our `ctlCustCombo` Customer Select control - so the control knows that this property page is available. There is a property on the `UserControl` of our Customer Select control called **PropertyPages**. If you click on the button that appears in the **Property** window for this property, you'll see a dialog appear that allows us to select which property pages our custom control can use:

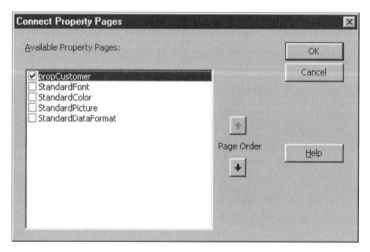

7   Select our new property page, as I have done in the screenshot here.

Notice that there are two buttons, to the right of the list of available pages, which allow us to move a selected page up and down in the list. The reason for this is that if we assign more than one property page to a control, then just one dialog is used to show them all, with tabs across the top to allow the user to choose exactly which page they wish to see. Moving the pages up and down in this list allows us to change the order of the pages on the tabs across the top of the real property page.

For now, though, all we need to do is make sure that our new property page is selected. Once it is selected, and the dialog is closed down, we can see it in action.

8 As always, make sure that there are no code windows or forms relating to the control that are open, and then bring the test form into view. Now select our custom Combo box control that's sitting in the test form. If you take a peek at the **Properties** window for this control, you should be able to see a new entry at the top, called **Custom**. This property provides users of our control with access to its property pages. Simply click on the ellipsis button to the right of the property in the **Property** window, and up it comes:

Our brand new property page doesn't actually do very much at the moment, but we've got our foot in the door. So close the dialog down, and bring up the code window for the property page itself. It's time to start looking at those two events that we saw earlier: `ApplyChanges` and `SelectionChanged`.

9 Okay, here's what we're going to do. We'll load up a list of the countries and regions that are in the database, and we'll put them into the Combo boxes on the property page for our users to select from. That way, the user won't have to type them in by hand.

This means we'll be performing some database access. Since the control itself already has an open database connection (from our earlier coding efforts), it makes sense for us to use that connection in the code for our property page. We therefore need to add a property to the control that will expose its existing database connection. Fortunately, this is easy enough to implement.

Bring up the code window for the `ctlCustCombo` control itself and add a simple DB property to it that will expose its database connection:

```
Public Property Get DB() As Database
    Set DB = m_dbDatabase
End Property
```

10 Now that we have that database property exposed, we can make use of it with some code in the property page.

Of the two events that we saw earlier (`ApplyChanges` and `SelectionChanged`), the most important one for us right now is the `SelectionChanged` event.

Let me explain. When we open up a property page, the chances are that we could have more than one copy of the control on a form selected at the same time. While the page is open, Visual Basic and many other development environments will actually let us go and select more instances of the control to apply the property page changes to. What this means is that a user could have three copies of our control on their form, select one, and bring up the property page. Then, with the property page on display, the user could hold down the *Control* key and click on the other two copies of the control that they have. At that point in time, we would have one property page actually serving more than one control. Not good - definitely not good.

> The `SelectionChanged` event lets us know when just this sort of thing happens. In fact, this event is triggered every time a property page is attached to a control, and that includes the very first time the page appears.

Once the `SelectionChanged` event occurs, we have access to a collection called `SelectedControls`.

`SelectedControls` is an array, if you like, containing every control that our property page is dealing with - even if we're only dealing with one control. It is through the `SelectedControls` array that we're able to set the actual property values on the control instances, based on the values that our users set into the property page controls. More than that, though, we can use the elements in the `SelectedControls` array to get at existing property values of controls - and that includes our DB property that we just exposed.

In the code for our property page, enter this event handler. I'll explain what's going on when you're done typing:

```
Private Sub PropertyPage_SelectionChanged()
    Dim recRS As Recordset

    Set recRS = SelectedControls(0).DB.OpenRecordset _
("SELECT DISTINCT country FROM customers", dbOpenSnapshot)
    recRS.MoveFirst

    Do While Not recRS.EOF
        cboCountry.AddItem recRS!country
        recRS.MoveNext
    Loop

    recRS.Close

    Set recRS = SelectedControls(0).DB.OpenRecordset _
("SELECT DISTINCT region FROM customers", dbOpenSnapshot)
    recRS.MoveFirst

    Do While Not recRS.EOF
        cboRegion.AddItem "" & recRS!region
        recRS.MoveNext
    Loop

    recRS.Close

End Sub
```

The first thing that happens here is that a recordset object, `recRS`, is created. We're going to need this to build up a list of the countries and regions that are already in the customer database, ready to be dumped into the two Combo boxes that we have on the property page.

Once that's done, we run the first query, selecting a list of all the `Unique` countries that are in the customers table, and then start to loop through the records in the query. This same line uses the `SelectedControls` collection:

```
Set recRS = SelectedControls(0).DB.OpenRecordset _
  ("SELECT DISTINCT country FROM customers", dbOpenSnapshot)
```

As I said earlier, we know that when this event occurs, the property page must be connected to at least one control on the form, and quite possibly more. We can get at these controls through the `SelectedControls` collection, so this line basically builds a recordset using the `DB` property that is exposed from the very first (and possibly only) control that the property page is connected to.

The rest of the code should now be fairly easy to follow. Once the recordset has been opened, the code loops through the records adding values into first the `country` Combo box, and then the `region` Combo box. Each time a new recordset needs to be created, the code uses the `DB` property of the first control in the `SelectedControls` collection to get at the database that's being used to perform the query on.

There are two important concepts that we need to understand here:

▶ If we need to initialize the controls on the property page, based on the existing property values in the control that the page is attached to, then the only place that we can really do this is in the `SelectionChanged` event handler. This event occurs as soon as the property page comes into view and is attached to a control on a form.

▶ In this event handler, if we need to access the properties of any controls connected to the page, then we must go through the `SelectedControls` collection. We CANNOT and MUST NOT name the controls explicitly in our code. It is, after all, up to the user to give our controls whatever names they see fit at design time, and we have no way when we write our code of knowing what the control names are going to be. All we can do is use the `TypeOf` command to work out what types of controls we have.

11 The `SelectedControls` collection is used to read values from the properties in our controls into the property page. Therefore, it makes sense that this same collection could be used to write the values back from the property page controls and into the properties of the controls with which the page is dealing.

That particular feat of magic takes place in the `ApplyChanges` event. Consider, for a moment, the property page for the **Data Bound Grid Control** (you'll need the **Components** dialog to find these DBGrid controls):

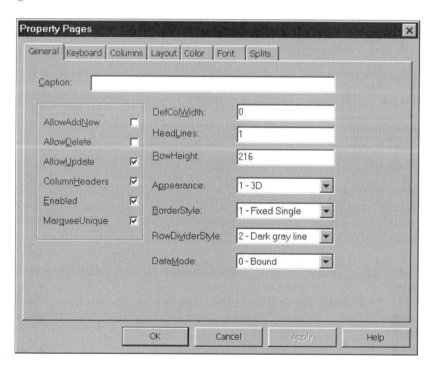

*Notice that, at the bottom there are both **OK** and **Apply** buttons. Now, as any experienced Windows user will tell you, both do similar jobs. They both, for instance, save any data that we enter into the dialog somewhere (whereas **Cancel** just discards it). The difference, though, is that the **OK** button will close the dialog down after it has saved that data, whereas the **Apply** button just saves the data and keeps the dialog open.*

Both the OK and the Apply button trigger the `ApplyChanges` event on a property page, so we don't really need to worry about whether the user pressed OK or Apply *per se*, within this routine. We just need to understand that they want to save their data.

The code that we'll write into the `ApplyChanges` event should therefore do two things:

▶ Firstly, it should validate the data that has been entered into the controls on the property page

▶ Secondly, providing the first part went well, it should save the data in those controls somewhere; in our case, into the properties of the underlying connected, and selected, control.

Type this code into your property page's `ApplyChanges` event, and again I'll explain it when you're done:

```
Private Sub PropertyPage_ApplyChanges()

    Dim TheControl As ctlCustCombo


    For Each TheControl In SelectedControls

        TheControl.LimitCountry = cboCountry.Text
        TheControl.LimitRegion = cboRegion.Text

    Next

End Sub
```

Let's take a look at this code. Since we will need to deal with the elements in the `SelectedControls` collection, in order to copy the values from the property page controls into properties of the attached controls, the first thing that we do is declare an object variable, called `TheControl`. This variable is of the same type as the control that the page administers. This last point lets us use the `For Each` loop to move through every element in the array, without having to waste time working out exactly how many items there are in the array before the loop starts.

The `For Each` loop then looks at each successive item in the `SelectedControls` collection, and temporarily puts it into our object variable, `TheControl`. Inside the loop, all we need to do is copy the property page's control values into the properties of this object variable.

When this event gets triggered (that is, when the user clicks on the OK or Apply buttons on the page) the property page is able to automatically update the properties of the controls to which it applies.

> *We don't need to worry about closing the form down afterwards, if the user clicked on the **OK** button, since that stuff is all taken care of for us, courtesy of Visual Basic.*

Devastatingly simple, isn't it? Granted, that's partly because we aren't doing any validation - but I hope you get the general idea. Do you want to see it working? Of course you do!

12 Close down all the code windows in the usual way, then bring up the form that has our control on it. Select the control and, in the Properties window, click on the button to the right of the Custom button to bring our new, fully functional property page into view:

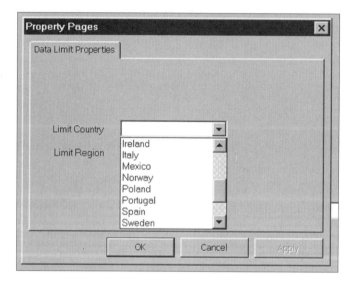

Hey, hang on a minute. How come that Apply button never gets enabled, no matter what we do with the Combo boxes on the form? I mean, shouldn't it get enabled when we select an item in the Combo boxes? After all, changes have taken place, and the normal Windows way of doing things when that happens is to enable an Apply button somewhere - to show that there are changes that need to be saved, isn't it?

13 The reason the Apply doesn't get enabled is that we need to write some more code to tell Visual Basic that changes have indeed taken place. Visual Basic doesn't know what our code is up to, or that the code and the controls on the form do indeed directly relate to properties on the controls to which the page is linked.

The way we'll do this is with the built-in `Changed` property of a property page. We simply set this property to `True` when things happen that will ultimately mean changes must be passed down to the related controls. In our case, this means that we're going to need to add some code into the click events of the two Combo boxes:

```
Private Sub cboCountry_Click()
    Changed = True
End Sub

Private Sub cboRegion_Click()
    Changed = True
End Sub
```

Enter these two event handlers into the code behind our property page, and try to bring up the page again. You'll find that the Apply button does indeed light up whenever you select an item from either of the two Combo boxes - indicating that there are changes to be saved.

The Changed property actually does a little more than that. It also provides a neat way to cancel the ApplyChanges event, should we need to do that.

A common use for the Changed property is within validation. Let's say we had some validation in our ApplyChanges event handler. We would typically want to check the values that the user entered and, if they got something wrong, display an error message of some kind. If we also set the Changed property to True at this point (it automatically gets **set** back to False whenever the user clicks on the OK or the Apply button) then we can Exit Sub without fear of Visual Basic closing the property page down. This is because Visual Basic sees that Changed is set to True, and says "Hey, the user hasn't got everything right - I'll keep this page open a while longer and give them a chance to correct their errors before they try and hit the OK or Apply buttons again." It isn't something that we need to worry about too much in our little example here, but I'm sure that you can see uses for this already in your own property pages.

Properties, Properties, Everywhere...

There are a few subtle things about properties that we haven't covered yet; things that we can take for granted on other people's controls, but are very easy to forget about on our own!

All controls are supposed to have a default property and, in Visual Basic 6, users expect to be able to see our properties categorized, as well as displayed in the more common alphabetical list. In addition, the Property window in Visual Basic 6 has a space at the bottom where our users expect to be able to see quick help on what a property does, or what it's used for. How can these things be achieved within our control?

Luckily, all these things, and more, can be achieved in Visual Basic through the use of just one dialog: the Procedure Attributes dialog. We can find this dialog by clicking the item of that name on the Tools menu within Visual Basic, and then clicking on the Advanced button on the dialog that appears:

I know, I know - it looks horrendous. It's not really. The **Procedure Attributes** dialog 'is our friend'.

The **Name** Combo at the top of the dialog allows us to choose the property that we want to manipulate in our control. Just drop it down and select something. At that point, we can associate that property with its very own property page by selecting a page from the **Use this Page in Property Browser** dropdown. Alternatively, we can assign the property to a property category, by selecting an item from the **Property Category** Combo list, or we can make the property the default property of the control, by clicking on the **User Interface Default** checkbox.

Simple huh! Have a play with it to get used to how it works.

Error Handling

Error control with ActiveX controls isn't quite as simple as it was with components, or indeed with normal objects. The idea behind error control in any kind of object is simple enough: the properties and methods on the object provide an interface to its functionality, and to its underlying data. Errors get raised when the object sees that something the user did with that interface was outside the bounds of what would normally be expected.

This still stands with controls but, in addition, they represent a part of the visual interface that the developer interacts with at design time. It is our job, as control developers, to make sure that this interface is consistent with the other controls that the developer is using.

Visual Basic provides us with a pretty handy set of pre-built error conditions that we can use to raise errors; for instance, all the "invalid property value" error dialogs are available, and so on.

We also need to make sure that any error dialogs that appear at design time contain the name of the control that the developer has set; we can do this using the name property on the **Property** window within the developer's environment (back to the `AmbientProperties` object again, I think).

Raising an Error within a Control

Actually raising an error within an ActiveX control is the same as raising it anywhere else. We simply do an `Err.Raise` command in our code where we want the error condition to occur.

The only thing that we really need to make sure of is that our control reports who it is properly. Suppose there are 15 copies of a control on a form, and one of them raises an error. Our users and development users will get pretty confused if we report the source of the error as something daft like `MyControl`, since that's what will appear in the error message box that pops up. Developers then tend to spend the next day or so trying to figure out:

> ▶ Which control raised the error, and

> ▶ Why we were too daft to provide the name of the control that they set at design time

This is where the `DisplayName` property comes in, within the `Ambient` property of a control. By specifying the value of this property as the source parameter, we can start to give our users useful error messages, making it easy for developers to track down exactly which instance of the control caused the problem. For example:

```
Err.Raise vbObjectError + 1, Ambient.DisplayName, _
    "Muppet, you got it wrong again"
```

It's the little touches like this that make our controls fit seamlessly with all the controls that a developer may be using, and which make the acceptance of our controls by prospective developers even less painful.

Pre-set Error Codes

The other thing we can do to make our controls seem to fit in more seamlessly is provide errors in a format that users are familiar with. If someone sets an invalid property value then it's no good if our code pops up a box saying **XYZ Property value error** is it now?

We can raise much more interesting errors than that, like **Invalid Property** just the same as Visual Basic can. We simply use some of the built in error constants that Visual Basic provides. Here's a table listing just a few of these error constants:

Error code	Description
CCInvalidPropertyValue	Trigger this when users try to put dumb data into properties, like text into numeric properties and so on.
CCSetNotSupportedAtRuntime	This one is great for those properties that we don't want our users to be able to set through code. Simply check the `RunMode` property of the `Ambient` object. If the control is in a running environment and shouldn't be, in order to set this property, raise this error.
CCSetNotSupported	Raise this for those properties that are Read Only. This is most often used for properties we implement that are Read/Write at design time, but Read Only at runtime (or vice versa).

Error code	Description
CCGetNotSupported	This one is used for Write Only properties. See CCSetNotSupported for its opposite number.
CCTypeMismatch	Use this when someone tries to put an invalid data type into a property. Using Variant properties, we can actually have the property change the type of data it needs on the fly in our code, and raise this error when the developer passes in the wrong kind.

Interface-less Controls

Most people, when they think of ActiveX controls, think of those cute little buttons in the Visual Basic toolbox which, when double clicked, provide a neat new GUI control for them to pass on to their users. However, it is possible to develop controls that have no runtime interface at all. At first, this may seem like a weird idea; after all, why develop ActiveX components if we don't want to expose any kind of user interface? I think we'll just have to get used to this idea though - and it isn't that weird really. Let me explain.

Developing an ActiveX control that doesn't have a user interface is a neat way of getting around some problems with ActiveX components. For example, let's say we had a component that needed to talk to a control in order for it to do its thing. A good example of this would be a web page link analyzer, which would go through selected web pages to make sure that all the links were valid. The easiest way to get such a thing working would be to make use of the functionality built into the Internet control that comes with Visual Basic. Two options would then present themselves:

We could develop our web page analyzer as a **ActiveX component**: then we would need our users to drop an Internet control on to their forms and set a property on our component such that we would know which Internet control it was using.

We could develop our analyzer as an **ActiveX control**: then we could embed the Internet control that the code was using inside our analyzer control itself. This way, our code would always know which Internet control to use. Furthermore, since we would not have implemented any kind of user interface, our development users could treat our analyzer just like an easy-to-use component (easy to use since they wouldn't have to do anything to instantiate it - other than draw it on the form that needed it).

There are more reasons why we would want to implement an interface-less control. Consider the Timer control that comes with Visual Basic. This control has no user interface - it simply doesn't need one! Since it's written as a control, though, rather than an ActiveX component, setting it up for use is easy: just drop the Timer on to a form, set the properties using the Properties explorer, and away we go! Isn't that much nicer than writing line after line of code to set up the interval and then enabling the control? After all, if we're going to use a Timer in that way we might as well use the Windows API timer calls instead, which defeats the whole purpose of a graphical development system somewhat.

Let's go and see how it's all done. It's actually very easy to accomplish these things, so we aren't going to do a long drawn out example this time around.

Defining the Design Time Interface

It may seem a little strange to talk about a design time interface for a control that is actually going to have no runtime interface. Regardless of whether or not the end user can see a control when the application is running, however, we still need to present a visual indicator that a control is on a form to the application developer.

Despite the keen intelligence of most developers, if we fail to provide some indicator at design time that a control has been created, most of them will click away on the icons in the toolbar in the vain hope that something will appear at some point. This is understandable. In the background, of course, Visual Basic is merrily creating more and more instances of our control on the developer's form.

The standard technique for a control with no runtime interface is to simply display an icon on the form that holds the control. Nothing complex here then. Let's try it out.

Try It Out - Creating the Design Time Interface for ActiveX Controls

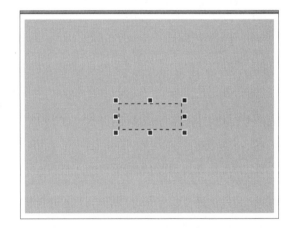

1 Start up a whole new ActiveX control project, and drop an image control on to the user control canvas when it appears:

2 Next, double click on the image control's **Picture** property to display the **Load Picture** dialog, and load up one of the sample bitmaps that comes with Visual Basic:

You should find these sample bitmaps in the \Graphics *subdirectory where you installed Visual Basic. Alternatively, you might find yourself searching on your hard disk, or in the* VB\Graphics *directory on Visual Basic's CDROM.*

3 Having loaded the icon, all we need to do now is to add some code to the control. At design time, all the user should be able to see when they draw the control on to their form is the icon that we just loaded, nothing else. Therefore, some code is required in the UserControl's Resize event:

```
Private Sub UserControl_Resize()
    Image1.Move 0, 0
    Width = Image1.Width
    Height = Image1.Height
End Sub
```

If we go ahead now and add a **Standard EXE** project to our project group, and load the control on to the form in that new project (using the same method – double clicking on **Picture** and loading the bitmap), then we'll find that only the icon appears. No matter how hard we try, the control will not allow itself to be resized at all. Each time we try, the resize code kicks in, making sure that the image appears in the top left corner of the control and that the control width and height are set to be the same width and height as the image itself.

However, if we now run our **Standard EXE** project, we'll find that the icon appears at runtime, which is not at all what we want! Let's do something about that now.

Hiding the Runtime Interface

Hiding that icon at runtime is a lot easier than you might think. In fact, those of you with a keen eye will probably already be thinking along the lines of making the control set its own Visible property to False, so that the control hides itself automatically.

Some of you may even have thought about adding to that idea with some code to examine the UserMode and setting the Visible property to NOT the value of the UserMode property. This would be logical, since at runtime that property is True (so we need False in Visible) and at design time that property is False (meaning that we want True in the Visible property). Happily, the solution is even easier than that!

Try It Out - Hiding the Runtime Interface for ActiveX Controls

1 Bring your user control back into view, and look at its properties in the Properties window:

2 Take a look at this screenshot and you'll see what we're after. There's a property called InvisibleAtRuntime. Set this to `True` and when a user runs a project that contains our control, the control will not appear at runtime!

Now, didn't I tell you that it was going to be easy!

Summary

In this chapter we took the whole idea of ActiveX controls a step further, introducing you to the delights of philosophy, property pages, and further objects and events that the control has access to when it wants to find out what's going on in the environment it's being hosted in.

You learned:

- Objects are not without their philosophical problems
- How to respond to changes in the environment
- All about the `AmbientProperties` object
- How to use built-in property pages
- How to create your own property pages
- About the **Procedure Attributes** dialog
- How to create the design time interface for controls
- How to hide the runtime interface of ActiveX controls

ActiveX components are code-only objects - we can only make use of it through code, and it only works when it has its interface poked and prodded by code in our application. ActiveX controls are different though. They do everything that a component does, plus they have their own user interface. So a developer using our control will interface with that control on two levels: through code, and through the design environment that they are working in (in our case, Visual Basic). In this instance, then, the introduction of property pages and making the control more "environment aware" are obviously great additions to the object-oriented way of working.

The property pages of ActiveX controls provide access to the interface of those controls on a graphical level. In effect, property pages are a graphical front end to the code interfaces we've already developed. Making the control aware of the environment that it's being used in is essentially giving the control scope to change itself, to use its own interface, in order that it fits in more with its new home.

We started this chapter of with a bit of armchair philosophy, and now, after a heft chunk of hard coding in-between, we seem to have arrived back at a set of thoughtful ideas and questions about where ActiveX components are taking us. Once thing is for sure though - after what we've covered in the last two chapters, you're now ready to incorporate ActiveX into your object-oriented programming.

In the next chapter, were going to have a more detailed look at the topic of object persistence, which keeps popping up in our discussions.

Why Not Try....

1 What is the `Ambient` (sometimes called the `AmbientProperties`) object?

2 What Visual Basic event lets us know that something has changed in the `Ambient` object's properties?

3 To what does the `UserMode` property of the `Ambient` object refer?

4 Does the `AmbientChanged` event take place if there is a change to the user control in the design time environment?

5 Rather than get real fancy here, let's just keep things simple by adding a Property Page to the user control that permits the user to change the Caption.

6

Object Persistence

Overview

So far in this book, there have been a few references to the topic of persistence. It's obviously an important issue in the world of object oriented programming, but what exactly is it? Well, each time an application uses an object an instance of that object is created. Now, persistence allows you to pass information from one instance (creation) of the object to the next instance (creation) of the object. Persistence can allow you to find out what values the object's properties had the last time the object was used. With persistence your objects can remember what they did the last time they were created – sounds useful to me.

This information is passed from one instance to the next by storing it in a bag, a `PropertyBag` to be exact. When you want to save information you place it into the `PropertyBag`, and when you want to read the information you retrieve it from the `PropertyBag`. In Visual Basic 5 only ActiveX controls were able to have persistence and property bags. In ActiveX controls persistence was essential because it allowed information to be passed from the copy of the control that was being used during the design phase of the application to the copy of the control that would be used at the run time phase of the application. In Visual Basic 6 any public creatable class can have persistence and property bags.

In this chapter we shall be covering:

- Persistence
- Property Pages
- Property Bags
- Read Property
- Write Property

Why do we need persistence ?

The first thing we need to do is explain why we need to store information between instances of our objects. An example using an ActiveX control will be perfect to show the importance of persistence. ActiveX controls are a special type of object: they can be placed on a form and used during design time and also be used at run time. This means that the control's properties can be set at both run time and design time. What does this mean in practice?

Let's consider a text box, which is really nothing more than a control that comes with Visual Basic. When you place a textbox onto a form you can set the properties of the textbox. You can set the height, width, text and other properties while designing your form. To be able to set these properties Visual Basic has to create an instance of the textbox that exists and runs during the design phase. So, when you run your application Visual Basic will destroy the instance of the textbox that was created for design time and create a new instance at run time.

To see how this works we will create two Visual Basic Projects. The first project will be a standard exe project used to test our second project, which will be an ActiveX control.

Below is a list of the important events of an ActiveX control that we will be using in this example:

Event Name	Description
ReadProperties	This event occurs when something might require the control to read the information that is stored in the `PropertyBag`. As the example will show, `ReadProperties` is called when the control is first loaded and when the control switches from design time to run time.
WriteProperties	This event occurs when something might require the control to write information to the `PropertyBag`. The example will show that this routine is called before the control is destroyed.
InitProperties	This event is called the first time the control is created. You can use this event to save default values.

Try It Out - Making an ActiveX Control without Persistence

1 Open Visual Basic, then select New Project from the File menu. Then select Standard Exe from the New Project window.

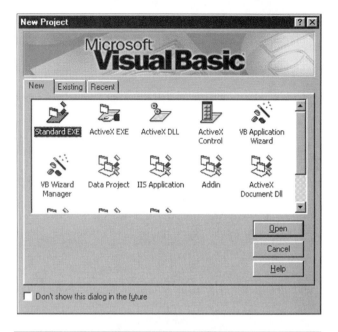

2 Next, return to the File menu and select Add Project. This time, select Active X Control from the Add project window.

Your project window should now look as follows:

You have now created a project group that can be used to build and test an ActiveX control.

3 Now go to the ActiveX control in the **Project Explorer** window, put the mouse pointer over **UserControl1** and right mouse click. You should see a list of selections, select **View Code** from the list.

The code window for your ActiveX control should now be open.

4 In the General Declarations section of the code window type.

```
Private strTextVariable as String
```

This will be a private variable global to our ActiveX control. We will use this variable to see what happens to values stored in private variables as the control goes from running at design time to running at run time.

5   In the top left corner of the code window select **UserControl** from the object dropdown list.

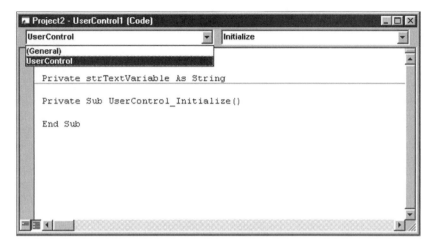

The UserControl_Initialize sub should now be in your code window.

Add the following message box to this sub:

```
Private Sub UserControl_Initialize()
MsgBox "The control is initializing" & vbCrLf & _
        "the value of strTextVariable is: " & strTextVariable
End Sub
```

6   Now, go to the event dropdown and select the **Terminate** event. Type the following code in the Terminate Sub:

```
Private Sub UserControl_Terminate()
    MsgBox "The control is terminating" & vbCrLf & _
        "the value of strTextVariable is: " & strTextVariable
End Sub
```

7   Now, we need to add the following code to the code window to create a property to set and get the values of the private variable strTextVariable:

```
Public Property Get TextVariable() As String
    TextVariable = strTextVariable
End Property
```

241

```
Public Property Let TextVariable(ByVal v_strNewValue As String)
    strTextVariable = v_strNewValue

End Property
```

Close the code window. If the usercontrol form is open close it, too.

8 If form1 is not open go to the Project Explorer window and double click on Form1 from Project1 to open it. Open the Visual Basic tool bar if it is not already open. You should see your control on the toolbar, double click your control to put it on Form1. You should get the message from the `intitialize` event as follows:

9 Click OK to close the message box. This shows that the control was initialized when you placed it on the form. Even though the form is in design mode the ActiveX control is initialized and running. `strTextVariable` does not have a value yet.

10 Now, go to the menu and click View and then Properties Window to open the property window. Select UserControl1 and in the TextVariable property type in "This is a test"

11 Now we're ready to run the project - run it by either pushing the *F5* key or going to the menu and selecting Run and then Start. You should see the following:

What has happened is the instance of the control that was running at design time is being terminated. A new instance, or to put another way, a new copy, of the ActiveX control will be created to be used while Form1 is running.

Click OK and you should see the following message:

Visual Basic has now destroyed the instance of the ActiveX control that we were using during the design phase of Form1 and created a new instance for the run time phase of the Form1. Notice what has happened to `strTextVariable` - the value has disappeared. The information did not get saved from one instance of the control to the next. Click OK and close the form and you will see the terminate event for the run time instance of your control:

Followed by the initialize event for the design time for the control:

Look in the Properties window at the value of `strTextVariable` for Control1 on Form1. Notice that the value we typed is gone. Delete the control from Form1 and you will see the terminate event fire for the last time. All references to this copy of the control are now gone. There is no persistance here. Let's take a look at how we can add persistence to our control object.

Adding Persistence to our ActiveX Control

We can now clearly see the problem. We would like the users of our control to be able to set properties during design time, such as our `strTextVariable`, and we want our control to remember those values. After all, it does not make sense for our user to put all the values in at design time and then have to put them all in again at run time. How do we pass this information from the design time instance of our control to the run time instance of our control?

One way we could do this is to write the information to a file somewhere. This sounds pretty good so far, but what happens when we place two copies of our control on a form? Copy1 and Copy2 will each have their own set of properties, so we will have to find some way to uniquely identify both controls and save the information on both controls to the file. Now imagine dozens of copies of your object on a form and imagine trying to uniquely identify each of them and writing and reading this information from a file. You can see that things are getting extremely complicated. Luckily, Microsoft comes to the rescue by giving us property bags and the `ReadProperties` and `WriteProperties` events. Let's take a closer look at these.

Property bags store information for each copy of your control. The really great thing about property bags is you don't have to worry about keeping track of which property bag belongs to which copy of your control when using them to store information during the transition from design time to run time. When going from design time to run time Visual Basic will save and retrieve the property bag for you. OK, so where do we find these wonderful bags? They can be found in the Read and Write properties of the control.

Property Bags have two methods, `ReadProperty` and `WriteProperty`, and one property, Contents.

> **ReadProperty** has two parameters, the second is optional:

> **Property Name** - Each item that is stored in the property bag will need some unique name to identify it. This name will be used to both store and retrieve this item from the property bag. The name can be any value but it is usually best to use the name of the item that is being stored in the property bag.

> **Default Value** - The default value is a value that this method will return if there is no item in the bag with the name used in Property Name parameter. If you leave out a default value and this item is not in the property bag an error is raised, so it is a good idea to use a default value.

> **WriteProperty** has three parameters, the last is optional:

> **Property Name** - The same as in `ReadProperty` except it is the name under which the item will be saved.

> **Property Value** - The value that will be saved in the property bag.

> **Default Value** - The default value passed is compared to the value you are setting Property Value to, if the values are different then an extra line of code is added to your project files. If the values are the same, nothing is written to the project files. Therefore using a default value can make your project files smaller.

> **Contents -** Returns or sets a byte array that represents the contents of the property bag. This property can be used to get the entire contents of the property bag and save the contents to a file, a database, etc. We can also fill the property bag by setting this property to a byte array.

When the ReadProperties and WriteProperties events occur in our code, they will respectively call the ReadProperty and WriteProperty methods of the Property Bag object. These methods will be called each time an item needs to be loaded from, or saved to the Property Bag.

Try It Out - Giving the Control Persistence

1 If Form1 is open in design mode close it.

2 Open the code window for UserControl1 again, select **UserControl** on the object dropdown and **ReadProperties** from the event dropdown. In the `ReadProperties` sub write the following code:

```
Private Sub UserControl_ReadProperties(PropBag As PropertyBag)
    strTextVariable = PropBag.ReadProperty("TextVariable")
    MsgBox "In read properties" & vbCrLf & _
        "the value of strTextVariable is: " & strTextVariable
End Sub
```

What does this code mean? It means that Visual Basic will supply the property bag for this particular copy of your control when Visual Basic raises these events. The `ReadProperty` method will retrieve the value of the item in the bag that has a key of `TextVariable` and set `strTextVariable` equal to that value. The item with a name property of `TextVariable` will be created during the `WriteProperties` method by using the `WriteProperty` of the `PropertyBag`.

Notice that we set the private variable equal to the value that was retrieved from the property bag. You may be wondering why we did not use the Let property. If we have several properties and there is some reference to another property in the Let and this property is not initialized yet, your Let property could fail. To prevent this we set the private variables directly and do not use the Let properties here.

We also did not use a default value. I have left the default value out so that we can see that the values are really being stored in the property bag, but it is good practice to put a default value there when doing normal coding.

3 Now, in the event dropdown of the code window select the `WriteProperties` event and write the following code:

```
Private Sub UserControl_WriteProperties(PropBag As PropertyBag)
    MsgBox "In write properties"
    PropBag.WriteProperty "TextVariable", TextVariable
End Sub
```

This will now write the value of `strTextVariable` to the property bag whenever the `WriteProperties` method is called. In this case we are using the Get property because all of the variables should be set and we do not have to worry about our Get property referencing something that does not yet exist. In a moment we will see when these two methods are called, but first let us add code to one more event for the UserControl.

4 Go to the event dropdown in the code window and select the InitProperties and put the following code:

```
Private Sub UserControl_InitProperties()
    MsgBox "The control is in init properties" & vbCrLf & _
        "the value of strTextVariable is: " & strTextVariable
End Sub
```

We will explain this bit of code in a moment.

5 Once again, close down the control and its code window, then open Form1. Double click on your ActiveX control in the toolbar. We get the message box from the `Initialize` sub of the control as before. This time, though, we also get something extra - we now see the `InitEvent` message box:

The `InitProperties` is called only once, when the control is first placed on the form. If there is anything special we have to do the first time the control is created, we can do it in the `InitProperties` sub. The first time the control is created there will be no property bag to retrieve information. Since there is no property bag, the `ReadProperties` event is not raised when the control is first created (first placed onto a form). Therefore the only way to set your properties the first time the control is created is by setting them in `InitProperties`. When the control is destroyed (such as when the application is run or the form is closed) `WriteProperties` is called and the information is stored in the `PropertyBag`. From that point on, the `ReadProperties` method will be called and the values can be retrieved from there.

6 Again go to the properties window and change the `TextVariable` property of UserControl1 to "This is a test". Now push F5 to run the application. You should see the following:

This time, before the runtime instance of the control was terminated the write properties was called. This means that the value of the `strTextVariable` is now in the bag.

7 Click **OK** and you should see the terminate event message:

The `PropertyBag` should now have the value of `strTextVariable`, "This is a Test", in the `PropertyBag` for the item with the name property `TextVariable`.

8 Click **OK** and you should see the `Initialize` event for the run-time copy of the control:

Notice that during the initialization of the control `strTextVariable` has no value. This makes sense, as we have not reached the point where the `ReadProperties` event has been called.

9 Click OK again and you should now get the message from the `ReadProperties` sub:

We have now entered the `ReadProperties` method and retrieved the correct value from the `PropertyBag`. It is important to realize that these properties were not set during the initialize event, so if you need to do something with these values while the control is loading it must be done during the read properties.

10 Click OK, close the form and return to design time. Click OK to the terminate event for the run time instance of our control and the initialize event for the design time instance of the control. Go to the property window and see that the property for **TextVariable** in **Control1** is still "This is a test".

I strongly recommend that the you now go back and run all of this code again but instead of using *F5* click *F8* (**StepInto** in the **Debug** menu) to step through the code line by line to see how every thing works and when each procedure is called. Place break points in the code to catch what is happening during design time. When you are done delete the control from Form1 and click OK for the `WriteProperties` and `Terminate` events.

What we have learned from this example is how to use property bags to save our information from one instance of our control to the next. We have discovered that the use of property bags allow us to have persistent information.

Property Pages

Wouldn't it be nice just to right click on your object during design time and get a nice customized form to pop up that allows you to change all of the properties? Perhaps some of you have noticed that when you right mouse click over certain objects and click properties that you do indeed go to a special form to enter property values in. Visual Basic gives you the ability to create your own custom forms to enter values of properties using what is called a Property Page. We will now add a property page to our example. The events in the property page that we are going to look at are:

Event	Description
SelectionChanged	When you put controls on your form you can select one of them or, holding the control key down and clicking on several controls, you can select more then one control. This event is called whenever your property page is open and you change which controls are selected. This event is also called when you change a property in the Visual Basic Properties window and when the property page is first opened. This is the event that is used to read the property values in when the control is loaded and when property values are changed in the property window.

Event	Description
ApplyChanges	This event happens when the user presses the OK button or the Apply button on the property page, or when property pages are switched by selecting tabs. This is the event that is used to update the properties to the new values that have been entered in the property page.

Property pages have one important property that we will need to use: the Changed event. Changed is a property of the PropertyPage that tells the PropertyPage that one of the properties for which the PropertyPage is responsible has changed. The first time the Changed property is set to True, the Apply button, (which will automatically be supplied to your property page) will become enabled. This will allow your user to click on the Apply button, which will in turn, trigger the ApplyChanges sub. You can then put code in the ApplyChanges sub to save the new information. This will all become a lot clearer if we actually try it out in Visual Basic.

Try It Out - Building a Property Page

1 Using the same project (Project2), start by opening the Properties window, putting the mouse arrow over project two and clicking on the right mouse button. From the drop down menu select Add and then Property Page or go to the Visual Basic menu and select Project and Add Property Page.

2 Select Property Page from the Add Property Page window:

3 You should now have a property page that looks like a form. Add a label on the form with a **Caption** property **TextVariable** and a text box with a **Name** property of txtTextVariable next to the listbox. The property page should look as follows:

4 Double click on the property page form to get access to the code window for the property page and select txtTextVariable from the object dropdown in the code window Now select the **Change** event in the event dropdown. Add the following code:

```
Private Sub txtTextVariable_Change()
    Changed = True
End Sub
```

We are setting the Changed property of the property page to let the property page know that one of the properties have been updated.

5 If there are any changes the ApplyChanges sub will save them.

```
Private Sub PropertyPage_ApplyChanges()
    SelectedControls(0).TextVariable = txtTextVariable
End Sub
```

What is SelectedControls(0)? Well, when you right mouse click over a control you are not only bringing up the menu but also selecting the control. You could push the control key and select multiple controls. Every control that you select goes into the SelectedControls() collection. If you had multiple copies of the same control (or different objects which use the same property pages) you could find out how many controls were selected by using SelectedControls.Count and then change the properties for each control. In this case, we are assuming only one control is selected and setting its TextVariable property to the new value. Notice that we used the Let property to set the variables. This is because we can only access public properties of the control through the SelectedControls object.

6 There is still one thing left to do. If the user has already set the properties we would like to retrieve those values and place them into our PropertyPage when the page loads. The SelectionChanged sub runs when the page is opened, so we can use it to initialize the PropertyPage with any values the properties has prior to the page running.

```
Private Sub PropertyPage_SelectionChanged()
    txtTextVariable = SelectedControls(0).TextVariable
End Sub
```

7 Now that our page is complete we need to make it a PropertyPage of our ActiveX control. Close the PropertyPage and open UserControl1 in design mode. Go to the **properties** window for UserControl1 and go to the **PropertyPage** property. Click on the PropertyPage property and you will see a button with three elipses. Click on this button and you will see the **Connect Property Pages** window.

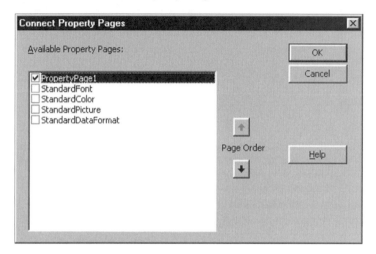

8 Now, select our PropertyPage called **PropertyPage1**. Then click OK and close the **Connect Property Pages** window.

9 Next you need to close UserControl1 and open Form1. Once again, place a copy of UserControl1 onto Form1. Place the mouse pointer over the control and right mouse click, and select **Properties**. Our new property page should come up - type in "This is a test" in the textbox. Did you notice how the **Apply** button became enabled as we started entering text?

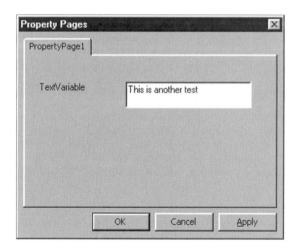

10 If you go to the Properties window and look at the **TextVariable** property for **UserControl1** you will see that it has been updated. If you change the value of the **TextVariable** property in the **properties** window you will see that the new value is now in the **PropertyPage**. If you now put a breakpoint in the `SelectionChanged` event you will see that it is called when you change the values of the properties in the Visual Basic properties window.

At this point we have created an ActiveX control that has persistence and a property page to update its properties. Microsoft does try to make it easier on the programmer by taking care of all of the default properties that our control has. Therefore you do not have to worry about passing the top, left, height, ... properties into your property bag - that is done for you automatically. You only have to worry about the properties that you add to your control. Do realize that you can pass any information you want into a property bag. As long as you give it a proper name to identify it, you can save it to the property bag. Therefore the property bag becomes a place to store any information that your control will need as it goes from one instance to the next.

The information in the property bag is actually stored in your project files. In this way the property bag with all of its information can be retrieved and changed during design time and retrieved when your project is about to run. The next obvious question is "If I change a property while my application is running, can I save that information in a property bag?" The answer is yes and no. During run time the `WriteProperties` method is not called, so you can not access the property bag associated with this control. What you can do is create your own property bag object and pass it into the `WriteProperties` and `ReadProperties` methods when you want to write and read information. But, to save this information from one instance of the control to the next you would have to save the property bag to a file yourself. We are actually going to do this when working with classes, so we will not demonstrate the technique here.

If we think about it, though, it makes sense that you can not save property bags at run time automatically. Imagine that I have an application that has ControlX in it. ControlX contains information on a particular user. If I use the application and put all of my information into the application, and the control saves this information in a property bag, it must somehow associate this information with me. If you use the same application on the same computer you will want the application to save the information and associate the property bag with you. If I now run the application, I want the application to retrieve the information associated with me, not you.

So, we can see the problem is that to use a property bag during run time to get persistence we need to have some way of associating it with some key value.

During design time Visual Basic automatically saves the property bag with the rest of the information on the control. What uniquely identifies each bag is the particular control that it is associated with, such as control1, control2, etc.

At runtime, Visual Basic has no idea what is going to uniquely identify this property bag; as what uniquely identified it is no longer what control it belongs to, but some other unique identifier, such as the user. So, if you want to save it at run time, you have to do it yourself and create your own system of associating a property bag with some key.

One place where it would be easy to use property bags at run time is when you are saving data that is shared by all instances of your control. If you are creating a control that handles invoices and this control needs sales tax information for every city, the sales tax information can be saved in a property bag. Any changes to the information will be needed by all of the controls, so you don't need any special way to identify which control needs this property bag.

Before finally moving onto classes, there is one more thing we can say about property bags in ActiveX controls. They are very useful for creating default values. If you use a Visual Basic ActiveX control in one of your applications, as we did with Form1, and then set various properties of the control at design time, then save these values into a property bag, when the control is compiled these values will become the default values for the control for this application. Every time the control is started it will retrieve the default values from the property bag.

If you want to find out more, I would recommend that you add a text box onto your form and a command button. Place a copy of the control on the form if there is not already one there. Write the necessary code in the click event of the command button to have the value of the controls `TextVariable` property set to the value in the text box. Run the application, enter a new value in the text box and click the command button to change the `TextVariable` property's value. Stop running the application and observe that the `WriteProperties` sub is not called. Restart the application - you will see that the changes you made at run time did not get saved.

A Persistent Class

In Visual Basic 6 we now have the ability to create a class that has persistence. Let us run through an example that allows us to build a persistable class.

> Let us imagine that our ActiveX control will calculate the total value of an invoice. We will need to know the taxes for various states. You will create a class called clsTaxes that will hold all of the tax information. The class will retrieve, set and save the values of the class' properties at design time and also at runtime, so the class will always have the most current information.

Visual Basic will add a `ReadProperties`, `WriteProperties`, and `InitProperties` subs into our code if we make our class public and persistable. We shall see how to do that in a moment. While these subs have the same names as the routines in an ActiveX control, they work differently in a class than in a control. ActiveX controls are placed on a form (or some other container) and so Visual Basic can save the property bag information into the project files containing the rest of the information on this control. Since the property bag is saved with the rest of the control's information Visual Basic always knows which property bag is associated with which control.

A class, though, is not being placed on a form or anything else for that matter. Visual Basic has no way of associating a class with a form or other container, therefore Visual Basic has nothing to identify the class. While Visual Basic might be able to call the `WriteProperties` and `ReadPropeties` events of your class, the property bag that is associated with this information will disappear for ever once that instance of the class is destroyed. This means that we cannot to rely on Visual Basic to call the `ReadProperties` and `WriteProperties` events when we need them, so instead we will call them ourselves. We will have to save the information in the

`Terminate` event before the class is destroyed, and retrieve the information from the same place when the class is initialized. The question is "Where should this property bag be saved?" In our example we will save it to a text file as binary information

Try It Out - Making a Persistent Class

1 Select Project2 then select Add Class Module from the Project menu. This will bring up the Add Class Module window, select Class Module.

The class should be added to your project and a code window for the class should now be open.

2 In the code window go to the object dropdown and select Class, go to the event dropdown and look at what events are available; you will see there is no ReadProperties, InitProperties or WriteProperties events listed.

3 Now, go to the properties window and change the name of the class to clsTaxes, change the Instancing to MultiUse and Persistable to Persistable.

To have persistence in a class we need to make it MultiUse, and to have persistance we need to set the Persistable property to Persistable. In the code window go to the left drop down list and select Class, go to the event dropdown and look at what events are available. You will see there is now a ReadProperties, InitProperties and a WriteProperties events.

4 We will now create properties to keep track of the New York, Connecticut, and Pennsylvania sales tax. We shall begin by placing private variables in our General Declarations section for each of the sales taxes.

```
Option Explicit
Private m_lngNYSalesTax As Long
Private m_lngConSalesTax As Long
Private m_lngPaSalesTax As Long
```

5 Next we will add the Get and Let properties for the three tax properties so we can set and get the values for the taxes.

```
Public Property Get NYSalesTax() As Long
    NYSalesTax = m_lngNYSalesTax
End Property
```

```
Public Property Let NYSalesTax(ByVal v_lngNewValue As Long)
    m_lngNYSalesTax = v_lngNewValue
End Property
```

```
Public Property Get ConSalesTax() As Long
    ConSalesTax = m_lngConSalesTax
End Property
```

```
Public Property Let ConSalesTax(ByVal v_lngNewValue As Long)
    m_lngConSalesTax = v_lngNewValue
End Property
```

```
Public Property Get PaSalesTax() As Long
    PaSalesTax = m_lngPaSalesTax
End Property
```

```
Public Property Let PaSalesTax(ByVal v_lngNewValue As Long)
    m_lngPaSalesTax = v_lngNewValue
End Property
```

6 Select Class from the object dropdown in the code window and select ReadProperties from the event dropdown. The ReadProperties will be coded the same as it was for the ActiveX control, we will set all of the properties to the values that are saved in the property bag. We will again set the private variables to the new values instead of using the Let properties in the ReadProperties method.

```
Private Sub Class_ReadProperties(PropBag As PropertyBag)
    m_lngPaSalesTax = PropBag.ReadProperty("PaSalesTax", 6)
    m_lngConSalesTax = PropBag.ReadProperty("ConSalesTax", 3.5)
    m_lngNYSalesTax = PropBag.ReadProperty("NYSalesTax", 5)
End Sub
```

7 The `WriteProperties` method will place the values of the properties into the property bag. However, there is one thing going on here that is not very obvious. Remember that when you pass parameters into a sub or function you can pass them in by value or by reference. The default is by reference, and since our `WriteProperties` method does not specify `byval` or `byref` it will use the default: by reference. This means that when the `WriteProperties` sub changes any of the property bags values it is also changing the values of the `PropertyBag` variable that was originally passed into the sub. If this not clear yet, it will be explained in more detail in the `Terminate` event.

```
Private Sub Class_WriteProperties(PropBag As PropertyBag)
    PropBag.WriteProperty "PaSalesTax", PaSalesTax
    PropBag.WriteProperty "ConSalesTax", ConSalesTax
    PropBag.WriteProperty "NYSalesTax", NYSalesTax
End Sub
```

8 We will next write the code for the `Class_Initialize` sub. If we want persistence in a class we will have to retrieve and save the information ourselves. A regular text file called `TaxData.txt` will be used to save the `PropertyBag` contents. Since Visual Basic is not supplying us with a property bag the `Initialize` sub needs to have a local `PropertyBag` variable that we can fill with the information in the text file. Once the `PropertyBag` is filled it can be passed into the `ReadProperties` method. The values that are coming back from the text file will be binary information, so we will need to open the file for binary reading and use a variant variable to hold the information. A byte variable will also be needed to pass these values into the `PropertyBag` `Contents` property. Type this into the `Class_Initialize` section.

```
Private Sub Class_Initialize()
    Dim varTemp As Variant 'To hold the PropertyBag Info from text file
    Dim byteArr() As Byte  'To pass the information into the PropertyBag
    Dim PB As PropertyBag  'A PropertyBag to hold the information
    ' Instantiate the PropertyBag object
    Set PB = New PropertyBag
    ' Read the file contents into a Variant.
    Open "C:\TaxData.txt" For Binary As #1
    Get #1, , varTemp  'Get the information
    Close #1
    ' Assign the Variant to a Byte array.
    If IsEmpty(varTemp) Then  'If there is no info varTemp will be empty
        byteArr = ""
    Else
        byteArr = varTemp
    End If
    ' Assign to the PropertyBag Contents property.
    PB.Contents = byteArr
```

```
      ' Call ReadProperties and pass in the PB with the info from the file
      Class_ReadProperties PB
      Set PB = Nothing
   End Sub
```

9 The `Terminate` event will save the values of the properties to the PropertyBag. Once again we will create a local PropertyBag variable and a variant variable to store the information from the PropertyBag and to place it into the text file.

```
   Private Sub Class_Terminate()
      Dim varTemp As Variant    ' Instantiate the PropertyBag object.
      Dim PB As PropertyBag
      Set PB = New PropertyBag
      Class_WriteProperties PB
      ' Assign the Contents of the PropertyBag to a Variant.
      varTemp = PB.Contents    ' Save to a text file.
      Open "C:\TaxData.txt" For Binary As #1
      Put #1, , varTemp
      Close #1
      Set PB = Nothing
   End Sub
```

Take special note of this line of code:

```
Class_WriteProperties PB
```

We mentioned earlier that we are passing the `PropertyBag` into the `WriteProperties` sub by reference. This means that if the `WriteProperties` makes any changes to the `PropertyBag` parameter that is passed into the sub, we are also going to make changes to the `PB` variable. When `WriteProperties` is filling the `PropertyBag` parameter with the values of the properties it will also be filling our `PB` variable with the values of the properties. So, after we call the `WriteProperties` sub, the variable `PB` will be filled with the values of our properties and these values can then be saved to the file.

Our class is now persistent, but to make this a little more useful we are going to create a property page to set the class' properties at design time. Unlike our ActiveX control, though, we can not assign a property page directly to a class.

However, this is not the end of the world. If our ActiveX control is going to use the class, then we can set the properties of the class through our ActiveX control. Let's see how this is done.

Try It Out – Setting Properties At Design Time

1 Start by closing the code window for the class and opening the code window for the ActiveX control. In the General Declarations section add the following line of code:

```
Option Explicit
Private strTextVariable As String
Public m_objPreferences As clsTaxes
```

m_objPreferences will be the private variable that will be the copy of clsTaxes that our ActiveX control will use. The property page will set the properties of this class through this variable's Get and Set properties, which we need to write next.

2 Let's add the Get and Set properties now:

```
Public Property Set TaxInformation(ByVal v_objNewValues As clsTaxes)
    Set TaxInformation = m_objPreferences
End Property
```

We are using a Set property instead of a Let because m_objPreferences is an object and we need to use Set when working with objects.

```
Public Property Get TaxInformation() As clsTaxes
    Set TaxInformation = m_objPreferences
End Property
```

3 We need to instantiate the m_objPreferences using the New keyword, so go to UserControl_Initalize and the following code:

```
Private Sub UserControl_Initialize()
    MsgBox "The control is initializing" & vbCrLf & _
        "the value of strTextVariable is: " & strTextVariable
    Set m_objPreferences = New clsTaxes
End Sub
```

4 We are now ready to build the property page that will set and get the values. Create a new property page (as before - go to the Visual Basic menu and select **Project, Add Property Page**). Change the **Name** property of the Property Page to **ppTaxes**.

5 Now place three labels and three text boxes on the form. Name the textboxes txtPATax, txtNYTax, and txtConTax. Change the caption of the labels to **PA SalesTax, NY Sales Tax,** and **Con Sales Tax**.

6 Next, open the code window for the new property page. Select PropertyPage from the object combo and ApplyChanges from the event combo. Enter the following code to save any changes made on the form to the appropriate properties of the control. Any changes we make to these properties will be saved to the text file when the Tax class is terminated.

```
Private Sub PropertyPage_ApplyChanges()
    With SelectedControls(0).TaxInformation
        .PaSalesTax = TxtPATax
        .NYSalesTax = TxtNYTax
        .ConSalesTax = TxtConTax
    End With
End Sub
```

7 Select SelectionChanged from the event dropdown. We will place code in the SelectionChanged sub to retrieve the current values of the class' properties.

```
Private Sub PropertyPage_SelectionChanged()
    With SelectedControls(0).TaxInformation
        TxtPATax = .PaSalesTax
        TxtNYTax = .NYSalesTax
        TxtConTax = .ConSalesTax
    End With
End Sub
```

8 Now, we have to add Changed=True to the Change sub of all of our textboxes to enable Apply command button of the property page. Type in the following code in the textboxes Change subs:

```
Private Sub txtConTax_Change()
    Changed = True
End Sub
```

```
Private Sub txtNYTax_Change()
    Changed = True
End Sub

Private Sub txtPATax_Change()
    Changed = True
End Sub
```

9   At last, it's time to test out our new property page. Before we can do so we need to make it available to our User Control. Do this as before (go to the UserControl1 Property page then click on the PropertyPage property, click on the button and check ppTaxes).

Now, close all the open windows and open Form1 again. If there is a copy of the ActiveX control on Form1 delete it, then place a new copy of the control on Form1, right mouse click over the control, and select **Properties**.

Now, select the second property pages tab. Enter new values into the textboxes, click apply and the click OK.

Close Form1. Closing the form will destroy the copy of clsTax. Reopen Form1 and open the property page for the tax information. If you have done everything correctly you should see the new values you placed in before. This means that these properties have persisted throughout the transition from design time to runtime – exactly what we wanted!

This is pretty handy stuff, but persistence has more uses in classes then just saving global data. Anytime you have an ActiveX control that contains a class with properties you want to persist you can use these techniques. Without persistence you could add the class' properties one by one to the ActiveX's property bag instead of creating a separate property bag for the control. Yet, it makes more sense to create a separate property bag within the class to persist the values. Instead of saving the class' property bag to a file you could save it as one of the ActiveX control's property bags items, but this is beyond the level of this example...

Summary

In this chapter, we've seen how persistence helps us to pass information from the design time instance of our control to the run time instance of the control.

We have learned how values we put in at design time disappear when we switch over to run time, how property pages allows us to make really great customized forms to change and view our ActiveX control's properties, and how the new Visual Basic classes can also have persistence.

In particular, in this chapter we have learned:

- How to make an ActiveX control persistent
- How to build a property page
- How to use a property bag
- How to build a persistent class

Persistence allows us to enter values in at design time that can be passed onto the run time phase of our control. Once the control is compiled these values then become the controls default values.

In the next chapter, we take a cue from some of the more philosophical issues that have been taking us by storm, and we return to an important and stabilizing base: this is the topic of object-oriented design. We have a set of powerful technologies at our fingertips; let's use them well, and let's learn to design our object-oriented programs with some care and clarity of thought.

Why Not Try....

1 What methods and properties does a Property Bag have, and what is their purpose?

2 What parameters are passed to the `ReadProperty` method and why?

3 What parameters are passed to the `WriteProperty` method and why?

4 Why is it good practice to supply your Property Bag with a default value?

6

Object-Oriented Design

Here's something we need to understand: our programming practice can only ever be as accomplished as the design work we put into our programs. Without a solid design behind them, our applications cannot be a complete response and solution to the particular problem at hand. No matter what powerful technologies we have at our fingertips, no matter how great Visual Basic may be in supporting object-oriented programming, and no matter how many excellent coding techniques we may have mastered (especially having read this book), without a good design our projects will not fully succeed.

Okay, now I've got off my soapbox, let's take matters into our own hands. In this chapter, we're going to take a good look at the design process - the groundwork to every application we write. We'll take a step back from all the great technologies and coding techniques that we've been exploring, and we'll come to appreciate just how critical the design phase is to the success of our object-oriented applications.

Of course, not many of us immediately appreciate this extra work the design process demands of us. But if we take the time to perfect our applications in these design stages, the cost of any changes we make, in terms of money and time, will be far less than the cost of changing a flawed product later on. Just as critically, if we design properly then our thinking will be clearer and our applications will be more robust. You see, really there's no such thing as object-oriented programming without at least some preliminary amount of design work to clarify the objects we're modeling. So this is an important chapter in our object programming careers.

We'll also discover, in this chapter, that a well-executed design phase in our programming can actually be very rewarding. Now that can't be bad can it?

In this chapter, you will learn about:

- Object-oriented design work
- Design methodologies
- Use case statements
- UML (Unified Modeling Language)
- How to use UML in object-oriented design

Why Do We Need to Design?

If we were to ask a builder to start construction on a new home for ourselves and our loved ones, we'd undoubtedly want to see some plans. It just isn't good enough for the builder to say, "Err...OK", and turn up on Monday morning to start laying down bricks. It doesn't work that way; it never has, and it probably never will.

You see, the thing is, houses are complex things to build, even though they're built in a clear, object-oriented fashion (you take a door from one company, a window from another, bricks from a third, and tie them all together). Houses are complex things, and we rely on them to provide us with warmth and shelter for years to come. Lots of thought needs to go into what they do and how they do it - before the blade of a shovel goes anywhere near a piece of earth.

It's funny, then, that there are still a lot of programmers out there, particularly of the Visual Basic variety, who will happily sit down and start churning out code after nothing more than a cursory mental glance at the solution. It's clearly very easy for programmers to think that building a program is simpler and more trivial than building a house.

The cost of many corporate development programs now runs into millions. With more and more people relying on the software they use each and every day as a part of their bread and butter income, a software development project actually becomes every bit as important as a new house! Odd, then, that programmers are often so laid back about the design of their applications.

> *Okay, let's get one thing out in the open straight away: I don't know any programmers who like to design things. I've never met a programmer who, faced with a new project, jumps two feet in the air and, with a spring in their step, starts drawing diagrams on a piece of paper.*

Yup, so design is not the most loved part of the development process. Yet if we put in the time to design our applications well, we can ensure that our developments run smoothly and that we have a clear idea of where the coding starts and stops on the actual project.

> *This last point is very important - it's very easy, otherwise, to get carried away with adding pointless new features to projects. In addition, if we design our applications correctly, we should be able to present the designs to our client, just as an architect would present house plans to his or her client. This can clarify a lot of legal issues for us if things happen to go wrong later.*

Just imagine if our house builders didn't plan the house they were creating, and they built the house but found that a wall was in the wrong place. The cost of the change would be far more than the cost of the change had it been made in the design phase, and the same is true in the world of programming.

> *And on a lighter note, get the design right and the application flows quite smoothly from it, and there is nothing quite like the buzz from shipping a working application on time and relatively bug free.*

From an object-oriented standpoint, there are some great tools and techniques out there which can add a little fun to the design process, and which also make sure that we're heading along the right track all the time. The most commonly used tool used with Visual Basic design work is Microsoft's own **Visual Modeler**. By a strange quirk of marketing torment, Visual Modeler (VM) is currently only available to users of Visual Basic 6 Enterprise Edition, but I hope this will change because it's too good a tool for everybody else to miss out on.

> *Appendix A takes you through your first steps with using Visual Modeler, if you can get hold of this great tool.*

Incidentally, Visual Modeler is actually a cut-down version of a product known as **Rational Rose**, a free trial of which you can download from their web site (www.rational.com) if you have an internet connection. It's worth looking into, regardless of the edition of Visual Basic that you own.

Pencil and paper are all we truly need for our object-oriented design work, however. If you can't get hold of any of these products, or you don't like the sound of them, that's really not a problem: pencil, paper, and your wits are all we need to start designing!

Design Methodologies

In the computer press, in other books, and in the corporate development world, you'll probably hear quite a lot of talk about **Design Methodologies**. You may even see me mention it once or twice! This stuff can start to get pretty scary if you engage in any newsgroup discussions on the Internet, and you could very well be forgiven for thinking that a design methodology is something akin to a religious belief – something that should be defended with your life, honor and soul! Now I'll say this just once: no design methodology is worth your life. Okay?

> *Simply put, a design methodology is an approach that can be used to produce a design for an application. In fact, almost any approach to designing an application could realistically be called a Design Methodology. Beasts, aren't they?*

Each method (methodologies are often referred to as **methods** by hip and trendy programmer types, like me) has its plus and minus points, and each is geared towards developing an application in a specific way.

The ever popular **SSADM (Structured Systems Analysis and Design Methodology)**, for example, works by analyzing the flow of data through an application and inventing routines, classes, modules or whatever else to effect the operations that take place on that data.

Some methods are specifically geared towards object-oriented development. It's very important, however, to be quite clear about what we mean here by 'object-oriented development'. We've already looked at this in some earlier chapters, so I'll just invoke one of our earlier definitions:

> *An object-oriented approach to design and development involves creating classes and objects which model real-world entities, their data, and the operations that take place in that data.*

This definition is, of course, pivotal. SSADM, on the other hand, would have us focus on the data on an invoice, such as the customer details, the invoice lines themselves, the date, and the price - all pure data. SSADM would then look at the various processes that an invoice might go through in a typical business. Where did the invoice come from? How did it get into the system? Where does it go when it gets in the system? What is the eventual output of data from the invoice (a check perhaps)? Here's a typical sort of SSADM diagram:

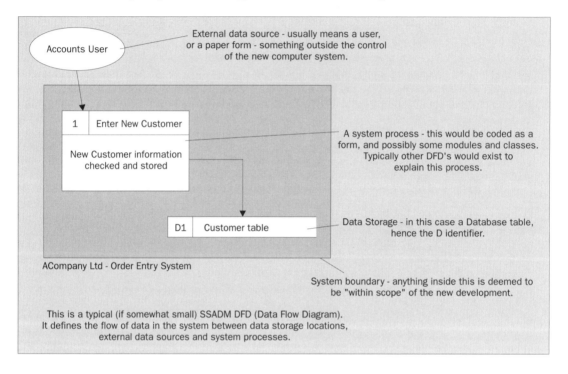

With an object-oriented approach, we'd have a single entity in the system known as an Invoice, its data exposed by properties, and the operations that act on an invoice exposed as methods (i.e. pay invoice, query invoice, enter invoice, etc.). The Invoice, here, is a black box with a clearly defined interface, and that's all we care about!

Typically, what goes on inside a black box does not concern a user of that box; but at a design level, the box will often reference other objects (products, order items, etc.), each with their own defined interfaces:

Contemplating this for a short while, it becomes very clear why we need to produce a design, or an object model of our application: the situation is just way too complicated to handle without one!

Each object that we define has methods and data. The data could easily be single instances of other objects, or perhaps even entire collections of other objects. In addition, those other objects have their own methods and data, but there is a strong possibility that some of the objects inherit functionality from yet more objects. Take it deeper and you need to define which objects represent our business area, which interact with the user (the user interface) and which are pure techie code type stuff for dealing with a database.

So there's a whole bucket and spade full of interaction here, and it's just not something any of us can easily keep in our head - or at least, not without introducing some flaws into our application at some point.

In addition, if we have some way of modeling all this stuff (graphically perhaps, or even in the form of simple English statements) it becomes a lot easier for us present our ideas to our clients. This is critical if we want to find out from our clients how well our intended design solves the problem before we start coding. And last but not least, a design model of what we're going to implement makes it easier for us to spot potential flaws in our understanding of the problem. So it's a no-brainer: design methodologies are our friends.

Object-Oriented Design

As I've already mentioned, there are a number of techniques out there which can help us in the design of an object-oriented application, and later in this chapter we're going to put a couple of them to good use.

Our discussion here will be a short introduction, simply a walkthrough of some of the most effective design methodologies available to us today. If you want to learn more, then take a look at any or all of these three titles - they're all on my bookshelf at the moment, and they're all from Wrox Press:

> **Professional Visual Basic 6.0 Business Objects**. This is a great book for those of you wanting to follow up on the topics we've introduced in this book. It looks at all the aspects of designing and deploying professional object-oriented applications in Visual Basic, from the perspective of a professional programmer. A great book to read after this one.

> **Instant UML**. This book is an excellent presentation of the full UML method, which we'll meet later in this chapter.

> **Clouds to Code**. This book doesn't specifically address Visual Basic, but it does provide a real-world case study of the total object-oriented development process.

My advice is to keep an eye on all the books on the shelf, but if you want to take the topics in this chapter and this book further, these books will guide you well.

Okay, now you know where we're at, let's start to explore some of the rather clever design techniques that are waiting for us out there.

Use Case Technique

The **use case technique** is one of the most popular tools for getting a handle on everything that needs to go into an application. It provides an easy way for us, as developers, to identify the objects that are in the real-world process we're trying to provide a solution for, and also the methods that take place on those objects. If we do it right, use case modeling can actually provide us with a very comprehensive set of requirements and specifications for a system, with surprisingly little effort.

The idea behind the use case technique is deceptively simple. Since most programmers are writing a system to fit in with, or replace, current real-world practices, the use case technique relies on identifying those practices and documenting them in a very straightforward manner.

For example, if we were writing a bank account administration system, we would write use case statements for processes such as opening an account, withdrawing money, and depositing money.

So what exactly does a use case statement look like? Well, let's look at making a withdrawal.

Use Case 1: Withdrawing Money

The customer is able to withdraw money by speaking with a bank teller. Provided there are enough funds in the account to meet the withdrawal amount, the bank teller will hand over the money.

The customer approaches the bank teller and tells the bank teller that he or she wants to withdraw money. The bank teller then asks for the account number and some proof of identity. The account number is fed into the computer and the bank teller waits for the account summary to appear. When it does the bank teller checks the available funds item on the account, and asks the customer how much money they wish to withdraw. If the requested amount is less than or equal to the amount of available funds, the bank teller will feed in the withdrawal amount to the computer and then remove the cash from a drawer and hand it to the customer. If the customer would like a withdrawal receipt, the bank teller prints one out and hands that to the customer with the money.

As you can see, a use case statement is nothing mystical or mysterious. It starts with a high level description of why the use case is needed and the process it describes, and then it goes ahead and describes that process in detail. The level of detail should be high enough for each individual step in the process to be identified, but not so detailed that we're actually approaching the complexity of program code. The use case statement should make no technical assumptions whatsoever; but it should leave the reader free to form their own conclusions about how they might implement it in code.

Something neat about that use case statement we just saw: it's fairly easy to identify some of the objects that are going to be in the final system just by identifying the **nouns** in the sentences. For instance, there's going to be a *Customer* object for sure, and maybe a *bank teller* object. There will almost certainly be an *Account* object, and we'll probably need to provide access, through properties or methods, to *Account* information about the *Customer*. This information is probably required so that the *Customer* can be identified by the *bank teller*. There will also be an *Account balance* and an amount of *Available funds* (which could be different to the balance if the customer has an agreed overdraft, for example).

The use case in this example is pretty high level, and would typically be used to write the **application specification.**

> *The application specification is a set of use cases that define every high-level process that a user of the application could do.*

Drill the application specification down into more detail, though, and we end up with a number of use cases covering such illustrious tasks as identifying a customer, grabbing account information, authorizing a withdrawal, and issuing cash. Each of these lower level use cases will eventually represent single methods in an object.

Use cases at the highest level typically represent one of the very first steps in application design, so they're frequently drawn up in collaboration with a panel of users. The analysts (that's us in this case) ask this panel of users lots of questions, and take notes about what the users require of the system. The analysts then go away and produce a set of high level use case statements that represent their understanding of the problem area. Now because these are at such a high level, they can easily be understood by our average user - who is then able to tell us, the analysts, whether or not we have an accurate grasp of the situation. By doing this, we dramatically reduce the chances of having to re-write our application, later on, due to a lack of understanding at this design stage.

UML

Use case statements help us to build up a picture of the objects, plus their methods, properties and events, within a real-world situation. All or some of these elements may be required in the final system. But now this is where something known as the **Unified Modeling Language** (**UML**) comes into the scheme of things, which can help us reach the next level of clarity and understanding about the system we're studying.

UML provides us with a graphical way to lay out the design of an object-oriented application. They say that a picture paints a thousand words, and UML is a fine example of this in practice. UML allows us to produce a diagram that, at a glance, will show the relationships between all the components in a system. More than that, though, a UML diagram also shows us where the use cases fit into the technical solution. This effectively provides us with a map between the real world and the world behind the screen.

UML is a huge subject, and there are plenty of books out there that cover the whole thing in-depth (I've already mentioned that **Instant UML** by Wrox Press is an excellent guide). However, you don't need to become a UML guru to be able to use it in your own designs, as we'll see later in this chapter. For those of you who can't wait until then, here's an example of what a typical UML model looks like - it does look a bit scary, but that's just part of its machismo, and we'll see what it all means later:

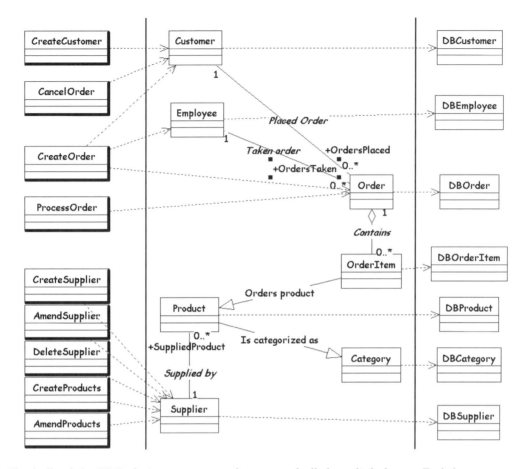

The bulk of the UML design process revolves around all those little boxes. Each box represents a form, a module, or a class. The different kinds of lines drawn between them indicate the relationships that exist between those elements. For instance, there may be situations where we need a collection of one class inside another - and there's a special kind of line in UML that we can draw between the two classes.

FYI **The diagram that we put together to indicate these relationships is called our object model.**

Later on in the design, these boxes are either drawn with lists of the properties and methods that each contains, or these properties and methods are listed on separate **object specification diagrams**, which are actually just boxes with lists of properties, methods and events written in them.

How we draw these models is up to us entirely. Most people use a pencil and a stack of paper. If we wanted to be more adventurous, we could represent each class in the model with a sticky note, and then attach cotton lines of different colors between the various sticky notes to show the relationships. This would give us the freedom to move things around until we were happy with our model and ready to draw the final design diagram. There is another alternative however.

Visual Modeler

I mentioned **Visual Modeler** earlier on in this chapter. The diagram you just saw was actually produced with it, but Visual Modeler is more than yet-another-drawing-program. Visual Modeler is a complete design tool that allows us to produce the full specification of any system we're working on by laying out the objects in the application and how they relate to each other, using the UML technique.

Appendix A gives you a full tour of Visual Modeler and how to use it.

Once our model is complete, we can just click a button and Visual Modeler will automatically generate a framework for our application, with all its objects plus their properties, methods and events in place. In fact, we can even use Visual Modeler to reverse engineer an existing application.

For reverse engineering, Visual Modeler analyzes the code in a Visual Basic project and produces a diagram with UML to matches what the application is currently doing.

Reverse engineering is great for those "after the fact" designs that we all do from time to time in response to the "Where's your documentation?" question that all development managers are trained to ask from birth.

As I mentioned earlier, Visual Modeler is currently only available to us if we have registered an Enterprise version of Visual Basic or Visual Studio on Microsoft's web site (www.microsoft.com). No doubt, with enough demand, Microsoft will make Visual Modeler available to everyone.

Since Visual Modeler isn't available to everyone, at the moment, we'll focus on designing applications with the pencil and paper in this chapter. But fear not - we have everything to gain from practicing these techniques by hand, and your newfound talents will transfer extremely well to any UML-based design tool should you manage to get hold of one.

The Northwind Problem

Remember our old friends, Northwind Traders? Well, they are back. Totally sick to the back teeth with the ineptitude of their current developers, they have turned to us (I guess they liked that ActiveX control we wrote for them a few chapters back) to create a complete product ordering and stock control system.

Northwind don't want any half measures either. Our brief is to automate every step of the Customer Order–Invoice-Dispatch cycle; but before we write a single line of Visual Basic code, Northwind would like us to produce a full object-oriented design of our project analysis to them.

Luckily for us, we've just heard about some neat tools called UML and Visual Modeler. Furthermore, we recently picked up some information about something that sounds just too cool, known as use case modeling. Armed with our newfound knowledge, we know just where to start.

Building a System Specification

A week or so has since passed, during which time we've been busy talking to people from Northwind about how they currently handle things. We also got ourselves a copy of the existing Access database, which they insist we must talk to with our new application. The biggest benefit of this phase, though, was the series of meetings that we held with the employees. These meetings gained us some valuable insights into the way Northwind works, and helped us produce a full set of use case statements describing the system and everything the employees get up to within it.

What do you mean you don't remember doing any of this? Just look at what you managed to produce:

1 - ORDERING A PRODUCT
Northwind maintains a catalogue of products, which is distributed to existing customers. The customers may then call sales representatives to place an order, using the product IDs in the catalogue.

The customer calls a sales representative and asks to place an order. The rep starts a new order form and enters his or her employee ID at the top, along with the customer ID and date.

The customer then lists the product IDs required, and the quantity of each. For each ID, the employee checks the stock sheet to determine if the product is in stock, and advises the customer if it is or is not, allowing them to change their mind. The customer is also told if any items are now discontinued, although they may still be in stock. If a product requested is discontinued, then the rep has to check other outstanding orders to ensure that it isn't already due to be dispatched - and lets the customer know.

When all of the product IDs have been entered, the customer chooses a preferred shipping company from a list that the representative gives. The rep enters the shipping company's ID on to the order sheet, and informs the customer of the total cost and shipping cost. The employee also enters the "required by" date on to the order, and hangs up the phone.

The order form is then sent to the warehouse for dispatch. An order acknowledgement sheet is produced and dispatched to the customer.

2 - PROCESSING AN ORDER
The warehouse person sorts the order sheets into ascending "required by" date order and then takes the first one.

The employee checks the items on the order against the stock sheets to ensure that all items required are in stock. If they are not, then the order sheet is passed across to the re-stock pile for processing.

The employee walks around the warehouse hunting for each item on the order. When each is found, the required quantity is removed from stock. If the stock hits the re-order level, then the amount ordered for re-stocking is equal to the amount necessary to fully re-stock the bin from the current level, but only if the re-ordering hasn't already been accomplished.

The employee then fills out the shipping details on the order, produces a shipping label, and attaches it to the box containing the ordered goods - ready for shipping.

3 - CANCELING AN ORDER

There are times when a customer will cancel their order in whole or in part. This is allowed so long as the order has not been processed and shipped. The customer calls a sales representative and gives them the customer ID. The rep then pulls out the customer's file to see a list of unprocessed orders. Then the customer gives the rep the order number, or product ID to be canceled.

If the customer gives an order number, then the order is destroyed in its entirety. If the customer gives a product ID number, then the product ordered is removed from the order. The rep then checks to see if the product has been ordered from a supplier. If it has, then the product order sheet is located and the amount on order is adjusted to reflect the canceled order. The rep cannot reduce the units on order to the point where the re-order level is compromised.

An order cancellation sheet is then produced and dispatched to the customer.

4 - STARTING A NEW CUSTOMER

New customers frequently call wanting to place an order. Before they can do this, however, they need to be registered with the system as customers.

The customer rings a rep and asks to start a new account. The rep then brings out a customer entry form and takes down the customer details. The rep then takes the customer's order, thanks the customer and hangs up, before producing a "Welcome to Northwind" letter and dispatching it to the customer with a catalogue of goods.

5 - ADDING SUPPLIERS

New suppliers can be added as a result of a sales call from the supplier, or because of a customer request. In both cases though, the new supplier needs to be contacted to confirm that they are able to supply Northwind with products - before the supplier details can be logged into the system. The supplier will also be required to send a product catalogue.

The clerk gets a new supplier file and fills out the supplier details with those supplied. The clerk will also bring up the company's web page (if they have one) on his or her computer to verify that the supplier exists; the clerk will attempt to verify the details that they have on the supplier.

The product sheets at this time will be blank, but since they are a part of the supplier's file, they are clearly on display to the clerk entering the supplier information.

6 - AMENDING A SUPPLIER

Suppliers frequently change address or other details and will normally let us know by a phone call or written letter. When that happens, the supplier's details on file need to be changed.

The clerk sorts through the supplier names in the filing cabinet until he or she locates the one required. The clerk then pulls out the file and amends the details with those just supplied.

7 - REMOVING A SUPPLIER

When a supplier goes out of business, or refuses to deal with Northwind any more, then future orders must not be allowed to go to the supplier, although its details should be maintained on the system for legal purposes.

The clerk searches through the names of suppliers in the system until he or she finds the one they want. They then stamp "DELETED" on the supplier's file and go through the product sheets of the supplier marking all the products discontinued.

8 - ADDING PRODUCTS

Suppliers will occasionally send through details of new additions to their product line, but more often than not the clerk will need to browse through updated catalogues to determine what the new products are, and add them to supplier product lists.

The clerk hunts for the supplier file based on the supplier's name, and when the clerk finds it, he or she grabs it and extracts the list of products from it. The clerk then searches for the product ID, and if the clerk finds that product ID he or she checks the details, and if necessary amends them.

If the clerk does not find the product ID, then he or she fills out a new product form, selecting a category for the product from one of the preset categories - and then places the product form into the file.

9 - AMENDING PRODUCTS

Suppliers occasionally amend the details of their product lines, with changes covering such things as a change of price and change of description. Changes to the product code need to be entered into the system as new products, and the old product line discontinued.

The clerk hunts for the supplier's file, based on the supplier's name, and when he or she finds it pulls out the product list.

When the clerk has found the product sheet for the product in question, he or she checks that the two codes match. IF they do not match then the old product is marked as discontinued, with a note pointing to the new one. For all other types of change, the original product sheet is amended to hold the new details.

That was just too easy! All we had to do was sit down with each department, find out exactly what went on, and write it down in simple English in order to build up a set of **requirements use case statements**. Now, as inevitably happens when we sit down with a group of users, some of the statements became a little tainted by the user's desires for new features to be included in the final product; but on the whole, we did a good job. The use case statements and the processes that they contain also happen to fit quite nicely with the existing Access nightmare that they passed to us.

You feel a warm glow, a buzz: we now have sufficient materials to move into some hardcore design.

Specification Refinement

With the requirements use case statements above, we now have what are known as **system requirements**. The use case statements that we got hold of represent a very high level view of what goes on at Northwind, and these are good enough to describe the system from a general everyday point of view. The next step is to produce **functional use case statements**.

Typically, system requirements represent more than one process. Adding a product to the system, for example, would require:

- Finding a supplier for the product
- Finding that supplier's list of products
- Searching for the product ID being added
- Updating existing products matching that ID
- Creating new products if there are no matching IDs

Functional use case statements describe each of these sub-processes in the same way that the system requirements describe each high-level process.

The steps we take to build up a complete set of functional use cases are identical to those for producing high-level statements, but with the obvious difference that the smaller the scope of each functional use case statement, the closer it will be to something that could be written in code. This process is also known as **specification refinement**.

Because the process of producing these more detailed functional use case statements is very similar to producing the high-level ones, but rather more in-depth, we aren't going to see that process here. I'm sure you get the general idea by now, and besides, Northwind is a simple enough operation that we can actually start to produce the design model with the case statements we already have. In the real world, though, since the problems we'll be solving will most likely be a great deal more complex than Northwind, it's usually essential to drill down into those functional use case statements.

Starting with UML

We're now ready to use UML to declare an object model. The first stage is to identify the objects themselves that are going to be in the system.

> *It's worth nothing that, as always, there is some overlap between the terms object and class. In the case of UML, we design the system from a working point of view, so everything we deal with is an object. When we come to write code from the object model, however, we will obviously turn each object into a class module in Visual Basic.*

So, how do we identify the objects that should be in the model? And once those objects are identified, how do we start to produce an object model with UML?

The simplest way is to pore over the use case statements for a while and produce a list of all the nouns. With a little time, and common sense, we should end up with a list of objects that we can start to draw on to a sheet of paper. This will be the beginning of our UML model.

From our use case statements, we have the following objects:

Product	Customer	OrderItem
Category	Employee	Supplier
Order		

Drawing these is simple enough. The symbol in UML for an object looks like this:

Notice how this is split into three parts. The top part is where we write the name of the object. The bottom two parts will hold the object's properties and methods.

If we're working with pencil and paper then it's actually quite a common practice not to write property and method lists in the box - since we just end up spending way too much time erasing the object and redrawing it in order to fit them all in! A much better plan is to have a separate sheet of paper for each object, and list the properties and methods of the objects on that. With this method, we can keep the high level diagrams quite tidy. You'll see what I mean in a moment.

Designing the Model - Step 1

So, having identified the objects that are going to be in the model, the next step is to actually draw them out. If you're following on, draw your objects on to the page so that your model looks like this (yes, I'm cheating and using a UML design tool instead of pencil and paper):

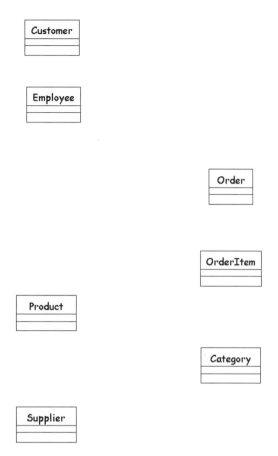

I've laid out the objects like this so that when we start to draw in the lines for the relationships, the model won't grow too confusing. In addition, there are still some other boxes to draw in.

Introducing Logical Tiers

UML is most often used in a multi-tier approach to design and development. What this means is that the model is produced from the standpoint that the application should be split into chunks, with each chunk dealing with a particular technical area. Most often, a three-tier approach is taken, with the UML diagram split into these logical tiers:

User Services   **Business Services**   **Data Services**

Confused? Okay, if we think of an application as three distinct parts joined together (user interface, business rules, and data access - three logical, thematic divisions), then we can get some really neat benefits in our application, in terms of maintenance, design, and extensibility. The idea behind it all is simple.

> *Make sure that any code you write references only one tier in the application. This way, you can easily break the application into separate executable portions, which can be reused by other parts of this or other applications. These executables can be implemented as ActiveX servers - which we know all about now from our earlier explorations into ActiveX.*

In addition, should the need arise to change an underlying technology (such as the database we're using) then we know that the changes to code will only affect one small group of objects in a particular tier.

The objects that we've drawn so far represent Business Services, in that they each represent something that the business deals with or produces as a matter of daily routine. The code in these objects should know nothing about the user interface of the application, and they should be totally free of any knowledge about the database. Instead, the user interface will use instances of these objects in order to display what it needs, and feed user input into the system. The business objects, in turn, will use instances of objects in the Data Services layer to get at their data, without having to rely on specific database, table, and field names.

In this way, the user interface could change without ever having an impact on the underlying way in which the application dealt with the business. The database could also be replaced with any new database that came along, without ever affecting the rest of the system. So long as the interface to the data services objects remains intact, then the rest of the code will compile and run fine. Neat isn't it?

> *There is, in fact, a lot more to these logical tiers within our applications than I have set out here. This is a fascinating and challenging area that all professional programmers today need to explore and form an opinion about. The follow on book to this one, Professional Business Objects with Visual Basic 6.0, contains a much fuller discussion of these tiers. We know all we need to know about logical tiers within our applications at this stage, so we're ready to move on to the next step in our design process.*

Designing the Model - Step 2

We can represent the three tiers in our diagrams by just drawing vertical lines down the page, dividing it into three chunks:

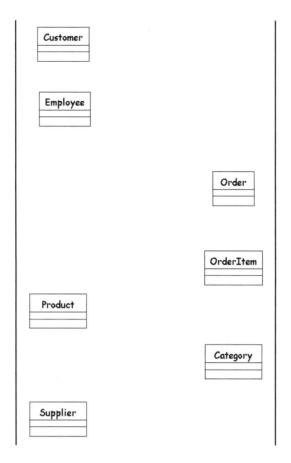

Hang on a minute. If the objects we have drawn represent the business services, then what about those other services? Let's look at the user interface first.

Modeling a User Interface

The most dynamic part of an application, during development, is the user interface. Users inevitably change their minds as to how things should look and behave on screen, and users have a nasty habit of forcing us lowly programmers to bend to their every graphical whim. For this reason, it's pretty tough to model the user interface, even at a form level.

We could go ahead and drop symbols of forms into our model - to represent Adding a product, Amending a product, and Deleting a product. It wouldn't be unheard of, at that point, for the user to come along and ask that all the forms be merged into just one multi-function form.

Instead, we use symbols called **Utility Modules** in UML to represent each of the high-level use cases. At coding time, all that needs to be done is to connect the forms themselves to the appropriate utility modules, which in turn make use of the business services objects, which in turn use the data services objects. In this way the forms are always totally detached from the rest of the system, and make use of the use cases themselves (in code form) to get their work done. The use cases shouldn't change, of course, unless the business goes through a major restructuring operation.

The symbol for a utility module looks like this; it's very similar to the symbol for a normal object in fact (who said UML was hard?).

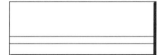

Note that the symbol is highlighted by a shadow to the right and below the symbol. This is how to distinguish it from the normal object.

Just as before, it's split into three parts, with the top part containing the name of the module (in this case the name of our high-level use case statements) and the bottom two segments containing lists of the properties and methods of the module.

Designing the Model - Step 3

Go ahead and drop utility modules on to our diagram - so that it looks like this now:

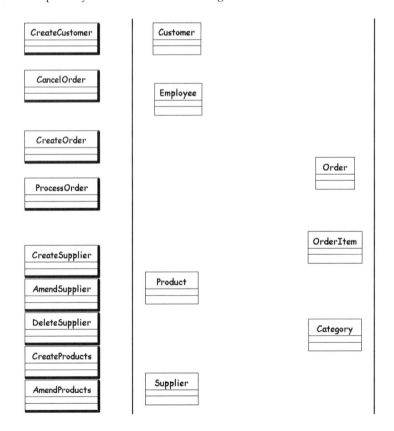

Data Services

Okay, so that sorted out the user interface for our diagram. What about those data services? We have the utility modules, which are eventually going to wrap up the functionality of the use cases we produced, and we have the objects themselves that represent the core of the business area that the application is supposed to support.

The **data services**, as their name implies, deal solely with the database and any other low level interfacing, such as serial ports. Each instance of a data service typically represents a single record in the database, but also provides methods and such like, to update and work with the rest - en masse, if necessary. Therefore, we're going to use one data object per table that we're dealing with.

Designing the Model - Step 4

In our case, all this equates to one data object per business object, so there is nothing too complex there. Drop some more objects into your paper model, in the data services column, so that it now looks like this.

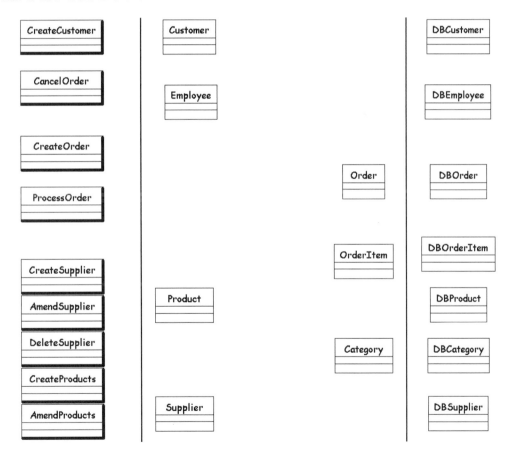

Now we have all our objects in our model. Let's just recap those objects:

> **Business objects.** The business objects are produced by scanning the use case statements for nouns. We need to use common sense here - if our use cases say something like "The sales person then gets the product out of the box to check it" that doesn't necessarily mean that we should put a "box" object into our model.

> **User services.** The user services typically relate on a one-to-one basis with the high-level use cases themselves. When we have code in them later, to deal with the methods and properties in the business and data services objects, we can simply attach the real user interface to these modules. We can then retain a system whose functionality is totally independent of any single user interface implementation, which is very cool.

> **Data services**. The data service objects typically relate on a one-to-one basis with the tables in the database, or at least with the queries that we'll use to get data in and out of whatever database we're using.

Let's look at how to draw in the relationships between objects in these three layers.

Dependencies

The first type of relationship that we need to be aware of is the **dependency** relationship.

 In a dependency, one object is dependent upon the methods and/or properties of another object in order to do its job.

For example, our Create Supplier use case is dependent upon the services of a *Supplier* object. This doesn't necessarily mean that the *CreateSupplier* module will have a permanent instance of the *Supplier* object available at all times – it could create one as needed; but it does mean that without the *Supplier* object the *CreateSupplier* module couldn't do its job.

In UML a dependency relationship is displayed as a dashed line drawn between two objects; the direction of the line indicates which object is dependent upon the other. The following diagram presents a dependency relationship between our *Customer* and a *CreateCustomer* module; and indeed, our *Customer* object is dependent upon the *CreateCustomer* module that will of course create it:

Designing the Model - Step 5

In our model, then, it's fairly easy to deduce that every business object is dependent on its data services counterpart in order to work. So, go ahead and draw some dashed lines in to show this, just like in my diagram:

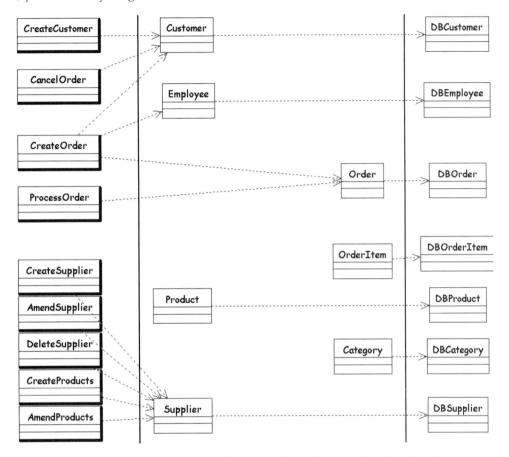

Notice how most of the user-services modules are dependent on the *Supplier* object, even though the supplier would not appear to be the center of Northwind's world. The reason for this is actually quite simple. Later on, when we put more relationships in, you'll see that it's actually the *Supplier* that makes available a list of its own products, and it is in relation to a *Supplier* that we amend, add and delete products; we do not work with a product object on its own.

Notice, also, how placing an order doesn't mean that there is a dependency on a product. The reason behind this is that the *Order* object provides access to *OrderItem* objects, which is another relationship altogether that we're going to draw in a short while. Each *OrderItem* in the system relates to a single product, so we can use an *Order* as a front end to the products that it references. This does make sense, since, when we place an order in the real world, we fill out an order sheet, and for each item entered on the sheet we relate it to a product at that point. Bear with me, it will become clearer in a minute.

Generalizations

This term sounds horrendous doesn't it? In Visual Basic terms, having a generalization relationship between two objects means that one object implements the other's interface, and can be expected to provide the same functionality as a result. Sounds very familiar, doesn't it!

> *In the more general world of object-oriented methodologies, generalization is also known as 'inheritance', 'sub-classing', or 'sub-typing'. Often, the generalization relationship is described as an "is-a" relationship between the two objects or classes. You should note that generalization is really a relationship between the classes of the objects.*

When a generalization is drawn, it's basically nothing more than a straight line with a solid arrowhead on the end (most people call them arrows since I guess there is nothing more embarrassing than being shot in the behind with a generalization):

The object that is pointed to is the one providing the interface; the object being pointed from is therefore a sub-type of the object being pointed at.

In the case of Northwind, this could work quite well. Looking at the diagram, each *Product* belongs to a category of products, so it makes sense to have the *Product* expose the *Category* object's interface as well, and incorporate an instance of its related category.

Furthermore, at Northwind each *OrderItem* could relate to a single product in the database; the *OrderItem* line would thus relate to a *Product*, showing how many of it were ordered. The *Product* itself shows its price and other information. The generalization would work quite well in this instance, showing that an *OrderItem* should expose the same interface as a *Product*. Users of an *OrderItem* object would then be able to get at all the information they needed about its associated product, because the *OrderItem* would be exposing the *Product* interface and thus contain the related instance of the *Product* object.

Designing the Model - Step 6

If we draw both of the generalizations that we've been discussing together in our diagram, we should end up with something like this:

Notice the words in the middle of the relationship lines? A picture paints a thousand words, but words and pictures are even better. It's quite a common practice to write the purpose of the relationship over the line to show exactly why the relationship is there in the first place. These words often end up being verbs about the various objects that they connect.

Associations

The next type of UML relationship that we'll define is a **general association**.

 In an association one object contains references to a set of other objects. The association relationship is best understood as a relationship between objects of the various classes.

This indicates that one object is a member of another, or perhaps part of a collection in another; but that's as far as it goes. There is no sharing of interfaces here, or anything even half as emotional - these two are just good friends.

Designing the Model - Step 7

Although it's one of the simplest types of relationship, from a conceptual point of view, explaining how to draw an association it is best done by demonstration:

Okay, let's explain what's going on here. The association is drawn as a straight line between the two objects and gets a name just as before. That's the simple part.

There's actually quite a lot being described here. First, note that there are two labels attached to the association line drawn between the two objects. These labels represent the name of the association as viewed from one end or the other. In this particular notation, the italicized name *Supplied by* refers to the association **from** Product **to** Supplier, while the non-italicized name with the "+" (+SuppliedProduct) refers to the association **from** Supplier **to** Product. Therefore, we can actually read the diagram - it's saying: "A Product is Supplied by a Supplier," and "A Supplier provides a SuppliedProduct Product." This last phrase doesn't roll off the tongue, but you get the idea.

In addition, we can improve the description by taking into account the **multiplicity** (actually multiplicities) of the association. These are the notations of 1 near the Supplier end of the association, and the more interesting 0..* near the Product end of the association.

> *The multiplicity of an association simply indicates how many of one object can be related to the other object through the same association. We always use the number/ notation closest to the object to characterize how that object relates to the other object.*

Therefore, the 1 near the Supplier object in the diagram means that we can say right off: "A Product is Supplied by **exactly one** Supplier." In the other direction, we read "0..*" to mean **0 to many**. Therefore, we can also read the diagram in the other direction of the association as: "A Supplier has **0 to many** Products as SuppliedProducts."

> *By the way, it is possible to be more specific, using notation such as **0..5** to represent that in an association there are none through 5 possible connections, but no more. The * in the example simply indicates **any** number.*

To recap: any association between two objects can thus be viewed from one end or the other, and there may be a name and a multiplicity assigned to the relationship in each direction.

There are a couple of other places where the Association relationship is useful in our model. The relationship between *Customer* and *Order*, for example, as well as the relationship between *Employee* and *Order*. It would be handy to be able to bring up a *Customer* and have a collection attached of all the *Order*s they had placed; and equally handy to be able to instantiate an *Employee* to see all the *Order*s he or she had taken.

Designing the Model - Step 8

Draw in these relationships in the same way we did with *Supplier* and *Product*, and our diagram should end up looking like this:

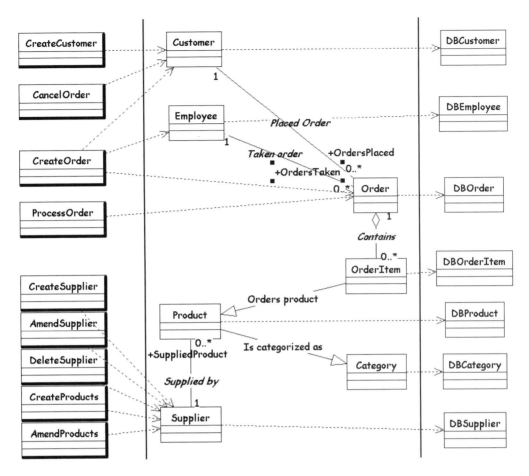

In this case, the *Customer* object will contain a collection of orders called *PlacedOrders*, while the *Employee* will have its own orders collection called *TakenOrders*. This approach of describing relationship is quite obvious once you get the hang of it, but totally obscure until that point (Windows was the same way for many people when it first came out).

Aggregation Relationships

The final type of relationship that we're interested in for now is the **aggregation** relationship. Aggregation is actually rather similar to the normal association relationship in many ways; we'll consider the differences now.

> *Aggregation intimately binds together objects so that one does not exist without the other. General associations relate objects that exist on their own outside the relationship, so whereas a general association has references to other objects, an aggregate is itself a container for other objects.*

An aggregation relationship can be read as 'consists of' or 'is made of'.

In our model, the relationship between an *Order* and the *OrderItems* is an aggregation, since an *Order* should contain a collection of *OrderItems* objects; furthermore, without anything in that collection of *OrderItems*, the *Order* object is basically meaningless.

Graphically, the difference between aggregate relationships and normal relationships is that for an aggregation relationship the end of the solid line is drawn with a diamond on it.

Designing the Model - Step 9

Draw our aggregate relationship between *Order* and *OrderItems* like this:

The diamond goes on the *Order* end in this case, indicating that an *Order* is made of *OrderItems*.

Summary

So there you have it, our completed UML model. We haven't covered everything there is to know about UML and drawing up a design model, but we've really got our heads into the Northwind situation by going ahead and building this model of what's going on. Those use cases were instrumental to this development, of course, but it's really our diagram now that will lead us forward, and help us get our heads around the Northwind scenario. I have full confidence that with a design diagram like this, we can move forward confidently to the implementation phase of our current work with Northwind.

We'll probably find ourselves coming back time and time again to this master design diagram. It is our spatial coordinates, it is our bearings, as we navigate through the maze of object interactions at Northwind. We'd be lost without this diagram, in all truth. Long live object-oriented design!

Okay, we haven't touched on properties and methods yet, but we'll cover those in quite some detail in the next chapter, when we actually get around to implementing the design.

In this chapter you have learned about:

- Design methodologies
- Use case techniques
- UML and a set of relationship diagrams
- How to build a system specification
- How to refine that system specification
- How to use UML to define objects and the relationships between them

Most essentially, however, you've learned how we can take hold of a new programming problem and translate it into a working set of analysis, and a working design diagram, that any professional programmer could take forward to the implementation phase of their application.

Let's head towards that implementation phase ourselves now, which is just waiting to happen in the next chapter. We'll carry forward the great stuff we've developed here.

Why Not Try....

1   Why isn't it a great idea to just start coding a Visual Basic Project?

2   Several popular Design methodologies were discussed in the chapter. What is the methodology that is Data Centric?

3   There are three Object Oriented Design methodologies mentioned in the chapter. Briefly discuss each one.

4   Summarize the Design Process used in Chapter 7 to solve the Northwind 'problem'.

6

Coding Objects to Our Design

Overview

In the last chapter, our good relations with the people at Northwind paid dividends, and we managed to establish an object design model for the application they've asked us to write. The question is, now we've got our working design, what exactly do we do with it? How do we move forwards from our object design to create the application itself? Well, it's the most natural thing in the world, but if you're not sure about the answer to that question then you're reading the right chapter.

Now we did take something of a shortcut in the last chapter, since we needed to gather as much information on OO design and UML as possible. In an ideal world, we would have spent weeks inserting the various methods and properties into the design model, as well as producing full requirements and functional use case statements. At the end of the day though, that would still have left us with the keynote question for this chapter: what now?

The obvious answer is: let's code! let's fire up Visual Basic and get typing! However, coding an application to fit a design requires a slightly different way of working. You see, our design imposes a structure upon our application, and if we've got the design right, this structure will benefit our project right across the board. Our gleaming new object model, if coded properly, brings with it the benefits of easy maintenance, easy expansion, and of course good clear development throughout. Realizing these benefits, though, does require that we remain true and aware to exactly what our design model requires us to do. Now that last bit requires a little extra effort from us - but it means our coding will be more effective, more logical, more professional.

So, in this chapter, we start out carefully and thoughtfully on the coding side of things. We must not lose sight of our design and what it asks of us as programmers. It's all too easy, you see, to take a shortcut here, employ a timesaver there, and before we know it we're way off track from our original design. Remember that example of building a house that we used as an analogy to good program design? Well now we're ready to build, and we must try to act like master builders.

Once again, there isn't really enough space in a single chapter to cover everything that we would ever want to put into the Northwind application. But that really isn't a problem. We'll tackle just one particular area of the application: the Suppliers object and its related forms and data classes. This way, we'll actually get the best of both worlds: we'll avoid having to step through every piece of Northwind's huge application, and at the same time we'll gain plenty of insight into where our design is taking us and what it means to actually write code according to that design.

So treat this as a glimpse of high end object-oriented programming. It's going to be quite hard work, and the code creation will at times seem uphill - but you'll see a great application being born, and you'll be right in there with me as we reach the crest of the hill and things start to get easier. You see, one of the great things about object-oriented programming is that once our objects are set up and working, things start to snowball: object relations proliferate, and modeling our real-world scenario starts to get easier. I hope you'll also appreciate how clean and carefully thought out the genesis of this application becomes - this is principled programming, and we've heading in the direction that will sooner or later lead us to professional programming.

In this chapter you will learn about:

- Implementing code from an object design model
- Cohesion and coupling in relation to object programming
- Coupling and cohesion in more detail
- Creating a Visual Basic Supermodel
- Building a framework with relationships, properties and methods
- Coding the relationships defined in UML
- Fleshing out code using an object-oriented approach
- Implementing object relations in object-oriented programming

Enough preliminaries, let's get going with the application.

The Rules

Rules? Yes - without a set of simple rules to follow we would soon find ourselves writing code that actually pulls wayward of the design model we've produced. There's a very fine and intricate set of relationships in there, between the various objects in our model. It's our job now to make sure that those relationships transfer properly into the code of our application. Rather laughably (but earnestly importantly), it's also our job to make sure that we don't write code that in one foul swoop could wipe out the benefits of the whole design process. You might think that's unlikely, but actually it's real easy.

There are two golden rules that I want to share with you, and they can be summed up in just two words: **coupling** and **cohesion**.

We've come across both these terms already in the book, but it's here at last that we're really going to see what they mean in terms of code.

> *Coupling refers to an object's dependency upon any specific application for its survival.*

For example, if we went ahead and produced a `Supplier` class that could not function without the help of two forms in the application itself, then we would say that the object was **tightly coupled** to the application. If we removed the class from the application and dropped it into another one, it probably wouldn't work, given its dependency on those two forms. What we're aiming for is a set of classes that are **loosely coupled**, classes that we can copy into other projects and make use of without a hitch.

Back to our good old black box idea. Remember our Television example? A Television is a fairly loosely coupled object, since we can easily transport it from room to room in our house, plug it in and use it. It is not dependent on the color of our carpets, and it really doesn't care whether or not the cooker is on. If it did, then it would be tightly coupled and nowhere near as popular as it is today. The coupling rule for objects in the real world is a very clear indication of how useful that object may be.

RULE 1: The more loosely coupled an object in the real world is to the environment around it, the more popular it will be. This is because more and more people will be able to buy that object and plug it into their own customized environments.

An Apartment, on the other hand, is an example of a tightly coupled object. It's firmly attached to a building, and most probably to one or two surrounding apartments. Attempt to remove it and you'll do irreparable damage to the building, the other apartments and your standing in the community. When you write object code, produce Televisions not Apartments.

Cohesion is just as important as coupling, and my second golden rule is all about cohesion. Let's establish a quick definition of cohesion right now:

> *Cohesion refers to how specialized an object is.*

Our Television, for example, is a strongly cohesive object. A Television is designed to do just one thing, and to do it well. It receives TV signals via an antenna or a cable, decodes the signals and displays them on a screen. A combined TV, video, and hi-fi unit, on the other hand, is not a strongly cohesive object. It performs more than one task. Here's my second golden rule:

RULE 2: Objects that do more than one task (weakly cohesive) rarely do any of the tasks as well as dedicated (strongly cohesive) objects.

This rule may explain why weakly cohesive objects are not as successful in the marketplace as highly cohesive objects.

Coupling and Cohesion in Design

Strongly cohesive, loosely coupled objects are a good thing to aim for - whether we have a form design for our application or not. However, with a UML design, coupling and cohesion also take on some new facets. Remember: our UML design is typically broken down into three distinct **logical tiers**, with objects in each tier being said to belong to user services, business services and data services.

Now, in order for our application to work, certain objects need to know about other objects - obviously enough. But it's tempting, when we first see this in an object model, and we hear the words cohesion and coupling ringing in our heads, to think the whole idea of having one object know about another object is contradictory to writing good re-useable code. How dare objects commit themselves to each other like that, we think to ourselves - as we start to get puritanical about these things.

Let's just stay cool about this for a moment. An Invoice is an object, and it contains items: lines on the Invoice that relate to products or services. Each of these Invoice items is an object in its own right, with or without an Invoice. However, an Invoice without Invoice lines is simply a printout of someone's name and address. So, for this example, and hundreds like it, we need to produce an object to manage the Invoice itself, and that object needs to be able to talk to a set of Invoice item objects. These item objects should be strongly cohesive, loosely coupled objects, which do nothing but provide information that their container (an Invoice) can use. In this instance, then, having one object know about and deal with another object is actually essential to keeping the first object cohesive. Now this is getting profound, don't you think?

Suppose we wrote an Invoicing class, for example, that knew about Invoice items, and thus was able to deal with the unit price of an item, available stock, and so on. Our Invoice object would be moving away from the world of invoices and into the world of stock management. It would no longer be cohesive. Profounder still.

However, those three tiers in our object model add another figure into the equation. When we're developing a **multi-tier** application, cohesion and coupling extend to the tiers as a whole. Now, first let me repeat that; and then let me explain.

> *When we're developing a multi-tier application, cohesion and coupling extend to the tier as a whole.*

In our design model, we have a Suppliers object in the business services tier. What this means is that we're going to produce a class that contains all the code to deal with a Supplier from a business standpoint. This class will contain methods to create a new Supplier, delete a current Supplier, change information on a Supplier, and provide us with properties that relate to a particular Supplier. The class provides everything someone in a business would need to know and deal with, to work with Suppliers. Should our Suppliers object know how to get at a supplier record in the Access database though?

It's tempting to answer yes. After all, how can we put properties into the business object to expose the supplier's name and address, unless it has access to the underlying database to get at that data? Think about this though. What happens when, a year from now, Northwind switches over to a SQL Server format database? If we were to code an all-encompassing Supplier object that could read and write Supplier data to a database, as well as provide all the code to implement the business rules that deal with a Supplier, then we would now find ourselves in the worrying position of having to change code in an object that is vital to the business.

This is a bad thing, and if you take a step back from it for a second, it's pretty easy to see that the object would not be cohesive, and that it would be tied to a specific format of database. Oops, we just broke the two most important rules. However, if we separate all the functionality that deals with databases out into a different batch of objects, arranging for them to live in the data services tier of our model, then wonderful things will start to happen in our lives. Take a look at this scenario.

The Supplier object in the business services tier talks to its counterpart in the data services tier to actually read and write to the underlying database. The Supplier object then knows nothing about, nor does it care about, database formats, SQL queries, and so on. **The Supplier object is now cohesive to the tier in which it lives.**

In addition, because the data access stuff is hidden away in a separate object, our original supplier object is now an independent, loosely coupled entity. This is most excellent - we're no longer breaking any rules, so I am happy.

Want to change from an Access database to a SQL Server one? Go ahead - you'll need to re-code the data services object, but the vital business services object need not change at all. Think of the massive amount of time that we're going to save just testing this. The business rules didn't change, only the database stuff did. We just need to test that the new database code works, and that the interface the new database object exposes works identically to its predecessor.

> *Let me put this all together into one statement: writing to an object model widens the scope of the cohesion and coupling. We therefore need to produce objects that are cohesive to their task, as well as to their logical tier.*
>
> *In addition, our objects need to be loosely coupled between logical tiers, in that an object in the user tier wouldn't implement business rules, and an object in the business tier wouldn't contain database code.*
>
> *Sound advice, meant well.*

Where Do We Start?

Have I still not answered that question? At the end of the day, it's really just a case of personal preference. Sorry to disappoint you, but the simple truth is that some people like to start with the business rules, while others prefer to start at the bottom, with the data services, and work their way up. In our case, we're going to start right at the top, with the relationships in the model. We'll then move into the business services tier.

A Visual Basic Supermodel

Before you do anything else, though, we need to invent our very own **supermodel**. This isn't as complex as it sounds - a Visual Basic supermodel, like its real-world counterpart, is an incredibly skinny thing that looks good but serves no easily definable purpose.

Try It Out - Creating a Visual Basic Supermodel

1 Start up Visual Basic and create a new project. When the default project appears, with its default blank form inside it, remove the form so that we have a blank, vague looking project.

Next up, we're going to add a class for each of the objects in the business and data services parts of our model. We'll also need standard modules to implement each of the use cases that we're writing code for. As we discussed, at the beginning of this chapter, we aren't going to develop every single facet of what could be a huge application in this chapter. You'd get bored, and anyway, the sheer bulk of the discussion would obscure some of the key points I'm trying to make in this chapter.

2 So, add fourteen class modules into our project (I've always wanted to say something like that) and name them `clsCustomer`, `clsDBCustomer`, `clsEmployee`, `clsDBEmployee`, `clsOrder`, `clsDBOrder`, `clsOrderItem`, `clsDBOrderItem`, `clsSupplier`, `clsDBSupplier`, `clsProduct`, `clsDBProduct`, `clsCategory`, `clsDBCategory`. Each of these classes maps directly to an object in either the business services tier or the data services tier in our model.

3 Next, add nine standard code modules to the project, naming them `modAmendProducts`, `modAmendSupplier`, `modCancelOrder`, `modCreateCustomer`, `modCreateOrder`, `modCreateProducts`, `modCreateSupplier`, `modDeleteSupplier` and `modProcessOrder`. One for each use case statement that we developed, in fact.

4 With that done, save this Northwind project as it stands, and you should find that your Project explorer now looks something like this:

How It Works

Granted, this does no work, in the traditional sense! It was very tempting to just go ahead and dump a form or two into the project to represent the user services, but we didn't. Recall our discussion about cohesion and coupling earlier in the chapter - everything should be as independent from everything else as is humanly possible (without writing code that is just plain weird of course). Now if we were to go ahead and drop some forms into the project at this point, and later put some code into those forms to handle everything from creating a supplier, to placing an order, then we'd be breaking our design and limiting the system already!

You don't believe me? If the user decided that they didn't like one of our forms, or that they would like a couple of our forms combined, then we'd have to start moving application logic around, just to satisfy a user interface requirement. That's not the best situation to find ourselves in - it's kind of like having to re-wire our house every time someone blows a light bulb.

Instead of writing code directly on to any forms, and blowing the whole model, we're going to use normal code modules.

Each module in the user services part of the model actually relates to a single use case statement. So we have modules there to create a supplier, amend a supplier, and so on. In code terms, each of these use case statements would actually have to be broken down into a number of distinct routines, just like our use case statements should have been broken down into more defined statements. It would be up to each of these routines, which deal with the methods and properties of the objects in the business services tier, to actually get something done. In addition, though, any forms in the application should do little more than connect to these routines, in response to user events on the form:

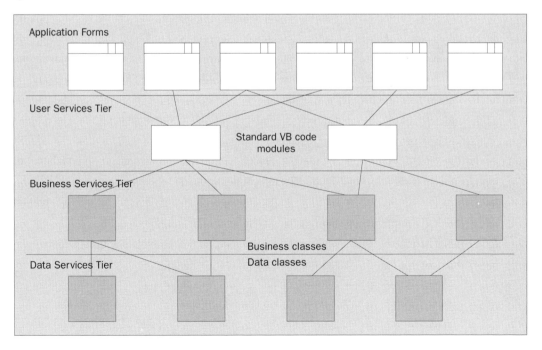

Sounds like a lot of hassle? Well I give you my word: it will save us in the end. Imagine that we had a form for creating a Supplier and another for amending Supplier information. Each of these forms did very little other than call the appropriate use case module's subroutines and functions. Now, what do you think would happen if we were asked to change the project so that the functionality encompassed by our two forms was moved into just one form? In this example, very little. The actual code of the application, the core logic which makes it do what it does, would not change. Only the forms would change. A new form would be created with new controls, new layout, and so on, but behind the scenes, all it would do would be to call existing routines in our use case modules. This means testing can be reduced, the likelihood of such changes introducing bugs is reduced, and our workload is significantly reduced. Does it still sound like a lot of hassle? I think not. In fact, I think it sounds like a very smart idea indeed, and I know it'll save us a lot of time and effort.

Now we can move into the next phase, which is to put a little flesh on to the bare bones of our application.

Relationships

The first thing that we need to do is to code up the relationships between the objects in our model.

> *In order to avoid wandering off the beaten track too far, I'm going to limit our discussion in this chapter to things that revolve around the* `Supplier` *object and any operations which need to take place to maintain it. This will keep our discussion crisper, and I know you'll be able to apply what we're learning here to the other parts of the application easily enough.*

Strangely enough, the Supplier object looks like an ideal place to start. Take a look at your model, and in particular that Supplier object:

As you can see, there is a relationship between a Supplier and its Products. Since a Product can only ever be dealt with as the result of a telephone conversation with a Supplier, it makes sense that our model copies this and uses the Supplier object as the interface to any Product. The relationship that we have in the model indicates that there is a "1 to 0, or many" relationship between a Supplier and its products, and that this is to be implemented in the Supplier object as a member called `SuppliedProduct`. How are we actually going to code this though?

Well, there are two distinct alternatives open to us. When I first got into object-oriented programming, it took me quite a while to get my head around the whole "real world" object thing. I ended up littering my code with objects that bore more relation to other objects in

Visual Basic (Recordsets, Databases and so on) than they did to objects in the real world. For this relationship, it would be very easy to add an object variable called `SuppliedProduct` to the Suppliers class that is nothing more than a wrapper around a recordset. In fact, I have been known to do this on more than one occasion.

In this case then, `SuppliedProduct` would provide a front end to every single product of a Supplier. It would use a set of methods and properties that look not a million miles away from the standard Visual Basic recordset, with methods to move to the first product, the next one, the last one and so on.

About a year ago, though, I found myself working on a project with a chap whom I can only describe as a bit of an Object god. When I tried to implement that way of working in the project that he and I were working on, a heated discussion on the subject of object-oriented programming ensued. I lost.

You see, our objects, and the way that we implement the relationships between them, should mimic the real world scenarios as closely as possible. In the real world, a Supplier would be based in a large building somewhere, with piles of boxes inside, each of which contained a Product. Since a Product is an object, the supplier would, in effect, be surrounding themselves with lots of instances of other objects. This is how we should be doing things.

Our Supplier object should have a **collection** of products, a group of related Product objects, each of which is independent of any other, and each of which can be interacted with as its own unique entity. So, the `SuppliedProduct` member that we presented in the design model needs to be a collection.

Let's start coding some of these relationships.

Try It Out - Adding the Relationships

1 Click on your new **clsSupplier** class in Visual Basic's Project explorer window to bring up the code window, and key in the collection:

```
Public colSuppliedProduct As Collection
```

2 Although we're only going to describe the `clsSupplier` stuff, in this chapter, we could quite easily go ahead and key in the relationships between the other classes in the same way. The `clsOrder` class, for example, is related to the `clsOrderItem` class in an identical fashion to `clsSupplier` and `clsProduct`: the `clsOrder` class contains a collection of `clsOrderItem`, which is called `colOrderedItems`.

3 The relationship between an
OrderItem and a Product on the
other hand is a little more complex.

According to our model, the `clsOrderItem` class **generalizes** the `clsProduct` class. In
real terms, an item on an invoice relates exactly to a single product. Now as well as
containing its own unique information, such as how many of the product were ordered,
most invoices will contain items to show us everything we need to know about a product
being ordered, such as its name, its code, its price, and so on.

The **Generalization** relationship covers this in UML, effectively telling us that the
`clsOrderItem` class implements the same interface as the `clsProduct` class. In addition,
since each `OrderItem` object at runtime relates to a single Product object at runtime, a
member in `clsOrderItem` is defined which stores the instance of the product to which it
relates.

The `clsOrderItem` object code therefore looks like this:

```
Implements clsProduct

Private m_objProductObject As New clsProduct
```

Each method on `clsProduct`'s interface that `clsOrderItem` implements would then just need
to call the method on the `m_objProductObject` member to do its job. This means that at
runtime if we have a `clsOrderItem` object, then we also have access to the `clsProduct` object
to which it relates, through the `clsProduct` interface on the `clsOrderItem` object.

Adding the Properties

Ultimately, everything in the model revolves around the objects in the business services tier.
After all, it's these objects that provide the core functionality of the system, the objects that in
effect run the business.

> *If we take this examination even further, however, then it could be said that
> ultimately everything is geared towards the data in the business services objects. So,
> what better place for our next stop on our journey of code!?*

The properties of a business services object more often than not relate to fields in a database.
Now those properties could combine more than one field to form a single property, or they
could translate a field value into something more useful from a business sense (customer ID
becomes Customer Name, for example). They could even consolidate data from fields in more
than one table. At the end of the day though, they relate to fields in a database.

Our clsSupplier object's properties, then, are quite easy to produce. The Northwind database itself has a Supplier table, and it is this that our clsSupplier class interacts with (indirectly of course, since all data access goes through the clsDBSupplier class in the data services layer).

> *If we were writing code for a system for which a database didn't yet exist, then we still wouldn't have too many problems in identifying properties to put in our objects. Most businesses, before they computerize, do everything around a paper chain: a collection of forms and crumpled bits of paper that effectively run their business. The items on these paper-based forms can be used to build up a list of properties very quickly indeed.*

In our Northwind project, the task is simple. Take a look at the Suppliers table in the Northwind database (you can use Visual Basic's **Visual Data Manager** add-in to do this if you don't have a copy of Access readily available on your machine):

We're basically going to need to produce properties for each field in the Suppliers table. I'm going to keep things simple here and just use Public variables in the clsSupplier class as the properties. As we'll see later, the use case modules validate data entered, so there is really no need to add another layer of code into our Supplier object to check values.

In the long term, however, this might not be the best solution. Although the use case modules will be responsible for checking data in this application, we cannot assume that every other application that makes use of the object will put similar checks in place. Ultimately then, you need to decide for yourself, in your own applications, whether to write property procedures and validate data with them, or not.

> *As a rule of thumb, property procedures are our friends - don't neglect them.*

That said, let's go ahead and take the easier option using `Public` variables.

Try It Out - Adding the Properties

1 Click on the `clsSupplier` class once again to bring its code window into view (assuming it isn't already in view). When it appears, add the following `Public` variables to the top of the `clsSupplier` class to implement its properties (also add the one `Private` variable I've listed here - as an internal reference):

```
Private lngSupplierID As Long
Public strCompanyName As String
Public strContactName As String
Public strContactTitle As String
Public strAddress As String
Public strCity As String
Public strRegion As String
Public strPostalCode As String
Public strCountry As String
Public strPhone As String
Public strFax As String
```

Adding a Method Framework

At this point, we have our project setup with the necessary modules and class modules in place. We've set up the relationships in code between classes, and we've even added properties to the classes (well, the one class we're looking at for now, anyway). Now it's time to start building a framework.

The method framework is just what it says - it's a collection of empty methods, with no code at all. With these in place, we have a framework into which we can plug code.

> *More than that though, developing a skeletal framework of methods gets the brain ticking over, and acts as an invaluable way to spot things you might have missed in the design, before you head down a path of heavy coding.*

In terms of the `Supplier` object, there are only a very few methods that we're actually going to need in the object. The use case statements that we mapped out way back at the beginning of the design process, in Chapter 9, are going to be implemented in the user services modules by calling the methods in the business services objects. So, what we need to do now is drill down on those use case statements and identify the lowest level functions that we need for each object.

In the case of our `Supplier` object, drilling down we can see that we're going to need a way to delete a supplier, store information (be it an update to an existing supplier, or information on a completely new one), and a way to locate an individual supplier based on their ID number. That's three methods that therefore belong to the `clsSupplier` class.

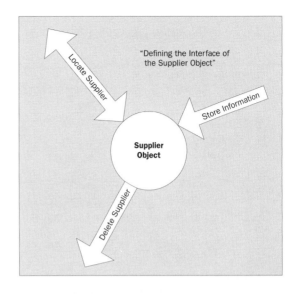

Try It Out - Adding the Method Framework

1 If it's not already open, bring up the code window for the `clsSupplier` class ready to start keying in code.

2 First, the `Find` routine. We're going to need to provide a way for users of the object to locate an individual supplier based on their ID number. Obviously, that routine is also going to need to be able to indicate to the calling code whether or not the find was successful. Therefore, a function is required. Key this in to the `clsSupplier` class:

```
Public Function FindByID(lngID As Long) As Boolean
' Locates a supplier based on their unique supplier ID number

End Function
```

Looks fairly painless, doesn't it? Producing a method framework is just a question of keying in the method definitions and working out what parameters those routines are going to need, and whether or not they need to return a value. In the case of our `FindByID` routine, here, it's obvious that the required supplier ID number is passed in as a parameter. Judging by the return value type, the routine will return `True` if the find was successful, `False` if not.

3 What about the routine to update information? Although the final application will allow users to create new suppliers, as well as change existing supplier information, we only really need one routine to save the information that the user enters. After all, a single instance of a `Supplier` object deals with just one supplier. It's pretty obvious that the `Supplier` object will know whether the information it is holding relates to an existing supplier or is for a new one. The code we write later can make this determination and then tell the data services objects whether they need to update an existing record or create a new one.

The `Update` routine is therefore going to look quite simple. Type this in to our `clsSupplier` class:

```
Public Sub Update()
' Gets the database object to save the changes to this object's properties

End Sub
```

This is great! Remember way back at the beginning of the book, when I first started talking about classes and objects?

> One of the golden rules of object-oriented programming that I mentioned back at the beginning of this book was that the interface to an object (its properties and methods) should be as easy to use as possible. The easier an object is to use, then more likely it is that other developers will use the object, instead of writing their own and increasing the company's maintenance burden.

This routine certainly looks like something most developers should be able to call without too much of a problem.

4   Finally then, the `Delete` routine. Once again, the `Supplier` object will already be referring to a specific supplier in the database, so the `Delete` routine should simply delete the currently loaded `Supplier`. Simple enough. Key this little routine in to the `clsSupplier` class:

```
Public Sub Delete()
' Deletes the currently loaded supplier, if there is one, from the database

End Sub
```

Wow! As easy and effortless as that was, we now have the complete interface of our `Supplier` object defined. Congratulations! That gives us time to tackle a rather more tricky issue now though.

Communicating Between Tiers

The next step is to tackle the framework of the data services objects, and to ask ourselves some very searching questions. Well, just the one searching question really.

The business services `Supplier` object relies on the methods of the `DBSupplier` object to get at stored information on suppliers. It uses the methods on the `DBSupplier` object to load up suppliers' information, to update existing information, to create new supplier records and of course to delete suppliers. How on earth are we going to get the mass of data that the `DBSupplier` object can come up with, into the `Supplier` object?

There are two solutions really:

- ▶ We could make the `Supplier` object know intimate details about the `DBSupplier` object, and copy property values from the `DBSupplier` object into the `Supplier` one at runtime.
- ▶ We could let the `DBSupplier` object have a fairly intimate knowledge of what properties exist on the `Supplier` object.

Which do we choose? Well, it's an arbitrary question. I chose to let the `DBSupplier` be aware of what properties exist in the `Supplier` object, in effect letting the `DBSupplier` object know which object is using it at any point in time.

Here's my reasoning behind the idea. The `Supplier` object runs the business side of dealing with suppliers. As a business, Northwind depends on certain information existing at any one point in time about a supplier. All suppliers have a name, for example; and an address, a telephone number, etc. The `DBSupplier` object, though, provides a neat front end to the `Suppliers` table in the database.

Databases are dynamic things; if we implement a set of properties in the `DBSupplier` object for the data on a supplier, are we going to change those property names when the database gets changed by an over eager DBA (Database Administrator person)? The obvious answer is "of course not", but we then end up in a situation where we have a class that is supposed to closely map to the database, but which actually exposes properties which bear no relation to the actual database. In addition, the `DBSupplier` object is obsessed with database work, shifting information from hard disk to application and back again. In the real world, would such an object care about field names and mapping them into properties?

Think of a car for a second. Does the engine know how its fuel system works? Does the fuel system know how the engine works? What actually happens in a car engine is that the engine has a connector for receiving fuel, and the fuel tank has a tube connecting it to the engine. The fuel tank's job, then, is 'to push fuel down that tube thing over there'. Our objects should work in the same way. Just as an engine can control the amount of fuel flowing, our `Supplier` object can control the flow of data between itself and the `DBSupplier` object. In addition, the `DBSupplier` object knows that any data it gets 'needs to be pushed into those properties on that object thing over there'.

What methods are we going to need to write in the `DBSupplier` class then? What data is it going to hold? Well, everything in this particular class revolves around one thing - a database. We're going to need to define a variable to deal with the connection to the database. That's easy enough, at this level of programming.

Try It Out - Connecting to the Database

1 Pop open the code window for the `clsDBSupplier` class and enter this code:

```
Private m_DB As Database


Private Sub Class_Initialize()

    ' Set up a connection to the Northwind database
    Set m_DB = Workspaces(0).OpenDatabase(App.Path & "\nwind.mdb")

End Sub

Private Sub Class_Terminate()

    ' Close the connection to the database
    m_DB.Close
    Set m_DB = Nothing

End Sub
```

Here we have a `Private` database variable in the class that's going to be used to deal with the connection to the database. In addition, the `Initialize` and `Terminate` events are coded up to actually connect to the database whenever the object is created, and to close the connection to the database when the object is released.

2 As always, the code relies on the fact that the `Nwind.mdb` database is in the same location as our project - so copy it there now to save any grief later on.

> *In Visual Basic 3 and 4, database work wasn't the fastest feature of Visual Basic. Opening and closing connections like this on the fly was something to be avoided, unless you really wanted to see the performance of your application dive down a large hole.*

> *In Visual Basic 6 though, things are very different. We can now have code that connects to a database and disconnects from it whenever the object is created or destroyed. Each routine in this class creates its own recordsets (opening and reading data from a table in the database) instead of having one central member permanently holding an open connection to a recordset. Visual Basic 6's database facilities are so fast that most users would barely even notice a drop in performance when a database is opened, or when a recordset is opened. This means that we can write neater, tidier code than before, and reduce the number of global and module level variables that we have floating around to deal with them.*

The next step, then, is to start to produce the framework methods that will perform the database work. Looking at the `Supplier` object that we were dealing with just a short while ago, it's already obvious that we're going to need routines that will:

> Find a supplier in the database

> Create a new supplier record

> Update an existing supplier

> Delete a supplier

Looking at the use case statements from the last chapter, we're also going to need some way of getting at a complete list of supplier names and IDs. Doing this means that a user of the system will be able to see the list, and select a supplier to deal with. Let's start coding.

Try It Out - Producing the Framework Methods

1 First, the `Find` routine of the `clsDBSupplier` class. This routine is going to need a Supplier's ID number passed to it, which it must then find, plus a `Supplier` object. Assuming the `Find` operation is successful, our `DBSupplier` object can then fill the fields in the business `Supplier` object with the data it just located. The routine therefore looks like this - go ahead and key it in to your `clsDBSupplier` class:

```
Public Function Find_Supplier(ByVal lngID As Long, _
                    supBusinessObject As clsSupplier) As Boolean
' Find a supplier record, and copy the data to the supBusinessObject passed in

End Function
```

Just as before, the routine is a function, returning True if the Find operation was successful, False if it was not. As I mentioned, this routine also expects to be passed a Supplier business object.

> *So what if we weren't dealing with a Supplier business object though, and we needed to call this routine anyway, perhaps from a different application? That's where the beauty of Visual Basic's object-oriented system comes in. We would just create an object that implemented the Supplier object's interface, and our routine would work quite happily with that.*

2 Next, the routine to create a new supplier record.

You should remember from when we looked at the `Supplier` object earlier, that it's up to code in the `Supplier` object to decide whether it needs to create a new record, or update an existing one, This decision is made when it does an update operation. Based on this decision, it can choose to call the `CreateNewSupplier` routine in the `clsDBSupplier` class, or an `UpdateExistingSupplier` routine.

In order to get the data into the `DBSupplier` object, we can just pass across a business object again. The `CreateNewSupplier` routine looks like this - once again, go ahead and key it in to our `clsDBSupplier` class:

```
Public Function CreateNewSupplier(supNewSupplier As clsSupplier) As Long
' Copies the properties in the supNewSupplier object into
' the fields in the Suppliers table in the database.

End Function
```

3 It makes sense, then, that the routine to update an existing supplier should work in a similar way. However, the update routine will also need to be told which supplier record to update, so it will expect to be a passed a supplier ID number:

```
Public Sub UpdateExistingSupplier(ByVal lngID As Long, supChangedData As
clsSupplier)
' Locates the supplier record specified by lngID
' and then copies the properties from supChangedData into it.

End Sub
```

4 The DeleteSupplier routine should be a similar no-brainer. It just needs to be told which supplier to go ahead and delete:

```
Public Sub DeleteSupplier(ByVal lngID As Long)
' Deletes the supplier specified by lngID

End Sub
```

5 Nearly there. The last routine we're going to need to add to clsDBSupplier is a routine to grab a complete list of supplier names and ID numbers. This is going to involve passing back a couple of arrays, one with the names and one with the ID numbers in; it therefore looks a little more complex, but not much:

```
Public Sub Get_Supplier_Names(lngIDNos() As Long, strNames() As String)
' Grab a list of supplier numbers and names and put them into
' the two variable length arrays that were passed in as parameters

End Sub
```

That's it - the framework for our data services object is now complete.

The Use Case Modules

The use case modules form a nice safe link between any forms in the application and the underlying business and data objects. By using a module to wrap up the sequence of events that take place in the high level use case statements, we're effectively freeing up the user interface to be whatever the user wants it to be. Changes to the user interface will not have an impact on the underlying code in any way, shape, or form.

First, the modAmendSupplier module. If you take a look back over the use case to amend a supplier in the real world, you'll see that we're actually going to need a few routines in here. Before we can even think of amending a supplier's information, for example, we need to scan a list to see which suppliers are on the database. Once we've spotted the supplier we're interested in, we'll need to select that individual supplier record. Finally, when the changes have been made, we'll need a routine to save those changes; in effect, to file them away.

First, let's take a peek at the routine to grab a list of supplier names. Since the module is designed to sit between forms and objects, it makes sense that any list grabbed from the data services objects should ultimately be dumped into either a combo box, or a list box, on a form. We can code up the framework for the routine with this in mind.

Try It Out - The Use Case Modules

1 Bring up the code window for the `modAmendSupplier` module and key this in.

```
Public Function CreateSupplierList(ctrListControl As Control) As Boolean
' Creates a list of suppliers in the supplied list control

End Function
```

The routine is a function in this case. If something goes wrong with grabbing the list from the data services object, then it can return a value of `False` so the user interface to reflect that there has been a problem. The routine also takes a single parameter, declared as a `Control`. Anyone calling this routine will be expected to pass in either a reference to a list box or a combo box. We'll put code in the routine later to check this, and fill the control with the list of supplier names.

2 Next up, the routine to select a supplier. Key this in to `modAmendSupplier`:

```
Public Function SelectSupplier(ByVal lngSupplierID As Long, supSupplierObject As
clsSupplier) As Boolean
' Selects a supplier record, ready for editing

End Function
```

Just as before, this is a function to let the user interface code calling the routine know if everything went to plan or not. Notice that the routine expects two parameters. The first is obviously the ID number of the supplier that needs to be found. The second is the `Supplier` object that we want the `SelectSupplier` routine to work with. It is this object that is used to actually do the search, and to hold the retrieved data should the find be successful.

3 The final routine we'll add to `modAmendSupplier` needs to be able to save amended data out since that is, after all, the underlying purpose of the module:

```
Public Sub SaveAmendments(supSupplierObject As clsSupplier)
' Tells the business object to accept modifications to a supplier

End Sub
```

Once again the routine takes a supplier object as a parameter - without it, it would have no way of knowing exactly which supplier needs updating, nor what information to update.

4 Next, it's time to look at the `modCreateSupplier` module. We're just going to need two routines in here - one to create a new `Supplier` object, and another to save the new data out to the database. By now, you should have a pretty good idea of what these routines are going to look like. Just in case though, I'll show you. Bring up the code window for your `modCreateSupplier` module and be ready to get typing.

5 First, the routine to create a supplier. Just as before, we're going need to pass a `Supplier` object to this routine so that it can clear it out ready to accept new information. Go ahead and key the following code in to the `modCreateSupplier` module:

```
Public Sub CreateNewSupplier(supTheSupplier As clsSupplier)
' Creates a new, empty supplier record

End Sub
```

6 Saving the data out is pretty straightforward as well. Unlike its counterpart in the `modAmendSupplier` module, we don't need to specify a supplier ID in this routine either, since we're creating a new supplier and expect the database to supply a new ID to us. So add this code to your `modCreateSupplier` module:

```
Public Sub SaveNewSupplier(supTheSupplier As clsSupplier)
' Tells the business object to save the new supplier information

End Sub
```

The system is really coming along now. There is framework code throughout, highlighting the different interfaces of each of our objects - and generally moving us a huge step closer to the warm and fuzzy feeling that comes with knowing what needs to be done to get fairly sophisticated object-oriented application running.

In our case, everything is quite simple. We need a form to front end everything and provide a user interface to the user; and we need to fill in the framework with the actual code that will do the work.

> *From an object-oriented standpoint though, the application is done!*

Adding the Forms

At this point, there is absolutely no reason why we can't start to add forms to the project. The framework of the application is complete, so we could even go so far as to put code in the form and the application would run, albeit not as well as its end-users had hoped.

Try It Out - Creating the Supplier Maintenance Form

1 Add a form to your project, and name it `frmSupplierMaint`. We're going to use this one form to handle everything there is to do with maintaining the company's list of suppliers. If we want to be adventurous, we can even add an MDI form to our project and set this `frmSupplierMaint` form to be a child. At that point, we would be approaching the user interface quality of the final application. It's not crucial to getting the point across though, so skip that if it doesn't appeal to you.

2 Now, on your form, lay out controls so that it looks like this:

Don't worry about getting your form to look identical to mine – as long as you have the same number of controls in roughly the same places, then you'll be fine.

3 In order that you can use the same code as myself, you might want to set the names, and other properties of the controls on the form as per the items in the table below.

Control	Property	Value
Supplier Combo box	Name	cboSupplier
	Style	2 – Dropdown list
Add supplier button	Name	cmdAdd
Edit supplier button	Name	cmdEdit
OK button	Name	cmdOK
	Default	True
Cancel button	Name	cmdCancel
	Cancel	True
Apply button	Name	cmdApply
Company name text box	Name	txtCompanyName
	MaxLength	40
Contact name text box	Name	txtContactName
	MaxLength	30
Contact title text box	Name	txtContactTitle
	MaxLength	30
Address text box	Name	txtAddress
	MaxLength	60
City text box	Name	txtCity
	MaxLength	15
Region text box	Name	txtRegion
	MaxLength	15
Postalcode text box	Name	txtPostalCode
	MaxLength	15
Country text box	Name	txtCountry
	MaxLength	15
Phone number text box	Name	txtPhone
	MaxLength	24
Fax number text box	Name	txtFax
	MaxLength	24
Top frame	Name	fraTop
Bottom frame	Name	fraBottom

4 Also, set the tab order so that it logically moves down the page in the proper field order - if you can't remember how to do this then take a quick look at the **VB Books Online**.

5 When you're done, you can save the form along with every other file in the project out to the hard disk. Time to start adding some more code in.

Filling in the Code

Okay, now that we have the framework of the application complete, we can go ahead and fill it in. To be honest, most of the object-oriented side of things has been covered by this stage. We've seen how to translate relationships in our object design model into Visual Basic code, and also how to put in place an object-oriented infrastructure that fits in well with the model. The bulk of the rest of the code that we're going to see through now is mainly technical - dealing with the database, the form controls, and generally getting the lines of communication up and running. We mustn't forget, however, to implement those business rules on the business tier. And there are still one or two tricks of the trade to be picked up yet. Read on through this jungle (aren't you glad we decided only to write a section of the application for this chapter?) and keep learning.

Let's have a quick recap of the object design model, as we formulated it in the last chapter:

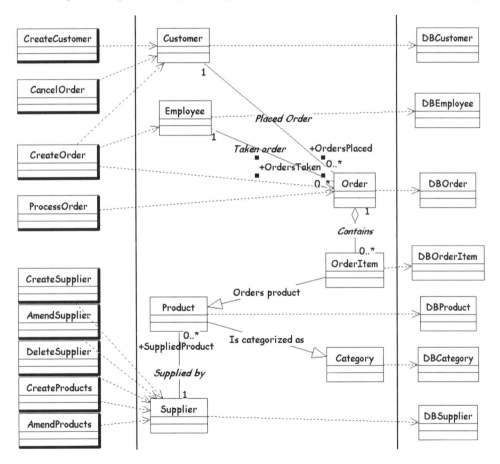

As I think I said somewhere else, we will often return to our object design model - it's our map and our best understanding of the territory we're trying to model with our object-oriented programming. Use it.

The DBSupplier Object

The best place to start is at the bottom of the model, in the data services tier.

Try It Out - The Find_Supplier Routine

1   In the Project explorer within Visual Basic, click on the `clsDBSupplier` class to open up its code window. There's a fair amount of typing to do, but nothing too complex. Let's start with the routine to find a specific supplier, the `Find_Supplier` routine:

```
Public Function Find_Supplier(ByVal lngID As Long, _
    supBusinessObject As clsSupplier) As Boolean
' Find a supplier record, and copy the data to the
' supBusinessObject passed in

  Dim recSuppliers As Recordset

    Set recSuppliers = m_DB.OpenRecordset _
("SELECT * FROM Suppliers WHERE SupplierID = " & lngID, dbOpenSnapshot)

    If recSuppliers.EOF Then
        Find_Supplier = False
        ' There was no supplier found matching the ID,
        ' so clear the data out
        With supBusinessObject
```

```
                    .strCompanyName = ""
                    .strContactName = ""
                    .strContactTitle = ""
                    .strAddress = ""
                    .strCity = ""
                    .strRegion = ""
                    .strPostalCode = ""
                    .strCountry = ""
                    .strPhone = ""
                    .strFax = ""

            End With
        Else

            ' A supplier was found,
            ' so set the fields in the supplier object up
            Find_Supplier = True

            With supBusinessObject

                .strCompanyName = "" & recSuppliers!CompanyName
                .strContactName = "" & recSuppliers!ContactName
                .strContactTitle = "" & recSuppliers!ContactTitle
                .strAddress = "" & recSuppliers!Address
                .strCity = "" & recSuppliers!City
                .strRegion = "" & recSuppliers!Region
                .strPostalCode = "" & recSuppliers!PostalCode
                .strCountry = "" & recSuppliers!Country
                .strPhone = "" & recSuppliers!Phone
                .strFax = "" & recSuppliers!Fax

            End With

        End If

        recSuppliers.Close

    End Function
```

How It Works

Although this code looks a bit tricky, it's actually very straightforward. This code is split into three parts.

▶ First, declaring a recordset, which we're going to use to grab the required supplier record from the `Nwind` database

▶ Second, copying values from the fields in the table to the properties of the `Supplier` object - passed into the routine as a parameter called `supBusinessObject`

▶ Third, the single line at the bottom of the routine that closes down the records

From an object-oriented standpoint, whatever happens when the search takes place, we need to make sure that the `Supplier` object that was passed in at the start of the routine is returned with valid content. This means that even if the search fails, we need to put something valid into the `supBusinessObject` object.

Glance at the code and you should see that it's quite obvious what's going on. If the search is successful, then the contents of the supplier record's fields are copied into the properties of `supBusinessObject`. If, on the other hand, the search fails, then the properties are all set to blank values. This makes sense - if we didn't manage to find the requested supplier then we have no data, and that's exactly what gets returned in the `BusinessObject` variable.

Try It Out - The CreateNewSupplier Routine

1 Let's key in the `CreateNewSupplier` routine now. Add this code to our `clsDBSupplier` class:

```
Public Function CreateNewSupplier(supNewSupplier As clsSupplier) As Long
' Copies the properties in the supNewSupplier object into
' the fields in the Suppliers table in the database.

    Dim recSuppliers As Recordset

    Set recSuppliers = m_DB.OpenRecordset("Suppliers", dbOpenTable)

    recSuppliers.AddNew
    SetRecordFields supNewSupplier, recSuppliers
    recSuppliers.Update

    recSuppliers.Bookmark = recSuppliers.LastModified
    CreateNewSupplier = recSuppliers!SupplierID

    recSuppliers.Close

End Function
```

How It Works

Again, nothing too complex there. The routine first opens up the `Suppliers` table in the Northwind database, and then uses the `Addnew` method to put the table into a state where it is ready to accept data for a new record.

That data is put into the record using a private routine that we haven't coded up yet, called `SetRecordFields`. This will take two parameters: the `Supplier` object with the data that we need to save, and the open recordset. All this routine does is copy values from the fields in the `Supplier` object into the fields of the `Supplier` record.

Once that is done, an `Update` is issued to save the changes, and the newly added record is found once again, using the recordset's `Bookmark` to move to the `LastModified` record. This is essential since we must pick up the newly assigned supplier ID which our routine returns, so that any code creating a new `Supplier` record can instantly see what the new supplier's ID number is.

Try It Out - The SetRecordFields Routine

1 We'd better code up that new `SetRecordFields` routine next. Key this in to your `clsDBSupplier` class:

```
Private Sub SetRecordFields(supTheSupplier As clsSupplier, recSupplierData As
Recordset)
' Copies the contents of the supplier object's properties out to the
' current record's fields

    With supTheSupplier

        recSupplierData!CompanyName = .strCompanyName
        recSupplierData!ContactName = .strContactName
        recSupplierData!ContactTitle = .strContactTitle
        recSupplierData!Address = .strAddress
        recSupplierData!City = .strCity
        recSupplierData!Region = .strRegion
        recSupplierData!Country = .strCountry
        recSupplierData!PostalCode = .strPostalCode
        recSupplierData!Phone = .strPhone
        recSupplierData!Fax = .strFax

    End With

End Sub
```

2 Just as I described, this routine copies property values into the fields of the current record in the passed in recordset. Why is this code in a separate routine and not embedded in the `CreateSupplier` routine? Well, by keeping it all in a separate routine it can also be used by the `UpdateExistingSupplier` routine. Let's key that one in to the same class:

```
Public Sub UpdateExistingSupplier(ByVal lngID As Long, supChangedData As
clsSupplier)
' Locates the supplier record specified by lngID
' and then copies the properties from supChangedData into it.

    Dim recSuppliers As Recordset

    Set recSuppliers = m_DB.OpenRecordset("Suppliers", dbOpenTable)

    recSuppliers.Index = "PrimaryKey"
    recSuppliers.Seek "=", lngID

    If Not recSuppliers.NoMatch Then

        recSuppliers.Edit
        SetRecordFields supChangedData, recSuppliers
        recSuppliers.Update

    End If

    recSuppliers.Close

End Sub
```

317

How It Works

This routine is understandably a little more complex, since it needs to first locate the `Supplier` record to update. This is exactly what the first part of the code does: opening up the `Suppliers` table, and then using the `PrimaryKey` to locate the supplier with an ID matching the ID passed into the routine (`lngID`). Assuming the seek was successful, the record is put into `Edit` mode and our old friend `SetRecordFields` is called to copy the property values of the `Supplier` object into the fields in the currently selected `Supplier` record.

We're nearly there. We can ignore the `Delete` routine at this stage, since in our little snippet of the entire application, we'll never actually allow the user to delete a supplier.

That just leaves us with the routine to grab a list of supplier names. This is used higher up the chain to build a combo or list box with a list of suppliers in, and gives the user a convenient method of choosing a supplier to work with.

Try It Out - The Get_Supplier_Names Routine

1 Type this little lot in to your `clsDBSupplier` class:

```
Public Sub Get_Supplier_Names(lngIDNos() As Long, strNames() As String)
' Grab a list of supplier numbers and names and put them into
' the two variable length arrays that were passed in as parameters

    Dim recSuppliers As Recordset
    Dim intCounter As Integer

    ' First, clear out the arrays
    ReDim lngIDNos(0)
    ReDim strNames(0)

    ' Next, grab a list of the supplier names,
    ' with their ID's from the database
    Set recSuppliers = m_DB.OpenRecordset _
("SELECT SupplierID, CompanyName FROM Suppliers ORDER BY CompanyName", _
    dbOpenSnapshot)

    intCounter = 0
    ' Start a loop through the list of suppliers
    Do While Not recSuppliers.EOF
        intCounter = intCounter + 1

        ReDim Preserve lngIDNos(intCounter)
        ReDim Preserve strNames(intCounter)

        lngIDNos(intCounter - 1) = recSuppliers!SupplierID
        strNames(intCounter - 1) = recSuppliers!CompanyName

        recSuppliers.MoveNext

    Loop
```

```
        ' Close the connection to the recordset
        recSuppliers.Close

    End Sub
```

2   Save your code.

How It Works

The most complex thing about this routine has nothing to do with objects at all. The routine looks nasty simply because it's dealing with variable length arrays.

The two arrays, one to hold the suppliers' names and the other to hold the suppliers' ID numbers, are passed into the routine as parameters. The code then opens up the `Suppliers` table, grabbing just the list of suppliers' names and IDs from the database. A loop is then used to move through each record in the new recordset, each pass through the loop increasing the size of these arrays by one before the new supplier name and ID are copied into the appropriate arrays.

> *It never ceases to amaze me how few people use variable length arrays, but they can be so useful at passing huge lumps of data around between routines; and they really aren't very hard to use. If you are a little bewildered though, take a peek at the only help at the* ReDim *command – that's the root of everything to do with resizable arrays.*

So, that's the `clsDBSupplier` class coded up. As I said at the start, there's really very little object-oriented code in there once the bulk of the code is written.

Apologies to those of you who fell asleep in the last section. However, there is something really interesting about what we just typed in. As we move closer and closer to the form, in terms of the design model, you will see two things happen. Firstly, you'll type less and less code, and that code which you do type just makes use of the methods in the lower level objects. Secondly, you'll find yourself dealing with the runtime management of objects more and more. The lower you go, the more technical it gets, the higher you go, the more you are concerned with using objects and little else. Fascinating - albeit in a dry kind of way!

The Supplier Object

The code in this section is distinctly more related to the world of object-oriented development than the stuff we just plowed through in the last section.

Try It Out - The Supplier Object

1   In the Project explorer in Visual Basic, click on the `clsSupplier` class to open up its code window, ready for us to fill in the framework methods that we have got in there. Just as before, since we aren't actually making use of the `Delete` functionality in this snapshot of the project, we're going to leave that routine blank. That leaves us just two routines to code up.

319

2 Let's get started with the `FindByID` routine, which the `Supplier` object can use to load itself up with a specific supplier's record information:

```
Public Function FindByID(lngID As Long) As Boolean
' Locates a supplier based on their unique supplier ID number

    Dim dbsSupplierData As New clsDBSupplier

    FindByID = dbsSupplierData.Find_Supplier(lngID, Me)

    ' If we managed to find the supplier based on their ID number, then
    ' update the internal ID number to keep track

    If FindByID Then lngSupplierID = lngID

End Function
```

The functionality to locate a specific supplier record in the database is contained in the `clsDBSupplier` class that we just coded. Naturally, the first thing that this routine needs to do is create an instance of that class. With that done, we can call the `clsDBSupplier`'s `Find_Supplier` routine.

There's something interesting to note about this call though. We pass two parameters across, the ID of the supplier that we want to find, and `Me`. `Me` is a special keyword that we can use in Visual Basic to refer to 'this object'. What the call is actually doing is passing across the ID number of the required supplier, and this instance of the `Supplier` object.

> *If you've done any work with MDI applications, then you've probably come across code before that uses the Me keyword. It's also used quite a lot in form event code as a way of saying 'This form'. It really means 'this object' and that's exactly how it's being used here.*

Assuming that the find routine returned `True`, we set the internal `lngSupplierID` member to be the ID of the supplier that we just found.

3 The `Update` routine is equally straightforward. Let's type its code in:

```
Public Sub Update()
' Gets the database object to save the changes to this object's
' properties

    Dim dbsSupplierData As New clsDBSupplier
    Dim lngNewID As Long

    ' First check to see if we are using a new supplier, or an
    ' existing one
    If lngSupplierID = 0 Then
```

```
            lngNewID = dbsSupplierData.CreateNewSupplier(Me)
            lngSupplierID = lngNewID

      Else

            dbsSupplierData.UpdateExistingSupplier lngSupplierID, Me

      End If

   End Sub
```

How It Works

Remember - this routine is responsible for automatically figuring out if it needs to create a new
`Supplier` record in the database, or update an existing one. It does this by looking at the
`lngSupplierID` member variable. If the `Supplier` object has just been created and then filled
with data from the user interface, then this variable would be 0, indicating a new record.
Anything else and we can assume that we have a `Supplier` record loaded.

After creating a `clsDBSupplier` object, the code examines the `lngSupplierID` variable to see
if we are dealing with a new or existing supplier. If it's a new supplier, then the
`CreateNewSupplier` method is called on the new `DBSupplier` object. If it's an existing
supplier we are dealing with, then a call is made to the `clsDBSupplier` class's
`UpdateExistingSupplier` method.

The Use Case Modules

Our next stop is with the use case modules, `modAmendSupplier` and `modCreateSupplier`.

Try It Out - The modAmendSupplier Module

1 Let's start with `modAmendSupplier`. Click on this module in Visual Basic's project explorer
to bring up the code window. The logical place to start in here is with the
`SelectSupplier` routine, so get typing.

```
Public Function SelectSupplier(ByVal lngSupplierID As Long, _
    supSupplierObject As clsSupplier) As Boolean
' Selects a supplier record, ready for editing

   Set supSupplierObject = Nothing
   Set supSupplierObject = New clsSupplier

   ' Select the supplier based on its ID into
   ' the supplier object passed
   SelectSupplier = supSupplierObject.FindByID(lngSupplierID)

End Function
```

2 The next routine to key in is the `SaveAmendments` routine:

321

```
Public Sub SaveAmendments(supTheSupplier As clsSupplier)
' Tells the business object to save the new supplier information

    ' Having completed the validation, it's now time to go ahead
    ' and save the changes

    supTheSupplier.Update

End Sub
```

3 Finally, we need to add some code to the `CreateSupplierList` routine, the block of
code that will fill a list or combo box with a list of supplier names for the user to choose
from:

```
Public Function CreateSupplierList(ctrListControl As Control) As Boolean
' Creates a list of suppliers in the supplied list control

    If TypeOf ctrListControl Is ListBox Or TypeOf _
            ctrListControl Is ComboBox Then

        Dim dbsSupplierData As New clsDBSupplier

        Dim strSupplierNames() As String
        Dim lngSupplierIds() As Long

        Dim intCounter As Integer
        Dim vntID As Variant


        ' Clear out the list control
        ctrListControl.Clear

        ' Grab the lists of supplier ids and names
        dbsSupplierData.Get_Supplier_Names lngSupplierIds(), _
            strSupplierNames()

        ' Now start to load up the list control
        intCounter = 0
        For Each vntID In lngSupplierIds

            ctrListControl.AddItem strSupplierNames(intCounter)
            ctrListControl.ItemData(ctrListControl.ListCount - 1) = vntID
            intCounter = intCounter + 1

        Next

        ' finally, clear out the data object
        Set dbsSupplierData = Nothing

        CreateSupplierList = True

    Else
        ' return a false, since the type of list control passed
        ' in was invalid
```

```
        CreateSupplierList = False
    End If

End Function
```

How It Works

The `SelectSupplier` routine is passed two parameters: the ID of the supplier that we wish to select, and a `Supplier` object. The contents of this `Supplier` object are of absolutely of no value here though, since the first thing the code does is set the object to `Nothing`. This has the result of terminating any instance of the object that might already be in the `supSupplierObject` variable. With that done, a new `Supplier` object is created and its `FindByID` method called. The net result, as we saw earlier, is that if the `Find` works then the `Supplier` object will come back with all its properties set to the right values. If it fails, then they will be reset to default empty values.

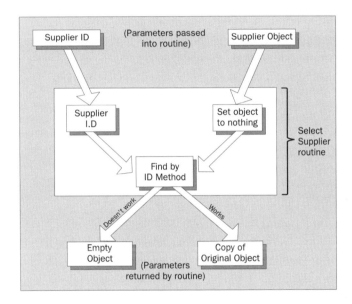

What about the `SaveAmendments` routine? You may be thinking, at this point, that if all the routine is doing is calling a single method on the `Supplier` object, then why on earth is the routine there at all? After all, the form could just as easily say `supTheSupplier.Update`.

The reason is simple. This is a use case module, the place where ultimately we will want to put code to implement the rules of the business. Right now, all we want to do when the routine gets called is have the object variable save its data. In the future, though, this routine could easily be expanded to update a system log, validate data, and do a hundred and one other things. Now imagine if every form that could update supplier information were simply allowed to call the `Update` method of the `Supplier` object directly, then such an enhancement would be a complete nightmare to put in place. We would need to search each and every form to see just which ones called that `Update` routine. By arranging for all the forms that update existing suppliers to call this one central routine, however, the changes are confined to a single block of code. Makes sense when you think about it that way, doesn't it!?

323

Last but not least, there's the `CreateSupplierList` routine (listed above). This looks nasty, but if you wander through the code line by line, it's actually quite basic stuff – there's just a lot of it.

Looking at the code behind `CreateSupplierList`, the routine first checks to see if the control passed to it is a combo box or a list box. These are the only two types of control that the routine will deal with. The rest of the code will only run if the control passed in is a combo or list control.

With that out of the way, the list control is cleared, and a `clsDBSupplier` object created so that the `Get_Supplier_Names` routine can be called. Finally, a loop is used to move through each item in the name and ID arrays, copying the names into the list control, and the IDs into the hidden `ItemData` array that every list control has. At runtime on the form, we can use this `ItemData` array, when the user selects a supplier, to find out the ID of the supplier they have selected.

Try It Out - The modCreateSupplier Module

1 The code that you need to key into the `modCreateSupplier` module is very similar to the `modAmendSupplier` module. Bring up the code window for the `modCreateSupplier` module now, and enter this:

```
Public Sub CreateNewSupplier(supTheSupplier As clsSupplier)
' Creates a new, empty supplier record
    Set supTheSupplier = Nothing
    Set supTheSupplier = New clsSupplier
End Sub


Public Sub SaveNewSupplier(supTheSupplier As clsSupplier)
' Tells the business object to save the new supplier information

    ' Having completed the validation, it's now time to go ahead
    ' and save the changes.

    supTheSupplier.Update

End Sub
```

How It Works

By now, that should all appear very straightforward indeed. The `CreateNewSupplier` routine just creates a new blank `Supplier` object, while the `SaveNewSupplier` routine just calls the `Update` method on that `Supplier` object to save the information out, just like in the `modAmendSupplier` module.

Take a look at this diagram – it shows how we are using these routines to provide links between the various objects in our application, thus leaving the objects free to sit there and be strongly cohesive.

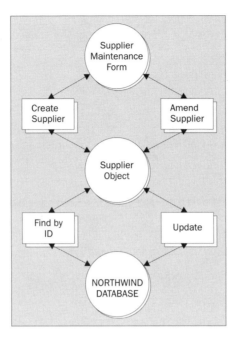

The Form

The final piece in the puzzle is to add the GUI code. The code that lives behind the form, that actually does all the work in terms of calling the other objects in the model to implement those use case statements we produced.

> *It sounds easier work, but this is the place where the object model can tie you up in one or two knots. Take care.*

Recall that we have normal code modules produced from the model to implement the main use cases that apply to the supplier (Amend, Create etc.). This is where the code goes to actually work with the Supplier object. All the form is truly interested in is:

- Can I show the user a list of suppliers?
- Can I show the user detailed information on the current supplier?
- Do all my bells and whistles work as they should?
- Do I respond to the other objects in the model correctly?

The form shouldn't have anything to do with the business itself, other than know where to go to ask for things to happen. Think of the form as a window on the files in your filing cabinet. It doesn't run the business; it only shows you the information you need to run your business, or at least a part of it.

So, the first stop is to add a couple of members to the form, so that the form knows who its current supplier is, and also whether it's being used to add or edit existing supplier information (it gets told this by a user clicking a button after all).

Try It Out - Coding the Form's Load Event

1 In the general declarations section of the form, add these few lines in to a new form:

```
Option Explicit

' Need a new member to hold the current supplier information
Public supCurrentSupplier As clsSupplier

' The form is being used for both adding and deleting suppliers.
' It therefore needs to know which mode it is currently being
' used in, in order to call the appropriate update routines.
Private blnAddingNewSupplier As Boolean
```

Of course, you can leave the comments out, but if you do type them in time after time, then you may find yourself forming an invaluable habit.

You may be thinking, especially after what I said earlier (about the form leaving the business side of things alone) that it's kind of strange to have an instance of the Supplier object belong to the form itself. We need this so that the form can display the Supplier information in its text boxes, and so that the form can feed any new information that the user enters into the properties of the Supplier object. It won't actually call any methods on the Supplier though, and will instead pass the Supplier object across to the code modules to do all the tough stuff. In effect, it is saying to each business model "Here, I have this supplier and my user wants you to do XYZ to it." In this instance, the form acts as a go-between. We'll see more of this later.

2 The most logical place to go next, then, is the form's Load event. When it loads, our user may well need to be able to get at a list of the suppliers available so that they can perform an edit operation. If all the user wants to do is add new data then this code won't have any adverse affects on them either.

Bring up the form's Load event and enter this code:

```
Private Sub Form_Load()

    ' Grab a list of supplier names and ids and load up the combo box
    Dim blnResult As Boolean
    blnResult = CreateSupplierList(cboSupplier)

    If Not blnResult Then
        MsgBox "An unexpected error occurred and a list" & _
        " of suppliers was not available. Please contact" & _
        " technical support as soon as possible", _
        vbExclamation, "Application Error"
    End If

    ' Disable the bottom frame, ok, cancel and apply buttons
    fraBottom.Enabled = False
    cmdOK.Enabled = False
    cmdCancel.Enabled = False
    cmdApply.Enabled = False

    ' Select the first item in the combo box
    If blnResult Then cboSupplier.ListIndex = 0

End Sub
```

How It Works

Just as I said earlier, the important thing to note about this code already is that it doesn't do anything which doesn't directly affect its own controls. It doesn't grab a list of suppliers, it asks another routine to provide it, and it doesn't do anything to the Supplier object at all – why would it?

All this code does is call the CreateSupplierList routine, and passes to that routine a reference to the combo box that we intend to use to show a list of suppliers. It's just asking another more knowledgeable routine to get a list of suppliers and dump them into a typical listing control. It does know though that if the routine returns a False value then something has gone horribly wrong. The form doesn't need to know exactly what went wrong, or what happened – all it cares about at that point is showing a message box to the user to let them know that something went wrong.

The rest of the code just disables the main data frame, so that the user can't change stuff without first asking, ready for him or her to choose to add a new supplier, select a supplier from the combo box, or elect to edit the currently loaded supplier information.

The next step in the functionality is to provide a way for the form to actually show supplier information, to get the `Supplier` object's property values out and into the text boxes on the form.

Try It Out - Showing the Supplier Information

1 Bring up your form's code window once again, and enter this little routine:

```
Private Sub ReloadData()
' Reloads data from the supCurrentSupplier object into the form fields
' Error handling is used in case the supCurrentSupplier object is empty

    On Error GoTo Reload_Data_Error

    With supCurrentSupplier

        txtCompanyName = .strCompanyName
        txtContactName = .strContactName
        txtContactTitle = .strContactTitle
        txtAddress = .strAddress
        txtCity = .strCity
        txtRegion = .strRegion
        txtPostalCode = .strPostalCode
        txtCountry = .strCountry
        txtPhone = .strPhone
        txtFax = .strFax

    End With

    Exit Sub

Reload_Data_Error:
    txtCompanyName = ""
    txtContactName = ""
    txtContactTitle = ""
    txtAddress = ""
    txtCity = ""
    txtRegion = ""
    txtPostalCode = ""
    txtCountry = ""
    txtPhone = ""
    txtFax = ""

    Exit Sub

End Sub
```

How It Works

This routine should be simple enough to follow with very little explanation – it just copies object properties to the text boxes on the form. The error handler might be quite interesting to some, after all, what could possibly go wrong with copying values from one place to another. Well, there could be instances where the `Supplier` object contains no data at all, such as at the start of the application. In this instance, the text boxes on the form will all be set to blanks, indicating that no `Supplier` is loaded.

Now we have a way to get information from a `Supplier` object into the form. The next step is to actually let the user loose with that combo box at the top of the form to select a `Supplier` to view.

Try It Out - Adding Code to the Click Event of the Combo Box

1 Bring up the combo box's `Click` event. The `Click` event is triggered whenever the user selects a new `Supplier`. It also gets triggered for the first time in our form's `Load` event, when we set the `ListIndex` property of the combo to 0 to select the first `Supplier` in the list. Code this up within your form:

```
Private Sub cboSupplier_Click()
    ' Grab the selected suppliers file and display the information in
    ' the bottom frame

    Dim blnResult As Boolean

    blnResult = SelectSupplier _
(cboSupplier.ItemData(cboSupplier.ListIndex), supCurrentSupplier)
    If blnResult Then ReloadData

End Sub
```

How It Works

Notice how small the code is.

> *At last, we're beginning to fully realize the benefits of an object-oriented approach. All the functionality to select a supplier, and then display its information, is now spread across methods in other modules.*

The first real line of code calls the routine to select a supplier. The code here is effectively saying, "Fill this `Supplier` object with information relating to supplier XXX."

Providing the result returned is `True`, meaning nothing went wrong, our `ReloadData` routine kicks in, filling the fields in the form with the information just retrieved.

> *How the information got retrieved, which tables the data came from, and so on, are not of a concern to the form – it simply calls high level routines that it knows exist elsewhere in the application.*

The application will still not run at this stage, since we need to implement two new routines. You should be getting a good feeling for how it is all coming together, so let's move on and get those buttons working.

First, the <u>A</u>dd new supplier button. If you look back over the use case for adding a new supplier, you'll see that the first thing that we need to do in the real world is create a new supplier sheet. In the application's world, a `Supplier` object has to be created. Once that is done, the user is allowed to enter data on to the sheet. The functionality for dealing with that entered data is invoked by the <u>O</u>K, <u>C</u>ancel and A<u>p</u>ply buttons at the bottom of the form, so all we are concerned with right now is allowing the user to enter data. We also need to give the user some kind of visual feedback to show what the form is expecting the user to do. In this Windows-centric world, this can be as subtle as simply enabling items on the form, and moving the cursor.

Try It Out - Coding the Add New Supplier Button

1 Code up the **Add** button's `Click` event on our form so that it looks like this:

```
Private Sub cmdAdd_Click()

    blnAddingNewSupplier = True
    CreateNewSupplier supCurrentSupplier
    ReloadData

    ' Disable the top frame and the two buttons it contains
    fraTop.Enabled = False
    cmdAdd.Enabled = False
    cmdEdit.Enabled = False

    ' Enable Cancel, OK and apply
    cmdOK.Enabled = True
    cmdCancel.Enabled = True
    cmdApply.Enabled = True

    ' Enable the bottom frame
    fraBottom.Enabled = True

    ' Move focus to the top text box
    txtCompanyName.SetFocus

End Sub
```

How It Works

Again, there's nothing too complex there, and the code remains very simple because it does nothing but set up the controls on the form, and rely on more knowledgeable routines to actually get the `Supplier` object ready to roll.

The first line just sets the `blnAddingNewSupplier` flag in the form to indicate that the form has been put in Add mode. Following that, a call is made to the `CreateNewSupplier` routine. Just as before, we pass across the `Supplier` object that the form owns, effectively asking the

`CreateNewSupplier` routine to put it into a state ready to accept new data. Once that is done, a call is made to `ReloadData`, which in this instance, because of the code in `CreateNewSupplier`, results in all the fields on the form being blanked out. This is a new supplier, after all, and the application has no idea of what data is actually going to be entered by the user.

Once that's all done, the top frame and its buttons are disabled. Then the bottom frame and its buttons are enabled, before the cursor is moved to the first text box. The result of this? The form is now ready for the user to enter some information, and the user has received some visual feedback that the state of the form has now changed.

The Edit selected supplier button works in much the same way. The user will have been expected to select a supplier before they clicked it (remember the form `Load` event selects a default supplier for them anyway, so there should be a supplier selected at all times whatever happens).

Try It Out - Coding the Edit Selected Supplier Button

1 The `Edit` button's `Click` event should look like this:

```
Private Sub cmdEdit_Click()

    blnAddingNewSupplier = False

    ' Disable the top frame and the two buttons it contains
    fraTop.Enabled = False
    cmdAdd.Enabled = False
    cmdEdit.Enabled = False

    ' Enable Cancel, OK and apply
    cmdOK.Enabled = True
    cmdCancel.Enabled = True
    cmdApply.Enabled = True

    ' Enable the bottom frame
    fraBottom.Enabled = True

    ' Move focus to the top text box
    txtCompanyName.SetFocus

End Sub
```

How It Works

Notice how it's almost the same code: the main difference is that the `blnAddingNewSupplier` flag is set to `False` to show that the form is not accepting new supplier information. There is also no call made to a routine to create or select a supplier – since the supplier has already been selected.

Great! Now our form allows users to select suppliers, and from there either create new ones, or edit the selected data. However, we still need code to go in the OK, Cancel and Apply buttons to deal with the edits that the user undertakes. Time to move on to those.

Just as before, the code to deal with these edits is implemented in modules external to the form, in order to implement the use case statements that we produced in the last chapter. For this reason, the code remains fairly simple, once again.

Let's take a look at the OK button. What should it do? Well, it needs to figure out if we are adding a new supplier, or editing an existing one. It then needs to copy the data from the form's text boxes into the properties of the Supplier object and pass that object to a routine to actually save the new supplier information, or amend the currently selected supplier. It also needs to take the form out of edit state, providing of course that there are no errors.

> *That's an interesting point incidentally. If the code in the form just needs to focus on the form itself, and know nothing about the business and its data rules, how can the form validate the information entered by the user? The simple answer is that it doesn't – validation is something that we would normally have entered into the use case modules earlier. It's the form's job to catch that error and display it to the user, no more, no less.*

Try It Out - Adding Code to the OK Button

1 Code up the OK button's click event like this.

```
Private Sub cmdOK_Click()

    Dim blnResult As Boolean

    ' Complete the transaction
    CopyEditsToObject
    On Error GoTo cmdOK_Error

    If blnAddingNewSupplier Then
        SaveNewSupplier supCurrentSupplier
        blnResult = CreateSupplierList(cboSupplier)
    Else
        SaveAmendments supCurrentSupplier
    End If

    ' Disable the OK, Cancel and Apply buttons,
    ' then disable the bottom frame
    cmdOK.Enabled = False
    cmdCancel.Enabled = False
    cmdApply.Enabled = False
    fraBottom.Enabled = False

    ' Enable the top frame, and also enable the add
    ' and edit buttons
    fraTop.Enabled = True
    cmdAdd.Enabled = True
    cmdEdit.Enabled = True
    cboSupplier.SetFocus

    Exit Sub
```

```
cmdOK_Error:
    MsgBox "There was an error with the data you entered." & vbCrLf & _
        Err.Description, vbExclamation, "Data entry error"
    txtCompanyName.SetFocus
    Exit Sub

End Sub
```

2 Now enter this code as well, which supports our `cmdOK_Click` method:

```
Private Sub CopyEditsToObject()
' Copies the edited field values on the form into the object
' ready for saving

    With supCurrentSupplier

        .strCompanyName = txtCompanyName
        .strContactName = txtContactName
        .strContactTitle = txtContactTitle
        .strAddress = txtAddress
        .strCity = txtCity
        .strRegion = txtRegion
        .strCountry = txtCountry
        .strPostalCode = txtPostalCode
        .strPhone = txtPhone
        .strFax = txtFax

    End With

End Sub
```

How It works

This code basically does the reverse of the `ReloadData` routine that we wrote earlier, copying the contents of the form's text boxes into the properties of the `Supplier` object, instead of the other way around.

Once that is done, an error handler is enabled to catch any validation errors that the other objects may pass back, and then either the `SaveNewSupplier` or `SaveAmendments` method is called. The bulk of the rest of the code does the usual enabling and disabling of user interface elements to prevent the user continuing to edit, and also giving them feedback that there changes have not been saved.

The Cancel button is even easier to code up. If you think about it, when a user cancels their edits they will really expect to see the form appear just as it was before they started to add the new record, or before they selected Edit. In this case, all we need to do is re-enable the top frame and its contents, disable the edit area, and redisplay the supplier currently selected in the combo box.

Try It Out - Adding Code to the Cancel Button

1 Add the following code, which does exactly what I just described:

```
Private Sub cmdCancel_Click()

    ' Reload the selected supplier
    Set supCurrentSupplier = Nothing
    Set supCurrentSupplier = New clsSupplier
    Dim blnResult As Boolean
    blnResult = SelectSupplier(cboSupplier.ItemData _
        (cboSupplier.ListIndex), supCurrentSupplier)
    ReloadData

    ' Disable the bottom frame, ok, cancel and apply buttons
    fraBottom.Enabled = False
    cmdOK.Enabled = False
    cmdCancel.Enabled = False
    cmdApply.Enabled = False

    ' Enable the top frame, and the add and edit buttons
    fraTop.Enabled = True
    cmdAdd.Enabled = True
    cmdEdit.Enabled = True

End Sub
```

How It Works

As you can see, the first couple of lines get rid of the old Supplier object and create a new one, asking the SelectSupplier routine to fill it with information about the supplier currently on display in the combo box. The rest of the code just deals with taking the form out of edit mode and back into selection mode.

Try It Out - Adding Code to the Apply Button

1 The final piece we need to code is the Apply button. In an application such as this, it is really nothing more than belt and braces for the user, providing them with a way to save the work they have done at that point and allowing them to continue working. For this reason, it's really nothing more than a cut down version of the OK button's code:

```
Private Sub cmdApply_Click()

    Dim blnResult As Boolean

    ' Complete the transaction
    CopyEditsToObject
    On Error GoTo cmdApply_Click_Error
```

```
            If blnAddingNewSupplier Then
                SaveNewSupplier supCurrentSupplier
            blnResult = CreateSupplierList(cboSupplier)
            Else
                SaveAmendments supCurrentSupplier
            End If


            blnAddingNewSupplier = False

            On Error GoTo 0
            Exit Sub

      cmdApply_Click_Error:

            MsgBox "There was an error with the data you entered." & vbCrLf & _
                Err.Description, vbExclamation, "Data entry error"

            txtCompanyName.SetFocus

            Exit Sub

      End Sub
```

2 Our application is ready to run.

How It Works

Again, the error handler is in there to deal with any validation errors that the support code may raise, just as in the **OK** button. The rest of the code just saves the object in the usual way.

Notice though, that immediately after calling the appropriate save routine, the blnAddingNewSupplier variable is set to False. This is essential. If we were adding a new supplier, then the first time we hit **Apply**, the new supplier record will be created. However, what happens if we hit the **Apply** button again after making further changes? Without resetting the blnAddingNewSupplier to False the **Apply** button would happily go ahead and create more new suppliers with exactly the same information that you previously entered – not a good situation, as I'm sure you can appreciate! Setting blnAddingNewSupplier to False after the first **Apply** means that any subsequent **Apply**'s are treated just as if the user was editing existing supplier information, which in fact they are.

We've now reached a significant point in the development of the Northwind application. We've completed the coding for the particular section of the application that we agreed for this chapter. What's more, it agrees with our two golden rules – the objects are weakly coupled and strongly cohesive.

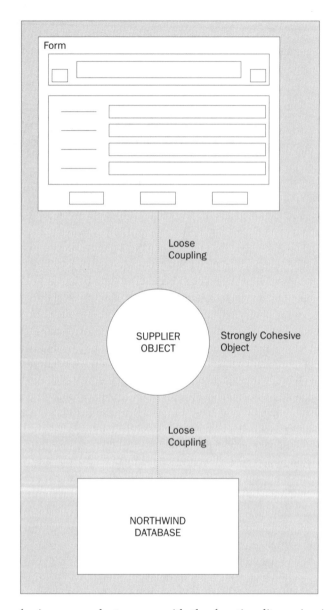

Our application so-far is now ready to run - with the functionality we've implemented thus far.

Don't forget to copy the Nwind.mdb database into the same directory as the project before you run the application, however, or the DBSuppliers object will have a nasty shock!

This is how my Northwind application looks like so far:

Summary

Well we covered a lot of ground in this final chapter. We took on board the full ramifications of the design model we developed in Chapter 9, and we've tried to stay true to the spirit of that model in our coding. Sometimes, that may have felt like we were going a little against the grain of our usual programming habits, but really, this is the professional way to proceed from having established our object-oriented design model.

I'll make no pretence: the coding was pretty hard work there when we started off, setting up our framework and gradually fleshing out the code. It was hard work, but then sometimes programming is - but notice how things started to really come together after a certain point. Once our key objects were in place in the application, it started to get easier to get them interacting and realizing the design model we intended to follow.

Furthermore, I have to say it, our application is pretty neat! We have sustained the three logical tiers our design asked of us, and our code implements these beautifully. While there's a lot of engine-room work going on behind the scenes in our DB classes, that action is logically separated from any activities defined at the business and interface levels. We have a very tidy application, and we're really working with objects as they work best.

In particular, I hope you're impressed with the way our forms, in this application, are so cleanly divorced from the nitty-gritty of the application. If we wanted to change our interface, it just would not affect the business and data tiers of this application in any troubling manner.

This chapter has offered you a glimpse at higher end object oriented programming with Visual Basic. It's quite rigorous, and it's a far cry from casually popping a few forms up and starting to create code off the top of our heads. This chapter, hard though it was, does offer you a vision. A happy medium between this rigorous approach and the more casual style we all know about is very healthy for a daily programming practice.

In this chapter we learned about:

- Implementing code from an object design model
- Cohesion and coupling in relation to object programming
- Building a framework with relationships, properties and methods
- Implementing object relations in object-oriented programming
- Adding object-oriented code to the `DBSupplier` object
- Adding object-oriented code to the `Supplier` object
- Adding object-oriented code to the use case modules
- Adding object-oriented code to the user interface form

In the final chapter of this book we shall be having an even more comprehensive look at how a real object oriented application is designed, coded and tested. We will also be looking at the world of **Business Objects** and **Utility Objects**.

6

Business and Utility Objects

Introduction

We'll begin this chapter by discussing exactly what are utility objects and business objects; if you read nothing else in this chapter, read this. What a strange thing to say I can hear you mutter, why wouldn't Peter want us to read this book cover to cover? Well of course, I'd be very pleased if you did just that, but I'm not going to hold it against you if you treat this chapter a little differently. You see, now that you've reached Chapter 11 you're familiar with all the basics of object-oriented programming, classes, ActiveX controls and components, UML and design methodologies. We've been there, seen that and done it. Now the fun really starts. Business and utility objects belong in the real world – they're not the stuff of hands-on step-by-step tutorials. So I'm not going to teach you them that way.

This chapter is really made up of five separate sections. First, there's the introduction to utility objects which I've already mentioned. Then we create a high-level design of each application in the Client Application Design section, using this design we can identify what objects we need. Then we go on to design our new utility objects in detail. Feel free to use these two parts of the chapter as an overview if you wish, although you may find that you want to take a closer look at the design if you begin writing the code in yourself.

Then we move on to looking at the actual code. You may wish to recreate these classes. If there seems to be more code than you can stomach, don't worry, you can still gain much from just reading through this section. I expect that there will be some of you that will want to try out this code yourselves, so at the very end I've included some user interfaces that use these classes. The more adventurous of you might like to try creating other interfaces to use these objects, but I'll leave you to try that out on your own.

Description of Utility Objects

Let's begin by discussing what we mean by a **utility object**. Recently many people have proclaimed that object-oriented software development technologies are a silver bullet that will solve all of the problems with creating robust applications on time. Many of these promises focus on how object-oriented technologies allow us to reuse objects. These people proclaim that the classes we create when building one application can be reused on future applications that deal with similar business entities. Often the focus of these promises of reuse center on **business objects**. In my opinion, utility objects are being overlooked in these discussions. While I feel that many of these promises have yet to be realized, I believe that there is progress in the industry. I also feel that utility classes are one of the best ways to begin to benefit from reuse.

In this chapter, I'm going to focus a lot of our discussion on utility objects. That doesn't mean that we're not going to cover business objects. In fact, two business objects will support each utility object that we'll create. I'd like the concept of business objects to take a back-seat in this chapter, so that they don't steal the limelight from our utility objects -but they are here every step of the way.

Definition of a Utility Object

When we design an application, we look for two specific types of objects that we can build to support our user interface. The two types are business objects and utility objects. Often these two types of objects work together. Here is a brief description of a utility object.

> *A utility object encapsulates the details of a function or process and allows the user of the object to interact with it using a simple and intuitive interface. Long before object technologies became popular, the tools that we are calling utility objects were sold as code libraries. These libraries provided developers with an Application Programming Interface, known as an API. These APIs were typically created for a specific language and often for a specific compiler. Today it makes more sense to create these tools using object-oriented technologies. By doing this we can create ActiveX DLLs using Visual Basic to package and distribute our tools. Through these DLLs, developers using many different languages can use these utility objects as they would any other object model.*

A big advantage of creating these tools using object-oriented technologies is that most developers find object models easier to work with than the typical API of the past. These objects, created from utility classes, do not model any real world entity like their counterparts, business objects; rather they encapsulate specific functionality that is often needed when creating applications.

Definition of a Business Object

We touched on the definition of a business object above, when we defined utility objects.

> *Business objects represent real-world 'objects' and concepts in a business. For example, you might have an Employee object, a Customer object and an Invoice object. All of these business objects have counterparts in the physical world. In the application, these objects interact with each other just as their physical equivalents do.*

Utility Objects vs. Business Objects

Now we will spend a little more time discussing the differences between utility and business objects. As we discuss these differences, remember that as with so many other things, there is not always a clear-cut distinction. Many of the objects that we identify during the design of an application could be classified as either type. In addition, it is quite common for a utility object to rely on a business object or visa versa.

The reuse of business objects is only just starting to become a reality. Often the problem is that when we create a business object, our design focuses on the needs of the current application. We create an object that will provide the services that we need at that time. It can be very difficult to look into the future and create the object to support other applications that may deal with the same object in a different way. Then when we begin the design of a new application that works with the same business entity, we try to reuse our object. At this point, we often find that we did not include all of the necessary properties and methods in the object to support our new application. Once we have discovered this problem, we are faced with three possible solutions.

> ▶ Modify the object and ensure that our old application still functions correctly
>
> ▶ Make a copy of the object as it currently exists and modify the copy to support our new application
>
> ▶ Start from scratch and build a new object to support our new application

There are technologies that help to overcome these problems, but we are only now beginning to see them really work.

While the reuse of business objects has been slow to fulfill its promise, utility objects have allowed easy reuse for years. Therefore, we will focus on utility objects in this chapter and the process of analyzing and designing an object model.

> *Although we will not cover it in this chapter, it is important to realize that these object models may be used from many different development environments including Visual C++ and Microsoft Excel. This and other books from Wrox Press will help you to understand the details of the development, but our focus will be on the procedures used to identify the objects and design their interfaces.*

The Application Suite

XYZ Financial Planners is a financial planning firm which assists its clients in all forms of financial management. Their clientele range from those who need help meeting their current obligations to clients with considerable means who are seeking assistance with retirement and investment planning.

The firm is looking for a simple yet comprehensive suite of financial applications that will assist them and their clients in gaining control of their current situation, evaluating loan options, and investment planning for both long and short term goals (such as retirement and children's college funds). The professional staff consists of individuals with varying degrees of experience and education.

The following list identifies the applications that will be delivered in the first version of this suite. In this chapter, we will follow the design and creation of a subset of these applications.

Current Situation Evaluator

This application is designed to show any client that the benefits of financial planning greatly outweigh the costs in any situation. It is intended to help the clients of XYZ Financial Planners determine the first steps to financial success and show how XYZ Financial Planners can help them in achieving even the most modest goals.

Using this application, the firm's employees can prepare personal financial statements and income projections for their clientele. The user of the Current Situation Evaluator software will enter information about the clients' assets and liabilities. This information will be analyzed to quickly identify the financial strengths and weaknesses of their clients. The Current Situation Evaluator will allow the user to include the projected effects of inflation.

This application is expected to be useful to the firm in introducing their services to potential clients. It allows the firm's representative to demonstrate to clients their real financial position. It demonstrates the potential benefits of using a financial planner and presents the opportunity to talk about the services that XYZ Financial Planners offers and how they can help to improve their client's current financial situation.

Loan Amortization

This application is intended to help the firm show a client the true cost of borrowing money. The user will enter the basic information required to calculate the payments and interest expense associated with a loan. An amortization schedule will be created showing the client the portion of each payment that will be applied towards reducing the principal balance. A summary of the total payments and total interest paid will also be shown.

An added feature will allow the user to specify an extra principal amount to be added to each payment. Extra principal payments cause a reduction in both the total amount paid and the term of the loan, and these savings will be emphasized in the summary. To assist the firm in highlighting the effects of changes to the components of the loan, different loan scenarios may be created and viewed side by side.

The application will allow the user to create these scenarios by changing the interest rate, the loan amount, the term of the loan, and the amount of extra principal payments. The client will then see the effects of these changes on the total amount of interest paid for each scenario. This application is expected to be very useful in helping those with current financial problems see the advantages of consolidating debt, aggressively paying off current debt and wisely choosing future debt.

Retirement Planning

With this application, the firm will have the ability to assist clients in identifying their future financial needs and creating a plan to achieve these goals. The user will be required to enter the basic information necessary to estimate the total amount of savings required at retirement. The application will also create a basic plan that will identify the current monthly savings required to reach the desired amount by retirement age.

This application will work similarly to the Loan Amortization application discussed above. The user will be able to create and compare multiple scenarios for the client to review. When creating each scenario the user will be allowed to supply differing values for the basic information required for creating a custom plan. These values include the desired monthly income during retirement, the age at retirement, the number of years the savings must last and the investment risk tolerance, which determines the estimated rates of return, for the before and after retirement periods. To assist the firm in highlighting the effects of the newly supplied values, the different scenarios may be viewed side by side. The client will then see the effects of these changes on the current monthly savings and on the total amount available during retirement for each scenario.

This application is expected to be very useful in helping the firm show clients the importance of planning for their future. It allows the firm's representative to introduce the planning services and the appropriate investment vehicles offered by the firm. By enabling the representative to emphasize the benefits of working with XYZ Financial Planners this application becomes a strong selling tool for the firm.

Investment Goals

With this application, the firm will have the ability to assist clients in creating a plan to achieve financial goals other than retirement. The main difference between this application and the Retirement Planner is that we only need to determine a single target amount. The user will be required to enter the basic information necessary to define their goal. These goals could include expenditures such as a child's college tuition or a sailboat to travel the world. The application will also create a basic plan to identify the monthly savings required to reach the desired amount.

This application will work much like the Retirement Planner application discussed above. The user will be able to create and compare multiple scenarios for the client to review. When creating each scenario the user will be allowed to supply differing values for the basic information required for creating their plan. These values include the desired amount, the number of years to save and the investment risk tolerance the user is willing to accept. To assist the firm in highlighting the effects of the newly supplied values, the different scenarios may be viewed side by side. The client will then see the effects of these changes on the required current monthly savings and on the total amount saved in the time specified.

This application is expected to be very useful in helping the firm show clients how they can achieve their life goals. It allows the firm's representative to introduce the many services and investment vehicles available. By enabling the representative to emphasize the benefits of working with XYZ Financial Planners, this becomes an additional selling tool for the firm.

Client Application Design

In this section, we will create a high-level design of each of the applications that we have described. The intent of doing this is not to create a full design of the client's system, but to show enough of the design to identify the objects that we will need to create. One of the main factors that we will look for in identifying the objects is the ability to reuse the object to create more than one of these applications. Another strong factor is the ability to reuse the object in applications for other clients in the future. Identifying these objects is a skill that is acquired and the best way to get it is to do it.

Our designs here will be very simple, consisting strictly of high-level **pseudocode** (English-like sentences that express what we're going to write in code).

Current Situation Evaluator

The following steps outline the flow of the Current Situation Evaluator:

```
Gather Information
        Information about each loan
        Information about assets - short-long term, liquidity
                We will utilize the Investment Planner to help quantify assets
        Information about current income
        Information about current expenses

Evaluate Each Loan - Use Loan Amortization
        Determine time to payoff
        Determine potential savings through early payoff

Evaluate Each Asset
        Determine current value
        Determine future value
        Determine liquidity

Determine Current Financial State
        Calculate monthly cash flow based on all income and all expenses

Determine Suggested Plans of Action (identify about 3 options)
        Review effects of loan consolidation
        If there is a positive cash flow
                Allocate current positive cash flow to liabilities vs. investments
                Ensure future success by focusing on appropriate investments
        Otherwise
                Prioritize payments for obligations
                Suggest expenses to be modified or eliminated

Display Information to User
        Show current cash flow
        Show current net worth
        Show suggested plans
                Show impact on current financial state over time
```

Loan Amortization

The following steps outline the flow of the Loan Amortization application:

```
Gather Information
        Amount borrowed
        Term
        Interest rate
        Extra payment amount
```

```
Calculate Periodic Payment
        This will not be affected by the amount of the extra payment

For Each Periodic Payment
        Identify principal
        Identify interest
        Identify remaining balance
        Keep a running total of interest payments

If Extra Payment Amount is Greater than 0
        For Each Periodic Payment
                Identify principal
                Identify interest
                Identify remaining balance
                Adjust remaining balance deducting the extra payment
                Keep a running total of interest payments

Display Information to User
        Show periodic loan payment amount
        Show total cost to borrow money
        Show total savings by making extra principal payments
```

Retirement Planner

The following steps outline the flow of the Retirement Planner application:

```
Gather Information
        Desired monthly income during retirement
        Years in retirement
        Years until retirement
        Assumed rate of return before retirement
        Assumed rate of return after retirement

Calculate Present Value
        This identifies the amount needed to fund the desired monthly payments
        after retirement

Calculate Future Value
        This will calculate the required periodic investment to reach the amount
        identified in the prior step

Accumulation Phase:
        For Each Periodic Investment
                Identify new balance
                Keep a running total of earnings

Distribution Phase:
        For Each Monthly Payout
                Identify new balance
                Identify total earnings
```

347

```
Display Information to User
        Show total amount required at time of retirement
        Show required periodic investment
        Show total amount of earnings prior to retirement
        Show total amount paid after retirement
        Show total earnings after retirement
        Show total earnings
```

Investment Goals

The following steps outline the flow of the Investment Goals application:

```
Gather Information
        Amount desired
        Years until needed
        Assumed rate of return

Calculate Future Value
        This will calculate the required periodic investment to reach the desired
        amount

For Each Periodic Investment
        Identify new balance
        Keep a running total of earnings

Display Information to User
        Show required periodic investment
        Show total amount of earnings
```

Identification of Utility Objects

It has taken us a long time to reach this section. The work we have done to this point is very important in the identification and design of our objects. When creating a new application, it is best to do a complete design of the application and then identify the objects that will support the design. Once these objects are identified, we can look for existing objects that we can reuse or design new objects when required.

To support the application suite that we have described above, we will need to create the following utility objects:

- Amortization object
- PresentValueOfAnnuity object
- FutureValueOfAnnuity object

We will also create several business objects that facilitate good design and modular programming, but as utility objects are so often neglected, I want us to focus our attention on them.

As we approach the end of this book, you're probably beginning to think about the next step in learning VB. If this chapter has whetted your appetite for business objects then why not take a look at Professional Visual Basic 6 Business Objects (ISBN: 1-86100107X) also from Wrox Press.

Design of Our Utility Objects

Now we need to discuss the design of the utility objects that we have defined. Some of these objects require that we create supporting objects for them.

As we review the following designs, you may think that we got lost somewhere. They do look very similar. This is intentional so don't worry. The financial calculations are similar to each other, and when the objects are used to build a user interface, the developer should not have to change his or her thinking when moving between them. Bear with me and realize that it is important to design each object even when they are so similar.

Amortization Object

As we've discussed above, one of the utility objects that we need to build to support the applications defined for our client is the Amortization object. This object will support the both Loan Amortization and Current Situation Evaluator applications. Also, this is a very common calculation that we may use often in our future work.

The following illustrates the public interface for the Amortization object:

        Properties:
                Amount
                Rate
                NumberOfPayments
                PaymentsPerYear
                ExtraPayment
                PaymentAmount
                TotalInterest
                TotalInterestWithExtra
                TotalNumPaymentsWithExtra
                PaymentDetails
                ExtraPaymentDetails

        Methods:
                Calculate

To support the PaymentDetails and ExtraPaymentDetails properties we will need to create two extra objects. The first supporting object is the Payment business object. This object will manage the information about each payment made during the term of the loan.

The following illustrates the public interface for the Payment object:

Properties:
      PaymentNumber
      PaymentAmount
      Principal
      Interest
      RemainingBalance

Methods:
      None

The second supporting object required for our design of the Amortization object is the Payments collection. This class is implemented as a wrapper around the Visual Basic standard collection object. We wrap the standard object to ensure that it will only allow Payment objects to be added. This collection will hold Payment objects for each loan payment.

Remember, we looked at collections in Chapter 4, when we discussed Object Hierarchies.

The following illustrates the public interface for the Payments collection object:

Properties:
      None

Methods:
      Add
      Count
      Item
      Remove

Now that we've identified the properties and methods of the Amortization object and its related objects, we can take this analysis a stage further and design the properties and methods in detail.

The first design that we will cover is that of the Payment object. Check it out!

This object's instancing should be set as "2-PublicNotCreatable"

PaymentNumber Property
      This is a long variable
      Read only for public interface
      Allowed to be set from within the DLL (Friend)
      This specifies which payment this object describes

PaymentAmount Property
      This is a currency variable
      Read only for public interface
      Allowed to be set from within the DLL (Friend)
      This is the total amount of the payment

Principal Property
> This is a currency variable
> Read only for public interface
> Allowed to be set from within the DLL (Friend)
> This is the portion of the payment that will reduce the outstanding balance

Interest Property
> This is a currency variable
> Read only for public interface
> Allowed to be set from within the DLL (Friend)
> This is the portion of the payment that goes towards paying interest

RemainingBalance Property
> This is a currency variable
> Read only for public interface
> Allowed to be set from within the DLL (Friend)
> This is the value of the outstanding balance after crediting this payment

The next design that we will review is for the Payments collection object:

> This collection's instancing should be set as "2-PublicNotCreatable"

Class_Initialize
> Create a member variable of type collection to do our work

Class_Terminate
> Ensure that the member variable is destroyed

Add Method
> Adds a Payment object to the collection

Count Method
> Returns the count of Payment objects from the collection

Item Method
> Returns the specified Payment object from the collection

Remove Method
> Removes the specified Payment object from the collection

Finally, we come to the design of our Amortization object:

Class_Initialize
> Create Payments object for the PaymentDetails property
> Create Payments object for the ExtraPaymentDetails property

Class_Terminate
> Set PaymentDetails = Nothing
> Set ExtraPaymentDetails = Nothing

Amount Property
>   This is a currency variable
>   This property is both read and write capable
>   The value must be greater than 0
>   It holds the amount of money borrowed

Rate Property
>   This is a double variable
>   This property is both read and write capable
>   The value must be greater than 0
>   The value must be less than 50
>   This is the interest rate for the loan.
>   It holds the interest rate and is set as a value expressed in number of percent (i.e. setting the value to 6.5 gives us 6.5% or .065)

NumberOfPayments Property
>   This is a long variable
>   This property is both read and write capable
>   The value must be greater than 0
>   This is the number of payments for the loan

PaymentsPerYear Property
>   This is a long variable
>   This property is both read and write capable
>   This value must be greater than 0
>   This is the number of payments due per year

ExtraPayment Property
>   This is a currency variable
>   This property is both read and write capable
>   This value must be greater than or equal to 0
>   This amount reflects extra payments applied to reduce the loan balance
>   If it is a zero then we will ignore it

PaymentAmount Property
>   This is a currency variable
>   This property is read only
>   This is the amount of the required payment
>   This is calculated by calling the Calculate method

TotalInterest Property
>   This is a currency variable
>   This property is read only
>   This is the total amount of interest paid for the loan as defined
>   This is calculated by calling the Calculate method
>   This ignores an extra payment

TotalInterestWithExtra Property
>   This is a currency variable
>   This property is read only
>   This is the total amount of interest paid for the loan with extra payments
>   This is calculated by calling the Calculate method

TotalNumPaymentsWithExtra Property
> This is a long variable
> This property is read only
> This is the total number of payments to pay off loan with extra payments
> This is calculated by calling the Calculate method

PaymentDetails Property
> This is a reference to the Payments object we defined earlier
> This property is read only
> Through this collection, the UI Developer can access information about each payment
> This collection is filled by calling the Calculate method

ExtraPaymentDetails Property
> This is a reference to the Payments object we defined earlier
> This property is read only
> Through this collection, the UI Developer can access information about each payment with extra payment
> This collection is filled by calling the Calculate method

Calculate Method
> This method will accept the following parameters
>> Amount
>> Rate
>> NumberOfPayments
>> PaymentsPerYear
>> ExtraPayment
> Each of these parameters is optional

> 'If the parameters are passed in then set our properties accordingly
> If Amount is non zero
>> Set Amount property equal to the input parameter

> If Rate is non zero
>> Set Rate property equal to the input parameter

> If NumberOfPayments is non zero
>> Set NumberOfPayments property equal to the input parameter

> If PaymentsPerYear is non zero
>> Set PaymentsPerYear property equal to the input parameter

> If ExtraPayment is non zero
>> Set ExtraPayment property equal to the input parameter

> 'Check to ensure that we have all of the required data
> If Amount <= 0 Then Raise Error to caller
> If Rate <= 0 Then Raise Error to caller
> If NumberOfPayments < = 0 Then Raise Error to caller
> If PaymentsPerYear <= 0 Then Raise Error to caller

```
'Calculate Periodic Payment
Set PaymentAmount = calculated payment
      PeriodicRate => (Rate/100/PaymentsPerYear)
      Factor2 => 1/(1+PeriodicRate)^NumberOfPayments
      Factor4 => (1-Factor2)/PeriodicRate
      Formula is => Amount/Factor4

'Calculate TotalInterest and Details for each payment
CurrentBalance = Amount
Counter = 1

For each Payment (count up to NumberOfPayments)
      Create a Payment object

      Set Payment.PaymentNumber = Counter
      Set Payment.Interest = CurrentBalance * PeriodicRate
      Set Payment.Principal = PaymentAmount - Payment.Interest
      Set Payment.RemainingBalance =
            CurrentBalance - Payment.Principal
      Set CurrentBalance = Payment.RemainingBalance

      Add Payment to PaymentDetails collection
      Increment Counter
Loop

' if we have an extra payment then calculate second payments info
If ExtraPayment > 0
      'Calculate TotalInterest and Details for each payment
      CurrentBalance = Amount
      Counter = 1

      While CurrentBalance > 0
            Create a Payment object

            Set Payment.PaymentNumber = Counter
            Set Payment.Interest = CurrentBalance * PeriodicRate
            Set Payment.Principal = PaymentAmount -
                  Payment.Interest + ExtraPayment
            Set Payment.RemainingBalance =
                  CurrentBalance - Payment.Principal
            Set CurrentBalance = Payment.RemainingBalance

            Add Payment to ExtraPaymentDetails collection
            Increment Counter
      Loop
End If
```

PresentValueOfAnnuity Object

Another utility object that we need to build is the PresentValueOfAnnuity. This object will support the Retirement Planning and the Investment Planning applications. As with the Amortization object, we begin by decided what properties and methods our objects will possess. Then we design our objects in greater detail.

The following illustrates the public interface for the PresentValueOfAnnuity object:

> Properties:
> > PayoutAmount
> > Rate
> > NumberOfPayouts
> > PayoutsPerYear
> > PresentValue
> > TotalEarnings
> > TotalPayouts
> > PayoutDetails

> Methods:
> > Calculate

To support the PayoutDetails property we need to create two extra objects. The first supporting object is the Payout business object. This object will manage the information about each payout that is made during the term of the annuity.

The following illustrates the public interface for the Payout object:

> Properties:
> > PayoutNumber
> > PayoutAmount
> > EarningsForPeriod
> > ReturnOfCapital
> > RemainingBalance

> Methods:
> > None

The second supporting object that is required for our PresentValueOfAnnuity object is the Payouts collection. This class is implemented as a wrapper around the Visual Basic standard collection object. We wrap the standard object to ensure that it will only allow Payout objects to be added. This collection will hold Payout objects for each payout for the life of the annuity.

The following illustrates the public interface for the Payouts collection object:

> Properties:
> > None

> Methods:
> > Add
> > Count
> > Item
> > Remove

Now, as before, we need to define our objects further.

The first design that we will cover is the design of the Payout object:

> This object's instancing should be set as "2-PublicNotCreatable"
>
> PayoutNumber Property
> > This is a long variable
> > Read only for public interface
> > Allowed to be set from within the DLL (Friend)
> > This specifies which payout this object describes
>
> PayoutAmount Property
> > This is a currency variable
> > Read only for public interface
> > Allowed to be set from within the DLL (Friend)
> > This is the total amount of the payout
>
> EarningsForPeriod Property
> > This is a currency variable
> > Read only for public interface
> > Allowed to be set from within the DLL (Friend)
> > This is the earnings portion of the payout for this period
>
> ReturnOfCapital Property
> > This is a currency variable
> > Read only for public interface
> > Allowed to be set from within the DLL (Friend)
> > This is the return of capital portion of the payout for this period
>
> RemainingBalance Property
> > This is a currency variable
> > Read only for public interface
> > Allowed to be set from within the DLL (Friend)
> > This is the remain value of the annuity after the payment

The next design that we will review is for the Payouts collection object:

> This collection's instancing should be set as "2-PublicNotCreatable"
>
> Class_Initialize
> > Create a member variable of type collection to do our work
>
> Class_Terminate
> > Ensure that the member variable is destroyed
>
> Add Method
> > Adds a Payout object to the collection
>
> Count Method
> > Returns the count of Payout objects from the collection

Item Method
> Returns the specified Payout object from the collection

Remove Method
> Removes the specified Payout object from the collection

Finally, let's design our PresentValueOfAnnuity object:

Class_Initialize
> Create a new PayoutDetails object

Class_Terminate
> Set PayoutDetail = Nothing

PayoutAmount Property
> This is a currency variable
> This property is both read and write capable
> The value must be greater than 0
> It is the amount of each desired payout

Rate Property
> This is a double variable
> This property is both read and write capable
> The value must be greater than 0
> The value must be less than 50
> This is the estimated rate of return
> It holds the rate of return and is set as a value expressed in number of percent (i.e. setting the value to 6.5 gives us 6.5% or .065)

NumberOfPayouts Property
> This is a long variable
> This property is both read and write capable
> The value must be greater than 0
> This is the number of periods for the annuity

PayoutsPerYear Property
> This is a long variable
> This property is both read and write capable
> This value must be greater than 0
> This is the number of periods per year

PresentValue Property
> This is a currency variable
> This property is read only
> This is the amount of the required to fund the annuity
> This is calculated by calling the Calculate method

TotalEarnings Property
> This is a currency variable
> This property is read only
> This is the total amount of earnings over the life of the annuity as defined
> This is calculated by calling the Calculate method

TotalPayouts Property
   This is a currency variable
   This property is read only
   This is the sum of all payouts over the life of the annuity
   This is calculated by calling the Calculate method

PayoutDetails Property
   This is a reference to the Payouts object we defined earlier
   This property is read only
   Through this collection, the UI Developer can access information about each payout
   This collection is filled by calling the Calculate method

Calculate Method
   This method will accept the following parameters
      PayoutAmount
      Rate
      NumberOfPayouts
      PayoutsPerYear
   Each of these parameters is optional

   'If the parameters are passed in then set our properties accordingly
   If PayoutAmount is non zero
      Set PayoutAmount property equal to the input parameter

   If Rate is non zero
      Set Rate property equal to the input parameter

   If NumberOfPayouts is non zero
      Set NumberOfPayouts property equal to the input parameter

   If PayoutsPerYear is non zero
      Set PayoutsPerYear property equal to the input parameter

   'Check to ensure that we have all of the required data
   If PayoutAmount <= 0 Then Raise Error to caller
   If Rate <= 0 Then Raise Error to caller
   If NumberOfPayouts < = 0 Then Raise Error to caller
   If PayoutsPerYear <= 0 Then Raise Error to caller

   'Calculate Periodic Payout
   Set PresentValue = calculated payment
      PeriodicRate => (Rate/100/PayoutsPerYear)
      Factor2 => 1/(1+PeriodicRate)^NumberOfPayouts
      Factor4 => (1-Factor2)/PeriodicRate
      Formula is => PayoutAmount*Factor4

   'Calculate TotalEarnings and Details for each payout
   CurrentBalance = Amount
   Counter = 1

```
For each Payout (count up to NumberOfPayouts)
        Create a Payout object
        Set Payout.PayoutNumber = Counter
        Set Payout.EarningsForPeriod = CurrentBalance * PeriodicRate
        Set Payout.ReturnOfCaptial =
                PayoutAmount - Payout.EarningsForPeriod
        Set Payout.RemainingBalance =
                CurrentBalance - Payout.ReturnOfCapital
        Set CurrentBalance = Payout.RemainingBalance

        Add Payout to PayoutDetails collection
        Increment Counter
Loop
```

FutureValueOfAnnuity Object

To support the Retirement, Investment Planning and Current Situation Evaluator applications in our application suite we need to provide a FutureValueOfAnnuity object. This object computes the future value of a steady stream of payments. The selected rate and term influence this calculation. We use this object to determine the required payments to reach our future financial goal. Because this formula is used in many financial calculations, it will again be very valuable in our bag of tricks.

The following illustrates the public interface for the FutureValueOfAnnuity object:

```
Properties:
        DesiredAmount
        Rate
        NumberOfInvestments
        InvestmentsPerYear
        InvestmentAmount
        TotalEarnings
        TotalInvestments
        InvestmentDetails

Methods:
        Calculate
```

To support the InvestmentAmount property we need to create two extra objects. The first of these objects is the PeriodicInvestment business object. This object will manage the information about each investment that is made during the funding term.

The following illustrates the public interface for the PeriodicInvestment object:

```
Properties:
        InvestmentNumber
        InvestmentAmount
        EarningsForPeriod
        CurrentBalance
```

Methods:
> None

We will discuss the design of this object in greater detail below.

The other object required for our design is the PeriodicInvestments collection object. This object is implemented as a simple wrapper around the standard Visual Basic collection object. Doing this allows us to create a collection that is guaranteed to hold only Installment objects. This collection will hold an Installment object relating to each investment made into the annuity.

The following illustrates the public interface for the PeriodicInvestments collection object:

Properties:
> None

Methods:
> Add
> Count
> Item
> Remove

Once more, let's enhance our design by providing more detail.

The first design that we will cover is the design of the PeriodicInvestment object:

InvestmentNumber Property
> This is a long variable
> Read only for public interface
> Allowed to be set from within the DLL (Friend)
> This specifies which investment this object describes

InvestmentAmount Property
> This is a currency variable
> Read only for public interface
> Allowed to be set from within the DLL (Friend)
> This is the amount invested in this investment

EarningsForPeriod Property
> This is a currency variable
> Read only for public interface
> Allowed to be set from within the DLL (Friend)
> This is the amount of earnings for this period

CurrentBalance Property
> This is a currency variable
> Read only for public interface
> Allowed to be set from within the DLL (Friend)
> This is the current value of the investment after this investment and earnings

The next design that we will review is for the PeriodicInvestments collection object:

This collection's instancing should be set as "2-PublicNotCreatable"

Class_Initialize
> Create a member variable of type collection to do our work

Class_Terminate
> Ensure that the member variable is destroyed

Add Method
> Adds a PeriodicInvestment object to the collection

Count Method
> Returns the count from the PeriodicInvestment objects in this collection

Item Method
> Returns the specified PeriodicInvestment object from the collection

Remove Method
> Removes the specified PeriodicInvestment object from the collection

Finally, look at the design for the FutureValueOfAnnuity object:

Class_Initialize
> Create a new InvestmentDetails object

Class_Terminate
> Set InvestmentDetails = Nothing

DesiredAmount Property
> This is a currency variable
> This property is both read and write capable
> The value must be greater than 0
> It holds the amount of money desired at a future date

Rate Property
> This is a double variable
> This property is both read and write capable
> The value must be greater than 0
> The value must be less than 50
> This is the assumed rate of return
> It holds the rate of return and is set as a value expressed in number of percent (i.e. setting the value to 6.5 gives us 6.5% or .065)

NumberOfInvestments property
> This is a long variable
> This property is both read and write capable
> The value must be greater than 0
> This is the number of investment periods

InvestmentsPerYear Property
> This is a long variable
> This property is both read and write capable
> This value must be greater than 0
> This is the number of investments per year

InvestmentAmount Property
> This is a currency variable
> This property is read only
> This is the amount of the required periodic investment to meet our target amount
> This is calculated by calling the Calculate method

TotalInvestments Property
> This is a currency variable
> This property is read only
> This is the total amount of investments
> This is calculated by calling the Calculate method

TotalEarnings Property
> This is a currency variable
> This property is read only
> This is the total amount of earnings realized
> This is calculated by calling the Calculate method

InvestmentDetails Property
> This is a reference to the PeriodicInvestments object we defined earlier
> This property is read only
> Through this collection, the UI Developer can access information about each investment
> This collection is filled by calling the Calculate method

Calculate Method
> This method will accept the following parameters
>> DesiredAmount
>> Rate
>> NumberOfInvestments
>> InvestmentsPerYear
> Each of these parameters is optional

> 'If the parameters are passed in then set our properties accordingly
> If DesiredAmount is non zero
>> Set DesiredAmount property equal to the input parameter

> If Rate is non zero
>> Set Rate property equal to the input parameter

> If NumberOfInvestments is non zero
>> Set NumberOfInvestments property equal to the input parameter

```
If InvestmentsPerYear is non zero
        Set InvestmentsPerYear property equal to the input parameter

'Check to ensure that we have all of the required data
If DesiredAmount <= 0 Then Raise Error to caller
If Rate <= 0 Then Raise Error to caller
If NumberOfInvestments < = 0 Then Raise Error to caller
If InvestmentsPerYear <= 0 Then Raise Error to caller

'Calculate Periodic Investment
Set InvestmentAmount = calculated payment
        PeriodicRate => (Rate/100/PayoutsPerYear)
        Factor1 => (1+PeriodicRate)^NumberOfPayouts
        Factor3 => (Factor1-1)/PeriodicRate
        Formula is => Amount/Factor3

'Calculate Periodic InvestmentAmount and Details for each payment
CurrentBalance = 0
Counter = 1

For each PeriodicInvestment(count up to NumberOfInvestments)
        Create a PeriodicInvestment object
        Set PeriodicInvestment.InvestmentNumber = Counter
        Set PeriodicInvestment.InvestmentAmount = InstallmentAmount
        Set PeriodicInvestment.EarningsForPeriod =
                CurrentBalance * PeriodicRate
        Set PeriodicInvestment.CurrentBalance = CurrentBalance +
                PeriodicInvestment.EarningsForPeriod + InvestmentAmount

        Add PeriodicInvestment to InvestmentDetails collection
        Increment Counter
Loop
```

Create Classes

In this section, we will see what all of our work has done for us. This is where we will actually create our objects in Visual Basic. I've said this already, but I'll say it once more as it's a point every programmer should know; planning and design are very important steps. Seldom will our plans and designs be implemented without changes and modification, but by doing a thorough analysis and design of our project we will be much more effective as we build our system.

Now we will discuss all of the code that must be created to implement each of the utility objects that we designed in the last section. There won't be many comments in amongst the code, as we shall be discussing each section in detail. However, when you actually write your own code, you should be liberal with comments, as these can serve to help you understand what you have done when you return to the code later.

Comments are so important, that I have some rules that I would like to suggest to you:

> First, describe the purpose of each file. Provide a general header that will allow someone to quickly understand the purpose of the file, which in our case will be a class. Included in this header should be a place to identify each change that is made to the file.

> Second, add a description to each procedure in the file. This again should be a general description of the purpose of the procedure.

> Finally, include general comments about what a section of code is doing.

I have found that when I work with code that has been around for a while, if there are any comments at all they are usually out of date and not relevant to the current version of the code. By writing code that is very readable (some would call this **self-documenting code**) and by having only general descriptions of the purpose of each file and procedure, the comments don't tend to become dated. This helps to ensure that the comments are relevant and useful when we return to maintain our code later.

Payment Class

Let's begin by looking at the `Payment` object. When Visual Basic starts create a new ActiveX DLL project and name the first class `Payment`.

It's good practice to use this standard header at the top of each file. Notice that we include the names of the original developer and an initial entry into the `Change History` section.

```
'
' Payment Class
'
' Created:  1998-09-10
'
' Created By:        Peter Wright
'
' Summary:  This class defines the Amortization object.
'           It provides the detailed information about
'           each payment made or due to be made over
'           the life of a loan
'
' Change History:
'       Developer       Date                Notes
'       PW              1998-09-10          Initial creation
'
```

The next section declares the member variables for this class. These are typically private variables (so they are not visible to the outside world) that maintain the state of the object. The user of the object has access to this state information through the properties and methods.

```
Option Explicit

Private m_lngPaymentNumber As Long
Private m_curPayment As Currency
Private m_curPrincipal As Currency
Private m_curInterest As Currency
Private m_curBalance As Currency
```

After the declaration of any module-level variables, we move on to the procedures that really create our object. We can break these into four sections:

- Class event handlers
- Property procedures
- Methods
- Supporting procedures

We can write headings in our code to indicate where procedures that belong to each of these four sections are placed. I recommend including these headers even when our object does not currently have any need for code in them. By doing this we keep each of our classes looking very similar and anyone that has to maintain the code at a later date can be sure they know where to find any code that they need to review.

```
' Create class event handlers

' Create the properties for our class

' Create the methods for our class

' Create the supporting procedures for our class
```

Now that we've discussed how code should be written, roll up your sleeves and let's get our hands dirty with some code. (Although I'll be concentrating on the actual code itself here, I hope that you practice the good-coding techniques I've mentioned so that they become second nature you.)

The Payment class has a series of `Property Gets` and `Lets` to read and write the properties we defined in our design. One point, in this class all of our properties have `Public` read access, but only `Friend` write access. Implementing the `Property Let` procedures as `Friend` allows any code within the DLL to access these procedures, but they will not be accessible outside of the DLL.

```
Public Property Get PaymentNumber() As Long
    PaymentNumber = m_lngPaymentNumber
End Property

Friend Property Let PaymentNumber(lngPaymentNum As Long)
    m_lngPaymentNumber = lngPaymentNum
End Property

Public Property Get PaymentAmount() As Currency
    PaymentAmount = m_curPayment
End Property

Friend Property Let PaymentAmount(curPayment As Currency)
    m_curPayment = curPayment
End Property

Public Property Get Principal() As Currency
    Principal = m_curPrincipal
End Property
```

```
Friend Property Let Principal(curPrincipal As Currency)
    m_curPrincipal = curPrincipal
End Property
```

```
Public Property Get Interest() As Currency
    Interest = m_curInterest
End Property
```

```
Friend Property Let Interest(curInterest As Currency)
    m_curInterest = curInterest
End Property
```

```
Public Property Get RemainingBalance() As Currency
    RemainingBalance = m_curBalance
End Property
```

```
Friend Property Let RemainingBalance(curBalance As Currency)
    m_curBalance = curBalance
End Property
```

There's nothing new here, we're just assigned reading and writing from properties, but let's run through what all these properties are for. The `PaymentNumber` property indicates the number of the payment for which this objects specifies the details. The `PaymentAmount` property is the periodic payment due for the loan - each payment object will have the same value. The `Principal` property is the amount that the loan balance is reduced by after this payment. The `Interest` property is the amount of the payment that is applied to the cost of the loan. Finally, the `RemainingBalance` property indicates the principal amount left on the loan after this payment.

Payments Class

This class defines the `Amortization` object. It provides a collection of `Payment` objects that describe each payment due for the loan. This collection class is **type safe** in that it only allows `Payment` objects to be added to the collection. We mimic the standard collection interface, but modify it as needed to only support our limited needs.

Again, we declare a member variable to maintain the object's state. `m_colPayments` is `Private` so that the outside world cannot see it.

```
Option Explicit

Private m_colPayments As Collection
```

The `Payments` class contains code in its event handlers. The following two routines just create the collection object and then set it to `Nothing` when the object is terminated. The routines are shown below:

```
Private Sub Class_Initialize()
    Set m_colPayments = New Collection
End Sub

Private Sub Class_Terminate()
    Set m_colPayments = Nothing
End Sub
```

The methods of the `Payments` class mimic the collection methods.

```
Public Sub Add(Item As Payment)
    m_colPayments.Add Item
End Sub
```

```
Public Function Count() As Long
    Count = m_colPayments.Count
End Function
```

```
Public Function Item(Index As Variant) As Payment
    Set Item = m_colPayments.Item(Index)
End Function
```

```
Public Sub Remove(Index As Variant)
    m_colPayments.Remove Index
End Sub
```

```
Public Function NewEnum() As IUnknown
    Set NewEnum = m_colPayments.[_NewEnum]
End Function
```

The `Item` method is the default method. To set this, select <u>T</u>ools-Procedure <u>A</u>ttributes-Ad<u>v</u>anced and set the **Procedure** <u>I</u>D to **(Default)**.

The **Procedure ID** of the `NewEnum` procedure should be set to **-4** and the **Hide this** <u>m</u>ember check box in the **Attributes** frame should be checked.

The `Payments` object is just a wrapper around the standard Visual Basic collection class that ensures that only `Payment` objects can be added. The only real code to note here is the implementation of the `NewEnum` function. This allows the user interface developer to use the `For Each` notation to iterate through our collection to process each `Payment` object that it contains.

Amortization Class

The final object that we needed to create to support our amortization requirements is the `Amortization` object. Through this object, a user interface developer is able to set the properties to the required values so that payment information about a loan can be calculated. Once the values have been identified, the `Calculate` method will determine the periodic payment, total interest to be paid over the life of the loan and the details about each individual payment.

As usual, we begin by creating member variable to maintain the object's state. These are all `Private` so they cannot be seen by the outside world. We also create private constants for error handling.

```
Option Explicit

Private m_objPaymentDetails As Payments
Private m_objExtraPaymentDetails As Payments
Private m_curAmount As Currency
Private m_dblRate As Double
Private m_lngNumPayments As Long
```

```
Private m_lngPaymentsPerYear As Long
Private m_curExtraPayment As Currency
Private m_curPaymentAmount As Currency
Private m_curTotalInterest As Currency
Private m_curExtraInterest As Currency

Private Const INVALIDAMOUNTERR As Long = vbObjectError + 1001
Private Const INVALIDAMOUNT As String = _
 "The amount of the loan must be specified"
Private Const INVALIDRATEERR As Long = vbObjectError + 1002
Private Const INVALIDRATE As String = _
 "The specified interest rate is invalid"
Private Const INVALIDNUMPAYMENTSERR As Long = vbObjectError + 1003
Private Const INVALIDNUMPAYMENTS As String = _
 "The number of payments must be greater than 0"
Private Const INVALIDPAYMENTSPERERR As Long = vbObjectError + 1004
Private Const INVALIDPAYMENTSPER As String = _
 "There must be at least one payment due each year"
```

Now let's take a look at the class event handlers. The `Initialize` event creates the `Payments` objects that will maintain the list of information about each payment. The `Terminate` event ensures that the memory for the objects is freed.

```
Private Sub Class_Initialize()
   Set m_objPaymentDetails = New Payments
   Set m_objExtraPaymentDetails = New Payments
End Sub
```

```
Private Sub Class_Terminate()
   Set m_objPaymentDetails = Nothing
   Set m_objExtraPaymentDetails = Nothing
End Sub
```

The `Amortization` object has a number of properties that we must write `Property Get` and `Property Let` routines for:

```
Public Property Get Amount() As Currency
   Amount = m_curAmount
End Property
```

```
Public Property Let Amount(curAmount As Currency)
   If curAmount <= 0 Then
       Err.Raise vbObjectError + 1001, _
     "FinancialUtility:Amortization:Amount", INVALIDAMOUNT
   End If
   m_curAmount = curAmount
End Property
```

```
Public Property Get Rate() As Double
   Rate = m_dblRate
End Property
```

```
Public Property Let Rate(dblRate As Double)
   If dblRate <= 0 Or dblRate > 50 Then
       Err.Raise INVALIDRATEERR, _
         "FinancialUtility:Amortization:Calculate", INVALIDRATE
```

368

```
      End If
      m_dblRate = dblRate
   End Property


   Public Property Get NumberOfPayments() As Long
      NumberOfPayments = m_lngNumPayments
   End Property


   Public Property Let NumberOfPayments(lngPayments As Long)
      If lngPayments <= 0 Then
         Err.Raise INVALIDNUMPAYMENTSERR, _
         "FinancialUtility:Amortization:Calculate", INVALIDNUMPAYMENTS
      End If
      m_lngNumPayments = lngPayments
   End Property


   Public Property Get PaymentsPerYear() As Long
      PaymentsPerYear = m_lngPaymentsPerYear
   End Property


   Public Property Let PaymentsPerYear(lngPaymentsPerYear As Long)
      If lngPaymentsPerYear <= 0 Then
         Err.Raise INVALIDPAYMENTSPERERR, _
         "FinancialUtility:Amortization:Calculate", INVALIDPAYMENTSPER
      End If
      m_lngPaymentsPerYear = lngPaymentsPerYear
   End Property


   Public Property Get ExtraPayment() As Currency
      ExtraPayment = m_curExtraPayment
   End Property


   Public Property Let ExtraPayment(curExtraPayment As Currency)
      m_curExtraPayment = curExtraPayment
   End Property


   Public Property Get PaymentAmount() As Currency
      PaymentAmount = m_curPaymentAmount
   End Property


   Public Property Get TotalInterest() As Currency
      TotalInterest = m_curTotalInterest
   End Property


   Public Property Get TotalInterestWithExtra() As Currency
      If m_curExtraPayment > 0 Then
         TotalInterestWithExtra = m_curExtraInterest
      Else
         TotalInterestWithExtra = TotalInterest
      End If
   End Property


   Public Property Get TotalNumPaymentsWithExtra() As Long
      If m_curExtraPayment > 0 Then
         TotalNumPaymentsWithExtra = ExtraPaymentDetails.Count
      Else
```

```
        TotalNumPaymentsWithExtra = PaymentDetails.Count
    End If
End Property
```

```
Public Property Get PaymentDetails() As Payments
    Set PaymentDetails = m_objPaymentDetails
End Property
```

```
Public Property Get ExtraPaymentDetails() As Payments
    Set ExtraPaymentDetails = m_objExtraPaymentDetails
End Property
```

Let's briefly discuss the purpose of each property and any interesting code issues.

The `Amount`, `Rate`, `NumberOfPayments`, `PaymentsPerYear` and `ExtraPayment` properties are all read-write. The `PaymentAmount`, `TotalInterest`, `TotalInterestWithExtra`, `TotalNumPaymentsWithExtra`, `PaymentDetails` and `ExtraPaymentDetails` properties are read-only and so don't have a `Property Let`. In addition, all the `Property Lets`, except for that of the `ExtraPayment` property, contain code to check that the property value is valid before writing that value to the property.

The `Amount` property just indicates the amount of money borrowed. The `Rate` property is the interest rate for the loan, which is expressed in percentages - for example 6.5 is 6.5% or .065 per year. The `NumberOfPayments` property identifies the number of payments to be made over the life of the loan. The `PaymentsPerYear` property identifies the number of payments that are required each year. The `ExtraPayment` property is included to show how adding an extra amount to each payment can effect the total cost of borrowing the money.

The other properties are all set when the `Calculate` method is called. The `PaymentAmount` property gives the required periodic payment for the loan. The `TotalInterest` property gives the total amount of interest to be paid over the life of the loan. The `TotalInterestWithExtra` property is only set if the `ExtraPayment` property is greater than zero. The `TotalInterestWithExtra` property gives the total amount of interest to be paid over the life of the loan if the specified extra payment is made. The `TotalNumPaymentsWithExtra` property is also only set if the `ExtraPayment` property is greater than zero - this property gives the total number of payments to be made if the specified extra payment is made. The `PaymentDetails` property returns a reference to a `Payments` object that holds information about each scheduled payment for the loan. Likewise, the `ExtraPaymentDetails` property returns a reference to a `Payments` object that holds information about each scheduled payment for the loan - however, this is only filled if there are extra payments to be made, and it reflects the effects of these payments.

Now let's move onto the sole method of our class - the `Calculate` method. This method is the workhorse of our class. This is where all of the information is generated and properties are set as required.

```
Public Sub Calculate(Optional curAmount As Currency, _
Optional dblRate As Double, Optional lngNumPayments As Long, _
Optional lngPaymentsPerYear As Long, Optional curExtraPayment As Currency)

    Dim dblPeriodicRate As Double
    Dim dblFactor2 As Double
    Dim dblFactor4 As Double
```

```
    Dim curCurrentBalance As Currency
    Dim lngCounter As Long
    Dim objPayment As Payment

    On Error GoTo CALCULATE_ERROR

    If curAmount <> 0 Then m_curAmount = curAmount
    If dblRate <> 0 Then m_dblRate = dblRate
    If lngNumPayments <> 0 Then m_lngNumPayments = lngNumPayments
    If lngPaymentsPerYear <> 0 Then _
        m_lngPaymentsPerYear = lngPaymentsPerYear
    If curExtraPayment <> 0 Then m_curExtraPayment = curExtraPayment

    If m_curAmount <= 0 Then
        Err.Raise INVALIDAMOUNTERR, _
        "FinancialUtility:Amortization:Calculate", INVALIDAMOUNT
    End If

    If m_dblRate <= 0 Or dblRate > 50 Then
        Err.Raise INVALIDRATEERR, _
        "FinancialUtility:Amortization:Calculate", INVALIDRATE
    End If

    If m_lngNumPayments <= 0 Then
        Err.Raise INVALIDNUMPAYMENTSERR, _
        "FinancialUtility:Amortization:Calculate", INVALIDNUMPAYMENTS
    End If

    If m_lngPaymentsPerYear <= 0 Then
        Err.Raise INVALIDPAYMENTSPERERR, _
        "FinancialUtility:Amortization:Calculate", INVALIDPAYMENTSPER
    End If

    dblPeriodicRate = (m_dblRate / 100 / m_lngPaymentsPerYear)

    dblFactor2 = 1 / (1 + dblPeriodicRate) ^ m_lngNumPayments
    dblFactor4 = (1 - dblFactor2) / dblPeriodicRate
    m_curPaymentAmount = m_curAmount / dblFactor4

    curCurrentBalance = m_curAmount

    For lngCounter = 1 To m_lngNumPayments
        Set objPayment = New Payment

        With objPayment
            .PaymentNumber = lngCounter
            .PaymentAmount = m_curPaymentAmount
            .Interest = curCurrentBalance * dblPeriodicRate
            m_curTotalInterest = m_curTotalInterest + .Interest
            .Principal = m_curPaymentAmount - .Interest
            .RemainingBalance = curCurrentBalance - .Principal

            curCurrentBalance = .RemainingBalance
        End With

        m_objPaymentDetails.Add objPayment
        Set objPayment = Nothing
    Next
```

```
        If m_curExtraPayment > 0 Then
            curCurrentBalance = m_curAmount
            lngCounter = 1

            While curCurrentBalance > 0
                Set objPayment = New Payment

                With objPayment
                    .PaymentNumber = lngCounter
                    .Interest = curCurrentBalance * dblPeriodicRate
                    m_curExtraInterest = m_curExtraInterest + .Interest
                    .Principal = _
                    m_curPaymentAmount - .Interest + m_curExtraPayment
                    .RemainingBalance = curCurrentBalance - .Principal

                    curCurrentBalance = .RemainingBalance
                End With

                m_objExtraPaymentDetails.Add objPayment
                Set objPayment = Nothing
            Wend
        End If

        Exit Sub

CALCULATE_ERROR:
        Err.Raise Err.Number

End Sub
```

Now let's look at this code in detail. As usual, we begin by declaring our local variables:

```
    Dim dblPeriodicRate As Double
    Dim dblFactor2 As Double
    Dim dblFactor4 As Double
    Dim curCurrentBalance As Currency
    Dim lngCounter As Long
    Dim objPayment As Payment
```

We then check to see if we need to set the properties to the input values:

```
    If curAmount <> 0 Then m_curAmount = curAmount
    If dblRate <> 0 Then m_dblRate = dblRate
    If lngNumPayments <> 0 Then m_lngNumPayments = lngNumPayments
    If lngPaymentsPerYear <> 0 Then _
        m_lngPaymentsPerYear = lngPaymentsPerYear
    If curExtraPayment <> 0 Then m_curExtraPayment = curExtraPayment
```

Then we ensure that we have the required information or send an error to the user:

```
    If m_curAmount <= 0 Then
        Err.Raise INVALIDAMOUNTERR, _
        "FinancialUtility:Amortization:Calculate", INVALIDAMOUNT
    End If
```

```
    If m_dblRate <= 0 Or dblRate > 50 Then
        Err.Raise INVALIDRATEERR, _
        "FinancialUtility:Amortization:Calculate", INVALIDRATE
    End If

    If m_lngNumPayments <= 0 Then
        Err.Raise INVALIDNUMPAYMENTSERR, _
        "FinancialUtility:Amortization:Calculate", INVALIDNUMPAYMENTS
    End If

    If m_lngPaymentsPerYear <= 0 Then
        Err.Raise INVALIDPAYMENTSPERERR, _
        "FinancialUtility:Amortization:Calculate", INVALIDPAYMENTSPER
    End If
```

Next, we calculate the periodic interest rate based on the rate and number of payments per year:

```
    dblPeriodicRate = (m_dblRate / 100 / m_lngPaymentsPerYear)
```

Then we use the periodic rate and other inputs to calculate the required payment:

```
    dblFactor2 = 1 / (1 + dblPeriodicRate) ^ m_lngNumPayments
    dblFactor4 = (1 - dblFactor2) / dblPeriodicRate
    m_curPaymentAmount = m_curAmount / dblFactor4
```

We compute each payment for the loan, keeping track of the current balance so that we can identify each payment's details:

```
    curCurrentBalance = m_curAmount
```

For each payment we create a `Payment` object and set its properties. We keep a running total of the overall interest paid in the member variable, `m_curTotalInterest`.

```
    For lngCounter = 1 To m_lngNumPayments
        Set objPayment = New Payment

        With objPayment
            .PaymentNumber = lngCounter
            .Interest = curCurrentBalance * dblPeriodicRate
            m_curTotalInterest = m_curTotalInterest + .Interest
            .Principal = m_curPaymentAmount - .Interest
            .RemainingBalance = curCurrentBalance - .Principal

            curCurrentBalance = .RemainingBalance
        End With
```

Having set `objPayment`'s properties we add it to the `Payments` collection and then set it to `Nothing`:

```
        m_objPaymentDetails.Add objPayment
        Set objPayment = Nothing
```

We now compute each payment for the loan, using the `ExtraPayment` value:

```
    If m_curExtraPayment > 0 Then
        curCurrentBalance = m_curAmount
        lngCounter = 1

        While curCurrentBalance > 0
            Set objPayment = New Payment

            With objPayment
                .PaymentNumber = lngCounter
                .Interest = curCurrentBalance * dblPeriodicRate
                m_curExtraInterest = m_curExtraInterest + .Interest
                .Principal = _
                m_curPaymentAmount - .Interest + m_curExtraPayment
                .RemainingBalance = curCurrentBalance - .Principal

                curCurrentBalance = .RemainingBalance
            End With

            m_objExtraPaymentDetails.Add objPayment
            Set objPayment = Nothing
        Wend
    End If
```

Finally, we finish our code with an error handler. In this case, we just raise all errors to the calling program, but we could add specific error handling if we wanted.

```
CALCULATE_ERROR:
    Err.Raise Err.Number
```

There really is not any magic code in these classes. What makes them special is the fact that they encapsulate a common financial formula.

Payout Class

The `Payout` class provides the detailed information about each payout from an annuity.

As with every other class, we begin by declaring our private member variables:

```
Option Explicit

Private m_lngPayoutNumber As Long
Private m_curPayout As Currency
Private m_curEarnings As Currency
Private m_curReturn As Currency
Private m_curBalance As Currency
```

Our `Payout` class contains only properties - no methods or event handlers. All of our properties here have `Public` read access, but only `Friend` write access.

```
Public Property Get PayoutNumber() As Long
    PayoutNumber = m_lngPayoutNumber
End Property
```

```
Friend Property Let PayoutNumber(lngPayoutNum As Long)
    m_lngPayoutNumber = lngPayoutNum
End Property


Public Property Get PayoutAmount() As Currency
    PayoutAmount = m_curPayout
End Property


Friend Property Let PayoutAmount(curPayout As Currency)
    m_curPayout = curPayout
End Property


Public Property Get EarningsForPeriod() As Currency
    EarningsForPeriod = m_curEarnings
End Property


Friend Property Let EarningsForPeriod(curEarnings As Currency)
    m_curEarnings = curEarnings
End Property


Public Property Get ReturnOfCapital() As Currency
    ReturnOfCapital = m_curReturn
End Property


Friend Property Let ReturnOfCapital(curReturn As Currency)
    m_curReturn = curReturn
End Property


Public Property Get RemainingBalance() As Currency
    RemainingBalance = m_curBalance
End Property


Friend Property Let RemainingBalance(curBalance As Currency)
    m_curBalance = curBalance
End Property
```

Let us now briefly run through what these properties relate to. The `PayoutNumber` property indicates which payout the `Payout` object describes. The `PayoutAmount` property is the periodic payout to be received - each `Payout` object in a `Payouts` collection will have the same value. The `EarningsForPeriod` property is the amount of earnings that the annuity had for the period. The `ReturnOfCapital` property is the amount of the payout that reduces the balance of the annuity. Finally, the `RemainingBalance` property indicates the principal amount left in the annuity after this payout.

Payouts Class

The `Payouts` class provides a collection of `Payout` objects that describe each payout scheduled for the annuity. This collection class is **type safe** in that it only allows `Payout` objects to be added to the collection. We mimic the standard collection interface, but modify it as needed to only support our limited needs.

In a radical change from our usual method of coding, we begin by defining a private member variable.

```
Option Explicit

Private m_colPayouts As Collection
```

Now we must add code to the `Initialize` and `Terminate` events of our class to handle the creation and destruction of our object.

```
Private Sub Class_Initialize()
    Set m_colPayouts = New Collection
End Sub
```

```
Private Sub Class_Terminate()
    Set m_colPayouts = Nothing
End Sub
```

Let's look at the methods of our object. These methods mimic the collection methods.

```
Public Sub Add(Item As Payout)
    m_colPayouts.Add Item
End Sub
```

```
Public Function Count() As Long
    Count = m_colPayouts.Count
End Function
```

```
Public Function Item(Index As Variant) As Payout
    Set Item = m_colPayouts.Item(Index)
End Function
```

```
Public Sub Remove(Index As Variant)
    m_colPayouts.Remove Index
End Sub
```

```
Public Function NewEnum() As IUnknown
    Set NewEnum = m_colPayouts.[_NewEnum]
End Function
```

As with our `Payments` class, the `Item` method should have its Procedure ID set to (Default). In addition, the `NewEnum` method should have a Procedure ID of -4 and the Hide this member check box must be selected.

PresentValueOfAnnuity Class

Through the `PresentValueOfAnnuity` object, a user interface developer is able to set the properties to the required values so that payout information about an annuity can be calculated. Once the values have been identified, the `Calculate` method will determine the periodic payout, total earnings to be earned over the life of the annuity and the details about each individual payout.

Let's start at the beginning with the declaration of our private member variables and constants:

```
Option Explicit

Private m_objPayoutDetails As Payouts
Private m_curPayoutAmount As Currency
Private m_dblRate As Double
Private m_lngNumPayouts As Long
Private m_lngPayoutsPerYear As Long
Private m_curPresentValue As Currency
Private m_curTotalEarnings As Currency
Private m_curTotalPayouts As Currency

Private Const INVALIDAMOUNTERR As Long = vbObjectError + 1001
Private Const INVALIDAMOUNT As String = _
 "The amount of the loan must be specified"
Private Const INVALIDRATEERR As Long = vbObjectError + 1002
Private Const INVALIDRATE As String = _
 "The specified interest rate is invalid"
Private Const INVALIDNUMPAYOUTSERR As Long = vbObjectError + 1003
Private Const INVALIDNUMPAYOUTS As String = _
 "The number of payments must be greater than 0"
Private Const INVALIDPAYOUTSPERERR As Long = vbObjectError + 1004
Private Const INVALIDPAYOUTSPER As String = _
 "There must be at least one payment due each year"
```

Now add code to our `Initialize` and `Terminate` events to handle the creation and destruction of our object:

```
Private Sub Class_Initialize()
    Set m_objPayoutDetails = New Payouts
End Sub
```

```
Private Sub Class_Terminate()
    Set m_objPayoutDetails = Nothing
End Sub
```

Now we must create the properties for our class:

```
Public Property Get PayoutAmount() As Currency
    PayoutAmount = m_curPayoutAmount
End Property
```

```
Public Property Let PayoutAmount(curAmount As Currency)
    If curAmount <= 0 Then
        Err.Raise vbObjectError + 1001, _
        "FinancialUtility:Amortization:Amount", INVALIDAMOUNT
    End If
    m_curPayoutAmount = curAmount
End Property
```

```
Public Property Get Rate() As Double
    Rate = m_dblRate
End Property
```

377

```
Public Property Let Rate(dblRate As Double)
    If dblRate <= 0 Or dblRate > 50 Then
        Err.Raise INVALIDRATEERR, _
        "FinancialUtility:Amortization:Calculate", INVALIDRATE
    End If
    m_dblRate = dblRate
End Property


Public Property Get NumberOfPayouts() As Long
    NumberOfPayouts = m_lngNumPayouts
End Property


Public Property Let NumberOfPayouts(lngPayouts As Long)
    If lngPayouts <= 0 Then
        Err.Raise INVALIDNUMPAYOUTSERR, _
        "FinancialUtility:Amortization:Calculate", INVALIDNUMPAYOUTS
    End If
    m_lngNumPayouts = lngPayouts
End Property


Public Property Get PayoutsPerYear() As Long
    PayoutsPerYear = m_lngPayoutsPerYear
End Property

Public Property Let PayoutsPerYear(lngPayoutsPerYear As Long)
    If lngPayoutsPerYear <= 0 Then
        Err.Raise INVALIDPAYOUTSPERERR, _
        "FinancialUtility:Amortization:Calculate", INVALIDPAYOUTSPER
    End If
    m_lngPayoutsPerYear = lngPayoutsPerYear
End Property


Public Property Get PresentValue() As Currency
    PresentValue = m_curPresentValue
End Property


Public Property Get TotalEarnings() As Currency
    TotalEarnings = m_curTotalEarnings
End Property


Public Property Get TotalPayouts() As Currency
    TotalPayouts = m_curTotalPayouts
End Property


Public Property Get PayoutDetails() As Payouts
    Set PayoutDetails = m_objPayoutDetails
End Property
```

Before we move on to discussing the Calculate method, let's quickly review the purpose of each of the properties above. The PayoutAmount property indicates the amount to be paid each period. The Rate property is the interest rate for the annuity, it is expressed in percentages - for example 6.5 is 6.5% or .065 per year. The NumberOfPayouts property identifies the number of payouts to be made over the life of the annuity. The PayoutsPerYear property identifies the number of payouts that are required each year - used to calculate the periodic rate. The PresentValue property is set when the Calculate method is called - this is a read-only property that tells the required initial investment for the annuity. The TotalEarnings property is also set when the Calculate method is called. It is a read-only property that gives the total amount of earnings over the life of the annuity. As with the `PresentValue` and `TotalEarnings` properties the `TotalPayouts` property is set when the `Calculate` method is called. It is also a read-only property that tells the total amount of payouts over the life of the annuity. Finally, the `PayoutDetails` property returns a reference to a `Payouts` object that holds information about each scheduled payout for the annuity.

The `Calculate` method is the only method in the `PresentValueOfAnnuity` class, but it is here that all of the information is generated. The format of the `Calculate` method of this class is very similar to that of the `Amortization` object, the difference being that the `Amortization` object is concerned with **payments** whereas the `PresentValueOfAnnuity` object is concerned with **payouts**. Let's take a closer look at this class then:

No surprises here, we're just defining our private member variables and checking to see if we need to set the properties to the input values:

```
Public Sub Calculate(Optional curPayoutAmount As Currency, _
Optional dblRate As Double, Optional lngNumPayouts As Long, _
Optional lngPayoutsPerYear As Long)

    Dim dblPeriodicRate As Double
    Dim dblFactor2 As Double
    Dim dblFactor4 As Double
    Dim curCurrentBalance As Currency
    Dim lngCounter As Long
    Dim objPayout As Payout

    On Error GoTo CALCULATE_ERROR

    If curPayoutAmount <> 0 Then m_curPayoutAmount = curPayoutAmount
    If dblRate <> 0 Then m_dblRate = dblRate
    If lngNumPayouts <> 0 Then m_lngNumPayouts = lngNumPayouts
    If lngPayoutsPerYear <> 0 Then m_lngPayoutsPerYear = _
        lngPayoutsPerYear
```

As before, we have to ensure that we have the required information or send an error to the user.

```
    If m_curPayoutAmount <= 0 Then
        Err.Raise INVALIDAMOUNTERR, _
        "FinancialUtility:Amortization:Calculate", INVALIDAMOUNT
    End If

    If m_dblRate <= 0 Or dblRate > 50 Then
        Err.Raise INVALIDRATEERR, _
        "FinancialUtility:Amortization:Calculate", INVALIDRATE
    End If

    If m_lngNumPayouts <= 0 Then
        Err.Raise INVALIDNUMPAYOUTSERR, _
        "FinancialUtility:Amortization:Calculate", INVALIDNUMPAYOUTS
    End If

    If m_lngPayoutsPerYear <= 0 Then
        Err.Raise INVALIDPAYOUTSPERERR, _
        "FinancialUtility:Amortization:Calculate", INVALIDPAYOUTSPER
    End If
```

Now we calculate the periodic interest rate based on the rate and number of payouts per year:

```
dblPeriodicRate = (m_dblRate / 100 / m_lngPayoutsPerYear)
```

Here we use the periodic rate and other inputs to calculate the required payout.

```
dblFactor2 = 1 / (1 + dblPeriodicRate) ^ m_lngNumPayouts
dblFactor4 = (1 - dblFactor2) / dblPeriodicRate
m_curPresentValue = m_curPayoutAmount * dblFactor4
```

Now we keep track of the current balance so that we can identify each payout's details:

```
curCurrentBalance = m_curPresentValue
```

In this next section of code, we calculate the `TotalEarnings` and `Details` for each payout, keep a running total of overall earnings and add the new payout to the `Payouts` collection:

```
For lngCounter = 1 To m_lngNumPayouts
    Set objPayout = New Payout

    With objPayout
        .PayoutNumber = lngCounter
        .EarningsForPeriod = curCurrentBalance * dblPeriodicRate
        m_curTotalEarnings = m_curTotalEarnings + .EarningsForPeriod
        .ReturnOfCapital = m_curPayoutAmount - .EarningsForPeriod
        .RemainingBalance = curCurrentBalance - .ReturnOfCapital

        curCurrentBalance = .RemainingBalance
    End With

    m_objPayoutDetails.Add objPayout
    Set objPayout = Nothing
Next

m_curTotalPayouts = m_curPayoutAmount * m_lngNumPayouts

Exit Sub
```

At the end of the `Calculate` method is error handling code:

```
CALCULATE_ERROR:

    Err.Raise Err.Number

End Sub
```

PeriodicInvestment Class

The `PeriodicInvestment` class provides the detailed information about each investment to be made over the life of an investment.

We begin by declaring the member variables to maintain the object's state. These variables are `Private` so that the outside world cannot see them.

```
Option Explicit

Private m_lngInvestmentNumber As Long
Private m_curInvestment As Currency
Private m_curEarnings As Currency
Private m_curBalance As Currency
```

The `PeriodicInvestment` class contains a number of properties. All of them have `Public` read access, but only `Friend` write access. Let's take a closer look:

```
Public Property Get InvestmentNumber() As Long
    InvestmentNumber = m_lngInvestmentNumber
End Property
```

```
Friend Property Let InvestmentNumber(lngInvestmentNum As Long)
    m_lngInvestmentNumber = lngInvestmentNum
End Property
```

```
Public Property Get InvestmentAmount() As Currency
    InvestmentAmount = m_curInvestment
End Property
```

```
Friend Property Let InvestmentAmount(curInvestment As Currency)
    m_curInvestment = curInvestment
End Property
```

```
Public Property Get EarningsForPeriod() As Currency
    EarningsForPeriod = m_curEarnings
End Property
```

```
Friend Property Let EarningsForPeriod(curEarnings As Currency)
    m_curEarnings = curEarnings
End Property
```

```
Public Property Get CurrentBalance() As Currency
    CurrentBalance = m_curBalance
End Property
```

```
Friend Property Let CurrentBalance(curBalance As Currency)
    m_curBalance = curBalance
End Property
```

As we've done with previous properties, we shall quickly review the purpose of each property now.

The `InvestmentNumber` property indicates which investment this object describes. The `InvestmentAmount` property is the periodic investment due for each period of the investment - each `PeriodicInvestment` object in a given collection will have the same value. The `EarningsForPeriod` property is the amount of growth of the investment for the period. The `CurrentBalance` property indicates the total value of the investment after this `PeriodicInvestment`.

PeriodicInvestments Class

The `PeriodicInvestments` object provides a collection of `PeriodicInvestment` objects that describe each periodic investment scheduled for the investment. This collection class is **type safe** in that it only allows `PeriodicInvestment` objects to be added to the collection. We mimic the standard collection interface, but modify it as needed to only support our limited needs.

Let's start at the beginning with our declaration of a private member variable.

```
Option Explicit

Private m_colInvestments As Collection
```

We need to include code in the `Class_Initialize` and `Terminate` events to handle the creation and destruction of our object.

```
Private Sub Class_Initialize()
    Set m_colInvestments = New Collection
End Sub
```

```
Private Sub Class_Terminate()
    Set m_colInvestments = Nothing
End Sub
```

Our `PeriodicInvestments` class contains several methods that mimic the collection methods. These methods are:

```
Public Sub Add(Item As PeriodicInvestment)
    m_colInvestments.Add Item
End Sub
```

```
Public Function Count() As Long
    Count = m_colInvestments.Count
End Function
```

```
Public Function Item(Index As Variant) As PeriodicInvestment
    Set Item = m_colInvestments.Item(Index)
End Function
```

```
Public Sub Remove(Index As Variant)
    m_colInvestments.Remove Index
End Sub
```

```
Public Function NewEnum() As IUnknown
    Set NewEnum = m_colInvestments.[_NewEnum]
End Function
```

As with the methods of our other collection classes, the `Item` method should be set as the default, and the `NewEnum` method should have the Procedure ID set to –4 and it should be hidden (this allows the user interface developer to use the `For Each` construct with this collection).

FutureValueOfAnnuity Class

Through the `FutureValueOfAnnuity` object a user interface developer is able to set the properties to the required values so that investment information about a future annuity can be calculated. Once the values have been identified, the `Calculate` method will determine the periodic investment, total earnings to be earned over the life of the annuity and the details about each individual investment.

As usual, we'll begin by looking at the declaration of member variables and constants:

```
Option Explicit

Private m_objInvestmentDetails As PeriodicInvestments
Private m_curInvestmentAmount As Currency
Private m_dblRate As Double
Private m_lngNumInvestments As Long
Private m_lngInvestmentsPerYear As Long
Private m_curExtraInvestment As Currency
Private m_curDesiredAmount As Currency
Private m_curTotalEarnings As Currency
Private m_curTotalInvestments As Currency

Private Const INVALIDAMOUNTERR As Long = vbObjectError + 1001
Private Const INVALIDAMOUNT As String = _
 "The amount of the loan must be specified"
Private Const INVALIDRATEERR As Long = vbObjectError + 1002
Private Const INVALIDRATE As String = _
 "The specified interest rate is invalid"
Private Const INVALIDNUMINVESTSERR As Long = vbObjectError + 1003
Private Const INVALIDNUMINVESTS As String = _
 "The number of payments must be greater than 0"
Private Const INVALIDINVESTSPERERR As Long = vbObjectError + 1004
Private Const INVALIDINVESTSPER As String = _
 "There must be at least one payment due each year"
```

Now we need to include code to create and destroy our objects in the `Class_Initialize` and `Terminate` events.

```
Private Sub Class_Initialize()
    Set m_objInvestmentDetails = New PeriodicInvestments
End Sub
```

```
Private Sub Class_Terminate()
    Set m_objInvestmentDetails = Nothing
End Sub
```

Now we need to code up some properties for our `FutureValueOfAnnuity` class:

```
Public Property Get DesiredAmount() As Currency
    DesiredAmount = m_curDesiredAmount
End Property
```

```
Public Property Let DesiredAmount(curAmount As Currency)
    If curAmount <= 0 Then
        Err.Raise INVALIDAMOUNTERR, _
        "FinancialUtility:Amortization:Amount", INVALIDAMOUNT
```

```
         End If
         m_curDesiredAmount = curAmount
      End Property


   Public Property Get Rate() As Double
      Rate = m_dblRate
   End Property


   Public Property Let Rate(dblRate As Double)
      If dblRate <= 0 Or dblRate > 50 Then
         Err.Raise INVALIDRATEERR, _
            "FinancialUtility:Amortization:Calculate", INVALIDRATE
      End If
      m_dblRate = dblRate
   End Property


   Public Property Get NumberOfInvestments() As Long
      NumberOfInvestments = m_lngNumInvestments
   End Property


   Public Property Let NumberOfInvestments(lngInvestments As Long)
      If lngInvestments <= 0 Then
         Err.Raise INVALIDNUMINVESTSERR, _
            "FinancialUtility:Amortization:Calculate", INVALIDNUMINVESTS
      End If
      m_lngNumInvestments = lngInvestments
   End Property


   Public Property Get InvestmentsPerYear() As Long
      InvestmentsPerYear = m_lngInvestmentsPerYear
   End Property


   Public Property Let InvestmentsPerYear(lngInvestmentsPerYear As Long)
      If lngInvestmentsPerYear <= 0 Then
         Err.Raise INVALIDINVESTSPERERR, _
            "FinancialUtility:Amortization:Calculate", INVALIDINVESTSPER
      End If
      m_lngInvestmentsPerYear = lngInvestmentsPerYear
   End Property


   Public Property Get InvestmentAmount() As Currency
      InvestmentAmount = m_curInvestmentAmount
   End Property


   Public Property Get TotalInvestments() As Currency
      TotalInvestments = m_curTotalInvestments
   End Property


   Public Property Get TotalEarnings() As Currency
      TotalEarnings = m_curTotalEarnings
   End Property


   Public Property Get InvestmentDetails() As PeriodicInvestments
      Set InvestmentDetails = m_objInvestmentDetails
   End Property
```

As we have done with other classes let's briefly discuss the purpose of each of these classes.

The `DesiredAmount` property indicates the target amount to accumulate. The `Rate` property is the interest rate for the investment, it is expressed in percentages - for example 6.5 is 6.5% or .065 per year. The `NumberOfPayouts` property identifies the number of payouts that to be made over the life of the annuity. The `InvestmentsPerYear` property identifies the number of investments that are required each year - used to calculate the periodic rate. The `InvestmentAmount` property is set when the `Calculate` method is called - this is a read-only property and it tells the required investment for the annuity. The `TotalInvestments` property is set when the `Calculate` method is called - this is a read only property and it gives the total amount of periodic investments over the life of the annuity. The `TotalEarnings` property is also set when the `Calculate` method is called - it is a read-only property that gives the total amount of earnings over the life of the annuity. The `InvestmentDetails` property returns a reference to a `PeriodicInvestments` object that holds information about each scheduled investment for the annuity.

Now let's move on to the `Calculate` method of the `FutureValueOfAnnuity` object. It's very similar to the `Calculate` methods of other objects that we've created so I won't go into too much detail.

```
Public Sub Calculate(Optional curDesiredAmount As Currency, _
Optional dblRate As Double, Optional lngNumInvestments As Long, _
Optional lngInvestmentsPerYear As Long)

    Dim dblPeriodicRate As Double
    Dim dblFactor1 As Double
    Dim dblFactor3 As Double
    Dim curCurrentBalance As Currency
    Dim lngCounter As Long
    Dim objInvestment As PeriodicInvestment

    On Error GoTo CALCULATE_ERROR

    If curDesiredAmount <> 0 Then m_curDesiredAmount = _
        curDesiredAmount
    If dblRate <> 0 Then m_dblRate = dblRate
    If lngNumInvestments <> 0 Then m_lngNumInvestments = _
        lngNumInvestments
    If lngInvestmentsPerYear <> 0 Then m_lngInvestmentsPerYear = _
        lngInvestmentsPerYear

    If m_curDesiredAmount <= 0 Then
        Err.Raise INVALIDAMOUNTERR, _
        "FinancialUtility:Amortization:Calculate", INVALIDAMOUNT
    End If

    If m_dblRate <= 0 Or dblRate > 50 Then
        Err.Raise INVALIDRATEERR, _
        "FinancialUtility:Amortization:Calculate", INVALIDRATE
    End If

    If m_lngNumInvestments <= 0 Then
        Err.Raise INVALIDNUMINVESTSERR, _
        "FinancialUtility:Amortization:Calculate", INVALIDNUMINVESTS
    End If
```

```
    If m_lngInvestmentsPerYear <= 0 Then
        Err.Raise INVALIDINVESTSPERERR, _
        "FinancialUtility:Amortization:Calculate", INVALIDINVESTSPER
    End If
```

Here we calculate the periodic interest rate based on the rate and number of payouts per year:

```
    dblPeriodicRate = (m_dblRate / 100 / m_lngInvestmentsPerYear)
```

Now we can begin to calculate the periodic payout. We use the periodic rate and other inputs to calculate the required payout.

```
    dblFactor1 = (1 + dblPeriodicRate) ^ m_lngNumInvestments
    dblFactor3 = (dblFactor1 - 1) / dblPeriodicRate
    m_curInvestmentAmount = m_curDesiredAmount / dblFactor3
```

Now we can begin to compute each periodic investment for the annuity. We must keep track of the current balance so we can identify each investment's details.

```
    curCurrentBalance = 0
```

Here we calculate the `TotalEarnings` and `Details` for each investment.

```
    For lngCounter = 1 To m_lngNumInvestments
  Set objInvestment = New PeriodicInvestment

  With objInvestment
    .InvestmentNumber = lngCounter
    .InvestmentAmount = m_curInvestmentAmount
    .EarningsForPeriod = curCurrentBalance * dblPeriodicRate
    m_curTotalEarnings = m_curTotalEarnings + .EarningsForPeriod
    .CurrentBalance = curCurrentBalance + .EarningsForPeriod + _
        .InvestmentAmount

    curCurrentBalance = .CurrentBalance
  End With

  m_objInvestmentDetails.Add objInvestment
  Set objInvestment = Nothing
    Next
```

Now we can set the `TotalInvestments` property:

```
    m_curTotalInvestments = m_curInvestmentAmount * m_lngNumInvestments

    Exit Sub

CALCULATE_ERROR:
    Err.Raise Err.Number

End Sub
```

We have now created an ActiveX DLL that we can use to build these and future applications. Select Ma<u>k</u>e Project dll and you will able to reference the `.dll` from future projects just by selecting the it from the <u>P</u>roject-Refere<u>n</u>ces dialog box. We will not delve into the details of how to create the DLL here, again our main focus has been to see what kind of functionality we can place into an object that we build with Visual Basic. All that we have let to do now is to see how we can use these objects to create useful applications. In the following sections we design and build two tools that will show you how easy it can be. We have worked hard to this point, it is now time to sit back and reap the benefits of that work.

Design and Building the Applications

Among the benefits that I want to emphasize with this discussion and illustration of utility objects is the ease with which user interfaces can be added to our project. Let's take a look at some simple user interfaces that use our utility objects.

Loan Amortization

The first step of our design is to determine what information we need to gather from our end user. Additionally, we need to determine what information our interface will display for our end user. We can borrow this information from the design work already completed:

```
Gather Information
        Amount borrowed
        Number of payments
        Interest rate
        Number of payments each year
        Extra payment amount

Display Information to User
        Show periodic loan payment amount
        Show total cost to borrow money
        Show total savings by making extra principal payments
        Show amortization schedule
                For normal payments
                For extra payments
```

Reviewing our design information above let's create two separate forms. We'll create our first form to allow the user to enter the required information. This form also displays the basic information that is calculated by our object. To keep the form from being overly cluttered we shall create a second form to show the amortization table.

The following table displays the controls needed on the first form. Notice that we have not included the labels in this chart. You should be very familiar with the design of a form and so should not need that information.

Need	Control	Control Name
Amount Borrowed	text box	`txtAmount`
Number of Payments	text box	`txtNumberOfPayments`
Payments Per Year	text box	`txtPaymentsPerYear`
Interest Rate	text box	`txtRate`
Extra Principal Payments	text box	`txtExtraPayment`
Payment Amount	text box	`txtPaymentAmount`
Total Interest Paid	text box	`txtTotalInterest`
Extra Payments Savings	text box	`txtExtraSavings`
Calculate Loan Information	command button	`cmdCalculate`
Calculate Amortization Schedule	command button	`cmdLoanAmortization`
Exit	command button	`cmdExit`

Here is a screen shot of the main form for this application:

With the form completed the last step is write the code necessary to complete the project. You can see that this form allows the user to enter all of the information that we require for calculating the loan payment and amortization details:

```
Option Explicit

Private m_objLoan As Amortization

' calculate the results and amortizations of the loan
Private Sub cmdCalculate_Click()
    ' create a new amortization object
    Set m_objLoan = New Amortization

    With m_objLoan
        ' set object properties
        .Amount = txtAmount.Text
        .Rate = txtRate.Text
```

```
            .NumberOfPayments = txtNumberOfPayments.Text
            .PaymentsPerYear = txtPaymentsPerYear.Text
            .ExtraPayment = txtExtraPayment.Text

            ' calculate the payment info
            .Calculate

            ' display results to user
            txtPaymentAmount.Text = Format$(.PaymentAmount, "##,##0.00")
            txtTotalInterest.Text = Format$(.TotalInterest, "##,##0.00")
            txtExtraSavings.Text = _
              Format$((.TotalInterest - .TotalInterestWithExtra), "##,##0.00")

        End With
End Sub
```

```
Private Sub cmdExit_Click()
    ' unload the form to kill the application
    Unload Me
End Sub
```

```
Private Sub cmdLoanAmortization_Click()
    ' bring up the amortization form with the payment details
    If Not m_objLoan Is Nothing Then
        Set frmAmortization.SetupForm = m_objLoan
        frmAmortization.Show vbModal
    Else
        MsgBox _
            "Cannot view amortization until you have calculated a loan."
    End If
End Sub
```

```
Private Sub Form_Unload(Cancel As Integer)
    ' ensure that we free up allocated memory
    Set m_objLoan = Nothing
End Sub
```

There, a simple user interface gives us all the detailed information that we want about our loan.

To see the amortization schedule we can proceed to the second form. On this form, whose screen shot is shown here, the user can specify which amortization schedule they want to view.

389

By selecting the desired option button at the top of the form the user can toggle between a view of the normal amortization schedule and one that reflects the difference resulting from making the extra principal payments.

Here's another table, showing the controls needed for our second form:

Need	Control	Control Name
Normal Payment Toggle	option button	`optNormal`
Extra Payment Toggle	option button	`optExtra`
Amortization Schedule	list view	`lvwAmortization`
Total Interest Paid	text box	`txtTotalInterest`
Exit	command button	`cmdExit`

Right click on the list view control and select **Properties**. Click on the **Column Headers** tab and type **Payment** into the **Text** box. Then click on the **Insert Column** button. Repeat the process with the other headings, i.e. **Amount, Extra, Principal, Interest** and **Balance**.

Here is the code for this form:

```
Option Explicit

Private m_objAmort As Amortization

' unload our form
Private Sub cmdExit_Click()
    Unload Me
End Sub

Private Sub Form_Load()
    ' view the normal amortization schedule on entry
    optNormal.Value = True
    FillListView
End Sub

Public Property Set SetupForm(objAmortization As Amortization)
    ' allow the calling form to pass us a reference to the
    ' amortization object
    Set m_objAmort = objAmortization
End Property

Private Sub FillListView()
    Dim curExtra As Currency
    Dim objPayment As Payment
    Dim objPayments As Payments
    Dim ltmItem As ListItem

    lvwAmortization.ListItems.Clear

    ' set up our variables to fill the list view
    ' with the proper information
    If optNormal.Value = True Then
        curExtra = 0
```

```
        Set objPayments = m_objAmort.PaymentDetails
        txtTotalInterest.Text = _
        Format$(m_objAmort.TotalInterest, "##,##0.00")
    Else
        curExtra = m_objAmort.ExtraPayment
        Set objPayments = m_objAmort.ExtraPaymentDetails
        txtTotalInterest.Text = Format$ _
        (m_objAmort.TotalInterestWithExtra, "##,##0.00")
    End If


    ' add a line to the listview for each payment
    For Each objPayment In objPayments
        Set ltmItem = lvwAmortization.ListItems.Add
        With ltmItem
  .Text = objPayment.PaymentNumber
  .SubItems(1) = Format$(objPayment.PaymentAmount, "##,##0.00")
  .SubItems(2) = Format$(curExtra, "##,##0.00")
  .SubItems(3) = Format$(objPayment.Principal, "##,##0.00")
  .SubItems(4) = Format$(objPayment.Interest, "##,##0.00")
  .SubItems(5) = Format$(objPayment.RemainingBalance, "##,##0.00")
        End With
    Next
End Sub
```

```
Private Sub optExtra_Click()
    ' only attempt to view the extra payment amortization
    ' if the extra payment is greater than 0
    If m_objAmort.ExtraPayment = 0 Then
        optNormal.Value = True
    Else
        FillListView
    End If
End Sub
```

```
Private Sub optNormal_Click()
    ' view the normal amortization schedule
    FillListView
End Sub
```

Again, the code behind this form should be self-explanatory to you. The purpose here is not to show you how to build a user interface, rather to show how easily we can incorporate our objects into one. The only notable code here is the fact that we will not let the user view a schedule for the extra payment unless the `Amortization` object shows that they enter a value for the extra payment.

Retirement Planner

The first step of our design is to determine what information we need to gather from our end user. Additionally, we need to determine what information our interface will display for them. We can borrow this information from the design work already completed:

```
Gather Information
        Desired monthly income during retirement
        Years in retirement
        Years until retirement
```

> Assumed rate of return before retirement
> Assumed rate of return after retirement
> Extra investments

Display Information to User
>> Show total amount required at time of retirement
>> Show required periodic investment
>> Show total amount of earnings prior to retirement
>> Show total amount paid after retirement
>> Show total earnings after retirement
>> Show total earnings

Reviewing our design of the retirement planner information above, let's create a single form for this application. The form will have two sections, the first allows the user to enter the required information and the second displays the results after the calculation has been completed. Of course, the whole reason for this form is to show how to use the utility objects that we created in this chapter.

Here's a screen shot of this form:

The following table displays the controls needed for this form:

Need	Control	Control Name
Desired Retirement Income	text box	txtMonthlyIncome
Payouts per Year	text box	txtPayoutsPerYear
Investments per Year	text box	txtInvestmentsPerYear
Years in Retirement	calculated	txtLifeExpectancy – txtAgeAtRetirement
Years Until Retirement	calculated	txtAgeAtRetirement – txtCurrentAge
Pre-Retirement Return	text box	txtPreRetReturn
Post-Retirement Return	text box	txtPostRetReturn

Need	Control	Control Name
Amount needed at Retirement	text box	`txtPresentValue`
Periodic Investment Amount	text box	`txtPeriodicInvestment`
Pre-Retirement Earnings	text box	`txtPreRetEarnings`
Total Payout in Retirement	text box	`txtTotalPayout`
Post-Retirement Earnings	text box	`txtPostRetEarnings`
Total Earnings – Pre and Post retire	text box	`txtTotalEarnings`
Calculate Information	command button	`cmdCalculate`
Exit Program	command button	`cmdExit`

With the form completed the final step is write the code necessary to complete the project. You can see that this form allows the user to enter all of the information that we require for calculating the retirement savings needed to reach the stated goal. The application that we delivered to our customer included many more options, but this will give you a feel for how to use the `PresentValueOfAnnuity` and `FutureValueofAnnuity` objects.

The following code listing is from this form:

```
Option Explicit

Private Sub cmdCalculate_Click()
    Dim objRetCalc As PresentValueOfAnnuity
    Dim objInvCalc As FutureValueOfAnnuity

    Set objRetCalc = New PresentValueOfAnnuity
    Set objInvCalc = New FutureValueOfAnnuity

    With objRetCalc
        ' set properties needed to determine amount required at retirement
        .PayoutAmount = txtMonthlyIncome.Text
        .Rate = txtPostRetReturn.Text
        .NumberOfPayouts = _
        (txtLifeExpectancy.Text - txtAgeAtRetirement.Text) _
        * txtPayoutsPerYear.Text
        .PayoutsPerYear = txtPayoutsPerYear.Text

        ' calculate the amount required at retirement
        ' we will also get the earning during retirement
        .Calculate

        ' set values on form
        txtPresentValue.Text = Format$(.PresentValue, "##,##0.00")
        txtPostRetEarnings.Text = Format$(.TotalEarnings, "##,##0.00")
        txtTotalPayout.Text = Format$(.TotalPayouts, "##,##0.00")
    End With

    With objInvCalc
        ' set properties needed to calculate the current investment needed
        .DesiredAmount = objRetCalc.PresentValue
        .Rate = txtPreRetReturn.Text
```

```vb
            .InvestmentsPerYear = txtInvestmentsPerYear.Text
            .NumberOfInvestments = (txtAgeAtRetirement.Text - txtCurrentAge.Text) _
            * txtInvestmentsPerYear.Text

            ' calculate the information to identify the current investments
            ' required to meet our goals
            .Calculate

            ' set values on form
            txtPeriodicInvestment.Text = _
            Format$(.InvestmentAmount, "##,##0.00")
            txtPreRetEarnings.Text = Format$(.TotalEarnings, "##,##0.00")
            txtTotalEarnings.Text = _
            Format$((.TotalEarnings + objRetCalc.TotalEarnings), "##,##0.00")
        End With

        Set objRetCalc = Nothing
        Set objInvCalc = Nothing
    End Sub


    Private Sub cmdExit_Click()
        ' exit the application
        Unload Me
    End Sub
```

There you go, now we have another simple user interface that gives us all the detailed information that we want about retirement planning. You can go ahead and use this one to see if you are on track for your early retirement!

Summary

Well, we've finally made it! It's been a long haul, but I hope you feel it has been well worth the trip. The utility objects that we have created with this project can be used repeatedly for other projects.

The ability to reuse these objects makes them very robust. We seem to always want more pay for less work. When building objects such as these, there is a lot of work up front, but there is a giant payoff when we can reuse them. You have seen just a taste of this with the test applications that we have built.

I've have tried to point out the differences between business objects and utility objects. Both are very useful and can help you create great applications. As you watch the development of the business object technology, be aware that utility objects are also available. The real difference that we see is that a utility object supports a well-defined function or process whereas a business object describes a business entity. The difference may seem slight, but it is much easier to fully implement the utility object and not find holes in it when you come back to use it in the future.

There are great advantages to building object to support your applications. These benefits are available even when reuse is not achieved. One of the best is the ability to create different user interfaces for your application with minimal work.

394

Do not underestimate the importance of design. While it can be very tempting to move into the coding process, do not short change yourself by moving forward too soon. If you go to the same effort that we have done here, you will spend less time preparing a superior product in the long run. You'll also be able to reuse your well-designed applications over and over. You'll definitely increase your efficiency and profits!

6

Working with Visual Modeler

Introduction

If you're lucky enough to have a copy of Visual Basic 6 Enterprise Edition, or even Visual Studio Enterprise Edition, then Microsoft are just aching to give you some goodies. Among them is Visual Modeler, a reduced-functionality version of leading UML design tool, Rational Rose.

Visual Modeler lets you draw out our UML designs in great detail, and covers everything from mapping out the relationships between objects to entering specifications for an object; it even allows you to specify the methods and properties of each object in our design model. When you're done, you just click a button and Visual Modeler will go away and create a skeleton Visual Basic application for you, leaving you to concentrate on plugging in the code that actually makes your application useful. More than that, Visual Modeler is one of the new design tools which support Reverse Engineering. With this little gem of functionality, we can even have Visual Modeler create a model of an existing application, giving us an ideal starting point to add much needed functionality to those old projects.

Aside from the obvious benefits that leaving paper and working on a computer screen bring, the close integration of Visual Modeler with Visual Basic makes the transition from design to coding a seamless one. Just as "keep it simple" is the credo for effective re-use of objects you write, by integrating Visual Modeler so tightly with Visual Basic, Microsoft have ensured that there is little reason to avoid using it in your own work. This means that, over time, more and more people will turn to Visual Modeler as their design tool of choice, and that makes it even more important that you get acquainted with it as soon as possible. So, if you haven't used it already, and you do have Visual Basic Enterprise, then now is the time to go and have a look at what's on offer.

This appendix gives a brief overview of what Visual Modeler is, and how to use it. If you have already read the chapter on UML design in this book, then the finer points of object-oriented design should already sit quite well with you. Visual Modeler takes this foundation of knowledge and just gives you a tool to "do it" on a computer.

Starting up Visual Modeler

If you're the proud owner of Visual Basic Enterprise or Visual Studio Enterprise you should have Visual Modeler installed on your machine – you should be able to locate it in C:\Program Files\Microsoft Visual Studio\Common\Tools\VS-Ent98, or wherever your Visual Basic Enterprise tools are installed. Load it up, and we're ready for action.

Starting out with Visual Modeler

The first time you run up Visual Modeler the sight of so many panels, toolbar buttons, and menu options can be a little daunting. However, if you are happy with the UML stuff we covered earlier in the book, then there is nothing here that should really scare you too much.

Tiered Service Model diagram, an overview diagram if you like that ultimately shows you all the objects in your model, and the tier that they fit in. More on this later, when you'll see how to actually start drawing diagrams.

The left side of the display is taken up with the **Browser**, a tree view that lets you "drill down" into the deeper levels of your diagram. Most of the work you do will revolve around the options underneath the Logical View item in the window, which provides you with access to the individual diagrams for each tier of the model. Expand it now and take a look:

If you keep on expanding the options underneath the Logical View item you should notice a trend. Each tier has a Package Overview diagram which you can select to view a diagram specific to the selected tier, or package. As you add classes into the model, something you'll see how to do shortly (so don't get so impatient and start staring out the window at the back there) you'll see entries appear in the tree for each individual class in the model, as well as the Package Overview diagrams.

Just as with any other Windows application from Microsoft, the top of the display is taken up with a menu and a toolbar. No great shocks there. They work just as you would expect them to, with the toolbar providing rapid one click access to commonly used items in the menu. I'm not going to go in depth on the toolbar right now - we'll look at it as we go along. However, if you want to explore a little on your own, then don't forget that you can hover the mouse pointer over an item on the toolbar to pop up a little ToolTip window containing help for you on what the button actually does. Feels like home already doesn't it?

Adding Classes

Of course, the real usefulness of a tool like Visual Modeler comes from its ability to let you drop classes into your design model and link them together. This is very easy to do. Make sure that you have the Logical View, Package Overview item selected from the browser, and the Three-Tiered Service Model diagram is on display, then turn your attention to the toolbar at the top of the screen:

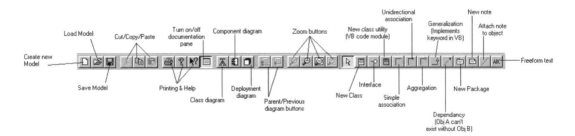

To drop a class into your diagram, just click on the New Class button and then click in the tier of your diagram where you want the new class to appear.

Once the new class appears, you can type in a name for it. Don't press *Return* when you are done typing the name though. Visual Modeler treats you pressing the return key as wanting to add a new line into the class' title, and will make any text that you already typed scroll up out of view. Instead, when you are done typing in the name, just click away from the new class.

You should also notice on the toolbar an icon to allow you to create a new **Class Utility**. Remember when we looked at these back in the design chapter? Class utilities are used in your module to symbolize anything that is not a true class, and are commonly used in Visual Basic to create forms or standard modules.

Creating a new class utility in Visual Modeler is exactly the same as creating a new class. Just click on the icon, then click in your model, and the new unit will appear, ready for you to type in a new name for it.

Looking at the diagram for a moment, it's hard to imagine how you might fit a complex diagram into the rather narrow columns that Visual Modeler gives you for the three tiers. Panic not. If you click and drag a class or class module near one of the tier separator lines, then Visual Modeler will automatically change the size of the tier in the diagram to accommodate your new change:

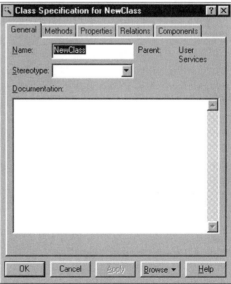

There is also quite a lot of information hidden behind each class and utility symbol that you drop into the diagram. Try double clicking on a class and the class properties dialog will appear:

This dialog serves a number of purposes, as you can probably guess by taking a quick glance at the tabs at the top. Using it you can add properties and methods to a class, change the options that affect how the class will be translated into Visual Basic code, and also view any relationships that have been set up between this and other classes. We'll look at each of these pages in more depth a little later. The first page though, the General page, is quite useful right now.

The General page contains just two options, but both are very important. The first is the class name, and it should be pretty obvious why this one is important; who would want to work on a project where all the classes were called Class1, Class2, and so on. The second is the Documentation area. This is just a free form text area where you can enter information on what the class is and does, essentially adding comments to your diagram. You can print all these out later to get a textual description of the objects in your model, which is of course invaluable in building up a useful collection of design documentation. Have a little play around with the dialog for a while. As I said, we'll be covering the various other pages a little later. When you are done, just click on the OK button at the bottom of the dialog to return to your diagram.

Adding Relationships

Once you have your classes laid out, the next stage is to obviously draw in the relationships between them. Visual Modeler supports all the normal UML relationships (associations, generalizations, aggregation, and dependencies). However, there are a few steps that you need to be aware of when you draw them. Let's take a look.

The 4 icons to the right of the new class and new class utility icons let you draw lines. If you have Visual Modeler loaded, start up a new project by selecting New from the File menu, and then go ahead and drop two classes onto the model:

To draw a simple association between the 2 classes, just click on the association line, then click and drag from class1 to class2:

The other types of relationship (generalization, aggregation, dependency and unidirectional association) all work in exactly the same manner. Click on the icon representing the relationship that you need, then click and drag from one class to another.

Once you have your association drawn, you can even click and drag in the middle of the line to put kinks in it. This serves no purpose when the time comes for Visual Modeler to go ahead and generate your code for you, but it can be very useful for keeping a neat order to your diagrams; they soon get pretty cluttered with lots of objects in the diagram, and even more lines connecting them:

Frequently, when you draw a relationship in, you will want to define members in either or both classes to actually represent the relationship in code. For example, with a simple association, that association may be in place because Class1 has a member of type Class2. You can define things like this just by double clicking on your new association line, which pops open the relationship specification dialog:

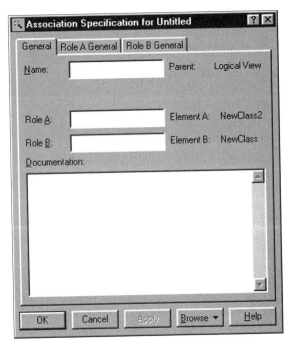

Actually there are three types of dialog: one for association and aggregation relationship, one for the generalization type of relationship, and one for the dependency relationship. Let's look at each in turn.

Association and Aggregation Specification Dialogs

The best way to get to grips with these things is to use them. Start up a new diagram in Visual Modeler, by choosing **New** from the **File** menu. When the blank Three-Tier diagram comes into view, drop two objects onto it, so that you diagram looks like mine:

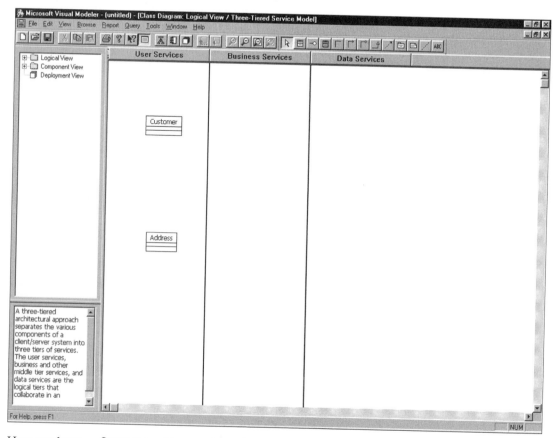

Here we have a **Customer** object, and an **Address** object; since in this hypothetical system, addresses are stored separate from the rest of the data in order to reduce duplication of data in the database (an employee could also be a customer and could also be a supplier - to store the address with each record in this instance would mean that there are three sets of duplicate data in the system).

Draw in a simple association relationship from the customer object to the
address object:

With the relationship drawn in, double click on the association's line to bring up the Association
Specification dialog box. When it appears, you might want to drag it to one side so that you
can still see your diagram underneath - we are going to explore this dialog and see its effect on
the diagram as well as make our changes:

The first thing to do is to give a name to the association, using the text box at the top of the dialog. This has no effect on the code that gets generated later, but it does add a level of readability to the diagram. The relationship between a customer and their address could be named "Resides at", so type that in and hit the **Apply** button:

Now its time to name the roles. When defining the names for the roles, you need to decide if the object named in the role relates to the other. So, in our case, does the Item in Role A, the Address class, relate to a customer? Of course it does - a customer resides at an Address after all. So, having decided that this role is important to our cause, the next step is to name it, effectively creating a member variable. So, name **Role A m_Address** and hit the **Apply** button:

Now the diagram is readable. There is a relationship between Customer and Address. A Customer resides at m_Address, which is an object of type Address. When the time comes to generate code, this m_Address variable will be created as a member within the Customer class.

Next up, does Customer relate to an Address? In other words, does an Address always have a relationship to a Customer, and is the Address aware of which Customer belongs to it? The answer here is no - an Address is a group of data which belongs to a Customer, but it should know nothing of who uses it and when. So, we can leave Role B blank, and when the code is generated we do not want to see a Visual Basic variable created to represent this role. Fortunately, the new version of Visual Modeler that comes with VB6 takes care of this automatically.

Now, we can look at the Role options. You will notice on the tabs at the top of the dialog that there are Role A General and Role B General tabs. Since we're only really interested in one role on this relationship, click on Role A General, to bring up its tab:

Now, this is where things can get a little confusing. As I mentioned earlier, Visual Modeler is a cut-down version of a larger product called Rational Rose, and this dialog actually comes direct from that product. Since Rational works with other development languages, such as C++, you will find from time to time options that do not work well with Visual Basic. The Role General page in the Relationship Specifications dialog is a prime example.

Selecting Public or Private for a role makes the member variable that you are creating either Public or Private within the class. However, Protected and Implementation do nothing.

As with the class specification, this page also provides an area for free-form text where you can type in a complete description of the role in question and thus explain your rationale to anyone reading your model at a later point.

Generalization Specification Dialog

The specification dialog for generalizations is very different. All generalization does is allow one class to implement the interface of another, and so there really is no need for naming roles and other such fun and games. However, there is quite a lot going on behind the scenes when you create a generalization with Visual Modeler.

Let's draw a couple of new objects on to the diagram, and link them with a generalization relationship. Go ahead and drop a **Vehicle** and **Car** object on to the diagram, as shown below:

In this instance, we have a generic vehicle class, that would presumably contain methods such as `Drive`, `Park`, `Start` and `Stop`, and we have a **Car** class that implements the same interface and presumably has some properties of its own, specific to a car.

Double click on the **Generalization Relationship** to bring up the relationship specification dialog once again:

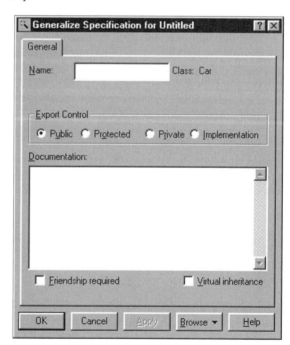

As you can see, it's considerable different to the Association and Aggregation specification dialogs. What Visual Modeler will do with this kind of relationship behind the scenes is create two classes in Visual Basic (Vehicle and Car) and in the Car class put in a new Vehicle member. Since the generalization relationship here forces the Car to implement the same interface as the Vehicle, Visual Modeler will also automatically drop in any methods and properties into the Car class which it needs to implement the same interface as the Vehicle. In addition, it will put code in to pass any calls to these methods and properties directly down to the matching methods and properties on the Vehicle member inside the Car class. You'll see this in action later on.

For now, just name the relationship "Is a kind of":

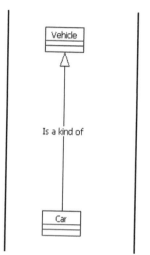

Once again, just by naming the relationship we add a nice level of readability to what was previously quite a confusing diagram. Here it's very easy for even an end user to see that a Car "Is a kind of" Vehicle. Who ever said UML was hard?

Dependency Relationships

The last kind of relationship to investigate in Visual Modeler is the Dependency relationship. This is actually the easiest one to work with, even though on the surface it would appear that it is the most complex (it has the most scary looking specification dialog). The reason for its ease is that Visual Modeler doesn't do anything to your code with this kind of relationship - as far as VM is concerned it exists only to add to your model's documentation.

Let's imagine that in our example so far we are going to make our Customers dependent on their Cars - perhaps our model is for a company which sells spares to motor racing companies. Draw a dependency from the Customer to the Car class, as shown.

Just as before, double click on the relationship to open up its **Specification** dialog:

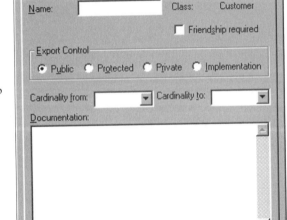

Looks horrendous, doesn't it!? The only options that you really need to worry about are the **Name** and the **Documentation** text boxes. You use these in the normal way. The **Cardinality** options are for the hardcore UML freaks who want to add even more information to their model. I'll concede that they are beyond me, and I tend to steer clear of team members who know what they mean (they are usually supremely wise analysts that make me feel humble). If cardinality is something you feel you should know about then go consult your nearest UML guru, or a book, such as **Instant UML** from Wrox Press.

For now, just Name the relationship Drives and then click the OK button to close down the dialog.

Multiplicity

The last thing that you will want to define for certain types of relationship is the multiplicity. As we saw earlier, you could have an Association between Class1 and Class2 because Class1 contains a member of type Class2. What if that member were a collection though? This is where multiplicity comes into play.

Let's drop yet another class on to our model - it doesn't really matter in which tier, since we are only playing around right now. Go ahead and add an Orders class to the model, then draw an association between it and the Customer. Don't forget to double click on the association after you have drawn it and set up the roles and name so that your association looks similar to mine. Also, don't forget to set up the Visual Basic options, just as before, so that only the Orders role will result in a Visual Basic data member getting created. Go back a couple of paragraphs if you can't remember how to do this.

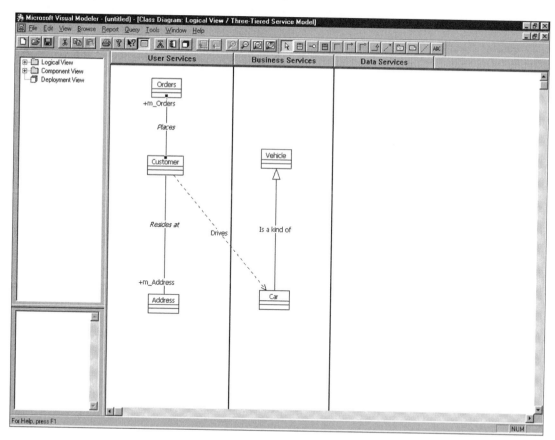

As you can see, the Customers class is set up here to hold a member of type Orders. This makes sense since, after all, a customer exists solely to place orders with our business. The problem is that most customers will want to place multiple orders over time, since our business is just so wonderful. So, instead of a single Orders member being in the Customers object, we need a collection.

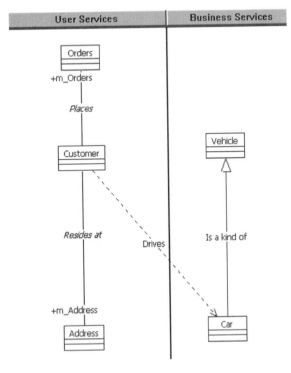

Right click on the Customer end of the relationship line itself and a pop-up menu will appear:

Select the Multiplicity option, just as I have done, and a sub menu will appear. Select 1 from the submenu. This tells Visual Modeler that in this relationship, 1 customer relates to...

Right click on the Orders end of the relationship, select Multiplicity from the popup menu and now select 0..*. 1 Customer now relates to.... 0 or many orders - a collection:

That's all there is to it! When we go to generate Visual Basic code in a little while, Visual Modeler will automatically create a collection in the **Customers** class called `m_Orders`. Anyone responsible for writing the final code into the **Customers** class will be able to easily glance at the model and see that the resulting collection is used to deal with **Orders** objects.

> *We are going to look at some of the other neat features of Visual Modeler now, before finally generating code for the model. Now might be a good time to save your hard work. Just click on the **File** menu and select **Save**, then save the project just as you would save something from anything other Windows application.*

Going Further

You now know how to do everything in Visual Modeler that we did on paper way back in Chapter 9 on design. However, Visual Modeler allows you to take things quite a bit further. Since Visual Modeler will ultimately produce Visual Basic code for you, it provides the necessary facilities for you to define the properties and methods of a class, as well as ways to control exactly how they are implemented in Visual Basic. And then, of course, there's the code generation wizard itself, the part of Visual Modeler that will actually go into Visual Basic and enter code for you. In addition, with Visual Modeler you can pay a great deal more attention to the individual tiers of your project and focus on diagrams specific to them, as well as creating your own (something Visual Modeler refers to as packages).

None of this is particularly hard to master either, thanks to the fact that the dialogs you use to accomplish most of these feats are all pretty much standardized in the way they look and behave, throughout Visual Modeler.

In an ideal world, you would sit with Visual Modeler for as long as it takes to get every tiny detail of the application mapped out in its entirety, and only then start to churn out the Visual Basic code to bring the application to life. While few of us actually get to work in an ideal world, it's still nice to see how it should be done, and that you have the tools to hand to do it.

Adding Properties

There are two ways that you can add properties to a class: you can either right click on the class and select **New Property**, or you can double click on the class to bring up the **Class Specification** dialog and use the **Properties** tab at the top to get to the properties page. There are buttons on the property page itself that let you add and delete properties within a class. This is actually the best way of doing it, since if you use the pop-up menu to add properties, you will be unable to specify the type of the property, or add any further information about it.

Lets add a property to the Vehicles class that we created earlier. Double click on the class to open up the class specification dialog:

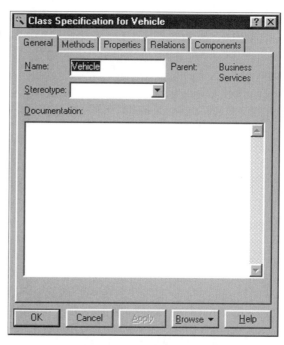

When the dialog appears, click on the Properties tab at the top to change to the Properties view, just as I have in the screenshot shown. This is where you can add your own properties to the class. Right click in the blank area in the middle of the dialog and a popup menu will appear. Select Insert and a new property will be created:

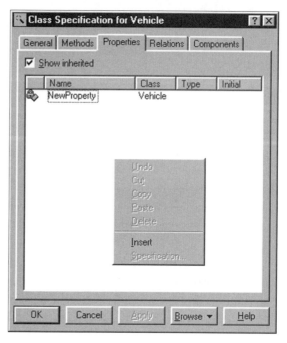

Initially the dialog will be waiting for you to key in a name for this property. Just press *Return*, then double click on the property and yet another dialog will appear - the Property Specification dialog:

Using this dialog you can specify a name for the property, as well as its data type, and also get at the Visual Basic options to control exactly what this property is going to look like when the code is generated. For now, set the name of the property to be NumWheels, and the type to be Integer. Obviously, since this is going to be a property, and not simply a private member of the Vehicles class, select the Public option button. You should end up with your dialog looking identical to this:

Now just click on OK to close down the class specification dialog and return to your model.

You should now be able to see the new property in your model:

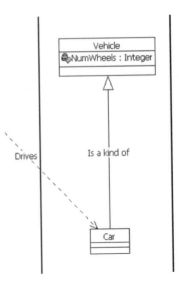

Adding Methods

Adding methods is almost identical to adding properties, with the obvious difference that you can now add parameters, as well as specify the return value type. Just as with properties, you have access to much more functionality and information if you double click on the class you want to add a method to, and then use the Methods tab in there to get at the Methods page. Right clicking on a class and selecting New Method simply provides you with a way to enter the method name, nothing more.

Let's add a method to our Vehicle class. Right click on the Vehicle class to open up the class specification dialog once again. When it appears, select the Methods tab at the top of the dialog:

As you can see, it looks very similar to the **Properties** page that we played with a short while ago. It works the same too. To add a method, right click in the blank area in the center of the dialog and select **Insert**. A new method will appear and the dialog will wait for you to enter a new name for it.

Just as you did with the properties, press *Return* and then double click on the new method to open up the method specification dialog:

The first page of the **Method** dialog, the one you see here, allows you to specify general information about the method. At the top you can enter the name for the method, and underneath that you can specify the type of the return value that the method will kick out. Leave it blank and Visual Modeler will think that your method is to be implemented as a subroutine. Enter a value, or select one from the drop down list, and Visual Modeler will code your method up as a function. Underneath this, just as with properties, is the export control frame, where you can elect to make your method `Private` or `Public`.

Key in Drive as the name of the method, and leave the return value blank, then click on the Argument tab at the top of the method specification dialog:

The Arguments page is where you can specify the arguments for your method, if any. It works in exactly the same way as the Property page. Simply right click in the page and select Insert to create a new argument. You are then able to enter a name for the argument, and double click on the Type column of your new argument to select its type from the list of available types.

Go ahead and enter a new argument now, call it sLocation. Then click on the Type field and enter String as the type, before finally clicking on the OK button:

Once you click on OK, you will be returned to the main Class Specification dialog, on the methods page that you were on a short while ago. Click OK again to close the dialog down and return to your model.

Just as before, the method will now appear in your model. To show the arguments for this method, you need to right click on the Vehicles class and then select Options from the drop-down menu, then check Show Method Arguments - they too should now appear in the model:

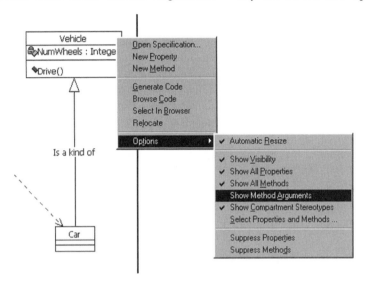

Generating Code

Once you have your model perfected, the next step is obviously to go and generate code using the Code Generation wizard in Visual Modeler. Don't expect too much though - all the wizard does is create a skeleton consisting of the classes and class modules that you specify, along with empty shells for any properties and methods that you specified, nothing more. It still never ceases to amaze me how many people think that when they hit the magic button, Visual Modeler should go right ahead and make some enlightened guesses as to the actually code that you are going to need as well. This doesn't happen; it just creates an empty framework for your code, according to the model that you created.

Before you start the code generation process, you need to make sure that you have the appropriate add-ins loaded up in Visual Basic – Load up VB, and select Add-in manager from the Add-in menu. Now you need to change the Load Behavior of Visual Modeler Add-in and Visual Modeler Menus Add-in. Both Add-ins should be set to Loaded and to Load on Startup. Now, return to Visual Modeler and select Generate Code from the Tools menu. After a short while, the following screen will appear:

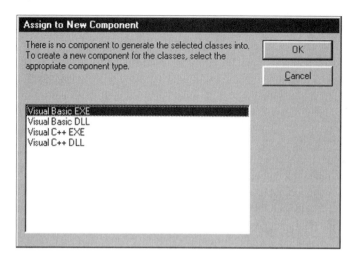

Select Visual Basic EXE to create the component, then click OK. Now an information page will appear - just click **Next** to move past this and on to the first real page of the wizard:

The **Select Classes** page, as the name suggests, allows you to select the classes that Visual Modeler should create code for. We want to code up all of them, so just leave the page as it is for now.

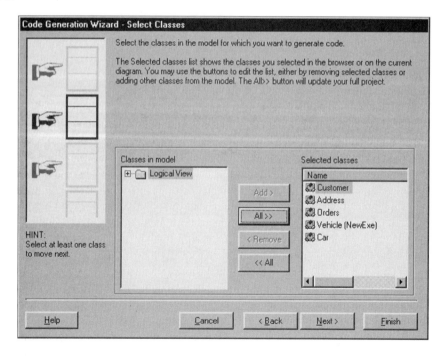

Now click on <u>N</u>ext, and you should see the following:

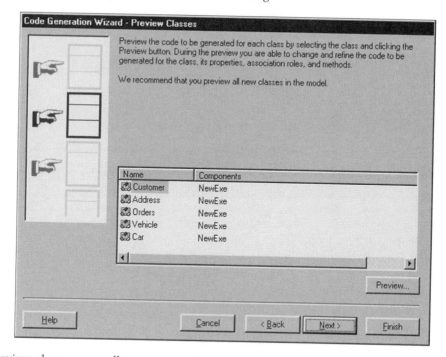

The preview classes page allows you one last glimpse at what is going to happen. Here Visual Modeler will list the classes and modules that it is about to go and create. You can even change exactly what Visual Modeler is going to do at this point by selecting a class and clicking the P<u>r</u>eview button. Do it now, select Vehicles and hit the Preview button.

The Class Options page shows you what properties are given to the class when you create it. Click Next:

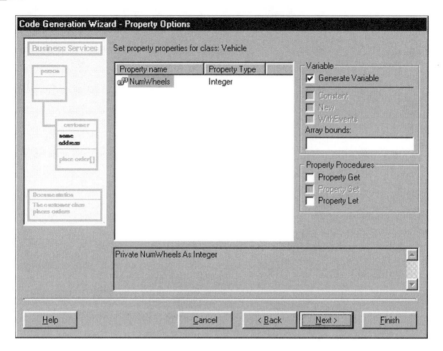

The Property Options page is very useful, showing you both properties that you created yourself, as well as properties and member variables that Visual Modeler is going to create for you. If Visual Modeler has decided to create a member variable where it shouldn't have, then you can use the Generate Variable checkbox to prevent this from happening. Just click on the unwanted variable and then clear the checkbox and Visual Modeler will no longer create the variable. Click Next again:

The Role Options page shows you any relationships that this class has with others that are going to result in the generation of code. In our model there is a class that relates to a Vehicle (a car) but vehicle relates to nothing, so this page is blank. Click Next one more time:

Finally the **Method Options** page shows you the methods in the class, their arguments, return types and so on. Click on the **Cancel** button now to return to the Code wizard, and when it appears, click the **Next** button once again. (Point and click programming - don't you just love it!?)

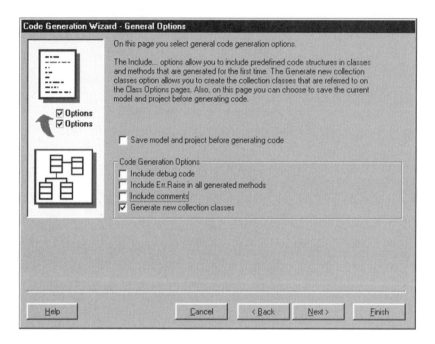

Almost done now. The **General Options** page allows you to tell Visual Modeler to include in debug code in the framework, error handlers, and comments on what the modeler did. By default all these options are checked, but the resulting code is pretty big and messy. For now, clear them all except for the **Generate new Collection Classes** option - remember we have a collection in place in the relationship between a customer and their orders. When you are done, click on the **Next** button just one more time (I promise that **Next** button will be done soon):

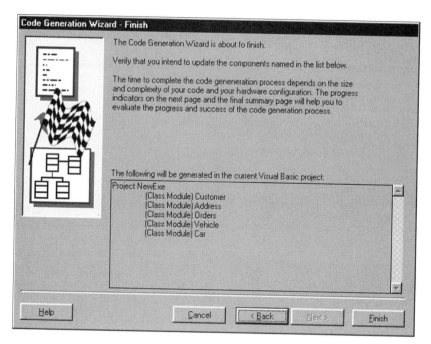

Finally, you'll be presented with a brief summary on what is about to happen to your Visual Basic project. There's not much to see, so click on the Finish button. The code generation wizard will now leap into life (well, crawl - its not the fastest process in the world) and generate your code skeleton for you in Visual Basic. Browse around the code for a while to see what Visual Modeler did, and refer it back to the model we created earlier:

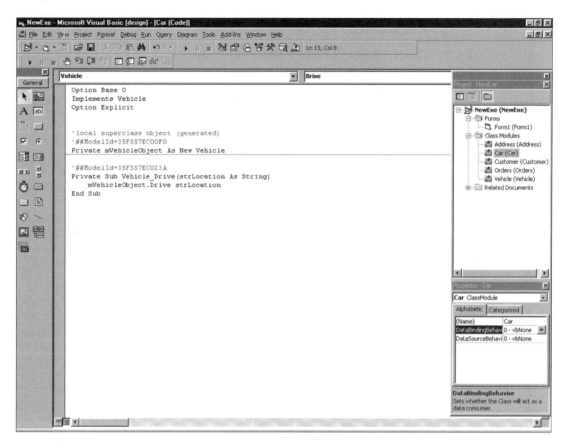

It shouldn't take too long for you to figure out what a fantastic time saver Visual Modeler can be. You now have the framework of an application that exactly matches a real UML model. Okay - the model itself isn't that much to be proud of, but you get the general idea. If this were a real commercial application, a huge amount of really mundane coding would now be complete, freeing your developers up to get on with the task of adding the functionality that counts.

Play around with the options that you set for the method, property and relationships some more, then regenerate the code again; its an excellent way to get acquainted with the way Visual Modeler does things, and the effect those things will have on your Visual Basic code.

A handy tip for those with a mind to explore. If you save the project before you make any changes, then if you find the changes really screw up your resulting Visual Basic code, you can hit the handy Revert to Last Save option on the Tools menu to get right back where you were before you did the changes.

This might not sound like too much of a big deal, but since the code generator will add members and properties to your model without your help, it can be a handy way of trying things out to see how they work, and then quickly removing the stuff that Visual Modeler will put into the model.

Reverse Engineering

The opposite to code generation is reverse engineering, a process whereby Visual Modeler will make a valiant attempt to produce a model of a loaded Visual Basic project. The results are not perfect, but they can be useful nonetheless. This is especially true if you are using Visual Modeler to come up with a rough object model for an existing project which you intend to refine to bring the project's documentation into the 90s.

The process is extremely similar to the Code Generation one. You just go to the Tools menu, select Visual Basic then Reverse Engineering Wizard and follow the on-screen prompts. It's very simple to use if you are already familiar with the Code Generation Wizard, so I won't bore you with the details here. By all means feel free to have a play yourself. In addition, you can get at the Reverse Engineering wizard from within Visual Basic itself – it's an item on the Add-Ins menu.

Now the reason I am just whizzing over this particular tool is simple. A lot of people who should know better think that the Reverse Engineering Wizard is a wonderful thing. After all, at last we have access to a tool that can provide us with documentation of a project once it has already been written. That in itself is not really a bad thing. After all, there are a lot of projects out there that could do with a bit of documentation. However, the attitude that really concerns me, and the reason why I tend to avoid going into too much detail on reverse engineering tools is the one that goes like this: "I can write my application best while sitting in front of a compiler. I think a tool which can produce the documentation management need, once I am finished writing the app, is a wonderful thing". There is a special circle in Hades for these people.

There is quite simply no way on earth that even the most talented programmer can hold in their head every minute twist and turn the code can take. There is no way that the even the very best among us could truly grasp the intricate details of even a reasonably sized project well enough to prevent themselves from duplicating their own work, or stumbling down blind alleys with code that should have been sorted out in design phase. Reverse Engineering wizards are a wonderful tool to document old systems that have no documentation, so that we can redesign them and get on with a new version. Anyone who says that they only need a tool like Visual Modeler because it can reverse engineer their code is either drunk, inexperienced, or just plain deranged. No matter how dull it is, no matter how much less glamorous it makes the job, there is no substitute for design before code. It is the cheapest and fastest way to spot flaws in a system, and the most effective way of getting developers off to a head start down the path to righteousness. By all means play with the reverse engineering wizard. The results it produces are nowhere near as clean and shiny as a model produced by hand, but there are instances when it is useful. However, never ever let yourself become sucked into the trap of using it to do documentation after the fact. That way lies a nasty reputation.

May I wish you the best of fortunes in your relations with Visual Modeler!

6

Database Programming: A Quick Refresher

OK, some of you may not feel too warm and happy about database code, so a quick refresher may be in order. It's only a quick one though, just enough to help you through some of the code you'll find in this book. Feel free to take a look at my earlier book, *Beginning Visual Basic 6* (especially chapters 13 and 14), also published by Wrox Press, if you want to learn more. You can also find lots of help by looking at Visual Basic's books online.

In a nutshell, a collection of objects comes supplied with Visual Basic that's known as the **DAO (Data Access Objects)**. These objects allow us to get at the information contained in local databases, particularly the Access format of database.

> *Here's a useful analogy that might help you think about databases. Each person you talk to is effectively a **database**, and each conversation that you have going with these people is known as a **workspace**.*

Visual Basic provides us with a default workspace that we can use to talk to databases, known as Workspace(0). If we really wanted to start more than one conversation with a database, or perhaps a set of databases, then we could start a new workspace (a new conversation). More often than not, people stick with their single default workspace.

Opening a Database

We can open a database with a simple statement like this:

```
Set MyDatabaseVariable = Workspaces(0).OpenDatabase("DatabaseName")
```

At this point, we have access to all the data in the database called DatabaseName.

Tables and Records

Whether you've dealt with databases in Visual Basic or not, you've probably heard about things called tables and records.

Imagine the database as a filing cabinet now. Each drawer holds related data (i.e. Customers, Orders, Suppliers). In the database world, each drawer would be known as a **table**.

Back in the real world, we wouldn't necessarily pull every file from the drawer every time we needed to deal with a customer. We would just pull one file (or a collection of related files) from the drawer, and this would be what we call a **record**.

Recordsets

Whether we want to deal with one or more records in Visual Basic it doesn't really make any difference - any data we pull out of a table is referred to as a **recordset**. A recordset is, rather predictably, a set of records. Individual records in the recordset relating to one 'thing' - perhaps one customer, for example.

We use the `OpenRecordset` method on a database object to create recordsets:

```
Set MyRecordsetVariable = MyDatabaseVariable.OpenRecordset("Customers",
dbOpenTable)
```

Notice the `dbOpenTable` bit on the end. `dbOpenTable` tells Visual Basic that, in this particular case, we want to deal with ALL the customers in the table.

Instead of `dbOpenTable`, however, we could have used `dbOpenDynaset` or `dbOpenSnapshot`. These are provided to allow us to work with just a SUBSET of the records in a table. So if we wanted to pull all the customers living in England, then this would be considered a `Dynaset` or `Snapshot`. The difference between the two is that we can make changes to `Dynaset` information, but we can only read `Snapshot` information - no changes allowed.

Indexes

If we go and grab a whole table with that `OpenRecordset` method, then we have the option of changing the order in which we read the information. We can do this using something known as the `Index` property.

When a database is created (before we even think about attaching Visual Basic to it) we create things called **Indexes**. Indexes sort the data in various ways and make it easy to locate individual records in the table.

Let's consider an example. There may be a `CustomerName` index on the `Customer` table that sorts the customers by their name. We can use this `Index`, with the `Seek` keyword, to get a particular customer, based on their name:

```
MyRecordsetVariable.Index = "CustomerName"
MyRecordsetVariable.Seek "=", "Fred Bloggs"
```

Here, we're telling VB that we want to use the `CustomerName` index, and that we're searching for a customer where the index matches the text of `Fred Bloggs`.

This only works for recordsets that we open with the dbOpenTable *keyword though, and even then the index that we use must already exist in the database. This means we have to run up Access and tell Access to create the index before our application can use it.*

SQL

If we're creating Dynasets or Snapshots then we can't use an Index. However, we can use a special programming language known as **SQL (Structured Query Language, pronounced Sequel)** to tell Visual Basic exactly which records we want, and which fields from those records we're interested in. For example:

```
Set MyRecordsetVariable = MyDatabaseVariable.OpenRecordset( _
    "SELECT * FROM Customers WHERE Country = 'England'", dbOpenDynaset)
```

The * means that we want every bit of information in each customer record - all the fields. The rest should be quite self-explanatory: SELECT... Customers... WHERE... their Country item of data is England.

SQL gets quite a bit more complex than this though - you can even use it to create recordsets consisting of information from two or more tables. Take a look at Visual Basic's online help for more information on the Select statement, then run up a copy of Access or the VisData application supplied with VB and have a play - its quite good fun and incredibly powerful.

6

Solutions

The following pages contain solutions to the exercises that are included at the end of each chapter. However, there are many ways of solving these problems, so don't worry if you have come up with different solutions. It is worth reading through these answers though, as you may find some good programming tips which you could use in your own code.

Chapter 1: Introducing Objects

1 A class is a template from which an object is created. We can create many objects based on a single class. When we create an object based on a particular class, we create an instance of that class.

2 Methods are routines to implement the services or procedures that we want our object to provide, such as the ShowInfo method described in the chapter.

Properties are attributes that describe an object, such as the Wheels property of the clsVehicle class. The designer of the object can choose what information they wish to make available about the object, and furthermore, what property values can be changed by the object's users.

3 A method is an action that an object is capable of performing. An event is an action that is recognized by an object, for which you can write code to respond to.

Starting with Visual Basic Version 5, it is now possible for the designer of an object to define and raise events emanating from the object. These raised events provide developers with feedback on what's happening to the object.

4 In Visual Basic, with the traditional structured approach to development, a programmer looks at the data that the application needs to deal with, and then works out what needs to be done to that data. This approach invariably results in a number of forms being produced for the user interface of the application. There will also be a set of routines that do the main work - either as events, or as subroutines that are called by events. The essential thing is that the focus of this structured approach lies purely with the data - and providing the user with the appropriate tools and facilities to maintain that data.

Instead of looking at the business data, and bolting an application on top of that, OOP relies on identifying the objects around which everything in an application takes place. With an OOP approach, abstract representations of real-world objects are used within our programs. Then we attach properties and methods to our objects and make events available to them.

5 Other programmers. This is something that confuses beginners to object-oriented programming. In the workplace, if you are savvy enough to be developing objects through the use of Visual Basic class modules, you most likely are doing so in order to provide their functionality to other programmers in your organization.

Therefore, it isn't the developer of the object who will ultimately be using it, but other programmers who will create 'instances' of the objects within their own programs---much like they instantiate instances of a command button on their forms.

6a Start a new Standard.EXE project. Add a class module to your project by selecting **Add Class Module** from the **Project** menu. After a short pause, a dialog box will appear. Select **Class Module** and then click on the **Open** button. Change the name of the class to clsEmployee.

We need to declare a Private variable for each one of the class' properties. Type the following lines into your clsEmployee class module:

```
Private m_strName as String
Private m_strDepartment as String
Private m_sngPayRate as Single
```

Now we need to code a Property Get procedure for each one of the class' properties.

```
Public Property Get Name() As String
    Name = m_strName
End Property

Public Property Get Department() As String
    Department = m_strDepartment
End Property

Public Property Get PayRate() As Single
    Name = m_sngPayRate
End Property
```

Now we need to code a Property Let procedure for each one of the class' properties.

```
Public Property Let Name(ByVal strName As String)
    m_strName = strName
End Property

Public Property Let Department(ByVal strDepartment As String)
    m_strDepartment = strDepartment
End Property
```

```
Public Property Let PayRate(ByVal sngPayRate As Single)
    m_sngPayRate = sngPayRate
End Property
```

6b Type the following lines into your `clsEmployee` class module:

```
Public Sub ShowInfo()

    MsgBox "Employee Name      : " & m_strName & vbCrLf & _
    "Employee Department: " & m_strDepartment & vbCrLf & _
    "Employee Pay Rate  : " & m_sngPayRate

End Sub
```

6c Type the following lines into the `General  Declarations` section of your `clsEmployee` class module:

```
Option Explicit

Public Event PayRateChanged(ByVal sngPayRate As Single)
```

Modify the `Property  Let` procedure of `PayRate` as follows. (Changed code is highlighted.)

```
Public Property Let PayRate(ByVal sngPayRate As Single)
m_sngPayRate = sngPayRate
RaiseEvent PayRateChanged(m_sngPayRate)
End Property
```

6d The declaration for an object `WithEvents` must occur in the `General  Declarations` section of a module. Accordingly, declare the object in the `General  Declarations` section of your form.

```
Option Explicit

Private WithEvents Employee As clsEmployee
```

Place a command button called `cmdOK` on your form, and place the following code in the `Click` event procedure.

```
Private Sub cmdOK_Click()

    Set Employee = New clsEmployee
    Employee.ShowInfo

    Employee.Name = "John Smiley"
    Employee.Department = "MIS"
    Employee.PayRate = 12.34
```

```
    Employee.ShowInfo

End Sub
```

Finally, the following code is the `PayRateChanged` event procedure of the `Employee` object. It should be typed into the form's code window.

```
Private Sub Employee_PayRateChanged(ByVal sngPayRate As Single)

    MsgBox "Payrate has been changed to : " & sngPayRate

End Sub
```

Now run the program, and click on the command button. When you do, a message box will be displayed showing you the current values for the `Name`, `Department` and `PayRate` properties. When the `PayRate` is changed, a message box will be displayed informing you that the `PayRate` property has changed, and finally a message box will be displayed showing you the new values for the `Name`, `Department` and `PayRate` properties.

Make sure you save `clsEmployee` as we shall be using it in a later example.

Chapter 2: Why Program With Objects?

1 They broke three rules which were introduced in Chapter 2.

Firstly, their code was not cohesive. Cohesive code means that there is one routine for one job. In Visual Basic terms, that means that one procedure does one thing. In their application, the Make It button tried to do a myriad of different things.

Secondly, their code was not loosely coupled (i.e it was tightly coupled!). Loosely coupled code means that the code is not explicitly linked to the user interface's controls. This means that we should be able to move the code from one application to another without too much trouble. When the Northwind programmers programmed this application, they wrote database code that was explicitly linked to the actual user interface button to make the invoice.

Thirdly, they didn't keep their code simple. They had huge routines, which can make for big problems from a maintenance and debugging point of view.

2 This statement is the common definition found for cohesion, and it's not a bad starting point. The problem, if there is one, is that the definition lacks a limitation on the word 'task.' What exactly is a task? For instance, strictly speaking, you can say that this code

```
Private Sub Command1_Click()

    Beep
    MsgBox "John, Mr. Gates will see you now"

End Sub
```

violates the tenant of cohesion since thee is more than one Visual Basic statement in the procedure. In this instance, what is the task? Is a statement the same as a task?

From a high level point of view, you can argue that the task in this procedure is to notify the user that Mr. Gates will now see them. This task is performed by presenting both an audible and a visual cue - two statements, one task.

3 The Northwind programmers, in their haste to get the program up and running, implemented very tightly coupled code. Not only is it highly coupled, but routines are repeated in many event procedures thoughout the application.

A good test to determine cohesion is to ask yourself how easy it would be to take some of your code, and use it in another application. Where are the problems? How much modification would be required?

In the Northwind application, for instance, there are explicit references to specific databases and locations, the database type, etc. Even if we didn't want to use the code in another application, imagine the difficulty if the database platform changed from Access to SQLServer, or Oracle.

Better to have written a single, highly cohesive routine to open a database and work with it, then the code we see in Northwind.

4 One good rule of thumb is the number of lines of code in a procedure. If your code goes over 15-20 lines, there's a strong chance that it could be broken down into smaller routines. Remember---shorter routines add a lot to the readability (and therefore maintainability) of your code.

Chapter 3: Object Oriented Development

1 Bearing in mind that this code is present in a re-usable class, and would be called when an instance of the class was created within a form, the purpose of raising the event DataChanged is to alert the calling procedure that something has caused the properties of the object to change - in this case, Public variables set aside to hold the values of the Titles table fields.

2 The procedure `Reload_Members` take place whenever the methods `MoveNext`, `MovePrevious`, `MoveLast` and `MoveFirst` are executed.

3   The properties are implemented as Public variables. Ordinarily, class properties are implemented as Private variables, and their values are either set by a `Property Let` subprocedure or retrieved using a `Property Get` subprocedure. This technique fully exposes the property to any code written by the program that instantiates the object.

4   The recordset is created in the `Initialize` event procedure for the class. This occurs when the class is first turned into an object.

5   The object is instantiated in the `Load` event procedure of the form. We now know that this causes the `Initialize` event of the class object to fire, which creates the `Titles` recordset.

6   By using the `With Events` declaration of the object, the `DataChanged` event procedure then appears in the procedures ListBox just like any other procedure available in our projects. At that point, we can use it in any way we deem fit.

How is it used? In this particular instance, the `DataChanged` event procedure is where we update the textboxes on the form with the object's properties (i.e. the underlying recordset's fields).

7   The code is totally independent of the data source. There isn't a hint, anywhere within the form's procedures, as to where the data is located.

Of course, what that means is that tons of programmers can write code using this class as intermediary between the form and the underlying database without concerning themselves with the intricacies of how it is obtained.

8   The only code that would need to be changed would be the `Class_Initialize` event of our class, where the actual location (and type) of our database is specified.

9   Start a new Visual Basic Standard.EXE project.

Add a class module to your project by selecting **Add Class Module** from the **Project** menu. After a short pause, a dialog box will appear.

Select **Class Module** and then click on the **Open** button---your new class module appears

Change the name of the class to `clsPerson`.

Type the following lines into your `clsPerson` class module:

```
Private m_strName as String
Private m_strAddress as String
```

Now we need to code a `Property Get` procedure for each one of the class properties.

```
Public Property Get Name() As String
    Name = m_strName
End Property
```

```
Public Property Get Address() As String
    Address = m_strAddress
End Property
```

Now we need to code a `Property Let` procedure for each one of the class properties.

```
Public Property Let Name(ByVal strName As String)
    m_strName = strName
End Property
```

```
Public Property Let Address(ByVal strAddress As String)
    m_strAddress = strAddress
End Property
```

Type the following lines into your `clsPerson` class module:

```
Public Sub ShowInfo()

    MsgBox "Name      : " & m_strName & vbCrLf & _
           "Address   : " & m_strAddress

End Sub
```

Test your class by placing a command button on your form, and placing the following code into its `Click Event` procedure.

```
Private Sub cmdOK_Click()

Dim Person as New clsPerson

    Person.ShowInfo

    Person.Name = "John Smiley"
    Person.Address = "222 Twain Street"
    Person.ShowInfo

End Sub
```

Now run the program, and click on the Command Button. When you do, a message box will be displayed showing you the current values for the Name and Address properties. Then, a message box will be displayed showing you the new values for the Name and Address properties.

10 Continue working with your project from question 9.

Add a class module to your project by selecting **Add Class Module** from the **Project** menu. After a short pause, a dialog box will appear.

Select **Class Module** and then click on the **Open** button---your new class module appears.

Change the name of the class to `clsCustomer`.

In order to implement the Interface of `clsPerson` into `clsCustomer`, type the following into your `clsCustomer` class module:

```
Option Explicit
Implements clsPerson
```

If you now try to run this project, you'll receive an error message indicating that you need to implement 'Name' for the interface `clsPerson`. In fact, you need to implement an interface for all of the properties and methods of `clsPerson`.

If you check the Object ListBox, you'll see that `clsPerson` appears, just as if it were an actual 'object' on the form. Select `clsPerson`, and then click the Procedures Listbox. You'll see entries for the `PropertyLet` and `PropertyGet` procedures for the two properties of `clsPerson`, plus an entry for the single method of `clsPerson` `ShowInfo`. Remember, the idea behind the `Implements` statement is to ensure that this project implements the same interface. That doesn't mean the same code within the implemented class, just the same methods and properties.

There's no need to do any typing here. Just select one of the procedures in the Procedures ListBox, and you'll create empty procedure templates for all the properties and methods in the class that you wish to implement here.

Do that now for all five of the procedures. As you do, notice that each of the procedure names in the Procedures ListBox become bold, indicating that they have now been implemented in our `clsPerson` class.

Now run the project. No compile errors---you've successfully implemented the interface of one class within another, although at this point, since all of the procedures are 'empty', we still have some work to do. Remember, Visual Basic doesn't implement true 'inheritance'---only interface inheritance.

Chapter 4: Object Hierarchies

The dog object will have a body object. The body object has a tail object, leg objects, and a head object. The leg objects have a foot object, which has several toe objects. The head object has eye objects, a nose object, ear objects, and a mouth object.

The ear object can lift, rotate and shake and listen to sounds. The mouth object can bark, yawn, bite, and drool and is either open or closed. The tail object has a color, spots, a position (up, down) and can wag and move.

Looking through this description we find many nouns: Dog, Body, Tail, Head, Eye, Nose, Ear, Mouth, Leg, Foot, and Toe are all nouns and so will all be objects. Since the leg, eye, ear, and toe objects all are objects that have multiple copies they will all need objects to manage them. While there is more then one foot object, each leg will only have one foot so there does need to be a class to manage the feet. Putting all of these objects together we get our hierarchy which would look as follows:

Dog Object

    Body Object

        Tail Object

        Head Object

            Eye Managing Object

                Eyes Object

            Nose Object

            Ear Managing Object

                Ears Object

            Mouth Object

        Legs Managing Object

            Leg Object

                Foot Object

                    Toe Managing Object

                        Toe Object

Each object would have its own set of special methods and properties.

The adjectives that describe the tail object are color, number of spots, and position and these will be the tail properties. The verbs associated with the tail object are wag and move and will be the methods for the tail object.

Finding the adjectives for the mouth object would give us the open property (which is either true or false). Looking at the verbs for the mouth object we would find a drool, bark, eat, bite and yawn methods and these will all be methods of the mouth object.

The ear-managing object will have an ear count property, and methods to access a particular ear and the properties and methods of that ear.

Write the rest of the description for the dog object using verbs and adjectives to describe the rest of the dog objects. Once your description is done turn them into properties and methods.

Chapter 5: Objects and ActiveX Components

1 An ActiveX component is a standard Visual Basic class placed in its own application, totally separate from any other application that make use of it. We call the ActiveX component application the **server** application, because it serves the other applications that call it. The applications making the calls to the ActiveX server are known as **client** applications, since they are clients of our ActiveX component server.

2 In real terms, IUnknown is not actually anything that we need to worry about too much. When we create a class module in Visual Basic, and we tell Visual Basic that we're going to expose it as an ActiveX component, Visual Basic puts the IUnknown interface in there for us: we never see it or have to deal with it.

3 Component binding is the process by which a client application loads up and uses a server's component. There are two types of component binding: Early binding and Late binding.

Which type of binding we use affects the facilities that Visual Basic provides for us during our development. The choice of binding type also affects the speed of the final application.

With late binding, we specify the name of the ActiveX component server, and the name of the interface after the program is actually running. This means that the Visual Basic compiler, does not check whether our calls are valid while we are writing the code in the client application to call the server application. All checking takes place when the program is running, as each call is made. This, as you can imagine, creates a huge overhead. Therefore, late bound objects are slow relative to early bound objects.

Early binding takes place as a program is being compiled. Therefore, type checking an object validation takes place before the program is run. Therefore, when the client application finally runs, without the overhead required to validate the object calls, the application runs much faster.

4 Start up a new project, by selecting **File-New Project**, and choose ActiveX DLL

As we saw in the chapter, when you select an ActiveX DLL project, you are presented with a single class module. Since we already have a class module we want to include in this ActiveX DLL, right click on **Class1** in the Project explorer window and choose **Remove Class** to get rid of the default class. Say **No** to the question concerning saving changes to **Class1**.

Now we need to add clsEmployee from Chapter 1 solutions (If you didn't create or save this class, It's time to get typing). Click on the Project menu and choose Add <u>C</u>lass Module. When the standard dialog appears, click on the Existing tab and find the clsEmployee class.

When you're done adding the class, the Project explorer window in Visual Basic will have changed to show you the new class in your project. As we did in the exercise in the chapter, click on the name of the clsEmployee in the Project explorer window and take a peek at the Properties window below. Notice that we now have an Instancing property.

Click on the Instancing property and drop down the list of options. Select MultiUse.

Right click on the name of the project in the Project explorer window, and select Project1 Properties to open the Project Properties dialog. Change the project name from Project1 to EmployeeServer.

When you've done that, click on the Component tab of the Project Properties dialog to display the component server options for the project: Select Project Compatibility and click on the OK button to close down the dialog.

Our ActiveX component server is now ready to be compiled. Save your project as EmployeeServer.vbp using the File-Save Project As menu option. Then click on the File menu again and select Make EmployeeServer.DLL.

5 Start a new Visual Basic Standard.EXE project.

Bring up the References dialog and reference the EmployeeServer.

Place a command button called cmdOK on your form, and place the following code in the Click Event procedure.

```
Private Sub cmdOK_Click()

Dim Employee As New EmployeeServer.clsEmployee

Employee.ShowInfo

Employee.Name = "John Smiley"
Employee.Department = "MIS"
Employee.PayRate = 12.34
Employee.ShowInfo

End Sub
```

Now run the program, and click on the Command Button. When you do, a message box will be displayed showing you the current values for the Name, Department, and PayRate properties. When the values change a message box will be displayed showing you the new values for the Name, Department and PayRate properties.

6 As we did at the end for the exercise at the end of Chapter 1, in order to place code in an event procedure triggered by a class module, we need to declare the object using the keyword WithEvents in the General Declarations section of a module. Place the following code in the General Declarations section of your form.

```
Option Explicit

Private WithEvents Employee As Employeeserver.clsEmployee
```

Modify the code in the click event procedure of the command button to look like this. Modified code is highlighted.

```
Private Sub cmdOK_Click()
```

```
Set Employee = New clsEmployee
Employee.ShowInfo

Employee.Name = "John Smiley"
Employee.Department = "MIS"
Employee.PayRate = 12.34
Employee.ShowInfo
```

```
End Sub
```

Finally, place the following code in the `PayRateChanged` event procedure of the `Employee` object.

```
Private Sub Employee_PayRateChanged(ByVal sngPayRate As Single)

MsgBox "Payrate has been changed to : " & sngPayRate

End Sub
```

Now run the program, and click on the Command Button. When you do, a message box will be displayed showing you the current values for the `Name`, `Department`, and `PayRate` properties. When the `PayRate` is changed, a Message box will be displayed informing you that the `PayRate` property has changed, and finally a message box will be displayed showing you the new values for the `Name`, `Department` and `PayRate` properties.

Chapter 6: Objects and ActiveX Controls

1 When we create an ActiveX control, we're typically not the programmer that will actually be placing it on a Visual Basic form somewhere. We're the designer of the control that will appear in someone's toolbox. Therefore, we need to consider the behavior of the control in the design time environment (when it's placed, sized, moved, etc on a form) as well as its behavior when it is run on that form.

2 Create a new project in Visual Basic in the usual way. When Visual Basic asks you what kind of project you want to create, choose ActiveX Control.

We need to place a Common Dialog control on the designer. If you don't see it in your toolbox, select the Microsoft Common Dialog control from the Project-Components menu of the Visual Basic main menu.

Change the Name property of the Common Dialog control to `dlgColor`, and set its `CancelError` property to True.

Place a command button on the designer. Name it `cmdColor`, and change its caption to 'Color Change'.

Now name the control designer itself, the same way you would a form. In this case, call it `ctlColor`.

Now we need to name the Project, and provide a project description. The name of the project affects the control's entry in the Windows registry, and the description is what users see when they go to the Components dialog to add the control to their project. Name the project `ColorControl`, and give it some kind of meaningful description.

Save your project using File-Save Project. When Visual Basic prompts you, save your actual control as `ctlColor.Ctl`, and your project as `ColorControl.vbp`.

3 Declare module level variables for the `Caption` and `Color` Properties by typing this code into the General Declarations section of the control.

```
Option Explicit

Private m_Caption As String
Private m_Color As Long

Event Click()
```

Next, code a Property Let and Get procedure for the `Caption` property.

```
Public Property Get Caption() As String

Caption = m_Caption

End Property
```

```
Public Property Let Caption(ByVal strCaption As String)

m_Caption = strCaption
cmdColor.Caption = m_Caption

End Property
```

Now code a Property Get procedure for the `Color` property.

```
Public Property Get Color() As Long

Color = m_Color

End Property
```

4 Place the following code into the control's `Resize` event procedure. This will ensure that when the control is resized, the command button 'fills up' all of the control, making for a nice and clean interface.

```
Private Sub UserControl_Resize()

cmdColor.Move 0, 0, ScaleWidth, ScaleHeight

End Sub
```

Place the following code into the control's `Initialize` event procedure. This will ensure that when the control is displayed, a caption equal to the name of our control is displayed.

```
Private Sub UserControl_Initialize()

m_Caption = UserControl.Name
cmdColor.Caption = m_Caption

End Sub
```

5 Place the following code into the `Click` event procedure of the Command Button.

```
Private Sub cmdColor_Click()

On Error GoTo ErrorHandler

dlgColor.ShowColor
m_Color = dlgColor.Color
RaiseEvent Click

Exit Sub

ErrorHandler:
    Exit Sub

End Sub
```

Pretty standard stuff here. Notice the use of the `ErrorHandler` in case the user clicks the Cancel button on the Common Dialog control. If the user makes a valid selection, then we set the value of `m_Color`, and 'raise' the click event procedure of the user control.

6 Make sure that you have closed the Designer window containing the user control.

Now go to **File** menu and add a new project to the project group. Make sure it's a Standard EXE project.

Before we drop the new control on our form, we need to change the way that Visual Basic deals with runtime errors. Click on the **Tools** menu in Visual Basic and select the **Options** item to bring up the Options dialog. Click on the **General** tab at the top of the dialog to show the error handling options for Visual Basic: select the **Break in Class Module** option.

Create a new custom control on the form using the icon at the bottom of the Toolbar.

When the control appears, it should have a caption of `ctlColor`, because of the code we placed in the control's `Initialize` event.

Resize the control on the form to see that the code in the control's `Resize` event is working properly.

Now take a peek at the Properties window for the user control. Note that there is a property called Caption (yes, that's the one we created), whose default value is equal to the ctlColor. Change the Caption property of the user control to something completely different.

Bring up the Code Window, select the user control, and then place the following code in the Click event procedure of the user control.

```
Private Sub ctlColor1_Click()

Me.BackColor = ctlColor1.Color

End Sub
```

Before we run the program, right click on Project1 and select Set as Startup.

Now run the program. Click on the user control. We may as well check the Error Handler first. Instead of selecting a color from the color palette, click on the Cancel button. What happens? If all is working properly, there will be no color change.

Click on the user control again, and this time select a color. What happens? The BackColor of the form is changed to your selection. Congratulations! You've created a functional ActiveX control.

However, did you notice that the Caption reverted to the default value of ctlColor?

7 Place the following code in the user control's ReadProperties event procedure. Notice the use of the default value for the Caption property.

```
Private Sub UserControl_ReadProperties(PropBag As PropertyBag)

With PropBag
    m_Caption = .ReadProperty("Caption", UserControl.Name)
End With

cmdColor.Caption = Caption

End Sub
```

Place the following code in the user control's WriteProperties event procedure. Notice the use of the default value for the Caption property.

```
Private Sub UserControl_WriteProperties(PropBag As PropertyBag)

With PropBag
    .WriteProperty "Caption", Caption
End With

End Sub
```

Chapter 7: Advanced ActiveX Controls

1 Ambient, defined in Webster's as 'surrounding', is an object that contains information regarding the surrounding environment of the user control.

2 The `AmbientChanged` event of the `User control` is triggered.

3 `UserMode` lets you know if the control is in the design or runtime environment. If `UserMode` is set to `True`, then the control is in a runtime environment. If set to `False`, then the control is in a design time environment.

4 No. Remember, `Ambient` means surrounding. This event is triggered for a change to everything but the user control.

5 Select the **ColorControl** project and then select the **Project-Add Property Page** menu option to add a property page to that control. You have two options. Select **Property Page**, and leave the **VB Property Page Wizard** for your own experimentation.

As you saw in the example in the chapter, this looks very much like an ActiveX control. As I mentioned, we're going to keep this simple, so just drop a label and a textbox on the property page. Change the Label's caption to **This is a Caption**, and call the textbox `txtCaption`.

Set the name of the property page to `propColor`, and set its caption property to `Color Control Caption`.

Now we want to attach the property page to our `ctlColor` control---so the control knows that this property page is available. There is a property on the UserControl of our Color control called `PropertyPages`. If you click on the button that appears in the Property window for this property, you'll see a dialog appear that allows us to select which property pages our custom control can use.

Select `propColor` as our new property page.

As always, make sure that there are no code windows or forms relating to the control that are open, and then bring the test form into view. Now select our custom control that's sitting in the test form. If you take a peek at the **Properties** window for this control, you should be able to see a new entry at the top, called **Custom**. This property provides users of our control with access to its property pages. Simply click on the ellipsis button to the right of the property in the **Properties** window, and up it comes.

At this point, changing the **Caption** in the Custom Properties Page doesn't do anything. That's our next step. Start by placing this code in the `SelectionChanged` event procedure of the Property Page. You may remember from the chapter that this code will ensure that when the Property Page is first displayed, the value for `Caption` is retrieved from the `Caption` property of the first selected control in the `SelectedControls` array.

```
Private Sub PropertyPage_SelectionChanged()

txtCaption.Text = SelectedControls(0).Caption

End Sub
```

So far so good---but this doesn't permit us to 'permanently' change the `Caption` property. To do that, place this code in the `ApplyChanges` event procedure of the Property Page. You may remember from the chapter that this code will apply the change to the appropriate property of each member of the `SelectedControls` array.

```
Private Sub PropertyPage_ApplyChanges()

Dim TheControl As ctlColor

For Each TheControl In SelectedControls
    TheControl.Caption = txtCaption.Text
Next

End Sub
```

Next you need to let the code the `Change` event for the textbox.

```
Private Sub txtCaption_Change()
Changed = True
End Sub
```

Now use the Property Page to change the caption of our user control and selecting OK. Voila! The caption of the control changed. But wait one moment. Did you notice that the `Caption` property in the Properties Window hasn't changed, even though we changed it via the Property Page and the control's caption has changed. We have just one more thing to do, and that's to modify the `PropertyLet` procedure of the user control by using the `PropertyChanged` method to notify the Property Window that the property has changed.

```
Public Property Let Caption(ByVal strCaption As String)

m_Caption = strCaption
cmdColor.Caption = m_Caption
PropertyChanged "Caption"

End Property
```

Chapter 8: Object Persistence

1 A property bag has a `ReadProperty` method, a `WriteProperty` method and a `Contents` property.

Objects may use the `ReadProperty` method to access the information stored in the property bag. The `WriteProperty` method is used to load information into the property bag.

The `Contents` property is simply the information stored in the property bag. By setting this property to a byte array, we can store and retrieve multiple items of information.

2 The `ReadProperty` method needs to be supplied with a property name and may also be supplied with a `Default` value. Each item in the bag has a unique `PropertyName` to identify it. The `Default` value is returned by the method if no item with the required `PropertyName` can be found.

3 The `WriteProperty` method again needs to be supplied with a `PropertyName` to identify the item, but it also needs to be given a `PropertyValue` – this is the value of the item that will be stored in the property bag.

4 The `ReadProperty` and `WriteProperty` methods use `Default` values for different purposes.

The `ReadProperty` method returns its `Default` value if no match can be found between the `PropertyName` supplied, and any identifiers currently in the property bag. The purpose of this is to prevent an error being raised whenever a requested item cannot be found. The user is still aware of the mismatch because the `Default` has been returned, but does not have to deal with error messages.

The `WriteProperty` method uses a `Default` value to check that a new `PropertyValue` is actually being added to the property bag. If the `PropertyValue` supplied differs from the `Default`, then it is put in the property bag and added to the project files. However, if a `PropertyValue` is the same as the `Default`, then it is not saved to the project files. This saves memory space and makes our programs more efficient.

If this is still unclear, imagine we wanted to save the `PropertyValue` of the `NumberofLegs` that a horse has. Ninety nine percent of horses would have the same value for this property. So, instead of saving lots of data exactly the same, we would set the `Default` value to four, and only save the exceptions to the property bag.

Chapter 9: Object Oriented Design

1 You should no more sit down and just start coding a Visual Basic project than you would start building a house. A house can be thought upon as a collection of objects (doors, windows, floors, ceilings, etc), but there still needs to be blueprint drawn up to specify the bounds of the system (i.e. the dimensions of the house), the properties and locations of the objects, etc.

2 The **SSADM** (Structured Systems Analysis and Design Methodology) works by analyzing the flow of data through an application and inventing routines, classes, modules or whatever else to effect the operations that take place on that data.

3 The **Use Case Technique** is one of the most popular tools for getting a handle on everything that needs to go into an application. Use case statements help us to build up a picture of the objects in a system, plus their methods, properties and events. The idea behind the Use Case Technique is deceptively simple. The Use Case Technique relies on identifying current real-world practices and documenting them in a very straightforward manner. The Use Case Technique starts with a high level description of why the use case is needed and the process it describes, and then it goes ahead and describes that process in detail. The level of detail should be high enough for each individual step in the process to be identified, but not so detailed that we're actually approaching the complexity of program code. A great benefit of the Use Case Technique is that it's fairly easy to identify some of the objects that are going to be in the final system just by identifying the nouns in the sentences.

Where the Use Case Technique leaves off, **Unified Modeling Language (UML)** picks up, helping us reach the next level of clarity and understanding about the system we're studying. UML provides us with a graphical way to lay out the design of an object-oriented application. Like a picture that paints a thousand words, UML allows us to produce a diagram that, at a glance, will show the relationships between all the components in a system. More than that, a UML diagram also shows us where use cases fit into the technical solution. This effectively provides us with a map between the real world and the world behind the screen.

4 Our first step is to develop a set of **Requirements Use Case Statements**, which are developed mainly through the use of employee interviews and observations. These **Requirements Use Case Statements** form the basis of formal **System Requirements** for Northwind. The **Requirements Use Case Statements** represent a high level view of what goes on at Northwind, good enough to describe the system from a general everyday point of view, but not quite what we need to start implementing the system.

The next step is to produce **Functional Use Case Statements**, which break down and describe the high level view of the **Requirements Use Case Statements** in more detail. The steps we take to build up a complete set of functional use cases are identical to those for producing high-level statements. However, the difference is that the smaller the scope of each functional use case statement, the closer it will be to something that could be written in code. This process is also known as **Specification Refinement**.

Next we use **UML** to declare an object model. The first stage in UML is to identify the objects themselves that are going to be in the system. The simplest way to do this is to examine the **Use Case Statements**, and produce a list of all the nouns. At the end of this stage we should have a list of objects that we can then draw on a sheet of paper. This is the beginning of our UML model.

At this point, the model is then broken into multi or logical tiers, along these lines: **User Services, Business Services, and Data Services**.

▶ **User Services** comprise the user interface of the system.

▶ **Business Services** are the business rules.

▶ The underlying database comprises the **Data Services** tier.

The objects that are drawn in the first stage of UML represent the Business Services tier, in that they each represent something that the business deals with or produces as a matter of daily routine. The code in these objects should know nothing about the user interface of the application, and they should be totally free of any knowledge about the database.

Next, we then represent the three tiers in our UML diagram by drawing vertical lines down the page, and dividing it into three sections - and then concentrate on the User Services. Many designers at this point would be tempted to drop symbols representing forms in the User Services tier. However, this is where the potential for user fickleness is strong. Today the user may want a form representing a single Business Service object - tomorrow, the user might ask that the same form interact with two Business Service objects.

Rather than drop symbols of forms into our model, instead we use symbols called **Utility Modules** to represent each of the high-level use cases. At coding time, we'll just connect these forms to these Utility Modules.

Now we turn our attention to the **Data Services**, which deal solely with the database. Each instance of a **Data Service** typically represents a single table in a database.

At this point we have now ideally identified all of the objects in the system, along with each Utility Module and Data Services. Now it's time to begin to identify and draw different types of relationships between the objects in the three tiers. There are a number of different relationships: Dependency, Generalization, Association, and Aggregation.

In a **Dependency** relationship, one object is dependent upon the methods and/or properties of another object in order to do its job. In UML, a dashed line drawn between two objects represents a dependency relationship. In the Northwind model, every business object is dependent on its data services counterpart in order to work.

Next we identify and draw **Generalization** relationships, where one object implements the other's interface, and can be expected to provide the same functionality as a result. In the more general world of object-oriented methodologies, generalization is also known as 'inheritance', 'sub-classing', or 'sub-typing'. Often, the generalization relationship is described as an "is-a" relationship between the two objects or classes. In UML, a solid line drawn between two objects represents a generalization relationship.

Next, we identify and draw **Association** relationships, where one object contains references to a set of other objects. This indicates that one object is a member of another, or perhaps part of a collection in another.

Finally, we identify and draw **Aggregation** relationships. Aggregation relationships are similar to normal association relationships in many ways, except that one of the objects cannot exist without the other.

With the objects on paper, and the relationships between them identified, our UML is complete.

6

Beginning
VB6 Objects

A

I

K

keys, methods 115

L

late binding 135
  see also ActiveX components, late binding
  advantages 152
  generic Object type, defining interface 136
  interface, defining with generic Object type 136
  QueryInterface 135
Let properties 113
LimitCountry, ActiveX design time properties 187
LimitRegion, ActiveX design time properties 187
ListCount, ActiveX control creation 187
load balancing, ActiveX servers 143, 167
  Distributed COM (DCOM) 167
Load event 26
logging extension, Northwind Traders. see extension, Northwind Traders
logical tiers, UML 294
  cohesion 294
  coupling 294
loose coupling 293

M

MDI forms. See Multiple Document Interface (MDI) forms
member routines 80
member variables 17
  m_ 17
menus
  MDI forms, adding to 75
methodologies, design 265
  see also design, OO program design
methods
  classes, adding methods to 19
  collections
    accessing 115
  keys 115
  object interface 9
    Function routines 9
    Sub routines 9
  Sub routines 19
    Public 19
Microsoft Access. see Access
Microsoft Data Bound List Controls, property pages 179
Microsoft Excel. see Excel
Microsoft Visual Modeler
  OO program design 265
  Rational Rose 265
modeling languages 267
  Unified Modeling Language (UML) 269
    see also Unified Modeling Language (UML)
MousePointerConstants, property pages 215

S

U

6

Beginning Visual Basic 6 Database Programming

Author: John Connell
ISBN: 1861001061
Price: $39.99 C$55.99 £36.99

The world is full of data and databases. This book will get you started with databases, whichever way you want to work with them in the future. I'll provide you with the background information and techniques that will give you a firm foundation for all your database work.

Every chapter is full of practical examples to reinforce your learning and give you working tools and applications. The aim is to build your knowledge and skills using the full range of capabilities available in VB 6 and get the most out of the strategic ADO functions.

This book is for everyone who wants to learn more about working with VB 6 and databases. Whether you've just learned to program with Visual Basic or you're after a briefing on the latest developments in VB ADO database programming, this book is for you.

Visual Basic 6 Business Objects

Author: Rockford Lhotka
ISBN: 186100107X
Price: $39.99 C$55.99 £36.99

This book is about the design of business software, following an object-oriented philosophy and using Visual Basic 5.0, and Windows technologies such as DCOM and MTS. It demonstrates a component-based, scalable, logical architecture that allows business code to be reused. Different UIs and back-end databases can then be added as circumstances dictate, with minimum disruption to core business code. We'll study a fully-worked example to demonstrate how we can create and implement a solid object model. Along the way, I'll cover a number of specific techniques that make this whole concept work well in the Visual Basic environment. In addition, I'll demonstrate some general architectural techniques that apply equally well to all development, whether it be for single-tier, multi-tier or Internet-based applications.

This book is aimed at experienced Windows application developers. It assumes you know how to program with Visual Basic, but takes the time to cover version 5.0 innovations and issues. It also gives full introductions to using server technologies like DCOM, MTS, SQL Server and ASP.

wrox

Register Beginning Visual Basic 6 Objects and sign up for a free subscription to The Developer's Journal.

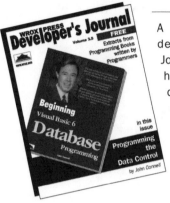

A bi-monthly magazine for software developers, The Wrox Press Developer's Journal features in-depth articles, news and help for everyone in the software development industry. Each issue includes extracts from our latest titles and is crammed full of practical insights into coding techniques, tricks, and research.

Fill in and return the card below to receive a free subscription to the Wrox Press Developer's Journal.

Beginning Visual Basic 6 Objects Registration Card

Name _____

Address _____

_____

_____

City_____ State/Region _____

Country_____ Postcode/Zip _____

E-mail _____

Occupation _____

How did you hear about this book?_____

☐ Book review (name) _____

☐ Advertisement (name) _____

☐ Recommendation _____

☐ Catalog _____

☐ Other _____

Where did you buy this book? _____

☐ Bookstore (name)_____ City _____

☐ Computer Store (name) _____

☐ Mail Order _____

☐ Other_____

What influenced you in the purchase of this book?

☐ Cover Design

☐ Contents

☐ Other (please specify) _____

How did you rate the overall contents of this book?

☐ Excellent   ☐ Good

☐ Average   ☐ Poor

What did you find most useful about this book? _____

What did you find least useful about this book? _____

Please add any additional comments. _____

What other subjects will you buy a computer book on soon? _____

What is the best computer book you have used this year?

_____

Note: This information will only be used to keep you updated about new Wrox Press titles and will not be used for any other purpose or passed to any other third party.

Check here if you *DO NOT* want a subscription to The Developer's Journal or further support for this book ☐

WROX PRESS INC.

Wrox writes books for you. Any suggestions, or
ideas about how you want information given in
your ideal book will be studied by our team.
Your comments are always valued at Wrox.

Free phone in USA 800-USE-WROX
Fax (312) 397 8990

UK Tel. (0121) 706 6826   Fax   (0121) 706 2967

Computer Book Publishers

NB. If you post the bounce back card below in the UK, please send it to:
Wrox Press Ltd. 30 Lincoln Road, Birmingham, B27 6PA

NO POSTAGE
NECESSARY
IF MAILED
IN THE
UNITED STATES

BUSINESS REPLY MAIL
FIRST CLASS MAIL   PERMIT#64   CHICAGO, IL

POSTAGE WILL BE PAID BY ADDRESSEE

WROX PRESS
1512 NORTH FREMONT
SUITE 103
CHICAGO IL 60622-2567